Varieties of Capitalism, Varieties of Approaches

Varieties of Capitalism, Varieties of Approaches

Edited by

David Coates

First published 2005 by
PALGRAVE MACMILLAN
Houndmills, Basingstoke, Hampshire RG21 6XS and
175 Fifth Avenue, New York, N.Y. 10010
Companies and representatives throughout the world

PALGRAVE MACMILLAN is the global academic imprint of the Palgrave
Macmillan division of St. Martin's Press, LLC and of Palgrave Macmillan Ltd.
Macmillan® is a registered trademark in the United States, United Kingdom
and other countries. Palgrave is a registered trademark in the European
Union and other countries.

ISBN 978-1-4039-1886-4 hardback

This book is printed on paper suitable for recycling and made from fully
managed and sustained forest sources. Logging, pulping and manufacturing
processes are expected to conform to the environmental regulations of the
country of origin.

A catalogue record for this book is available from the British Library.

Library of Congress Cataloging-in-Publication Data
Varieties of capitalism, varieties of approaches / edited by David Coates.
    p.   cm.
   "[This book is] the product of a conference held at Wake Forest
University in North Carolina in 2002"—Introd.
   Includes bibliographical references and index.
   ISBN 1–4039–1886–4 (alk. paper)
   1. Capitalism—Congresses.   2. Comparative economics—Congresses.
   I. Coates, David.

   HB501.V356 2005
   330.12′2—dc22
                                                          2004053453

Printed and bound in Great Britain by
CPI Antony Rowe, Chippenham and Eastbourne

Contents

v

List of Contributors

Greg Albo, Assistant Professor, Department of Political Science, York University; and Director of its International Political Economy Summer School; with research interests in comparative and Canadian political economy: author of many widely cited research articles including 'Competitive austerity and the impasse of capitalist employment policy', *The Socialist Register 1994* and 'European industrial relations: impasse or model', in E.M. Woods *et al.* (eds), *Rising From the Ashes: Labor in the Age of Global Capitalism*.

Robert Brenner, Professor and Director, Center for Social Theory and Comparative History, University of California at Los Angeles; with research interests focused on early modern European history, and Marxist theory. Author of, among other works, *The Economics of Global Turbulence: A Special Report on the World Economy 1950–1998* (New Left Review 229, 1998) and *The Boom and the Bubble: The US in the World Economy*.

Stephen Broadberry, Professor of Economic History at the University of Warwick; with research interests in the comparative economic performance of Britain, the United States and Germany in the nineteenth and twentieth centuries: author of, among many works, *The Productivity Race: British Manufacturing in International Perspective 1850–1990*, 1997.

Vivek Chibber, Assistant Professor of Sociology, New York University; with research interests in economic sociology, Marxian theory and the sociology of development: author of, among other works, 'Building a developmental state: the Korean case reconsidered', *Politics and Society* (1999); and *Locked in Place: State-Building and Late Industrialization in India* (2003).

David Coates, Worrell Professor of Anglo-American Studies, Wake Forest University: author of, among other works, *The Question of UK Decline* and *Models of Capitalism: Growth and Stagnation in the Modern Era*; and the editor of *Economic and Industrial Performance in Europe, Industrial Policy in Britain* and the three-volume *Models of Capitalism: Debating Strengths and Weaknesses*.

Travis Fast, a doctoral candidate in Political Science at York University, Toronto. His research interests are the political economy of advanced capitalism, with a focus on North America, the restructuring of the state and unemployment policies.

Sam Gindin, Currently holds the Packer chair in Social Justice at York University, Toronto, Canada; formerly Director of Research and assistant to the President, Canadian Auto Workers Union: author of, among other works, 'Turning points and starting points: Brenner, left turbulence and class politics', in L. Panitch and C. Leys (eds), *Working Classes, Global Realities* (*The Socialist Register 2001*).

Colin Hay, Professor of Political Analysis, Research Director and Head of Department, Department of Political Science and International Studies, University of Birmingham, UK: currently directing the ESRC funded project on 'Globalisation, European integration and the European social model', which is part of the ESRCs (Economic and Social Research Council) One Europe or Several? research program: author of, among other works, *The Political Economy of New Labour* and co-editor of *Demystifying Globalization*.

Michael Kitson, Fellow of St. Catherine's College, Fellow at the Cambridge-MIT Institute (CMI) and at the Judge Institute, Associate Director of the CMI's National Competitiveness Network, and University Lecturer in Business Economics: author of many research publications on economic policy and performance, including (with Jonathan Michie) *The Political Economy of Competitiveness: Essays on Employment, Public Policy and Corporate Performance*.

Martijn Konings, Received MA degrees in Political Science and Economics from the University of Amsterdam, and is currently a PhD candidate in the Department of Political Science at York University. His thesis is a comparative enquiry into the relation between finance and political development in the US and Germany.

Cathie Jo Martin, Professor of Political Science, Boston University: author of, among other works, *Stuck in Neutral: Business and the Politics of Human Capital Investment Policy* and *Shifting the Burden: The Struggle over Growth and Corporate Taxation*.

Leo Panitch, Canada Research Chair in Comparative Political Economy and Distinguished Research Professor of Political Science at York University, Toronto, Canada: co-editor of *The Socialist Register* and author of, among other works, *Renewing Socialism: Democracy, Strategy and Imagination* and (with Colin Leys) *The End of Parliamentary Socialism*.

Jonas Pontusson, Professor of Government, Director of the Cornell Summer Program in International Business, and Advisor to the International Political

Economy Program, Einaudi Center, Cornell University: author of many articles on labor politics, wage inequality and welfare-state retrenchment, and co-editor of, among other works, *Unions, Employers and Central Banks* (with T. Iversen and D. Soskice).

Introduction

There is no more important issue in the advanced capitalist world these days than that of how best to organize a successful economy. The old issue of 'capitalism versus socialism' is currently off the agenda. The issue of 'capitalism versus capitalism' currently is not.

Policymakers and intellectuals both face the same issue – which variety of capitalism works best. Because they do, the new and important sub-discipline of comparative political economy is now rich in studies of why and how different advanced capitalisms organize and perform in distinctly different ways. The explosion in the *volume* of studies on varieties of capitalism has been the striking feature of the relevant literature of late; but what that literature still lacks is a careful consideration of the *organizing frameworks* and *methodologies* that underpin it. The route to a full understanding of the nature of contemporary capitalism, and of the strengths and potentialities of its various institutional forms, does not lie simply through the addition of more discrete studies: those in large measure we now have. It also lies through a careful reflection upon, and a comparison of, the competing understandings currently available to us on how economic success is to be measured, how evidence about that success is to be mobilized, and how economic performance of whatever quality is to be conceptualized and explained?

This book is the first major attempt yet made to generate that reflection and comparison. The product of a conference held at Wake Forest University in North Carolina in 2002, it brings together leading exponents of all the major approaches to the 'variety of capitalism' issue. The book contains chapters written from within mainstream economics, within the currently highly influential school broadly labeled 'the new institutionalism', and within radical scholarship of a Marxist kind. Each approach is laid out and evaluated separately. Each approach is illustrated by chapters on key national case studies. Each approach is compared and evaluated against the others. The whole collection is united by an opening chapter on paradigms of explanation, and by a closing analysis of their relative strengths and weaknesses.

The conference was motivated, and the book is driven, by the same set of concerns. The first is that much of the best scholarship in the critical area of comparative political economy is still fragmented between different disciplines and different intellectual traditions, with remarkable little interchange of arguments (or even relevant research literatures). The second is that in consequence, much graduate work in the field goes on without any serious and systematic examination of the intellectual frameworks shaping research design, and without exposure to parallel debates occurring in other disciplines and traditions of scholarship. The third is that within particular disciplines and traditions, big and exciting debates are underway, to which only their direct participants and their students are easily exposed. (We have in mind particularly the debates around the Hall and Soskice volume on *Varieties of Capitalism* and the debate in more radical circles around the work of Bob Brenner – debates which deserve a wider and less directly committed audience.)

The book explicitly examines, reflects upon and applies dominant and different paradigms of explanation to the key question of why advanced capitalisms vary in institutional form and in competitive performance. The book has been constructed as a set of separately authored but closely coordinated chapters. Collectively, these chapters combine writing by leading figures and talented newcomers in the field of comparative political economy and they bring together North American and European intellectuals. That combination then enables a number of the key participants in important debates in comparative political economy to reflect upon the strengths and weaknesses of the positions to which they adhere; and as they do so, to generate new lines of research and suggest new syntheses of approach and conceptual framework.

It is the view of all the contributors to this book that an interchange of this kind (one that is theoretically, conceptually and methodologically comparative and reflective, as well as empirically focused) is particularly appropriate at this juncture in the development of the field, given the weight of detailed research monographs now emerging: monographs that are not, in the main, comparative and reflective in this way. It is the associated hope of all the contributors to this book that the chapters gathered here will then help stimulate just such a sensitivity to questions of approach and method in the next generation of research students in this field.

In the preparation of this book, immense debts have been gathered: debts to the other participants in the original Wake Forest conference, and debts to the academic leadership of Wake Forest University itself. Thanks in particular are owed to Paul Escott who, as Dean of the Undergraduate College at Wake Forest, provided the funding for the conference. Thanks are also due to the conference's other participants: Klaus Armingeon, Jim Cronin, Peter Hall, Marty Hart-Landsberg, Chris Howell, Herbert Kitschelt, Joel Krieger, William Lazonick, Mary O'Sullivan, David Soskice, John Stephens, and Ian Taplin. The responsibility for the final outcome of the conference that they graced does not, however, lie in any way with them. It lies elsewhere. It lies, in the first instance, with the authors of the chapters that follow; and it lies in the end with me as their editor. It is simply to be hoped that those who attended the conference, as well as those who did not, can find something of lasting value in this, its outcome.

David Coates
Wake Forest University
June 2004

1
Paradigms of Explanation

David Coates

> Today the vast majority of economists and sociologists are largely ignorant of each other's work and intellectual inheritance and, despite significant encroachments from each side into the other's territory, the core of the two subjects are moving apart. On balance, I believe that our understanding of the modern world has been seriously impaired by this division of intellectual labour.
>
> Ingham (1996a: 244)

The differential post-war performance of advanced capitalist economies has become an issue of such importance that it has generated a large and ever-growing academic literature of its own. Since 1945 the major economies have grown in different ways and at different rates; and so too have the literatures describing them. Traditionally, discussions of the determinants of economic competitiveness and growth were understood to be a monopoly of economists (and economic historians). Economic performance was not something that was thought to lie within the purview of other disciplines within the social sciences. More recently, however, that has changed. New literatures have emerged alongside, and to a large degree invisible to, mainstream economics. Political scientists, comparative industrial sociologists, radical geographers, management gurus, educationalists: all have added their voice to the big debate on the varieties of capitalism and their relative performance. There is in consequence now no shortage of *explanation* of why some post-war capitalist economies have performed better than others. There is however a shortage of *agreement* on those explanations, and an equivalent shortage of material that *maps* those disagreements for newcomers to them. It is with the provision of such a map that this chapter is primarily concerned.

Paradigms of explanation

Four features of the literature on the post-war competitiveness and growth performance of advanced capitalist economies seem immediately apparent.

First, the literature contains a distinct range of disagreement on *how economic performance is to be conceptualized and measured*: a range that stretches from the narrowly economic to the broadly social. Second, it contains a distinct range of disagreement on what constitutes *appropriate methodologies* for the explanation of economic performance, however conceptualized and measured; that is, a range that stretches from the isolation of discrete economic factors to the analysis of interconnected social systems. Accordingly there is, third, considerable disagreement within the relevant literature on the range, nature and significance of the *evidence* necessary for assessing the adequacy of the explanations on offer; and, finally, those explanations themselves vary in the *theoretical frameworks* from which they emerge and within which they are either explicitly or by implication set. Under all four of these features of the literature we now face, it is possible to find major texts whose mix of *concepts, methods, evidence and theory* is highly unusual because it is idiosyncratic. The Hegelian-inspired work of Fukuyama (1995) is a case in point; but in the main, the best of the material on offer uses concepts, methods, evidence and theory in a consistent and more orthodox way. There are differences of view, that is, but the differences are systematic and consistent: and they are because here, as in much of the social sciences, the debate is characterized by the existence within it of *distinct paradigms of explanation* (and of politics).

One way of grasping the necessarily paradigmatic nature of academic scholarship in the social sciences is to deploy the image of spotlights beaming down upon a stage. At the core of the image is the notion of the stage lit from different points high above the stage itself. In such a theater, each spotlight throws a particular part of the stage into clearest relief, and leaves slightly darker and unexplored areas caught in the center of the other beams. In such a universe of stages and lights, general intellectual progress comes from the examination of the conceptual and theoretical structures within each spotlight, and from a comparative assessment of their relative strengths and weaknesses. So in the specifics of this case, if we are fully to grasp why economic performance differs between particular national capitalisms, we need to understand what is going on within each beam of light (what concepts and theories each contains), what the strengths and weaknesses of each beam turn out to be, and what – if any – illuminates most of the stage on which all of them are at play.

The current debate on how and why economic performance differs between varieties of capitalism is one organized around three main poles, three main spotlights.

1 It contains a debate, largely within mainstream economics, centered on disagreements between 'old' growth theory and 'new', in which growth accounting and economic modeling are the major methodologies, and in which the theoretical universe deployed stretches from Smith (1776) to Joseph Schumpeter (1942).

2 It contains a second debate, largely centered in political science, in which comparative institutional analysis and detailed individual case studies are the predominant methodologies, and in which (the relatively underdeveloped) theoretical universe is anchored in something called 'the new institutionalism' (and through it, no doubt, in some indirect way in the work of Max Weber).

3 It contains a third debate, largely confined to vestigial radical political circles and journals, in which the prevailing methodology is historical materialism, and in which the theoretical frameworks deployed are predominantly Marxist in origin.

Each debate is fierce within itself, and each debate also overlaps (in conceptual devices, literatures, and evidence) with material on the margins of the others; but ultimately each of the literatures within each spotlight conceptualizes performance (and indeed the economy producing it) differently. Each understands its academic tasks as entirely different in kind; each looks for and develops different forms of evidence; and each accepts as adequate different levels and kinds of explanation. Each debate, that is, is anchored in a particular intellectual paradigm.

Of course, the divisions within the literature with which we are concerned here are not just paradigmatic ones. There are divisions too of academic disciplines and sub-disciplines. Historically, much of the debate about why economies perform in different ways has been a dialogue of the deaf, precisely because it has been organized as a series of sealed discussions within *disciplines*; and even now, as those disciplinary boundaries weaken, much of the debate goes on in discrete and relatively sealed *area literatures*, organized around specific regional questions or concepts or theories. There are, for example, large and separate literatures on the 'decline of the UK economy' written by economic historians, political scientists, cultural historians, international relations specialists, educationalists, industrial relations specialists, and management scholars: literatures which then dialogue with each other only occasionally and at the margin (Coates 1994). That discipline fragmentation within the literature on the UK economy could no doubt be replicated with ease in literatures focused on other national economies. Likewise, within the growing sub-discipline of contemporary political economy, we find a debate largely focused on Western Europe – around questions of welfare capitalism, liberal market economies and coordinated market economies. We find a debate largely focused on Southeast Asia – organized around the role of the state. There is a debate, predominantly among scholars of Latin American economies – organized around dependency theory; and so on. Those debates too are largely self-referential ones.

Even so, the basic cleavages of knowledge here are genuinely paradigmatic in nature. In discipline after discipline, in area study after area study, the underlying choice between frameworks of thought is predominantly the same and the basic choices of conceptual apparatus and theoretical explanation are remarkably consistent. Time and again scholars face the same basic decisions. Should they explain differential economic performance by deploying the categories of *markets, production functions, growth factors, and externalities*; or by using notions of *cumulative causation, endogenous and exogenous variables, technological compatibility, and social capabilities*; or by talking of *social embeddedness, path dependency, and comparative institutional advantage*; or by thinking of the world in terms of *social structures of accumulation, class forces, capital accumulation, and modes of production*? As we start to explore varieties of capitalism and varieties of performance, those are our choices too. For we need a language to analyze economic growth and its social consequences; and the language necessarily comes, as languages always do in the social sciences, with considerable theoretical baggage buried inside it.

There is also one other general thing to note as we begin this stocktaking of existing scholarship in the area of comparative economic performance. That is, that things are changing, and for the better. Major texts do now cross discipline and paradigm walls, and much of the key literature sits at the interface between paradigms. In fact, of late, the exchange between paradigmatic positions – and the attempt to find new syntheses of concepts, methods, explanations and theories – has been extremely creative in this field. As the remainder of this book will demonstrate, much valuable work has been (as is being) done at the interface of mainstream economics and the new institutionalism; and much valuable work has been done (and remains to be done) at the interface of the new institutionalism and Marxism. The fact that the previous paragraph gave us four strings of concepts, and not simply three, suggests that the interface between paradigms, as well as the content of each paradigmatic spotlight, is worthy of study and evaluation. This volume of essays has been collected for that reason, and that reason alone: on the general understanding that there is much to be gained from seeing this set of literatures in paradigmatic/spotlight terms, from exploring the underlying premises and associated methodologies of each paradigm, and from clarifying the choices of explanatory framework and content that each offers. If we are fully to understand how capitalisms vary, and with what consequences, we need to know our paradigms: which is why this chapter has as its main task a preliminary mapping of their content.

Market-focused analyses

The debate on why the growth performance of advanced capitalist economies has differed in the post-war period sits alongside a parallel debate on the determinants of economic growth in general. That wider debate is one that goes on *within* mainstream economics (between old and new growth theory). It is one that goes on *at the edge* of conventional economics (among other schools within the mainstream, particularly Schumpeterian and post-Keynesian); and it is one that goes on *beyond* conventional economics (among various schools of radical political economy).

In mainstream economics at least, there is a clear neoclassical orthodoxy on how economic growth occurs. It is an orthodoxy built around a view of *markets* as optimal economic and social allocators. It is one that conceptualizes economic activity as the coming together of discrete actors/factors in a linked set of markets; and it is one which then understands the central relationships at play in any economy as relationships organized in distinct 'production functions'.

$$\text{Growth} = f(\text{land, labor, capital, and enterprise})$$

in production functions, in which the use of specific economic resources is inevitably subject, over the long term, to the law of diminishing returns. In such a view of the world, economic growth occurs by either moving along an existing production function (using existing technologies to the full) or, via technological progress by a movement of the entire function to an entirely higher level; and economic growth over time is conceptualized as the combination of those two movements. With the world understood in this way, differential growth patterns can ultimately only be explained as a consequence of the difference in production functions: as a consequence of differences in either the quantity of factors deployed or the quality of their individual characters and general interconnections. The broad thrust of this approach is that the untrammeled interplay of market forces should produce both economic growth over time and (through a long-term redeployment of resources triggered by diminishing returns) an eventual convergence of economic growth paths; such that, if growth and convergence do not occur, analysis must inevitably focus on the location of inadequacies in factor supply/quality, or seek out (and press for the removal of) barriers/ blockages to the free interplay of these factors in untrammeled markets.

Early in the development of the debate on why growth rates differed in post-war capitalist economies, this broad approach inspired two widely cited and influential studies, each replete with its own methodology and open-ended research agenda. The first was Denison's (1962, 1967) advocacy of growth accounting as the route to the understanding of the determinants of economic growth. In Denison's growth accounting methodology, the sources of growth were conceptualized as 'factor inputs' (capital, land, and labor) and factors affecting 'output/unit of input'. The latter, for Denison, included 'advances in technological and managerial knowledge, gaps between optimal and actual distributions of resources', 'levels of demand', 'economies of scale', and 'barriers to the optimal distribution of resources imposed by governments, businesses or labor unions' (Denison 1967: 9–10). The characteristic form that growth accounting took in Denison's hands (and still takes in the hands of later growth accountants) is the long and careful specification of how each factor is to be calculated, followed by the building of scores for each, culminating in the creation of tables giving each factor a weight/ number for each country in turn. Growth accounting, as practiced by Denison, calculated the impact of technological progress as that portion of total output that could not be explained after calculating the contribution of all other factors (i.e. the residuum). The contribution of the 'advance of knowledge' to economic growth was computed as the value of the residuum in the most advanced economy (in Denison's case, the USA), with the remaining gap else-where explained in terms of 'catch up' (as the result of the diffusion of the US technology). Later growth accountants, and Denison himself, persistently sought to find other measures to reduce that residuum; but throughout, the general approach has remained the same. By comparing tables of numbers between successful and unsuccessful economies, growth accounting seeks to isolate factors whose presence or absence holds the key to growth in particular cases; in a world in which the general list of factors mobilized in growth accounts provides an overall specification of the factors vital to the growth equation.

The other widely cited contribution from within this general approach has been Olson's study of *The Rise and Decline of Nations* (Olson 1982). Written in part because of its author's dissatisfaction with orthodox growth accounting, and explicitly positioning itself within the conceptual universe of neoclassical economics, Olson's work constituted an initially much-cited explanation of growth accounting's missing residuum, an explanation that emphasized the way in which 'the retardants to growth may be rooted in social institutions, rather than technology, preferences or resource endow-ments' (Bowles and Eatwell 1983: 217). The Olson thesis was that the more established a democracy the more likely was it to acquire special interest groups that limited growth because they served only special interests. According to Olson these special interests (because they were not all-encompassing in their constituencies) were more likely to reduce than to increase efficiency, were more likely to block rather than encourage inno-vation, and were more likely to prioritize wealth distribution than wealth creation. 'The hard core of the argument [was] that various interest groups develop modes of collective action to further their particular interests, and increasingly over time their activities distort the efficiency of resource allocation to a very important degree' (Maddison 1995a: 86). For Olson, countries with low rates of growth were likely to be those whose system of special interest groups had not been broken by war or revolution. That was why, for him, the UK's rate of economic growth slowed after 1945, and that of West Germany did not. Good Federalist Paper-style liberal that he was, Olson offered us a view of growth blocked by factions: both by strong cartels and by strong trade unionism.

It should be noted that Olson's argument and approach, though still widely cited, was never fully accepted even by scholars comfortable with the conceptual and theoretical universe that he occupied; and was found even less attractive by scholars anchored in different paradigms. Even his theoretically near neighbor, Maddison, while sympathetic to his analysis of the UK's growth problems (blaming trade unions was, after all, very popular in neoliberal circles in the UK in the early Thatcher years) was quick to criticize Olson's approach for its omissions: particularly its failure to allow for economies' different 'distance from the technological frontier', and hence capacity for growth through 'catch-up'; and its silence on variations in the tempo of growth over time within any one economy, particularly the issue of post-73 sluggishness, in the context of stable systems of interest groups (Maddison 1995a: 86, 90). This last omission was very much the thrust of other critiques too – that, as a theory 'about the determinants of disparities in long-run economic growth' Olson's work 'was much less satisfactory as an explanation of the post-73 downturn' (McCombie and Thirlwall 1994: 87). They were not alone in rejecting his work as theoretically inadequate and empirically flawed, and in criticizing him for ignoring the Schumpeterian view that big companies, in situations of imperfect competition, are the best triggers of growth. Elbaum and Lazonick did so too, in relation to Olson's analysis of the UK economy: arguing that the UK economic decline was triggered by the very fragmented structures of industrial organization that Olson favored – structures 'that left British industry too reliant on market coordination in an era in which competitive advantage went to those business organizations capable of planned coordination' (Elbaum and Lazonick 1984: 319). Scholars examining post-war Germany and Japan have been similarly critical (Friedman 1988; Reich 1990: 5): and the latest in a line of general reviews of Olson's argument now available to us (Unger and van Waarden 1999) reinforces these earlier views that Olson's work, though elegant, remains profoundly flawed.

Denison's growth accounting has, by contrast, proved far more resilient; but it too has serious limitations as a route to a full understanding of why growth rates differ, as even its more sympathetic critics regularly concede. Two criticisms in particular have had (and continue to have) huge force in the wake of Denison's scholarship – the taxonomy/depth criticism and the endogenous/exogenous one – both of which have moved the debate away from the study of isolated economic factors in abstract markets toward a more institutionally-sensitive analysis of the determinants of economic growth.

Denison himself was well aware of the limited explanatory reach of growth accounting as he practiced it: conceding from the outset that there was 'no room in my classification for such more ultimate influences on growth as birth control, tax structures, the spirit of enterprise or planning, to name but a few' (Denison 1967: 315). Maddison has made this point many times: 'that growth accounting at best takes us to the *proximate* causes of growth, not to *ultimate* causes', on which growth accounting leaves us with 'an embarrassing area of ignorance' (1995a: x). In fact, serious doubts remain, and debate flourishes, about the adequacy and meaningfulness of growth accounting's treatment of even proximate causes. The 'objectivity' and empirical adequacy of some of the measures used to isolate factors is a matter of perennial dispute, and certainly the scale of the residuum in the early studies raised questions about whether those early attempts were any kind of explanation at all. But that notwithstanding, 'ultimate causes' lie beyond the easy reach of even the most methodologically sophisticated and theoretically sensitive forms of growth accounting: and yet they remain critical to any explanation of the differential performance of post-war capitalist economies. Here is Maddison's own list of ultimate causes, written by the scholar widely regarded as the outstanding growth accountant of his generation.

> An investigation of ultimate causality involves consideration of institutions, ideologies, socio-economic pressure groups, historical accidents, and national economic policy. It also involves consideration of the international economic order, foreign ideologies or shocks from friendly or unfriendly neighbors. (Maddison 1995a: 103)

Equally telling has been the argument that early growth accounting was weak as an explanation of economic growth to the degree to which it treated growth factors as independent of each other, and brought technical progress in (as its main explanatory factor) from outside: there, but unexplained. As Abramovitz and others have argued, the factors isolated by Denison interact. 'They support one another and make joint rather than separate contributions' (Abramovitz 1989: 28). Measuring them separately might undervalue them, by failing to see their contribution to the role of other factors; or it may over-value them, by not accounting for their dependence on others: and either way, the whole disaggregating approach pulls analysis away, back from any examination of how factor-interaction can trigger endogenously generated growth performance. In consequence, Maddison, Abramovitz, and others have preferred to focus on the ways in which the *interplay* of Denison's growth factors has/has not enabled some economies to 'leap forward', others to 'fall back', and the entire pack of advanced economies to either converge or remain on distinct growth trajectories. In consequence, the growth accounting approach has of late spawned a rich 'convergence' literature (Abramovitz 1986; Baumol 1994). It is a literature full of careful examinations of the post-1945 surge of productivity growth and its diffusion across advanced capitalism from the US economy which triggered it. It is a literature replete with the recognition of the 'advantages of backwardness', and with the role of 'catch-up' in the Western European and Japanese post-war growth story. It is also a literature sensitive to the way in which the capacity of an economy to 'catch-up' depends on the fit between some of growth accounting's key factors (not least natural resource endowment and technological congruence) and a string of less easily quantifiable social characteristics: what Baumol termed 'ancillary variables'

(1994: 62) and Abramovitz 'social capability' (1994). But just like Maddison's list of ultimate causes, Abramovitz's definition of 'social capability' has proved to be, by his own admission, 'a vague complex of matters, few of which can be clearly defined and subjected to measurement' (1994).

> It includes personal attributes, notably levels of education.... but it also refers to such things as competitiveness, the ability to cooperate in joint ventures, honesty, and the extent to which people feel able to trust the honesty of others. And it also pertains to a variety of political and economic institutions. It includes the stability of governments and their effectiveness in enforcing the rules of economic life and in supporting growth. It covers the experience of a country's business people in the organization and administration of large-scale enterprises and the degree of development of national and international capital markets. (Abramovitz 1994: 88)

In a word, the importance of 'social capability' in the explanation of growth differentials, like the specification of Maddison's ultimate causes, opens the road to the study of institutions: to what Maddison himself described as 'part of the historian's traditional domain... or the sociologist' (Maddison 1995a: 103). Not all growth economists feel comfortable making that journey, but those that do have made an enormous contribution to our understanding of differential economic performance, as we will now see.

In search of institutions

The intellectual journey away from neoclassical understandings of why some economies perform more adequately than others has been a journey in search of, and then through, the study of institutions: the economic institution of the firm initially, but eventually social, cultural and political institutions as well. The further the journey taken by individual scholars, the greater the rupture they have been obliged to make with the governing premises and methodologies of neoclassical economics. For some, the move has been marginal, though still immensely significant. This has been particularly the case with the work of Oliver Williamson, and the resulting emergence (or more accurately re-emergence) of schools of institutional economists. These are schools whose members still in the main operate within the dominant assumptions of methodological individualism, still proceed primarily by the construction of abstract models, and still see their role as explaining growth differentials through the isolation of differential patterns of individual rationality and choice. For others, the rupture has run deeper, and the movement from the abstract modeling of neoclassical economics has been greater. There the goal has been to understand different patterns of economic performance by *embedding* that performance in different histories and social contexts. Between the dominant paradigms now structuring the debate on the differential performance of different varieties of capitalism, that is, stand literatures that can be positioned in relationship to one another by the relative weight they place on the economic and the social: literatures that at one end allow only the entry of organizational variables into a universe still conceived in market terms, to literatures which see markets as necessarily socially constructed. Between the main paradigms stand literatures labeled 'institutional economics' and 'the new economic sociology'. Those literatures are occasionally in dialogue; but more normally their reference points are back to the mainstream of the separate disciplines (economics and sociology) in which their major practitioners were initially trained.

Once the walls of neoclassicism are breached, however, there is an inexorable logic to the direction of movement. It is, however, not an uncontested logic. On the contrary, it sits alongside what is often referred to as an all-encompassing 'economic imperialism' (Hodgson 1996: 383): the set of assertions by convinced neoclassical economists that the ontological premises on which they 'do' economics are universally applicable, and that in consequence *rational choice modeling* is the quintessentially scientific methodology for the whole of the social sciences. Much of social science is currently struggling under this ideological onslaught. But for those economists and others who are not convinced that the route to knowledge lies through the plucking 'of axioms of behavior . . . from the air' through which to construct 'general theories impoverished in terms of their concreteness, relevance and practical application', analysis is then inexorably pulled toward an examination of 'the features and institutions that characterize a given economy' (Hodgson 1996: 382–3). If such analysts then go that extra inch, and remove the assumption of inevitable diminishing returns that lies at the heart of the neoclassical deployment of Pareto-optimality as its measure of efficiency, then it quickly becomes feasible for them to anticipate the establishment of self-sustaining differential growth paths. It becomes possible for them to follow Veblen, and to see processes of 'cumulative causation' at work in different capitalist economies over time, and to talk of virtuous and vicious cycles of growth and stagnation (Hodgson 1996: 410). It even becomes possible for them to follow Marx, to see the logic of combined but uneven development at work in those same economies, and even to talk of the development of under-development. Once the wall is breached, the floodgates are genuinely open: and how far they go depends on how far they want to swim.

For across the entire intellectual/political spectrum – from Conservative to Marxist – the most general shared critique of neoclassical economics is that its market-focused explanations of differential economic performance rest on inadequate premises about human motivation, and ignore the necessarily social nature of market processes. It seems not to matter if you are a Hegelian or a Schumpeterian, the point is the same. Neoclassical economics is at best only '80% correct...there is a missing 20% of human behavior about which neoclassical economics can give only a poor account'; since 'as Adam Smith well understood, economic life is deeply embedded in social life, and it cannot be understood apart from the customs, morals and habits of the society in which it occurs. In short, it cannot be divorced from culture' (Fukuyama 1995: 13). 'If businesses were merely factors of production,' Best has written, if they were merely 'land, labor and capital, combined in a firm to economize on coordination costs, the task would be a straightforward technical exercise'; but they are not. 'The problem is that firms are social institutions with unique cultures' (Best 1990: 21–2).

The claim here, from the critics of neoliberalism, is that human beings are more complex actors than the ontological presuppositions of neoclassical economics allow. Their behavior is shaped by more than instrumental calculations of how best to maximize the level of individual short-term profits. It is shaped by judgments of morality and feeling. It is affected by the definitions and understandings social actors impose on their economic activity. It is molded by issues of uncertainty and insecurity, and by concerns that can be long term and qualitative in nature. Because all this is so, neoclassical economics is said by its critics to be 'not only strictly inaccurate, but also insufficiently specific. Its universality is spurious and its specificity is unrepresentative of the characteristic relations and structures of modern socio-economic systems' (Hodgson 1996: 386). Thus the route is open to the view that markets should be studied (and can only properly be studied) as social institutions, working best in particular social contexts. The route is also open to the view that those contexts may be precisely those *not* engendered by the application of untrammeled market principles. For markets left to themselves generate insecurity, inequality, and short termism, as well as resource efficiency, innovation, and growth: and because they do, the way is also open to explanations of differential economic performance that make neoclassical economics part of the problem rather than part of the solution. It is open to explanations that prioritize a range of *social* variables as keys to economic success, and to those that emphasize the *fragility* of successful social structures of accumulation. Indeed the pass is even open, as we shall see, to arguments that ultimately link economic under-performance within any one capitalist economy to structural contradictions of capitalism as a global system, and which treat resurgent neoliberalism as a sign of the problems now facing a post-Fordist capitalism, rather than as a new and stable solution to them.

So there is a journey of infinite length here: whose first landing stage is the now well-established field of institutional economics. The center of gravity of institutional economics is but an inch away from that of neoclassical economics as a whole. As it is now well-documented, neoclassical economics had no adequate explanation of the existence of its key component actor – the capitalist firm – at least had no adequate explanation until Oliver

Williamson developed his arguments about 'transaction costs'. By reactivating a strand of economic argument foreshadowed in the inter- and post-war writings of Coase, Williamson's work triggered a renewed willingness among institutionally-minded economists to use the presuppositions and methodologies of neoclassical economics methodological individualism to explain the emergence and behavior of key economic institutions, particularly that of the firm, and to incorporate institutional variables into their explanations of economic growth. The 'characteristic project' of the resulting 'new institutional economics', as Williamson labeled it, 'has been the attempt to explain the emergence of institutions, such as the firm or the state, by reference to a model of rational individual behavior, tracing out the unintended consequences of human interactions' (Hodgson 2001: 247). The writings of Milgrom and Roberts are one important case in point. Theirs is genuinely innovative work on the economics of organizations that explicitly deals 'with firms and organizations as they really are' (Milgrom and Roberts 1992: xiii), applying traditional forms of economic analysis to the full set of issues confronting firms: from internal issues of coordination, organizational design, and managerial motivation to external questions of contracting, business alliances, and corporate control and governance. The work of Alesina and others on the impact of political variables on economic performance has been equally innovative here (Alesina and Rosenthal 1995; Alesina, Roubini with Cohen 1997).

The other seminal figure in the revival of institutional economics has been Douglass North. His 1971 jointly authored *Institutional Change and American Economic Growth* (Davis and North 1971; also North 1990) marked the beginning of a systematic attempt to explain the general relationship between economic institutions and economic growth by bringing the conceptual apparatus of neoclassical economics to bear on the economic history of the United States. As he argued later, on this view 'the key to growth' lay with 'efficient economic organization'; and efficient organization itself entailed 'the establishment of institutional arrangements and property rights that create an incentive to channel individual economic effort into activities that bring the private rate of return close to the social rate of return' (North and Thomas 1973: 1). The resulting neoclassically-inspired institutional economic history has left its practitioners equipped and willing to tackle 'such diverse topics as transitions from socialism to capitalism and economic development'. They simply have done so – and often have done so very simply – aware that 'institutions matter', and accordingly predisposed to argue that since, in their terms, 'the institutional framework of a nation determines the level of transaction costs', it will also 'in turn determine how well markets function' (Yeager 1999: 159). Equipped with theoretical equipment of this kind, it is not perhaps surprising that the new institutional economists have quickly reproduced the level of certainty characteristic of neoclassical economics, but with a slightly refined agenda: one that sees the key to economic growth in both transitional and developing economies as the creation of 'an institutional framework that lowers transaction costs and creates incentives for dynamic efficiency' (Yeager 1999: 45), and one that is sensitive to the capacity of different institutional mixes to generate path dependency – understood here as 'sub-optimal behavior' created by 'lock-in effects' (Magnusson and Ottoson 1997: 2).

Such analysts are not the first generation of institutional economists to be aware of the possibility of path dependency, or of the manner in which processes of cumulative causation can generate virtuous and vicious cycles of economic growth. Those things had been obvious years before to the 'old' institutionalist schools of economics associated with Veblen and Myrdal: but with the revival of these insights by this new generation, the agenda of professional economics has widened again slightly. Contemporary academic economics has retreated an inch from 'the propensity of most neoclassical theorizing for narrow, institution-free, formalistic way[s] of analyzing economic life' (Magnusson and Ottosson 1997: 1). Of course, the whole intellectual tradition remains wedded to the building of formal models, and continues to assert the superiority of models whose set of variables gain elegance through parsimony; but at least now the debate on the determinants of economic growth has been extended to include institutional factors. The much-cited new growth theory puts explanatory weight on investments in human capital and purposive Research and Development (R&D) (Romer 1986; Lucas 1988), and is prepared to explain the persistence of different growth paths by reference to issues such as schooling, fertility rates, public policy, and the rule of law (Barro 1997: xi); and in that way, mainstream economics has come of late to contain work that brings formal model building and institutionally-sensitive economic history together to explain (and to glorify) capitalism's 'free market innovation machine' (Baumol 2002). It is work, as with Baumol, that is occasionally ambitious in its coverage and detail: but more normally it is work that continues to treat institutions in a highly stylized and extremely limited way.

The economic imperialism associated with this explosion of institutional economics, with what Ingham (1996a: 261) has termed the 'second version' of this imperialism – rational choice modeling being the first – has also triggered a powerful defensive counter-move from within the ranks of professional sociology. For rather than simply accept that, with a dash of 'transaction costs' thrown in, the methodologies and assumptions of neoclassical economics could expand infinitely to encompass the entirety of comparative political economy, new schools of economic sociologists have recently emerged to insist that the rupture achieved by Williamson with the dominant paradigms of professional economics was still far too mild. And it was very mild. Williamson himself is on record as saying that sociology merely studies the 'tosh' of economic life (Ingham 1996a: 262), agreeing with the earlier and often-cited Samuelson dictum that 'economics studies the rational and leaves the irrational residue to sociology' (Ingham 1996b: 552). Not surprisingly, sociologists have argued otherwise; criticizing the new institutional economics for both its functionalism and its 'undersocialized' understanding of human agency. The much-cited 1985 Granovetter article on 'the problem of embeddedness' began this counterattack: using the Duesenberry quip – that 'economics is all about how people make choices' while 'sociology is all about how they don't have any choices to make' (Granovetter 1985: 485) – to argue that, because economic activity is socially embedded, 'economic actions, outcomes and institutions are affected by actors' personal relations and by the structure of the overall network of relations' (Ingham 1996b: 554) into which they are set. Nearly two decades after that first counter-defense, there is now an extensive body of research material subsumed in the 'new economic sociology' to parallel the 'new institutional economics' (Granovetter and Swedberg 1992; Smelser and Swedberg 1995); with both bodies of material in their different ways committed to the view that economic growth is linked to the manner in which market processes and institutional structures interact, and is not in any simple sense simply the product of the quantity and quality of non-socialized market interactions alone.

The new institutionalism

There is a sense, however, in which the literatures on why growth rates differ, and those on varieties of capitalism, do have different centers of gravity. The ruling orthodoxy in the debate on economic growth these days is definitely a neoliberal one, whereas in the current state of scholarship on varieties of capitalism, the center of gravity lies neither in nor on the margins of the neoclassical paradigm. Of course not all professional economists and economic historians are wedded to the neoclassical paradigm; and economists working within subordinate schools of economic thought (primarily Schumpeterian and post-Keynesian) have shown a greater willingness than their neoclassical colleagues to incorporate the role of institutions into the center of their analysis. For those of us concerned with explaining the differential post-war economic performance of advanced capitalist economies, the most important of the work inspired in part by Schumpeterian economics has been that of Lazonick (1991, 1992, 1994a,b); though Porter's widely cited work is also to be located here (Porter 1990). The best of the post-Keynesian material has come from Hutton (1994, 2002). But these are still minority voices in an economics profession dominated by a neoclassical paradigm that is structurally intolerant of the possibility of variety. Since variations from the neoclassical norm – of free and unregulated markets – are as likely as not to be treated by scholars working at the core of that paradigm as defects, not as alternatives, the 'varieties of capitalism' literature has in general been the product of scholars trained in other social science disciplines – particularly by those who carry, with greater or lesser degrees of personal ease, the label of 'the new institutionalists' (Thelen and Steinmo 1992; Hall and Taylor 1996; Immergut 1998; Thelen 1998). It is they, and not the more conventionally trained growth economists, who have been prepared to study in detail the degree of path dependency guaranteed by the internally sustained interplay of institutional variables within particular capitalisms; and it is they who have been prepared to insist on the resulting capacity of autonomous capitalist models of a more regulated kind to survive and prosper alongside liberal capitalism (Crouch and Streeck 1997: 1).

In terms of its ruling ontologies and epistemologies, this new institutionalism has positioned itself in the broad philosophical space between the 'methodological individualism' of the neoliberal tradition and the structuralism of historical materialism. Not that there is anything particularly new about that space. In one sense it has been the quintessential home of the entirety of radical non-Marxist social science: in Europe certainly after Weber, in the US certainly after Veblen. It just is that this center ground has been, and remains, wide enough to invite a range of different approaches: indeed its eclecticism, and its openness to alternative ways of analyzing societies, has often been singled out as one of its greatest strengths by scholars drawn to it. For our purposes here, that space has been a meeting point for at least two broad approaches to the core questions of capitalist variety and growth differentials. One, coming from neoliberalism, has sought to soften the abstractedness of formal economic modeling by incorporating modeling techniques and rational-choice premises into analyses that recognize the existence and importance of economic (and political) institutions: a sort of '*soft rat. choice*'. The other, coming off more structuralist approaches, has sought to break the economic determinism of vulgar Marxism by adding autonomous institutional variables that filter and shape social interests. In political science, this approach has normally carried the label of *historical institutionalism*; in sociology, it is variously labeled as organization theory or *sociological institutionalism*. The sweep of both these approaches has been far wider than the literature on growth differentials and capitalist models, which is why it seems legitimate to treat 'new institutionalism' as genuinely paradigmatic in character and scope; but both have focused on issues of growth performance and institutional variety in capitalism in ways that neoliberal scholarship, broadly speaking, has not.

As Peters has correctly observed, 'some components of the new institutionalism are more compatible with the assumptions of the dominant individualistic approaches to the discipline than are others' (1999: 2); and not surprisingly, the form of new institutionalism that sits closest to the methodological individualism of neoclassical economics, as Peters himself has observed, has been *rational choice institutionalism*. The key bridging work here of late has been that produced by Iversen and Soskice. We now possess a body of research arguing that 'even under rational expectations, macroeconomic policies and institutions have long-term effects on unemployment and distribution of income' (Iversen 1999, 2000); and we also have research material linking the distribution of levels of social protection between national capitalisms to different training regimes, and to the different individual rationalities triggered by each – material that then defends forms of social protection as functional to competitiveness (Estevez-Abe *et al.* 2001; Iversen and Soskice 2001). Dialoging directly with rational expectations economics, and using the modeling and statistical apparatus obligatory in that discipline, such rational choice institutionalism is currently building a powerful defense of European welfare capitalism against the 'TINA imperialism' of the neoliberal Right, and sending powerful signals to center-left governments on how best to defend welfare systems in an age of global capital, flexible production technologies and deindustrialization (Iversen 1999: 171; Soskice 2000). It is also cohabiting with other strands of new institutionalist thinking – particularly historical and sociological new institutionalism – which, in the existing non-economic scholarship on varieties of capitalism and their relative economic performance, is now on the point of establishing itself as a new orthodoxy in its own right. Economists with an interest in institutions might dialogue with sociologists with an interest in markets, and look radical when set against the orthodoxies of neoclassical economics; but away from the rarified atmosphere of economic departments, it is historical institutionalism that is the prevailing orthodoxy, or quickly becoming so. Among the key elements of that new orthodoxy are arguments of the following kind.

First, that neoclassical orthodoxies notwithstanding, economies have to be understood as socially embedded cluster of institutions. They are not things that can be meaningfully studied in abstraction from that social context, for markets are not the same everywhere. On the contrary, as empirical study regularly demonstrates, core institutions inside different economies have different characteristics; and because they do, economies vary in (among other things) 'the character of the state governing them, the character of their labor relations systems, the organization of their financial systems, and their legal/regulatory frameworks' (Zysman 1994: 258). In consequence, it is simply neither possible nor legitimate to 'observe a single institutionalized market – finance or labor – and conclude that similar arrangements will have the same consequences' (Zysman 1994: 256) everywhere.

Second, that because economies are socially embedded in this way, the interests of their component elements cannot adequately be grasped except by situating them within the socially embedded whole. For not only does 'each economy consist of an institutional structure', each economy is also an 'institutional organization of politics and markets' which then 'defines the choices of each actor', 'sets down patterns of constraint and incentive', and so induces 'routine behaviors from companies and government' (Zysman 1994: 258). In fact, the claim is often made here that economies are best thought of not simply as clusters of institutions but as clusters which are themselves organized hierarchically, in the sense that the character of the whole is disproportionately influenced by the principles and practices developed by each economy's core institutional nexus – an institutional nexus which will differ, economy from economy, in both the type and character of its component elements.

Such socially embedded and hierarchically structured institutions are then understood as system parameters, with differing degrees of ability to trigger high rates of economic growth. A new institutionalist approach to why growth rates differ characteristically closes in on institutionally-induced differences of economic performance as key here: with competitiveness fixed (as with Abramovitz earlier) in the 'fit between... institutional capacities and the possibilities of the global market' (Amable 2000: 649) – fixed, that is, to use Hall and Soskice's powerful language, by the 'institutional complementarities' that then give particular economies 'comparative institutional advantages' (Hall and Soskice 2001: 17, 36). On this understanding of why modern economies perform differently, it is the manner in which institutions combine that is central. Analysts need both to 'recognize the joint effect of a series of institutions and modes of organization on the whole economy' and be sensitive to the possibility that 'different structures of institutions may... perform roughly the same – in terms of an economy's growth rate... – in spite of having separate components which may look very different when compared to one another because the relative efficiency of an institutional structure depends on the way the different components operate together' (Amable 2000: 655).

The new institutionalist scholarship expects national economies to perform differently, and *not* to converge, because of the possibility of path dependency in growth performance over time, and because of the existence of parallel 'virtuous' and 'vicious' circles of growth and decline that pull and keep economies apart. The result, if the bulk of the new institutionalist scholarship is right, is the necessary emergence and persistence of different national economies and different national trajectories – each with its own origins back in time, each with its own track record of evolution and change. As Hollingsworth put it, 'a society's social system of production is very path-dependent and system-specific' (Hollingsworth 1997: 266). There are broad types of such national economies – the new institutionalist literature of late has made much of the distinction between liberal and coordinated market economies (Soskice 1990a,b, 1991, 1999) – but even within those broad categories, from a new institutionalist perspective national variations are to be expected, welcomed, and observed over time. For there are historically induced differences of institutional form here: 'the particular historical course of each nation's development creates a political economy', as Zysman has it, 'with a distinctive institutional structure for governing the markets of labor, land, capital and goods'. The claim here is that 'distinct national paths of economic development and particular technological trajectories are an outgrowth of an institutionally specific context within which each economy operates' (Zysman 1994: 279). Or, as Hall and Soskice have argued more recently – in a chapter replete with diagrams of path-dependent interaction (what they term 'complementarities across sub-systems') – that 'differences in the institutional framework of the political economy generate systematic differences in corporate strategy across Liberal Market Economies (LMEs) and Coordinated Market Economies (CMEs)' (Hall and Soskice 2001: 16, 28, 32); and necessarily so.

Beyond institutionalism

It is hard to overstate the importance, in both academic and political terms, of the work of the new institutionalists as a bulwark against the intellectual and policy-making imperialism of economic theory of a neoclassical kind. The whole school has provided – and is providing – rich and sophisticated research data on a variety of post-war economic growth trajectories; and is arming a new generation of research students with the conceptual apparatus of *path dependency, social embeddedness*, and *institutional complementarity* through which to explore the residual strengths of more managed, and more socially equitable, forms of capitalist organization; but the new institutionalism is itself not problem-free. On the contrary, it too has now come under challenge, both from within its own ranks and from its left, for a series of linked weaknesses that limit, in the view of its critics, the power of its rebuttal of neoliberalism.

Internally, the major criticism now beginning to be heard is one of 'institutional determinism'. Colin Crouch's has been the major voice here, pointing to the danger that the very power of the Hall and Soskice advocacy of institutional complementarity and comparative institutional advantage might blind students of comparative political economy to the existence of what he terms 'fruitful incoherencies within empirical social systems' (Crouch and Farrell 2002: 6). 'To a considerable extent,' Crouch (2001) has written, 'the utility of the concept of path dependency depends on what we understand by the analogy of the path'. Make it too tight, and it ceases to be 'a useful analogy for complex societies without clear directing centers and with uncertain knowledge of their futures' (Crouch 2001: 112). But treat it in a wider and looser way – more in the manner of a medieval route or pilgrimage – then it is better able to deal with a world in which 'institutional systems, far from being coherent, are characterized by redundancies, previously unknown capacities, and incongruities, which very frequently provide the means through which actors – whether firms, policy entrepreneurs or others – may seek to tackle new exigencies', and through which indeed those very actors may initiate 'institutional change and adaptation' by 'breaking the path rather than continuing along it' (Crouch and Farrell 2002: 120).

This propensity to 'institutional determinism' in the literature on varieties of capitalism is itself contingent on the presence/absence in specific pieces of academic research of other additional propensities. The propensity to institutional determinism is likely to be at its greatest in studies which treat the institutional logics mapped out in particular ideal-typical typologies as exhaustive of the actual processes at work in particular national economies. It will clearly be at its least evident where scholars recognize that though, for example, the US economy may be a liberal market or uncoordinated market economy in the majority of its sectors, it also contains a huge military-industrial complex which has quite a different relationship to the coordinating role of the state. Moreover, institutional determinism is likely to be a feature of studies in which national economies are treated in isolation one from another, and in which they are not placed on any map of the global economy as a whole. Additionally, the propensity to institutional determinism is likely to be maximized in studies whose research design assumes – but does not question – the degree to which processes and practices developed within any one national economy take precedence over processes and practices brought *into* that national economy from outside: in studies, that is, which undervalue the importance in contemporary economic life of the changing technologies, work processes and forms of corporate organization that now cut across national boundaries. And lastly, the propensity to institutional determinism in any particular study is likely to be influenced by the degree to which its research design is, explicitly or by accident, top-down in its anchorage; since the great danger of too 'functionalist' a mapping of institutional complementarities is that the role, experience, and resistance of labor to the changing requirements of capital will then be systematically excluded or marginalized in the descriptions and explanations of capitalist models on offer, and the degree of institutional coherence and strength exaggerated accordingly. As scholars like Thelen have noted, 'sectoral variations, global positionings, cross-national influences and class tensions are all likely to be casualties of too mechanistic an adoption of the logics of institutional complementarities, and yet all are vital if the story of modern economic systems is to be grasped and explained in full' (Thelen 2003: 28).

This is not the first time, of course, that this argument has been put. A similar call to widen the explanatory frameworks of historical institutionalism, and to extend its dialogue with rational choice institutionalism to 'engage in a sustained analysis of contemporary capitalism', was made with great elegance and extreme care in 1995, by Jonas Pontusson (1995b). His critique was at once methodological and substantive. His was a critique of method, one that noticed that the underlying thrust of the new institutionalist case – 'that institutions, as distinct from structures, matter' (Pontusson 1995b: 127) – was not something that a methodology based primarily on empirical case studies could easily address. It was also a critique of substance. For Pontusson noted the existence of a reluctance to open 'the black box of economic variables' in even the strongest historical institutionalist studies under review: studies in which the 'sketchy treatment of the forces behind and the effects of globalization,' as he put it, 'stands in marked contrast to [the] careful analysis of political institutions' (Pontusson 1995b: 130). He was led to write this.

> The study of comparative capitalism poses a ... fundamental challenge to the historical institutionalist tradition for it requires us to attend to a range of variables, such as factor endowments and the concentration of capital, that cannot be characterized as institutional variables without rendering the concept of institutions vacuous. ... The point ... is not to deny that institutions matter but to argue ... that underlying structures shape the configuration and operation of political and economic institutions [and to press for an] approach [which] provides the basis for an understanding of the systematic power of capital and also enables us to analyze the interests of collective actors and how these interests change over time. (Pontusson 1995b: 120)

The whole logic of the Pontusson argument in 1995 was that the focus of scholarship should be widened to take in institutions *plus* structures – an extension that would then open a route to a renewed concern with the uncovering of 'structural power relations' and the provision of 'a basis for an analysis of economic interests and the forces that shape them' (Pontusson 1995b: 143).

There are at least two broad ways to effect that extension of scholarship. One is to draw heavily on work that explicitly deploys Marxist categories of analysis. The other is to draw instead on what might be termed 'left institutionalism': that body of scholarship on varieties of capitalism and their growth potential that sits on the left face of the new institutionalism, and is written by scholars – including Pontusson himself – with their own linkages to, pasts in, or dialogue with, mainstream Marxism. This particular interface has recently been extraordinarily productive of scholarship of outstanding quality: scholarship which in many ways has reproduced (and indeed has often been produced by scholars who, in their early days, were heavily involved in) the 1970s debates around Marxist theories of the state, economic determinism, and the analysis and specification of classes. After all, the new institutionalist scholarship has not been simply a reaction to neoclassical economics. It has also been a reaction to class-based explanations of European welfare systems; and on its left face, it has generated bodies of scholarship that were prepared to incorporate class-based analysis into their explanations while insisting in addition on a degree of autonomy for political variables, and for international ones. The work of Huber and Stephens (2001) has been exemplary here (also Kitschelt *et al.* 1999), as has that of Pontusson (1992, 2000) himself; but in truth the list is longer, and has its presence in the exciting work of a new generation of scholars (Chibber 1999; Hay 2000).

What that material has among things done, and is now doing, is to probe two features of the growth story of different capitalist models that a focus on their institutional dynamics alone tends to obscure. One is the centrality of capital-labor tensions to the various capitalist models. The other is the manner in which the interaction between capitalist models, and their shared experience of common global trends, has latterly corroded the viability of the particular internal settlements between classes on which the contemporary models rest. It is those features of the contemporary economic condition which Marxist scholarship in this field privileges for analysis, inviting the new institutionalist scholarship as it does so to dialogue with a coherent and distinct paradigm of analysis to its left.

The economics of global turbulence

As an intellectual tradition, Marxism has traditionally been less concerned with variations in the institutional structures of particular national capitalisms than with the general dynamics of capitalism as a mode of production. Like neoclassical economics, it has tended to argue that all cats are gray in the dark, and that it is with the general feline characteristics of capitalism that intellectual work and political struggle ought properly to be concerned. But in the process of addressing those concerns, a body of Marxist material has emerged that has much to say – sometimes explicitly, more normally by implication – about both how particular national capitalist economies vary, and why.

For as Howell has noted, in the recent explosion of scholarship on both the manner in which the institutional characteristics of contemporary capitalism vary in different national contexts, and the degree to which changes in the global economy of which they are a part may now be eroding that variation, 'in the broadest sense the best of that literature oscillates around *two* distinguishable approaches to the analysis of contemporary capitalism' (2001a), not around one.

> The first of these approaches, and the more influential, emphasizes variations between contemporary cases, and assumes rough similarity over time (as a result of path dependence, institutional incentives and the like). The second approach, by contrast, emphasizes that the key variations occur in types of capitalism over time (through periodizations organized as long waves, stages, regimes, and so on), and assumes some rough similarity between contemporary cases. (Howell 2001a: 1)

As that second approach, Marxism has tended to generate periodizations rather more easily than typologies; but its periodizations have established very distinct types of capitalism nonetheless. In the past, when the language of the international communist movement dominated left-intellectual thought, the periodization was characteristically one between *liberal, monopoly*, and *state-monopoly* forms of capitalism (Jessop 1982). More recently, however, regulation theory has given us categories of *Fordism* and *post-Fordism* (Aglietta 1979; Boyer 1990); world systems theory has distinguished *core, semi-periphery* and *periphery*; and a strand of American Marxist scholarship has recommended that we analyze the post-war US economy (and other similar economies) as particular *social structures of accumulation* based on limited capital-labor accords (Kotz *et al.* 1994). The roots of these conceptual distinctions lie back in the writings, not simply of Marx himself, but of those later Marxists – from Lenin and Trotsky to Dobb, Sweezy and Mandel – who were keen to understand (and transcend) capitalism as a global system marked by combined but uneven development. In all those formulations, the particular character of class relations has been held to be formative of the institutional configurations prevalent in particular periods; and in all of them, those institutional configurations are understood to be in the end vulnerable to structurally rooted contradictions between the classes so related. In fact, the more orthodox the Marxist scholarship, the greater has been the propensity to treat the 'varieties of capitalism' which preoccupy the new institutionalists as simply different versions of a common mode of production, and to see each model as equally prone as the rest to experience internal contradictions, and eventually decline and decay.

The sources of that decay have been differentially described by a series of Marxist scholars, but ultimately they always come to rest on contradictory class relationships: contradictory class relationships between sections of the dominant capitalist class, and/or contradictory class relationships between capitalists and proletarians. The general tendency of work produced within this intellectual tradition has been to explore the differential growth rates achieved by particular national capitalisms by examining the character of their dominant rather than their subordinate classes: to look, in particular, at the relative weights of industrial, commercial, and financial bourgeoisies, and at the nature of the relationship between them; and to link those dominant class patterns to the place occupied by each particular national capitalism within the developing matrixes of capitalism as a global system. It has also been a general tendency of scholarship produced within this tradition to go beyond the capital–capital relationship which is the central concern of much of the best of the new institutionalist literature, to focus instead on the tension between capital and labor. And, of course, being Marxists, analysts operating within this tradition have invariably done more than merely examine the sphere of *circulation* (where most institutional analyses of financial systems stop) or the sphere of *exchange* (the sphere privileged by neoclassical economics). They have invariably linked both those spheres to the social relationships dominant in the underlying sphere of *production* from which commodities initially emerge, and in which – on a Marxist understanding of capitalism – the structural contradictions of the whole mode of production are ultimately to be located.

The result has been the generation of a series of studies that have proved more sensitive than much of the new institutionalist literature to what Henderson once termed 'the dark side of the miracle' (Henderson 1993: 213): the processes of labor exploitation that fueled the remarkable growth stories of successful capitalist models rapidly chasing the US (Burkett and Hart-Landsberg 1996, 2000). The result has also been the generation of a series of studies that, by treating capitalist models as accumulation regimes, have emphasized the necessary fragility of the class accords at their core, and so have been less persuaded than much of the new institutionalist material about the long-term viability of either LMEs or CMEs in an age of global capital (Kotz *et al.* 1994; Aglietta 1998). The world systems variant of this broad Marxist tradition has recently generated an important work on the character of both the US and Japanese economies: a work that has explained the character and contradictions of their institutional configurations and growth performance by placing each on a longer, and heavily theorized, temporal and global trajectory (Arrighi 1994). The insights of regulation theory have now been applied to a whole string of national capitalisms, from the British to the Japanese; in the general context of an approach which understands that the changing pattern of accumulation globally, and the changing size and balance of class forces at the global level, opens and closes the spaces for the arrival and survival of particular varieties of capitalism (Howell 1992, 2001b; Boyer 1996, 2001; Boyer and Yamada 2000) We also now possess an important body of material of a more orthodox Marxist kind: one that has combined an analysis of class tensions with a typology of accumulation strategies to argue the general vulnerability of European welfare systems to a globally induced tendency to ratchet-down wages and working conditions (Albo 1994; Panitch 1994; Coates 2000). And of late the Marxist approach to varieties of capitalism and their performance has generated its very own, and very fierce, 'Brenner debate' (Brenner 1998, 2002a).

So here too is a rich body of material on which to build explanations of institutional variation and differential growth performance in contemporary capitalism. It is a body of material largely sidelined in mainstream discussions of varieties of capitalism, discussions that seem more comfortable at the moment to dialogue with neoliberalism than with Marxism. The huge strength of the Marxist approach is its propensity to place particular national capitalisms in a larger global picture, and to explore issues of stability and performance through the lens of class competition – both horizontally and vertically conceived. Maddison, quoted earlier, admitted to embarrassment about the level of ignorance that growth accounting possessed about the ultimate causes of growth performance. Marxism, of course, admits to no such embarrassment.

The issue of choice

Clearly the three main paradigmatic clusters discussed in this chapter drift toward different measures of performance. For mainstream economists, the range of legitimate performance indicators seems to stretch from Gross Domestic Product (GDP) to the Human Development Index (HDI), so opening the debate on growth performance between economists to social issues, if only in a highly restricted and easily quantifiable form. The new institutionalist scholarship is sensitive to (and comfortable with using) these indicators, but invariably goes further in the social direction (exploring welfare rights as well as competitiveness). Marxism is the most eclectic of the three approaches on its measures, using all these quite regularly but also privileging class experience as its measure, being willing to explore 'the dark side' of accumulation – hours, work intensity, job security, even stress at work – in ways that few new institutionalists do. One way of putting this comparative point might be to talk of a movement as we go across the paradigms from static 'technical efficiency' to 'dynamic efficiency', then to 'structural efficiency', and ultimately to 'class efficiency'. The movement is certainly from the narrowly economic to the social, from the quantitative to the qualitative, and from the visible to the hidden.

The three approaches also differ in paradigmatic depth. Both liberalism and Marxism have fully worked through ontological positions, and systematically linked epistemologies and governing concepts. Both are in that sense grand theory, working outward from premises toward empirical generalizations. To go back to the imagery of the stage and its illumination, they each work coherently down the spotlight, with clear linkages between their initial general premises and the resulting detailed individual analyses. The new institutionalism is not grand theory in that sense. It is much more middle-range theory, with its ontological and epistemological underpinnings less obvious, less explicitly thought through, and less uniform. The movement of analysis in the new institutionalist scholarship is much more up the paradigm, from empirical generalization to middle-order conceptualization or categorization. Typological forms of explanation (models) are more common here, as are explanations rooted in the logical interplay of linked concepts that lack any basic driver. In terms of the imagery of spotlights, and paradigmatic cones, the direction of movement is backward from empirical generalization, not forward from ontological premise. The three approaches in this sense differ qualitatively, not just quantitatively.

Moreover, the three approaches have their own definite and distinct logics, each moving inexorably to predictable conclusions (and hence politics).

The first paradigm focuses attention almost exclusively on markets, and on barriers to their effective deployment. Its explanation of lack of growth ultimately always has to be market failure. Its expectation has to be generalized prosperity and capitalist convergence. The second paradigm pushes us toward institutions that innovate. Its explanation of lack of growth has to be institutional inadequacy. Its expectation has to be path divergence, and the persistence of difference. The third paradigm pushes us toward convergence of outcome, and toward fragility of institutional difference. It expects varieties of capitalism to succumb to systematic and general tendencies within capitalism as a mode of production, and the growth potential of all capitalist types to be crisis-riven and ultimately cyclical.

There are well-established ways of choosing between such paradigms; and those will be rehearsed in the editorial afterword to this book. But in the end the proof of the pudding is always in the eating; and it is time now to feast on chapters that will illuminate the various strengths and weaknesses of the paradigms of explanation on offer here. You are invited to read on, and to come to your own sense of which, if any, works.

Part I
The Approaches Explained

2
Measuring Capitalism: Output, Growth and Economic Policy

Michael Kitson

Over 70 years ago, Keynes (1930) published an essay in optimism predicting that within a century the standard of life in progressive countries would be between four and eight times higher, and the 'economic problem' would have effectively been solved. Individuals would then appreciate that: 'avarice is a vice, that the exaction of usury is a misdemeanour, and the love of money is detestable, that those walk most truly in the paths of virtue and sane wisdom who take least thought for the morrow...We shall honour those who can teach us to pluck the hour and the day virtuously and well, the delightful people who are capable of taking direct enjoyment in things, the lilies of the field who toil not, neither do they spin' (Keynes 1930).

Keynes was spot on with his arithmetic: Gross Domestic Product (GDP) per capita in the UK is now approximately four times greater than it was in 1930 and if growth continues at current rates, GDP will be 6 or 7 times greater by 2005. And for the other 'progressive' (advanced) countries of the world the rate of increase has been higher and may continue to be so. But Keynes's understanding of the human condition is more questionable, and particularly, usury and the love of money remain as the foundations for orthodox economic analysis. Neoclassical economics, which is the prevailing orthodoxy, is based on the assumption that agents in an economy behave in a self-interested way to maximise their utility – and the pursuit of self interest will ensure the optimum outcome. And the optimum outcome will be a higher rate of economic growth. Thus, policymakers need to focus on making markets more efficient to improve prosperity.

This chapter takes an alternative perspective. First, it suggests that the focus on GDP as an indicator of prosperity is flawed and that advanced countries need to focus on a range of indicators. Second, explaining changes in GDP by theory based on neoclassical assumptions is insufficient as it imposes the notion of 'sameness' on varieties of capitalism. More dangerously, such theories imply that the liberal market model is superior, thereby reducing the role of economic policy to merely making markets more 'efficient' in the narrow neoclassical sense of the concept.

Economic measurement: national income accounting

The focus or benchmark of economic policy is economic growth, usually measured by the increase in GDP (or its close relation, Gross National Product (GNP)) – one of the key measures in national income accounting. When adjusted for the size of population, this measure is taken by many as the best indicator of the standard of living. The problem is that the standard of living in the advanced countries now has little relationship with GDP or other associated measures, instead it has been influenced by health, education and good family relations.

Modern national income accounting developed during the 1930s following the Great Depression, but it became established during the Second World War when it was an important part of war planning. There were earlier attempts to measure the size of the economy. Thomas Petty in England produced the first estimates of national accounts in 1665, and policy underlined Petty's purpose as he was trying to estimate the taxable capacity of the nation. As emphasised in the chapter by Broadberry, sectoral change is a key characteristic of economic development and this is reflected in economic analysis and measurement. In France, the Physiocrats, who considered that agriculture was the source of a nation's wealth, focussed on measuring agricultural production. For Smith (1776), in Britain, the first industrial nation, the focus was wider and included manufactures. Smith did, however, exclude services from his analysis of the wealth of nations, as they did not produce a tangible product. For Marshall (1890), however, one of the founding fathers of neo-classical economics, it was utility rather than tangibility that was important, and services provided utility and they could be measured by their market price.

The modern version of national income accounts evolved during the interwar period in the UK and the US, in particular as a tool for war planning. In the US, in the early 1930s in the Commerce Department, Simon Kuznets developed a uniform set of national accounts which evolved into GDP. Kuznets, however, had reservations about the national accounts that he helped to create. In his first report to Congress, in 1934, he concluded that: 'The welfare of a nation can scarcely be inferred from a measurement of national income'. In the UK, Keynes had been calling for official national income statistics since 1937 (Skidelsky 2000: 71). Using the work of Colin Clark and Erwin Rothbarth, Keynes made estimates of the UK national income (Keynes 1940a,b) and the first set of the official UK national accounts were produced in 1941.

Following the Second World War, Keynesian demand management dominated economic policy formulation. And central to demand management was measurement of the components of demand (consumption, investment, government and net trade) that summed to national income. By evaluating the behaviour of the components in national income, policymakers could decide which policy lever (fiscal or monetary) to pull and when to pull them. As the economy was considered to be similar to a hydromechanical device, it could be illustrated by one – the Phillips machine, designed by Bill Phillips, a New Zealand-born engineer turned economist, was created to model the circular flow of income in a national economy. In the Phillips machine, the flow of water through plastic pipes represented the movement of funds in an economy, and the collection of water in various holding tanks represented the various components of national income. Undoubtedly, the Phillips machine was a useful pedagogic device until Keynesian economics went into retreat in the 1970s from both the policy agenda and economics courses in universities. But whether an economy should be represented as a machine where you pour money in one end and wait for it to appear in tanks elsewhere is questionable – history, institutions and behaviour may also be important. Despite the retreat of Keynesian economics and demand management in the 1970s, the powerful legacy of national income accounting remains. If 'it's the economy, stupid' then GDP, and its increase, is how you normally measure 'it'.

The most important indicator, but can we measure it?

Although economic growth is the most important indicator, there are empirical problems in measuring it accurately, and obtaining reliable measurements of GDP are problematic for a number of reasons.

First, it is very difficult to measure the output of services (such as banking, health, education and so on), which are the largest share of GDP in the advanced countries. As no physical output is produced, measures frequently depend on input indicators (such as labour or the wage bill) and this can lead to a failure to correctly capture productivity movements and their impact on the output of the sector.

Second, it is increasingly difficult to measure the output of manufactured products because as they become more sophisticated their attributes are more difficult to quantify: for example the power of computers has changed so rapidly that many perceive that the statistics underestimate the contribution of information and communication technology (ICT) to national output and growth. For instance, Moore (1965) from Intel noted that the complexity of minimum-cost semiconductor components had increased exponentially since 1959. In the 1980s, Moore's Law became commonly interpreted as the doubling of microprocessor power every 18 months, and in the 1990s, it became associated with the claim that computing power at fixed cost was doubling every 18 months. Moore's Law has been used to highlight the rapid change in ICT but whether this change has adequately been picked up in the statistics is moot – as is whether it should. Statistical inadequacy may explain the paradox observed by Solow (1987) that 'you can see the computer age everywhere but in the productivity statistics'.

Attempts have been made to capture the impact of technological change on output using 'hedonic' price indexes. Denison (1989) has argued that in the US such price indexes have fallen too fast and overestimated the real growth in ICT, although Griliches (1994) and Triplett (1999) believe that such estimates are a 'major advance' (Griliches 1994: 6). Even if computer power is correctly captured in the statistics, what if such power is unlikely to be used? More powerful and more complex technologies are being used for typing and adding up – and although some tasks may be accomplished quicker, the technological bottleneck is more likely to be in the human brain not the machine.

Third, there is the aggregation problem: how to combine the outputs of a variety of different goods and services (say, computer software and hotdogs)? The answer is by creating index numbers of output and weighting the items together depending on their relative size in production, expenditure or income – but such weights change and this creates the problem of whether to use base-year weights or current-year weights – and there are strengths and weaknesses in either approach.

Fourth, GDP and related measures do not take into account economic activity that does not involve a legitimate financial transaction – so they ignore the black economy but also many other forms of legitimate activity such as housework and some childcare. Distortions may arise over time when types of activity move from the informal economy (where they are not recorded) to the formal economy (where they are). For instance, if parents decided not to look after their child themselves but to employ a nanny or childminder – measured national output would increase even if there were no real change in the level of activity. Such changes may be important in the advanced countries due to increased female participation in the workforce and because of changes to lifestyle.

Even if we can measure it, is it useful?

GDP and its various derivatives are the most commonly used measures of growth and they may not adequately reflect the standard of living or prosperity.

First, some components of GDP (investment and some parts of expenditure by Government and on imports) are postponed consumption which will (hopefully) benefit future generations, but do not have a direct impact on the current standard of living although they will indirectly benefit those who earn income through such expenditures.

Second, GDP takes no account of the environmental impact of economic activity. An alternative 'Green GDP' would take into account the depletion of natural resources, environmental degradation and long-term environmental damage, which will affect the standard of living and the quality of life of future generations.

Third, there is no account taken of the distribution of income. There are various measures of inequality (such as the Gini coefficient) and means of adjusting crude GDP data to allow for the adverse impact of inequality on social welfare (such as the Atkinson index [Atkinson 1970]). US economic performance since the early 1990 would be revised downwards if account were taken of the rise in inequality during this period.

Fourth, GDP includes many items that may not be good indicators of the standard of living. For instance, deteriorating health that is treated may be shown as higher output of health care, and a high crime rate may lead to a high output of policing and legal services. Furthermore, having the financial power to purchase more goods and services may improve well-being but other factors may be more important (health, education, social cohesion and so on). The limitations of using GDP have led to the development of better or more appropriate indicators. The Human Development Index (HDI), which combines GDP per capita with life expectancy and literacy levels, is frequently used as a superior indicator for less developed countries. Nordhaus and Tobin (1972) constructed a Measure of Economic Welfare (MEW) which excludes defence and some of the other regrettable necessities of capitalism from the calculations. Other attempts to produce superior measures that take into account environmental and social factors includes those by Daly and Cobb (1989) for the USA and Jackson *et al*. (1998) for the UK. But despite these improvements, GDP on its own remains the crucial headline indicator for the developed countries and for the policymakers within them.

The limitations of GDP are most apparent when it is compared with other indicators of the standard of living or well-being. In his analysis of the economics of happiness, Layard (2003: 3) concludes that 'GDP, is a hopeless measure of welfare. For since the War that measure has shot up by leaps and bounds, while the happiness of the population has stagnated'. International comparisons show that once a country has reached an average GDP level of $15,000, its level of happiness is independent of income (Layard 2003). It seems that although GDP may be useful in assessing the standard of living in middle-income countries, it is of less use for the advanced countries. The factors that have a positive impact on happiness are job security, employment, a stable family environment and good health (Blanchflower and Oswald 1999; Di Tella *et al*. 2002). The policy agenda that focussed on happiness would attach a high priority to increasing jobs, reducing job insecurity and reducing stress in the work place. Additionally, hours worked would be reduced and geographical labour market flexibility discouraged to improve family life. Public expenditure would be increased in areas of health and education, and redistribution would be important to increase social cohesion and to improve the welfare of those on low incomes (whose happiness is linked to income). This is a policy agenda that is very different to the modern orthodoxy, which focusses on increasing GDP through increasing labour market flexibility, encouraging risk taking and limiting the role of the state.

From measurement to growth theory

What causes GDP to change has occupied much of the attention of a range of academic economists but the orthodox explanations of economic growth are firmly based on neoclassical economics. Thus, whereas national income accounting developed in tandem with Keynesian demand management, growth accounting developed along with growth theory. According to Say's law, one of the cornerstones of neoclassical economics, supply creates its own demand. Thus, the market acts to efficiently allocate resources (capital, labour and so on) and there is no demand problem such as involuntary unemployment. Without the demand problem (or the Keynesian problem) what economists need to be concerned with is what determines supply.

The most influential explanation of economic growth is the model developed independently by Solow (1956) from the USA and Swan (1956) from Australia. It is perhaps symptomatic of the hegemony of American economics that the model is now commonly known as the Solow model (for example, Mankiw [2003], and Gylfason [1999]). The Solow–Swan model shows how growth in the capital stock, growth in the labour force and advances in technology interact; and how they affect a nation's total output. The supply of goods is based on a production function that describes the relationship between inputs (capital and labour) and output. Many versions of the Solow–Swan model uses a Cobb–Douglas function which displays constant returns to scale but displays diminishing returns to a single factor (that is if capital is kept constant and labour increases, the incremental increase in output will be smaller with each additional unit of labour).

In the Solow–Swan model, only technological change can explain *persistent* increases in per capita growth. The simplest assumption about technological progress is that it increases the efficiency of labour – it is labour-augmenting technological progress. Where does technological progress come from? In the Solow model, it is exogenous – it is 'manna from heaven', or more precisely manna from scientists and engineers.

Although only technology can explain economic growth in the long term, changes to other economic variables can explain the level of output and short-term changes in the growth rate as an economy moves from one level to another (a 'growth transition'). For instance, capital stock is a key determinant of the economy's output, and capital stock can change leading to economic growth. If the savings rate is high an economy will have a large capital stock and a high level of output, but if the savings rate is low, the economy will have a small capital stock and a low level of output. Higher savings lead to faster growth in the Solow–Swan model – but only temporarily: an increase in the savings rate raises growth until the economy reaches a new steady state. Population growth can also be considered within the Solow–Swan model. In the steady state with population growth capital per worker and output per worker are constant. The model indicates that countries with high population growth (with no change in capital) will have lower levels of capital per worker and thus lower output per worker.

There are a number of important implications of the Solow–Swan model. First, the investment rate is a key determinant of whether a country is rich or poor. Second, a country with a high population growth will have a low level of income per person. Third, economies with the same steady state but with, say, initially different capital stocks should converge on the same income per capita levels (so have different growth rates). But this may not happen due to 'conditional convergence' – countries gravitate to different steady states because of crucial differences – in savings rates, population growth and institutional factors.

One of the major critiques of traditional growth theory is that it does not explain the causes of persistent growth. As persistent growth is due to technological change, which is exogenous, it does not shed light on what it was developed to explain. This limitation is one of the factors that led some economists to try and explain growth as an endogenous process (see p. 37–38). Although it cannot explain the existence of economic growth, traditional neoclassical theory can explain variations in growth. Different savings rates and different population growth rates will lead to different steady states and there may be movement from one steady state to another. But within this framework is the assumption that different countries use the same production function: that is, they use the same combinations of labour and capital. This is an assumption that is divorced from common sense (see Grossman and Helpman 1994). The whole notion of a production function is an abstraction which sheds little light on, and more likely distorts, understanding of the production process. For instance, capital and labour are assumed to be substitutes when in many cases they are complements (workers need to use machines). Capital is considered to be homogenous when in reality it takes many forms, and is embodied in real assets where it is 'lumpy' and difficult to reverse. Labour is also considered to be homogenous, whereas labour markets are segmented and skills and working conditions and practices vary. And in the traditional Solow–Swan model, diminishing returns to capital means that the growth rate cannot be explained, but in many parts of the economy, constant or increasing returns are an important characteristic of production and distribution. There is also a whole series of further problems concerned with whether micro-production functions can be aggregated to give any sort of meaningful macroeconomic relationships. As Felipe and McCombie (2003: 2) point out: 'essentially it boils down to the question – does it make sense to sum the inputs and outputs, of, say, oil refining and the textile industry and estimate a function that somehow purports to represent the technological parameters, such as the aggregate elasticity of substitution, of this combined industry?'

The response of neoclassical economics to these weaknesses has been to tweak a few of the assumptions and when estimating growth to add a few more 'explanatory' variables. But the overall framework remains intact. Not that neoclassical economists (well not all of them) believe their framework is a good picture of reality, as Solow (1966: 1259–60) admits:

> I have never thought of the macroeconomic production function as a rigorously justifiable concept. In my mind, it is either an illuminating parable, or else a mere device for handling data, to be used so long as it gives good empirical results, and to be abandoned as soon as it doesn't, or as soon as something better comes along.

Many would argue that the production function is not illuminating but does it give good empirical results?

The Solow–Swan model is confronted with the data in three ways: calibration, where the parameters of the model are determined by data from national income accounts; growth accounting, where growth is decomposed into its various components; and estimation, where the models are subject to econometric evaluation to determine the explanations of growth (on the latter two, see p. 39–41). At a very basic level, there is some consistency between the model's predictions and the stylised facts of economic growth. First, there is some evidence that is consistent with the notion that investment rate is a key determinant of whether a country is rich or poor. Second, there is evidence that is consistent with the notion that countries with a high population growth will have a low level of income per person. But third, there is less evidence that is consistent with this notion of absolute convergence, as countries that start poor tend to stay poor.

At a more detailed level, however, the predictions of the model become much less consistent with the data. First, there is the failure to predict the large global differences in income. A calibration of the model indicates that it could explain a twofold variation in income between rich and poor nations – not the tenfold variation that appears in the data (Mankiw 1995). Second, as noted above, data does not show absolute convergence but there are some studies that show 'conditional' convergence (see Mankiw *et al.* 1992); but the rate of convergence suggested by the model is twice that of the rate suggested by the data. Third, if poor countries are poor because they have small capital stocks, then capital should flow to such countries because the marginal product of capital will be higher – but it does not.

Developments in growth theory

The limitations of the Solow–Swan model have led to revisions – but importantly, the underlying framework remains. There have been three main adjustments to the model: first, a redefinition of capital; second, dropping the assumption of decreasing returns to capital; and third, introducing the notion of institutions and social capability.

Capital, in the traditional model, is the economy's stock of equipment and structures (such as machines, factories and offices): in more recent versions of the Solow–Swan model, capital is taken to have broader meaning and includes human capital (reflecting skills, education and training). The inclusion of human capital increases the total share of capital in the production function and this helps some versions of the Solow–Swan model to better confront the data – as calibrated versions of the 'augmented' models can better explain the variations in income, the rate of convergence and why capital does not flow to poor countries (Mankiw 1995). But when the models are subject to estimation, to evaluate the size and significance of behavioural relationships, human capital tends not to be important (see Benhabib and Spiegel 1994; Pritchett 1996) although this may reflect the limits of obtaining reliable measures (on which, see Crafts 2002), econometric testing and the importance of the institutional context for evaluating the impact of education.

Even with capital being more broadly defined, the augmented Solow–Swan model implies that economic growth will approach the rate determined by the exogenous rate of technological progress. And although the model can explain some differences in growth rates as the result of economies having different steady states, the existence of persistent differences in growth rates, and in some cases, evidence of divergences in growth rates, cannot be easily accommodated on the model. New neoclassical growth theories, such as Romer (1986, 1990, 1994) and Lucas (1988), have attempted to resolve this deficiency by incorporating increasing (or non-decreasing) returns to capital. The major contrast between traditional and 'new' neoclassical models is that the latter treat technical progress as an endogenous element of the economic system – an element that can be influenced by corporate strategies, investment behaviour and public policies.

A simple change in the specification of the production function can radically alter the predictions of the growth process. The so-called AK models ($Y = AK$, where Y is output, K is the capital stock and A is a constant) assume constant returns to capital, so increasing the capital stock will increase output at a similar rate and increased savings will, therefore, lead to continual growth. The AK model is the simplest form of endogenous growth model. In other vintages, the proximate sources of growth vary but the main focus is on the generation of knowledge. The models of Arrow (1962) and Lucas (1988) suggest that there is 'learning by doing' where technological progress is a result of the act of producing. In such models, all firms collectively benefit from a higher level of aggregate capital stock because there is more 'learning' but there may be little incentive for individual firms to increase investment, as the gains will accrue to all firms not just the one making the investment. In Lucas's (1988) model, it is investment in human capital that generates spillover effects to the rest of the economy. In Romer (1990), the growth of ideas is related to current stock of ideas and level of employment in the research and development (R&D) sector. Endogenous growth models suggest that policies which promote investment, or at least certain kinds of investment (such as R&D expenditure and investment in education) may be able to influence the long-term growth rate.

For some, endogenous growth models are in a category that is theoretically distinct from the traditional Solow–Swan framework (the UK Chancellor of the Exchequer famously referred to government policy being based on 'post-neoclassical endogenous growth theory'). But they are all firmly grounded in the neoclassical paradigm: they assume full employment and, to the endogenous growth process, the competitive process is often reduced to simplified alternative specifications of market structure – monopolistic competition, oligopoly and so on. Also, such models ignore the inter-relatedness of many forms of investments – it may be the case that it is not just about 'ideas' but having the equipment and know-how to exploit such ideas.

Neoclassical models can explain 'why growth rates differ' in many different ways: because steady states are different; the movement from one steady state to another; endogenous growth; and perhaps, because institutions and history matter. Abramovitz (1986) and Abramovitz and David (1996) stress the role of technological congruence and social capability in the growth process. According to Abramovitz (1986: 406) changes in technology are 'more congruent with the resources and institutional outfits of some countries but less congruent with those of others'. Social capability is a society's ability to assimilate technology and realise its potential and is determined by institutional and social structures as well as market structures. A lack of social capability can be due to perverse incentive structures which dissuade agents (such as workers, producers and government) in the economy from engaging in the most efficient and productive way (as prescribed by the neoclassical paradigm) and due to vested interests hindering the growth process. Olson (1982) has suggested that vested interests can create 'institutional sclerosis', leading to a resistance to the changes that are necessary for an economy to realise its growth potential. For North (1990), one of the leading proponents on the New Institutional Economics, successful economies required a strong network of property rights, efficient market structures and democratic and decentralised decision-making. A related concept is 'social capital' which has some similarities to social capability although it has emerged independently and it has not been incorporated into formal models to the same extent as many other explanations. Social capital is a broad concept which consists of norms, networks and relationships that help determine society's social interactions (Puttnam 2000). In a similar vein, Fukuyama (1995) has argued that the success of private sector business depends on high degrees of social trust.

Assessing the social, political and institutional factors can give important insights into the growth process and its variations across time and space (on which, see Coates 2000). Whether issues which are normally in the realm of political economy can successfully incorporated into formal models of economic growth is more questionable. There is the problem of measurement (of social capital, trust and so on) but, more importantly, the assumption in such models of empirical regularities which have universal policy applicability.

Explaining growth: accounting, estimation and data mining

The original growth model of Solow and Swan led to the development of growth accounting to decompose growth into its factor inputs (capital and labour) and what is left: the Solow residual. The Solow residual (sometimes referred to as total factor productivity (TFP) or multi-factor productivity (MFP)) is typically taken as a measure of technical progress – but it may include entrepreneurship, managerial ability and 'other elements' (Barro 1998: 1). Perhaps so many other elements that, as Abramovitz (1956) observed, it is a 'measure of our ignorance'. A feature of the early investigations of growth accounting was the large size of the Solow residual. Solow (1957) estimated that only 12.5 per cent of growth in output per capita in the US during the period 1909–1949 was due to factor accumulation. Thus 87.5 per cent of growth was explained by technical progress, which, of course, is not explained by the model. Later studies indicated that there were measurement errors in earlier studies and that if adjustments were made to allow for much of technical progress being embodied in capital goods then the residual was lower (Denison 1962; Jorgenson and Griliches 1967). Although endogenous growth models have arguably undermined the Solow–Swan model, recent studies have developed the growth accounting framework to encompass strands of endogenous growth to allow for increasing returns and spillover effects (Barro 1998).

Growth accounting is a product of neoclassical economics – and it can give useful insights if it is accepted that main processes in economic life are captured in a Fisherian world of intertemporal consumption, saving and investment behaviour. But if the economy is not best represented by a production function, where the marginal product relations apply, then the statistics thrown up by the data may have been generated by entirely different processes to those modelled (on which, see Harcourt and Kitson 1993). Thus, the components of growth are unlikely to simply reflect resource endowments, technology and how close markets are to the neoclassical ideal. Instead they are the product of the effectiveness of institutions and the state, economic policy, competences of firms, the level of demand and, in particular, how these mechanisms and processes interact over time and space. Furthermore, such processes and their interactions will vary significantly between nations and within nations. A growth accounting exercise can shed little light on such a variety and the complex processes underpinning it. It is more likely to obscure, or assume away, the important variations that are essential – but albeit difficult – to understand.

There are further issues regarding measurement – not only are there difficulties in aggregating capital goods and treating labour as homogenous but the residual is measured as just that – a residual, so any errors in measuring output, capital and labour will be captured in the measure of 'technical progress'. More elaborate techniques have been deployed to isolate the components of growth but with little consensus concerning the results. In his survey of TFP studies of East Asian growth, Felipe (1999) concludes: 'this work has become a war of figures. From the crudest calculations to the most detailed studies... In many cases these are straight exercises in data mining... It seems that re-working the data can show almost anything.'

If data mining is apparent in growth accounting it is endemic in the empirics explaining the causes of economic growth. There are now a plethora of econometric studies, which attempt to compare the growth performance of different countries based on the various neoclassical models (for surveys of this expanding literature, see Durlauf and Quah 1999; Temple 1999). Despite the power of modern econometrics and the availability of large and easily manipulated datasets, the key conclusions emerging from such studies is that growth is more complex than can be understood by universal models.

As Solow (1988) observed, 'every piece of empirical economics rests on a substructure of background assumptions that are probably not quite true... Under those circumstances, robustness should be the supreme econometric virtue; and over-interpretation is the endemic econometric vice.' But very few variables in growth equations are 'robust', that is, variables that are significant across a range of empirical specifications. Instead a variable that is found significant in one specification becomes insignificant in alternative specifications that use different time-periods, different countries or different econometric techniques (Levine and Renelt 1992). For instance, human capital variables are consistently insignificant or fail to pass tests of robustness – they are 'fragile' (Pritchett 1996). But this does not constrain many advocates of neoclassical growth models – they just ignore the significance tests or blame the data (after all, human capital is difficult to measure). The variables that tend to be most robust are investment and measure of political stability. But this may reflect other issues with the empirics. For example, a positive correlation between growth and investment may be because investment increases growth or that growth increases investment or an additional variable increases both (the simultaneity problem). A second problem is that the independent variables used to explain growth might be correlated with each other (the multicollinearity problem). Thus, high growth economies may have high investment, high rates of school enrolment and strong and stable institutions, but it is difficult for multiple regression techniques to identify the key drivers (Mankiw 1995) and, more importantly, the interaction effects between the variables.

The growth of the 'growth literature' has led to the inclusion of a range of social and institutional indicators as independent variables – trust and religion being the latest fads. This can lead to further econometric limitations such as the 'degrees of freedom' problem. A more important limitation is the assumption of common causal relationships across countries and across time. As Brock and Durlauf (2001) observe: 'does it really make sense to believe that a change in the level of civil liberties index, has the same effect on growth in the United States as in the Russian Federation?' Institutional reforms have different impacts and work through different mechanisms in different countries at different times. For example, the market reforms introduced in Russia had a very different impact to similar reforms introduced in other Eastern European countries (Stiglitz 1999).

The poor empirical performance of neoclassical growth models is not surprising, given the variety of growth experiences across a variety of economies. Neoclassical models are fundamentally based on the vision of how an ideal liberal market economy behaves. As Hammermesh (1990: 274) observes: 'the cultural imperialism of American empirical economics should not blind us to the possibility that the structure that describes a relationship in the U.S. may not be representative of some (any?) other economies'.

Assessing neoclassical growth models

The neoclassical growth model and its variants are based on the usual restrictive assumptions of neoclassical economics – simplified notions about market structures with economic behaviour being based on the principle of constrained maximisation. The reality is that economies, or more precisely the workers, firms and governments within them, do not behave as neoclassical economics predicts. Traditional neoclassical growth theory largely ignores the role of institutions and history as being important determinants of the growth process or reduces them to simple independent variables. Furthermore, neoclassical models are based on what Kenny and Williams (2001) refer to as 'ontological universalism' and 'epistemological universalism'. Ontological universalism is the notion that all economies and economic processes are similar and comparable. For instance, this notion of 'sameness' means that the cause-and-impact of a rising capital stock should be similar in different countries, so, in economists' terms, they will have similar investment functions. Epistemological universalism indicates that, in principle, the process of economic growth is governed by a series of universal economic rules and such rules are not a reflection of time or location. Thus, neoclassical economics, reflecting the 'physics' envy on which much of it is based (on which, see Kitson and Michie 2000), is grounded in a search for scientific laws which precludes it from providing much insight into what drives growth in varieties of capitalism. Additionally, by the very nature of its assumptions, which implicitly indicates that in most (if not all) cases, free markets are allocatively efficient, only one form of capitalism – the liberal market form – ensures the optimum outcome, and to the extent that nations deviate from this there is a need for corrective action.

It would not be a big issue if neoclassical models remained in academic silos and neoclassical economists just continued to mimic their colleagues in the sciences. But the neoclassical creed has seeped so exorably into the political domain that it dominates economic policy, especially in the liberal market economies (see US Government (various issues); HM Treasury 2000). Some neoclassical economists remain sceptical about the usefulness of growth theory, especially the new variants, to inform public policy. Commenting on the problems of measuring the externalities predicted by many new growth theories, Mankiw (1995: 309), who is author of one of the most successful and ubiquitous textbooks in macroeconomics and currently (2004) Chairman of the Council of Economic Advisers to the US President, concludes: 'modern growth theory does not offer any clear policy prescriptions ... policy makers who want to foster economic growth would do well to heed the first rule for physicians: do no harm'. But this conclusion is slightly less 'modest' than the author claims: doing 'no harm' refers to not engaging in the intervention that can be inferred from some endogenous growth models. If growth is endogenous and if policymakers can identify the key sectors that provide increasing returns or externalities, then they should direct resources to these sectors. Although the case for such intervention is unproven, for some neoclassical economists, 'doing no harm' has an explicit meaning – unfettered free markets will ensure the optimum outcome, and the role of the state is to sort out market failures and provide some provision for those individuals who get trampled by the competitive process.

The policy implication of neoclassical growth theory is 'the importance of being efficient', as what is good for economic efficiency is good for economic growth (Gylfason 1999). So what is good for efficiency? The following is based on Gylfason (1999) but there are many similar prescriptions from the new growth theorists (see Sala-i-Martin 2002). First, the liberalisation of trade because of the usual implications of the orthodox theory of comparative advantage (on the limitations of this, see Kitson and Michie 1995). Second, privatisation because we 'suppose private output is better' then we 'suggest some hypothetical efficiency gains from privatisation' (you cannot fault the logic!). Third, macroeconomics stabilisation such as restrictive monetary and fiscal policies to reduce the distortionary impact of inflation. Fourth, investment in education and health, to improve human capital. In summary: 'free trade, stable prices, private enterprise, a well educated and healthy labour force, and diversified exports ... are all conducive to increased economic efficiency and growth. Whether nations grow faster or slower than their neighbours is, therefore, in large measure, but not wholly, a matter of choice' (Gylfason 1999: 110). Thus, choose the path of liberal or uncoordinated markets and grow fast and become rich. Whatever the rhetoric – neoclassical growth theory, endogenous growth or Washington Consensus – the implications are clear: only one form of capitalism works best.

Growth: some alternative perspectives

Beyond the neoclassical straightjacket

The neoclassical paradigm is based on the behaviour of one capitalist system, which is subject to verification using mathematical models. This generates a series of general laws about economic behaviour, where national-specific factors are either neglected or treated as simplified independent variables where their impact will be the same across time and space. The assumption of sameness may facilitate mathematical manipulation and econometric testing but does little to help understand why capitalist systems differ.

The above does not mean that economic models should never be used. Some degree of simplification is required to understand how economies behave. But analysing the 'stylised facts' of economic growth should be grounded in real world issues. Economies cannot be adequately represented by neoclassical models: demand is important; markets do not behave as suggested in simplified textbooks; the steady state is a mythical place which is never reached; causal mechanisms interact, are unstable and vary across time and space. In summary, there are varieties of capitalism. To understand such a variety requires insights from different disciplines and from different paradigms of economic thought. Below are some of the insights from the broader church of economics that are ignored by neoclassical models.

Keynesian endogenous growth

Although increasing returns have been incorporated into recent neoclassical models of growth, they have been integral to many alternative approaches to growth, stretching back through the works of Kaldor (1966, 1970, 1972), Myrdal (1930, 1957), Young (1928) and Marx (1867) to Smith (1776). They took time to penetrate the domain of neoclassical economics because it was difficult to get the math right. Alternative approaches, however, do not depend on the assumptions of the neoclassical approach: full employment is not normally assumed and economic growth is not solely determined by exogenously given factor endowments and exogenous or endogenous technology.

Increasing returns and economies of scale are particularly important in cumulative causation models which help explain how trade performance can lead to divergences in economic growth (see Kaldor 1972). In such models, a nation that is successfully competing in foreign trade can expect that the advantage of an expanding market will increase its competitiveness – including cost competitiveness and other non-price factors, such as product quality, customer service and technological development. Thus, demand and supply interact to influence the path of economic growth. Growing economies, for instance, will be able to invest in capital and skills enabling them to improve processes and products. Conversely, a nation with poor performance in international trade can expect a trend of deteriorating competitiveness and declining markets – with a lack of investment and a dwindling skill base likely to constrain future growth. Thus, while not explaining initial imbalances, the existence of economies of scale indicates why such imbalances may generate virtuous or vicious circles of growth.

In neoclassical models, divergences from 'equilibrium' can be rectified through price adjustment and/or the correction of market failures. Cumulative causation approaches suggest that economies do not behave like this. First, history is important (as recognised in recent path-dependent models), such that the quantity and quality of factors of production accumulated from the past influence what can be produced in the future. This is inconsistent with conventional equilibrium theory which asserts that an economy is only constrained by exogenous variables (with the exception of technology in the new growth theories). Additionally, it implies that it is difficult and expensive to reverse many economic decisions. If a factory is closed or if a market is lost, it is difficult to regain the status quo ante. Second, the impact of economic shocks may not only have a once and for all impact on long-run capacity, but may lead to cumulative changes.

A cumulative causation approach may be taken to suggest that economies may be permanently locked in to a slow or a fast growth path. This would be misleading as well as inconsistent with the 'stylised facts' of growth. Although cumulative processes may generate forces that encourage divergences in growth, other forces may temper or ameliorate such effects. For instance, the international transfer of technology may allow the adoption of new techniques – improving the performance of weak economies. Additionally, successful countries and regions may find that they are 'locked in' to certain techniques of production or have become overcommitted in certain sectors, which will constrain their future growth performance. Furthermore, a change in policy regime may improve the growth path of a relatively weak economy, and if particularly successful may create the conditions for a virtuous circle of growth – and such a policy change does not necessarily require the freeing up and liberalisation of markets. A cumulative causation approach indicates the forces that generate divergences in growth but such divergences will also be influenced by institutional factors, policy and the technological system.

Cycles and growth

Demand is also important in influencing the business cycle, which in turn can also influence economic growth. Yet, in most conventional economics, the phenomena of economic growth and the business cycle are analysed independently: business cycle theorists analyse detrended data and considered the trend as exogenous; whereas growth theorists focus on understanding long-run deterministic growth trends using equilibrium models. Developments in economics, however, have called into question this traditional division.

There has been a re-evaluation of previous approaches, such as those of Schumpeter (1942) and Goodwin (1967), which view growth and cycles as unified phenomena.

Developments in economics have produced a variety of approaches that can help in the understanding of the relationship between growth and the business cycle, including the real business cycle literature and the concept of hysteresis where short-term shocks have persistent impacts. The notion of hysteresis is usually applied to the labour market whereby a recession-induced increase in unemployment results in a rise in the long-term rate of unemployment, such that when the recession has dissipated unemployment does not fall back to its pre-recession level (see Blanchard and Summers 1988; Ball 1997). The mechanisms which cause this change are the creation of a cohort of long-term unemployed who find it difficult to re-enter the labour market; a change in the wage bargaining process (the insider–outsider model); and the loss of productive capacity through capital scrapping. The notion of hysteresis can, however, also be applied to the production process and technological development. Positive hysteresis may occur when a temporary boom may not only increase output in the short-run, it may increase research and development and learning by so doing, which in turn will put the economy on a higher growth path. In other models, however, a temporary recession may be a 'virtue' as inefficient firms are bankrupted, freeing resources for newer and more efficient firms and organisational inefficiencies are reduced – a process of 'creative destruction' to use Schumpeter's (1942) terminology.

Conclusion

There are varieties of capitalism and a variety of paradigms of economic analysis. Increasingly, however, only one paradigm – neoclassical economics – is used to quantify and evaluate economic processes and policies. Neoclassical economics dominates the discipline both in the literature and in educational establishments where the tendency is to *train* economists to manipulate models rather than *educate* them to understand economic and social processes. And this dominance is apparent in policy formulation where the focus is on power of market forces to efficiently allocate resources. Thus, the role of the state is limited to dealing with problems of 'market failure', 'agency problems' and, if a social conscience dares to dislodge the logic of the market, some redistribution to help the 'deserving poor'. The assumptions and framework of neoclassical economics inevitably lead to the conclusion that liberal market economies are superior. The limitations of neoclassical economics, however, are now only rarely acknowledged and they are often buried in a fog of mathematics and econometric techniques. Furthermore, the insights from alternative paradigms and other disciplines are only on the fringes of the policy agenda or are subject to the neoclassical takeover, stripping them of their insight and relevance (a prominent example is the attempted takeover of geography creating the vacuous 'new economic geography').

This chapter opened by recalling a note of optimism that was written more than 70 years ago – it ends with some pessimism that modern orthodox economics can contribute much to understanding the 'economic problem'. If economics is going to contribute to understanding the varieties of capitalism, it must embrace the important insights from alternative paradigms and from other disciplines. It must also be recognised by economists – and more importantly by policymakers – that the pursuit of faster economic growth and higher GDP may not increase prosperity and well-being.

Note

Parts of this chapter were presented at conferences at Wake Forest University, North Carolina and London Guildhall University. I would like to thank participants at both conferences for helpful suggestions and David Coates for comments on various drafts of this chapter and to Can Ozdemir for many useful discussions. This chapter draws on research funded by the Economic and Social Research Council (project L138251038). The usual disclaimers apply.

3
Beyond Bone Structure: Historical Institutionalism and the Style of Economic Growth

Cathie Jo Martin

Explaining economic growth is a bit like trying to account for beauty. Beyond the obvious 'chacun à son gout' is a debate about what really matters. While neoclassical economists (and their esthetic equivalents) might argue that bone structure is everything, historical institutionalists might insist that growth (like beauty) reflects a certain sense of style. Indeed, institutionalists bring into the growth equation all sorts of factors neglected by their economistic colleagues: not least institutionally determined relations between employers and workers, patterns of cooperation among firms, systems of financing, and the opportunities or constraints created by the structures and policies of government. They do that because the succinct explanation for cross-national differences in growth rates, provided by historical institutional analyses, is that institutional divergence produces variations in economic performance. Institutions create incentives for firms to undertake certain types of strategies for economic production. The emerging differences in production processes lead to divergent policy outcomes. Although, in an ideal world, countries might be expected to converge on the best model, in practice institutional systems become entrenched. Because each model has its own sets of benefits and detriments, and of winners and losers, institutional configurations and path dependencies are difficult to alter.

Yet as this chapter will show, any such bipolar portrayal of historical institutionalists – as those who move beyond the bare bones of economic structure to search for the textural sources of growth – while demonstrating the approach's general distance from mainstream economics, also does a disservice to the riches (and alas flaws) of the tradition. For historical institutionalists are a varied lot, dispersing widely along the structure/agency continuum. Some vest institutional structures with the sort of irrefutable logic that makes outcomes all but certain – here institutional determinism might be said to replace economic determinism. Others (stressing the history part of historical institutionalism) view institutions and policy legacies as constraining, rather than determining, individual strategy. Such analytic divisions among institutional scholars then influence individual views of growth trajectories: their distinctiveness, their amenability to change, and their ultimate functionality. They also produce variations (and arguably shortcomings) in such scholars' understanding and forecasting of economic growth. Paradoxically, in fact, historical institutional approaches suffer from problems of too much structure at one end of the continuum and too little predictive power at the other: a varying predilection for structure and agency that hampers the ability of historical institutionalism as a whole to anticipate changes in (and the future direction of) economic growth. Historical institutionalism, as we will now show, has much to say about *past* patterns of economic performance; but less to say about how those performances may be affected in the future by capitalism's perennial tendency to crisis.

Breaking away from neoclassical economics

Historical institutionalists stand apart from even the most sophisticated neoclassical economists in their more developed and nuanced understanding of the role of institutions in shaping economic growth. Scholars sympathetic to this approach argue that because an element of indeterminacy governs how individuals or nation states view their material conditions and seek to improve their economic circumstances, institutional influences have a profound impact on the development of individual strategies or policy vehicles for achieving economic expansion. Historical institutionalism as a broad intellectual tradition builds on the assumptions of institutional economics, and draws from social movement theory, economic history and political sociology. The early heroes of this discipline – not least Weber (1947) and Polanyi (1944) – remind us of a less materialist era with their integrated vision of political economy, their nuanced conceptions of the state, and their group-oriented views of a society governed by ruling passions as well as interests. Several key assumptions differentiate (broadly speaking) the historical institutionalist view from its intellectual competitors.

- First, an individual's interests cannot be derived automatically from his/ her economic conditions because a range of potential preference positions are consistent with any material circumstance. Starting from an assumption of relative indeterminacy, historical institutionalists seek to identify the extra-economic factors that bring individuals or collectivities to align their fortunes with one set of actions over another.
- Second, institutions (and ideas) are important independent (or at least mediating) variables in the articulation of interests or preferences. Institutions, groups, and networks are critical to the cognitive processes-shaping preferences, as they selectively expose members to new ideas and

foster broader political identities (Granovetter 1985; Scott 1985; Touraine 1985; Snow, Rochford *et al.* 1986). Business associations, for example, have been shown to shape their members' preferences in addition to representing members' interests (Turner 1982; Grimm and Holcomb 1987; Martin 2000). Institutions privilege some sets of interests over other sets; for instance, by defining the rules of engagement in the public sphere, institutions make some policy solutions more plausible than others (Hall and Taylor 1996).

- Third, timing, sequencing and path dependencies shape interests (Pierson 1994; Orren and Skowronek 2004). As with Ray Bradbury's butterfly, dynamics set in place (perhaps fortuitously) at point 't' will be causal at 't + 1'. Choices made at critical junctures or points of political upheaval often lead to institutional arrangements and policy solutions that lock in subsequent choices (Skocpol 1985; Weir 1992; Pierson 1993). Thus scholars writing in this tradition view national economic and social initiatives as largely defined and constrained by the past.
- Fourth, strategic choice – especially on the part of state actors – plays a (varying) role in historical institutionalist theories. For example, far from unfolding according to a natural dynamic of their own, markets require institutional support for their creation and perpetuation; the invisible hand of the market is heavily guided by state regulations (Polanyi 1944). Thus, macro assumptions about markets parallel the micro insights about individual preferences – social construction is an essential ingredient – and indeed, the institutions shaping markets create a set of incentives for individual actors to pursue certain types of economic strategies (Hall and Soskice 2001).
- Finally, from these assumptions follows a recognition of diversity of national models of growth: institutions, strategies, and policies differ across broader institutional settings. These institutional arrangements and strategic choices may or may not be functional, as institutional development is often precipitated by contingent circumstance. Thus, the notion that countries will converge on the optimal institutional arrangements ignores both the permutations in origin of their systems and the institutional stickiness that reinforces institutional and policy trajectories.

This generic portrait of historical institutionalism obscures subtle distinctions pertaining to both the divergence of this broad approach with others and the varieties of analyses within the tradition itself. Hall and Taylor (1996) specified three types of historical institutionalism and Campbell and Pedersen (2001) added a fourth – rational choice, sociological, historical institutionalism, and discursive institutionalism – while Thelen (1998) has recently argued that the subtle distinctions between subfields are fading: that, for example, ever-expanding points of commonality between rational choice and historical institutionalism are weakening stereotypical distinctions. Rational choice approaches once (rather predictably) fixed preference in material conditions, viewed institutions as functional, and sought universal theories rather than empirical truths; while historical institutionalism emphasized social construction, located institutional development in the historical contingencies, and used facts to generate (at best) mid-range theories. Yet both sides have pursued a strategy of 'creative borrowing' (Thelen 1998) and works today may be sorted along a continuum in their views of the relative indeterminacy of expressed preferences.

Rather than offering another mediation on the permutations of institutional theory, given these fine extant works (Hall and Taylor 1996; Immergut 1998; Thelen 1998; Campbell and Pedersen 2001), this chapter will focus on the lessons of historical institutional analyses for varieties of economic growth, on the methodological or empirical strategies that have been used to isolate institutional effects, and on the shortfalls of institutional analysis in capturing shifts in capitalist trajectories. The following sections offer examples of historical institutional efforts to account for variations in economic growth rates across countries, regions, firms, or points in time. It takes up in turn the studies of corporatism, American political development and varieties of capitalism (VoC), in an effort to examine how each accounts for variations in economic growth.

Corporatism and the politics of association

The first deeply influential wave of institutional analysis in comparative political economy was the study of corporatism as a system of business and labor representation. Puzzled that capitalist democracies with broadly similar economic systems had varying rates of economic growth, scholars turned to the organization of societal groups to examine how associational patterns shape societal inputs into the political process (and thereby influence public policy). Contrary to the literature drawn from neoclassical economics, with its tendency to see groups as barriers to growth, they quickly surmised that countries with corporatist business and labor organizations were better able, than those without, to reconcile social and economic goals and to develop public policies best suited to shifting economic conditions (Shonfield 1965; Schmitter 1981; Lembruch 1984; Katzenstein 1985; Esping-Andersen 1990; Soskice 1990a; Wilson 1990; Streeck 1992; Crouch 1993). The benefits of corporatism extended to several different features of social partners' engagement with the governmental process: the organizational *characteristics of the groups*, the mechanisms for bringing the groups into the *policymaking process*, and the impact of the system on *policy outcomes* (Molina and Rhodes 2002).

The scholarship on corporatism suggested that institutional characteristics of business and labor organizations (such as scope, exclusivity, and degree of centralization) influence how these labor market partners engage in political processes and unify to achieve collective goals. The scholarship argued that corporatist associations are more centralized, more encompassing, less voluntary, and less competitive than their pluralist counterparts and therefore better able to promote collective action for shared goals (Schmitter 1981; Wilson 1990). Likewise, such scholarship argued that political deliberation should be of higher quality in social corporatist groups because the associations focus participants' attention on broader, shared concerns. Members receive assurance that they will not be punished for committing to these broader goals because corporatist peak associations adjudicate among conflicting demands and bind firms to negotiated decisions. When peak associations include most firms in a country, members do not have the luxury of leaving and joining another group, should the association not satisfy narrow policy demands. Thus, so the corporatist literature suggested, encompassing groups are more likely to cultivate norms of trust and cooperation and to generate support for broad collective concerns than associations with a more narrow membership (Katzenstein 1985; Rothstein 1988; Streeck 1992; Putnam 1993; Visser and Hemerijck 1997).

On this argument, the benefits of corporatism extend beyond the characteristics of the groups, to the manner in which business and labor are brought into the policymaking process. In pluralist systems, social partners provide input primarily through the legislative process; however, in corporatist settings, they may also serve on advisory commissions of administrative governmental agencies and develop rules and regulations through the collective bargaining process (True 1992; Mosley *et al.* 1998). Moreover, iterative corporatist patterns of interaction create a positive sum game for business and labor in tripartite or collective bargaining settings: because the groups foster a long-term perspective and guarantee compliance, each side is more willing to take positions that will benefit the broader economy (Wilensky 1976; Streeck and Schmitter 1985; Crouch 1993; Hicks and Kenworthy 1998; Mosley *et al.* 1998).

Consequently, scholars of corporatism generally agree that countries with encompassing employers and labor organizations are more likely to produce collectively beneficial policy outcomes than those without such groups (Wilensky 1976; Streeck and Schmitter 1985; Kendix and Olson 1990; Crouch 1993; Hicks and Kenworthy 1998). In the area of economic performance, corporatist labor and employer associations with centralized systems of collective bargaining have been able to focus members' attention on shared macroeconomic goals: for example, achieving wage and price restraints in exchange for stable employment and non-inflationary growth (Calmfors and Driffill 1988; Lijphart and Crepaz 1991; Henley and Tsakalotos 1992). Although much of the conventional writing on the welfare state held that weak or divided business led to greater social provision because strong employers defeat social initiatives (Castles 1978), the logic of corporatism suggests that well-organized managers are more likely to favor social programs that contribute to human capital and economic growth (Streeck

1992; Martin 2000). Swank and Martin (2001) found empirical evidence of this relationship between corporatist organizations and the welfare state. Scholars writing in this tradition also developed theories of sub-national variation. They found dynamics at the policy or sectoral levels that contradicted national patterns, while also confirming the corporatist insight that higher levels of organization yield more collectively beneficial policies (Wilks and Wright 1987; Coleman and Jacek 1989; Grant 1989; Soskice 1990a; Campbell *et al.* 1991; Hart 1992).

Finally, the scholarly literature on corporatism suggested that corporatist institutions enable employers to compete on the basis of higher value-added production strategies than those available to firms in pluralist countries. With a diversified quality production strategy, firms manufacture customized, quality-competitive goods that generate much higher profit margins. While mass production strategies entail few institutional supports and are thereby available to companies in institutionally poor countries, diversified quality production strategies can only be used in societies where institutions support cooperation and coordination. Corporatist business and labor associations foster the coordination that brings firms to share cutting-edge technologies, so necessary to these production strategies in the economic battle against foreign competitors. These corporatist groups are also said to foster the cooperation between labor and management that is essential to investments in productivity and human capital (Streeck 1992). The growth trajectories in these regulated economies are at least as impressive as those where capitalism is given freer rein (Calmfors 1990).

To summarize, scholars writing in this tradition believe corporatist institutions contribute to high growth rates more than pluralist ones by bringing business and labor to express broad support for policies aimed at fostering economic growth, even if they must forgo their narrow interests in obtaining particularist concessions from the state. The greater coordination and control achieved by economy-wide wage negotiations leads to better income policies: business and labor groups agree to restraints on wage and price increases. Tripartite channels lead to increased compliance with (and easier implementation of) economic and social programs that create the conditions for enhanced growth rates; thus firms and workers might be induced to invest in training programs that expand human capital and enable strategic investments in high value-added manufacturing sectors. Finally, firms can compete in higher value-added sectors when corporatist institutions enable the cooperation and coordination necessary to the production strategies of managed capitalism.

American political development: bringing the state back in

Meanwhile, across, the Atlantic another provoking wave of historical institutional analysis was building in the subfield of American political development.

Groundbreaking work by scholars such as Skocpol and Skowronek sought to isolate how state structures shaped alternative paths to economic growth and social provision. Scholars of corporatism recognized the importance of the state in licensing interest groups and setting the rules for tripartite negotiations, but it was in American political development studies that state structures and actors rose to center stage. Indeed, 'bringing the state back in' initially included a subtext ambition of taking employers and other interest groups back out. State autonomy (or freedom from the interference of pressure politics) was viewed as essential to bureaucrats' capacities to choose functional economic strategies and to choose wisely (Skocpol 1985).

According to scholars sympathetic to this strand of historical institution-alism, the state matters in several ways to cross-national differences in economic and social policies. First, the broad institutional structures of government (related to the separation of powers, relations between federal levels, and the number of veto points) define the degree to which govern-mental actors are insulated from interest group pressures (Skocpol 1985; Immergut 1990; Huber *et al.* 1993; Hacker and Pierson 2002). State struc-tures demarcate internal governmental conflicts, as politicians and bureau-crats develop interests according to their intra-governmental institutional interests. When state actors, especially bureaucrats, are relatively insulated from interest group pressures, they have greater freedom to formulate policy in accordance with their separate goals and interests and tend to make more effective (and less political) policy decisions (Nordlinger 1981; Skocpol 1985).

So, for example, in the realm of economic policy, Steinmo (1993) argued that the decision-making structures (and veto points) in Sweden, Britain, and the US made for very different tax policy outcomes. The American fragmented system of political authority produced a complex and inefficient tax code, with considerable nominal progressivity but very little *de facto* redistribution. The rather insulated Swedish state structure delivered an elegant, simple system that included very flat rates (somewhat surprising, given the considerable power of organized labor) and an emphasis on consumption taxes, designed for investment and economic growth. Consti-tutional structures also have an impact on interest group organization. For example, countries with a highly fragmented state institutional structure tend to develop highly fragmented business organizations. In systems with multiple veto points, managers can try to influence policy until they find a sympathetic hearing. Alternatively, when access to government deliberations is limited, managers must discipline themselves to achieve success in their few opportunities for input and learn to work together to wield influence in the political arena (Coleman 1988; Martin 2000).

Second, policy legacies create blueprints for future economic and social initiatives and structure divisions among interest groups. Prior choices have policy ratchet effects, making future preferences about policy path-dependent. An adaption process makes individuals to feel comfortable with, and accustomed to, their national approaches to policy problems. Although economists urge us to write off sunk costs, prior investments make it psychologically hard to set out in new directions (Skocpol 1985; Weir 1992; Pierson 1994; Swank 2001). Path-dependent processes are more complicated than a simple closing of options, since policymakers retain a degree of political choice (Huber and Stephens 2001).

In the area of economic policy, Weir and Skocpol (1985) made a path-dependent argument to account for the different trajectories of Keynesian deficit spending in Britain and Sweden. Both countries experienced a collapse of the economy, driving desperate bureaucrats (well acquainted with Keynesian ideas) to lose faith in traditional theories of public finance. Yet while Swedish policymakers quickly embraced Keynesian macroeconomic policies and developed big public works projects, Britain delayed implementing Keynesian policies until after the Second World War. Weir and Skocpol (1985) attributed these differential responses to bureaucratic infighting and policy legacies from before the Great War. British Labour's attachment to a cash unemployment benefits system prevented experimentation with a more radical public works program because bureaucrats and party stayed true to their past policy initiatives (Weir and Skocpol 1985).

Finally, politicians' more short-term political strategies for winning business support are said to influence corporate preference development, mobilization, and participation in state programs (Katzenstein 1978; Martin 1991, 2000; Walker 1991). For example, in the area of US post-war corporate tax policy, government policy entrepreneurs sought to build business support for wildly different approaches to corporate taxation. The state actors accomplished this feat by introducing major employers to fundamentally different logics of economic growth and information about the distribution of the tax code. These entrepreneurs then mobilized their business allies to engage in partisan battles over the legislative future of the tax code. Rather than insulating themselves against capture by business interests, these policy entrepreneurs actively elicited corporate assistance in their partisan battles. Yet this use of corporate allies to augment the limited political power of the ruling governmental faction ceded jurisdictional public authority to business interests, and accelerated the siphoning off of fiscal resources of the state to private interests (Martin 1991).

To summarize, the general consensus in the American political development strand of historical institutionalism is that higher levels of state autonomy and capacity are beneficial to economic growth, because fewer political and economic resources will be diverted away from the collective good to narrow special interests. Policy choices are also deeply influenced by prior solutions to political problems made (often for contingent reasons) at historical critical junctures. To understand the degrees of freedom that a country has to respond to current issues challenging economic growth rates, we need to assess past choices and the structural autonomy of the state. Seemingly dysfunctional growth policies can be attributed to the attraction of familiar paths enduring well beyond their proven utility.

Varieties of capitalism and functional complementarities among institutions

An exciting recent historical institutional approach has developed with the investigations of Hall and Soskice and their collaborators into the varieties of capitalism (Hall and Soskice 2001). Building on corporatist insights, the VoC literature argues that there exist choices on how to organize the production of goods and that these choices are related to the institutions that have an impact on markets, or to what they call the institutional framework of the production process. The primary objects of investigation in this approach are the strategic choices of individual actors (especially firms). Specifically, the authors seek to identify how national institutions create incentives for employers to choose one type of production strategy over another (Regini 1995; Visser and Hemerijck 1997; Culpepper 1999; Estevez-Abe *et al.* 2001; Hall and Soskice 2001; Manow 2001; Mares 2001; Wood 2001).

Diverging from corporatist studies that focus primarily on business and labor associations, the VoC scholars identify four major institutional systems: the financial system, the industrial relations system, the education and training system, and the inter-company system. Differences in these systems are said to account for the variation in the strategic behaviors of individual actors: for example, why workers in some countries get more skills than workers in other countries, or why firms in some countries are more innovative than firms in other countries. These institutional differences add up to two broad models of economic production: coordinated market economies (CMEs) and liberal market economies (LMEs). These two models of advanced capitalist economies each rely on a fundamental production regime, each of which has an entirely different logic of company economic competition. Employers in CMEs realize that in addition to deriving economic advantage from physical and factor components, they can enhance their competitive positions with institutional arrangements that encourage information exchange and consensus. Consequently, CME firms choose to compete in high-skills market niches (not available to LMEs with their lower skill levels), and desire government interventions that contribute to the expansion of skills, such as high levels of social protection and policies fostering cooperative labor relations. Alternatively, in LMEs (the US being the key example), labor-management relations are contentious, neither workers nor employers have incentives to invest in skills, and competitive strategies entailing a high-skilled, productive workforce are discouraged.

Scholars writing in the VoC tradition have yielded fascinating empirical accounts of the incentives shaping firms' and workers' behaviors in diverse institutional settings, and have shown how these contribute to enormous differences in national growth trajectories. For example, unemployment in Germany is notoriously high, and Thelen (2001) offers startling insights into this state of affair. All things being equal, market forces and the enormous untapped labor pool should erode the rigid labor regulations and hefty minimum wage that constrain economy expansion. Yet German employers have done little to push for these reforms because labor market rigidities have benefits for their productive strategies: rigidities and high wages contribute to the high levels of productivity and workplace cooperation so vital to competition in high equilibrium markets. Estevez-Abe *et al.* (2001) draw attention to the stark differences in workers' incentives to invest in skills in CMEs and LMEs. Under conditions of high levels of unemployment and employment protections, workers will make risky investments in firm-specific skills, while few protections inspire only general skills creation. Casper (2001) illustrates how fundamental differences in contract law make German firms much more likely to pursue forms of non-market coordination than their American counterparts (Casper 2001).

To summarize, the VoC literature suggests a dualistic world where the rules of the game diverge markedly across models. Although economic growth is achievable under either regime, the strategies that make sense in a LME are entirely wrong for a CME and vice versa. Indeed, countries that attempt reforms deviating from their historical model run into problems because institutional complementarities reinforce strategies and prevent easy change. Although countries (such as Australia and New Zealand) seem capable of moving from greater to lesser coordination, the opposite trajectory seems especially difficult to accomplish. Thus, Ronald Reagan's famous slogan 'stay the course' might be the epithet of choice for this scholarly tradition, as both economic GDP and employment growth tend to be weaker in hybrid countries. Yet beyond these observations about the institutional stickiness of the past, the VoC approach offers limited guidance about the future strength of growth performance in LMEs and CMEs.

Varieties of historical institutional studies

As the three examples laid out above demonstrate, historical institutional arguments about the causes of and variations in economic growth are not of a single piece. Two dimensions partition these institutional studies of growth: the degree of agency or historical contingency permissible in the key independent variables; and the object of explication or level of analysis of the dependent variable.

First, historical institutional analyses can be segregated according to the degree of agency permitted in their causal mechanisms. Some institutional accounts include little room for agency: here the structural characteristics of key institutions are said to produce a certain set of outcomes. Institutional arrangements have a certain functional logic that dictates certain types of policy choices and channels actors toward certain types of strategic choices. As Thelen (1998) suggests, the origins of institutions are often (although not always) viewed as functional solutions to a set of problems. The assumption of functionality also accounts for the persistence or 'stickiness' of the system, helping the institutional system to endure. Alternatively, other historical institutional analyses identify path dependencies as the critical explanatory factor causing policy outcomes. Although path-dependent explanations often begin with institutions, there is an assumption that the policy solutions will persist even when the institutional design changes. Thus, contrasts in British and Swedish labor market policy can be traced initially to the divergent patterns of institutional control over labor market and unemployment problems and then to policy trajectories that continued even after the institutional patterns shifted (Weir 1992; King and Rothstein 1993). Institutional explanations emphasizing path dependencies share with their more structuralist counterparts an expectation of enduring legacy or stickiness of the policy-making process, but the former includes rather more room for agency and historical diversity than the latter. Institutions and initial policies are often happened upon for contingent reasons, counter-factuals are used to reflect on what might have been under a slightly different set of circumstances, and policy legacies in these accounts may ultimately prove to be dysfunctional. Ultimately, the factors precipitating path dependencies may be more fortuitous than fortunate.

Second, historical institutionalist analyses diverge in their object of explanation: while some scholars use institutional explanations to account for macroeconomic or macro policy outcomes, others seek to account for the strategic choices of individual actors at the micro level. For example, some corporatist investigations demonstrate that features of collective bargaining systems are important to rates of inflation and economic growth; thus, an analysis of institutional structures is used to shed light on an observed macroeconomic phenomenon (Calmfors 1990). In comparison, the VoC scholars seek to introduce the micro link to macro policy, by observing how institutional structures shape the strategic choices of employers and workers (Hall and Soskice 2001; Mares 2001). These individual choices may add up to support for one kind of incomes policy over another, but there is a common effort to identify the micro processes of the relationship between institutional structure and policy outcomes.

These dimensions produce four cells of possible institutional explanations. The studies of corporatism and the VoC trace outcomes to the structural characteristics of significant institutions, while the historical institutionalism in the American politics subfield pays greater attention to policy paths set into place by agency and historical contingency. While the literature on corporatism and American political development largely attempts to explain macroeconomic and policy outcomes, the VoC literature focuses on the

Table 3.1   Types of historical institutional analyses

Type of causal variables	Object of explanation	
	Macroeconomic outcomes or policy	Micro strategies or choices
Structural characteristics of institutional forms	Corporatism Shonfield, Streeck case studies or cross-national quantitative	Varieties of Capitalism Hall and Soskice theory-driven argumentation some statistical analysis
Path dependencies Institutions viewed as arriving from historical contingencies or agency	American Political Development literature Skocpol, Skowronek historical case studies, use of counterfactuals	Social Movement Theory Martin work on firm preferences

strategic choices of employers as an object of explanation (as well as an intervening variable) (see Table 3.1).

Historical institutional explanations differ as well in terms of the institutions, given analytic precedence and research attention. While the corporatist literature places a priority on employer and labor associations, VoC scholars focus on a broader set of institutions. American political development has been rather more concerned with state institutions, and particularly how state institutions and actors have shaped the expression of private interests. While corporatist scholars have made great use of cross-national statistical analysis, the American political development literature has relied more on historical and archival inquiry, and the VoC literature has utilized theory-driven argumentation and case study, albeit with important exceptions (Gingerich and Hall 2001; Iversen 2001).

Meditations on historical institutional approaches

Historical institutional theories have contributed much to the illustration of past growth policies and outcomes, yet one wonders about their utility for future economic trajectories. The weaknesses of historical institutionalism might affect its ability to clearly see trends, possibilities and time bombs in economic growth trajectories. We now consider criticisms of the approach and its visionary gaps about the future of economic growth.

An initial problem with both the structural and historical versions of historical institutional analysis is their tendency to explain continuity more easily than change. Studies of corporatism and VoC that underscore the functional benefits of institutional structures are especially prone to this failing, although even those recognizing historical contingency in the development of policy paths are hard pressed to account for deviations from those paths. If macroeconomic and policy outcomes are largely determined by functional institutional structures, one wonders why anyone would want to deviate from the status quo. The tendency to view institutions as functional and their origins as intentional is often erroneous: institutional relations have frictions as well as functional interdependencies, especially when different parts of the overall institutional system have been created at different points in time (Hall and Taylor 1996; Goldstein 1988; Thelen 1998). The absence of agency in these models raises questions about how change might be brought about even if desired. As Coates writes in the introduction, this tendency toward institutional determinism creates a solidification of explanation that the theory was initially supposed to overcome.

The difficulties of accounting for change are compounded by a second problem, the scarcity of model types: in a dichotomous world of corporatism versus pluralism, LMEs versus CMEs, one can hardly expect abstract models to fit closely with real-world national economies or to capture diversity at the sectoral and regional levels. Yet by not fitting in this way, the model types can pull analysis away from critical areas of difference *within* countries treated as exemplars of one model or the other. For example, how are we to read the USA as a pure LME when it contains so fully developed a military-industrial complex that shows many CME features? Institutional models also tend to minimize economic influences on institutional development (Pontusson 1995a). Thus, business organization in America is fragmented in part because of the deep sectional divisions in the US economy. Although the absence of encompassing labor and employers' associations have reinforced tendencies toward a LME, this institutional effect has economic structural roots.

Rigidities in institutional analyses are especially problematic in light of the many forces of convergence in the international political economy and concomitant challenges to the functional logic of these governing institutions. At issue is whether the benefits of corporatism, coordination, and comprehensive welfare states will persist with the decline of managed capitalism. Globalization is complicating national policies aimed at macroeconomic stabilization and social provision (Esping-Andersen 1996; Kitschelt *et al.* 1999; but see Iversen 2001; Swank 2001). Technological change is creating a growing gap between skilled and unskilled, and public and private-sector workers (Lash and Urry 1987; Longstreth 1988; Lange *et al.* 1995). The traditional benefits of corporatism reflected not only the presence of encompassing organizations, but also the strength of unions in exposed sectors who had strong incentives for wage constraints. With the ascendency of white-collar and public sector workers, typically concentrated in non-exposed sectors, exposed-sector workers have less influence and thus there is less impetus for macroeconomic constraint (Crouch 1990). Post-industrial societies with their shifting skills and needs have greater cleavages within both labor movements and business communities; and this split may be complicating peak association efforts to negotiate economy-wide wage agreements and decentralizing collective bargaining (Crepaz 1992; Katz 1993; Due *et al.* 1994; Pontusson and Swenson 1996; but see Wallerstein *et al.* 1997; Perez 2000; Thelen 2001). European Union (EU) integration is narrowing the jurisdiction of national policy and limiting the scope of agreements achieved through both collective bargaining and tripartite negotiations; and peak associations for labor and business at the EU level seem to have much less representational power than their counterparts at the national level. Neither the Union of Industrial and Employers' Confederations of Europe (UNICE) nor the European Trade Union Confederation (ETUC) have been accorded negotiating mandates by their member organizations (Greenwood *et al.* 1992). For all these reasons, corporatist forms of interest intermediation may be losing ground in public policy negotiations (Streeck and Schmitter 1985; Sandholtz and Zysman 1989; Christiansen and Rommetvedt 1999; Kitschelt *et al.* 1999).

A third problem with many historical institutional analyses (and primarily with path dependent explanations) is the tendency toward post-hoc explanation or tautological reasoning that loses predictive power. Path dependencies, although true, may be true by definition: we ascertain these essential truths after the fact. Lessons derived from the past can be positive or negative and one cannot predict in advance the moral of the story. There is also the problem of incorporating theoretically into the concept of path dependencies the introduction of new ideas that by definition challenge older policy paradigms. The dissemination of ideas from other regimes is an important source of policy innovation. One wonders whether path dependencies and institutional arrangements are more functional and more predictive at one point of time than another. How do these institutional solutions survive the passage of one economic era to the next? Indeed, the independent variables of both institutional structures and policy legacies are better at explaining continuity than accounting for change. Path dependencies are at once too predictive and not predictive enough, in their inability to accommodate radical shifts.

A fourth criticism of much of the historical institutionalist writing concerns its lack of a micro foundation (Pontusson 1995b; Hall and Taylor 1996). The predictive power of rational choice theorists is greatly enhanced by the discipline's clearly specified set of incentives or processes that are applicable to various levels of analysis. Although historical institutionalist analysts make claims about the macro-effects of institutional arrangements, little theoretical or empirical work has been down to establish the validity of these claims at the micro or individual level. It is true that the VoC scholars have attempted to develop a theory of firm strategy specifying how institutions shape individual employers' interests; however, this approach cannot account for inter-firm variations within national settings. The model points to essentially different logics of firms across regime types, but derives these logics from system-level institutional distinctions; thus, there is no place in the theory for variation *among* firms within national model types.

Recent historical institutional scholarship has responded to these varied criticisms. To address charges of institutional determinism and functionalism, scholars have shifted conceptually from how institutions determine outcomes to how they shape processes, thereby introducing greater contingency into predictive models. Attempting to specify how institutions shape processes of engagement, Thelen has recently argued that social pacts between business and labor need to be renegotiated. Different patterns of business association may have a divergent effect on this process, but the outcomes are by no means assured. Visser and Hemerijck (1997) and Scharpf and Schmidt (2000) have studied how corporatist patterns of interaction further the task of economic adjustment, focusing on the processes by which pro-growth coalitions and agreements are negotiated and the institutional structures giving rise to these processes. Their work suggests that, like a good marriage, the processes of negotiation, information-sharing and communication – rather than de jure agreements (such as pre-nuptials) – may be most important to long-term success.

In response to the charges that the institutional models are too encompassing and fail to capture diversity, others have tried to separate the various institutional effects contained in the broad models. Investigating the durability of corporatist forms of collective bargaining, Wallerstein *et al.* (1997) have disaggregated the corporatist model, showing that union coverage (density) has increased in many countries, even while the concentration of union power (concertation) has declined. In a similar vein Soskice (1990a) and Golden (1993) have both rejected centralization as the institutional factor essential to propitious wage bargaining, preferring respectively coordination and union monopoly (or the lack of competition between multiple unions for members).

Scholars have also struggled to come to terms with the post-hoc nature of path-dependent analysis. In an effort to understand precisely *which* paths matter, Orren and Skowronek (2004) have develop a hierarchical ordering of paths dependencies, and selected a subset of paths in American history that have been linked to a genuine transformation of governing authority. This enables them to develop generalizations about significant paths for the area of political development, and we could envision a similar undertaking for studies of economic growth. In the same vein, works on temporal changes, interaction effects, and periodicity are currently struggling to identify *when* paths matter, with the recognition that the salience of institutions and path legacies as independent variables change over time (Baumgartner and Jones 1993; Pierson 1994).

Recent scholarship has also struggled to identify the micro foundations of macro institutional structures, in particular looking at how structures might inspire micro processes of engagement in the political sphere. Jones (2001) has conceptually moved beyond the impact of institutional arrangements on incentives, to examine their effect on cognitive processes. I have sought conceptually and empirically to identify how structures of business association and welfare regimes shape firms' formation of their preferences (Martin 1995, 2000). This empirical work has the advantage of allowing us to move beyond tautological arguments, because theories and the validity of causal relations can be tested. In a study of Danish and British active social policies, I found that differences in business organization and welfare regimes had a profound impact on employers' willingness to participate in the program. While Danish employers belonging to a corporatist business association were significantly more likely to participate, belonging to a pluralist business association did not bring British firms to participate in the programs. Danish employers reported that their corporatist associations were enormously important in providing information about the programs and in helping firms to link these programs to larger concerns about the skilled labor pool. The UK employers, by contrast, did not (Martin forthcoming). This kind of empirical, micro-level institutional analysis can be fruitful in allowing us to evaluate whether the institutions said to influence individual actors during the golden age are losing their salience in these post-industrial, shifting times.

A final criticism (taken up in Chapter 4) is perhaps most vexing for historical institutional analysis. In its effort to free growth from economic determinism, historical institutionalist scholarship has tended to neglect the economic realm, paying insufficient attention to capitalist crisis tendencies and other broad movements in the political economy. But the essential question before us now is whether we are at such a point of broad transformation that paradigmatic change overwhelms model variations and old paths cease to hold true. Brenner (1998) has argued that capitalist crisis tendencies may be so overwhelming economies at the present that all bets are off and cross-national permutations are pushed to the margins; and if that is so, then in the final analysis, social science research will need a broader theory of the relationship between structural changes in the economy and institutions as a mediating influence, than that currently on offer by historical institutionalists.

4

Contesting the 'New Capitalism'

Greg Albo

For some time now, students of comparative political economy have been preoccupied with interpreting the new phase of capitalism that has followed the post-war boom and been dominated by neoliberal ideas and policies. This has meant, on the one hand, a number of declarations of political endings: the end of corporatism, the end of the nation state, the end of Modell Deutschland, and so on. And, on the other hand, numerous forecasts of a 'new capitalism': post-Fordism, cosmopolitan democracy, diversified quality production, the borderless world, and so on. Behind these bold, if often misguided, formulations have been three fundamental research questions about the 'new capitalism'. First, what is the character of the new processes and activities of adding and realizing value? Second, what has been the resulting transformations in the pattern of exchanges in the world market and in the relationship between its constituent states? Third, what mediating role has been played by the variety of institutionalized relations of capitalism in these developments, and are these relations tending towards convergence or divergence of national 'models of capitalism'?

The theoretical stakes in addressing these questions – with their focus on specifying the spatial and temporal variations of capitalist development – have always been high. They have guided the neoliberal defence of *exchange* as the essential expression of human nature and thus the necessity of global convergence towards an institutional regime protecting capitalist property rights and liberalized markets (Bhagwati 2004). They have shaped the institutionalist concern for the parameters for differentiated *distributional* bargains, social networks, and governance institutions, in societies where property rights and productive assets remain private and market allocation of new investment predominates (Hall and Soskice 2001). And they have informed the Marxist concern with historically specifying and locationally situating capitalist *social relations*, the balance of social forces, the limits of liberal democracy, and potential agendas for structural transformation (Wood 1995).

For Marxian political economy, theorizing the specific varieties of capitalism across history and in different social contexts does not begin with deductively deriving models of individualized market exchanges or inductively generalizing from institutional and distributional particularities. Capitalism must be theorized in terms of its historical development as a specific form of social relations, a particular mode of production with its own logic of reproduction. In an abstract but essential way, capitalism is the social relations of generalized commodity exchange: one class only has available the sale of its labour power to earn its means of subsistence and social necessities, and directly produces the social product; another class controls the means of production through the institutions of private property as legitimated by states, purchases labour power to put this capital into use, appropriates the social product produced, and attempts to realize the value of the product, including its surplus value, through the circulation of commodities in the world market. For Marxian political economy, the study of comparative capitalisms always invokes conceptions of exploitation, social classes, national social formations, and an encompassing world market. It is to this debate contesting the conceptualization of the 'new capitalism', and in particular the Marxian assessment and contribution, that we now turn.

Lineages of comparative political economy

In comparative political economy, this debate has, in fact, a very long lineage. It is worthwhile to recall some of this history. For all the main traditions of political economy have seen the production of a 'new economy' as something inherent in capitalist development, and capitalism's relationship to modernity as a whole.

In the founding statement of the neoliberal *exchange*-based position, Smith (1776: 477) discovered the new economy of his day in that 'capitalists led by an invisible hand had to promote an end to which was not part of his intention' (Smith 1776: 477). In such a market, private pursuits produced public value and the wealth of nations – what Smith called, 'the great multiplication of all the arts' (Smith 1776: 15). Free exchange was, for Smith, a necessary imperative for development. In forwarding his classical synthesis, Mill contended that even though 'laissez-faire...should be the general practice' (Mill 1965: 950), 'it is not admissible that the protection of persons and that of property are the sole purposes of government. The ends of government are as comprehensive as those of social union' (804–5). For Mill, the new property relations of capitalism allowed a variety of *distribution* relations to be instituted. Social distribution was limited neither by the requirements of market exchange nor by class structures but only by political will.

In contrast, Karl Marx staked his position on the *social relations of capitalist production* as a whole. Capitalism was given explicit conceptualization as a continual displacement and transformation of social relations on a world scale: 'all that is solid melts into air' and 'the breaking down of all Chinese walls' in the well-known phrases of *The Communist Manifesto* (1848). Marx gave this view more systematic presentation in *Capital* where the accumulative imperatives of capitalists compel adoption of strategies of continual revolution of the means of production:

> the development of capitalist production makes it constantly necessary to keep increasing the amount of capital laid out in a given industrial undertaking, and competition makes the immanent laws of capitalist competition to be felt by each individual industrial capitalist as external coercive laws. It compels him to keep constantly extending his capital, in order to preserve it, but extend he cannot except by means of progressive accumulation. (1961: 592)

For Marx, the market imperatives imposed by capital accumulation always had to be examined in the context of the specificities of history and class relations, of time and place.

The development and consolidation of monopoly capitalism in the late nineteenth century brought a host of theorizations about the new trajectory of capitalism. The formation of neoclassical economics, for example, consolidated a focus on rational individual economic agents, pursuing their self-interest in an endless series of exchanges as a theory of capitalist development, irrespective of the arrival of monopolies. The theorization was consistently of a convergence of prices, production functions, and outcomes as capitalist exchange became generalized. In the view of Walras, governments should enforce competitive markets as 'production in a market ruled by free competition...will give the greatest possible satisfaction of wants' (1954: 255). In contrast, institutionalists such as Weber, Veblen, and Hobson rejected the neoclassical reduction of society to exchange although, like Mill, not necessarily the capitalist organization of the economy. Instead, they noted a range of organizational developments, including monopolies and government bureaucracies, that were displacing pure market exchange by non-market authoritative allocations of resources, for good or ill depending upon the assessor. Weber identified the ceaseless extension of instrumental rationality through both technological and organizational evolutions as an integral aspect of capitalist development. But for Weber, economic action was always dependent upon differentiated complexes of values of distinct societies at different times. The plurality of institutionalizations of these values formed the variability of capitalist societies, conceptualized as ideal types of characteristics differentiated, according to a principle of variation embedded in the evolution of instrumental rationality, as the central calculus of capitalist development (Gerth and Mills 1958: 66–9).

For Marxian political economy, theorists such as V.I. Lenin, Nikolai Bukharin, Rudolph Hilferding and Karl Kautsky were preoccupied with the way that finance and monopoly capitalism led to imperialist contestation over the division of the world market. These writers, and indeed political actors, were divided over the economics of imperialism and the degree to which 'world trusts' could overcome imperialist rivalry. But they agreed that there were tendencies inherent within capital accumulation to both the internationalization of capital and a stratification and division of the world market into competing states. Bukharin best captured the simultaneous processes of capitalist development as follows: 'together with...the inter-nationalisation of capital, there is going on a process of "national" inter-twining of capital, a process of "nationalising" capital' (1972: 80).

The post-war formation of welfare states under the guidance of Keynesian economic policy brought a host of new theorizations in an effort to penetrate the implications of the 'new collectivism' of capitalist societies. Neoliberal writers like Hayek (1944) and Friedman (1962) warned that the expansion of the state sector of the 'new capitalism' would thwart individual incentives and freedoms. Hence, to the extent that they interfered with market pro-cesses, states varied in how far along they were on a common road to ruin. Institutionalists, too, found a new pattern of convergence. In this case, how-ever, convergence met with a favourable assessment as the new state-managed capitalism also allowed for Mills's vision of alternate distributional bargains being struck within different representative polities. Institutionalists mainly quarrelled over what variables, or pattern of values, to give causal weight to, with some emphasizing a managerial 'technostructure' and others a more general logic of industrialism (Goldthorpe 1984). Even Shonfield's pivotal text highlighting variations in national economic policymaking in the central economies observed that 'there is a certain uniformity in the texture of these societies...and even more markedly in terms of their behaviour over a period of years' (1965: 65).

Against the view that somehow the tendencies governing capitalist accu-mulation were being superseded by either negatively or positively perceived impediments to exchange and state policies, Marxist accounts held firm that the economic imperatives of accumulation and the class relations of capitalism remained perfectly intact, at least in the case of the advanced capitalist countries. Instead, they argued that what needed to be explored were not tendencies of societal convergence – which for the institutionalists included convergence also of non-capitalist societies through the stages of modernization – but the impact and mediations of the new organizational structures on the patterns of capitalist accumulation. This standpoint was famously put, against the fury over the 'end of ideology and capitalism as we know it', in the contending interpretations of Baran and Sweezy (1966), Mandel (1975) and Aglietta (1979). These texts returned thinking to capitalist development in the context of the hierarchical relations between states as aspects of the world market, a market increasingly dominated by the competition between multinational corporations and rivalry between new centres of accumulation in Europe, Japan, and the US. If these texts insisted on the continued variation of capitalist development in the world market – its uneven and combined development – there was an equal case being made that capitalist democracy and class relations remained salient features to be explored in opposition to the various institutionalist theses of managerialism ending class divisions. These were the themes, of course, of Miliband (1969); and the entire Marxist state debate of the 1970s focussed on the specific modalities of the state and the variations of national class compromises across the advanced capitalist countries (Carnoy 1984). These debates clarified, in opposition to linear views of advancing exchange or socio-technological evolution, that locating post-war regimes and their common impasse by the 1970s required a periodization of the phases of capitalism. It required that scholars conceptualize the more abstract universal characteristics of capitalism as a specific historical form of organizing societies; locate the particular developments of different phases of capitalist development; investigate singular – or comparative – cases of class relations and social formations in their many concrete patterns of determination; and see each level of analysis as informing the other as a process of real – as opposed to idealized – abstraction of the real movement of historical capitalism.

The current debate over the contours of the 'new capitalism' within comparative political economy has re-posed similar conceptual issues. In terms of economic developments, the high-technology means of production and its consequences for the production of value, the organization of work and the circulation of commodities, has been the critical development. This has gone alongside, and in turn spurred, new financial innovations that have multiplied the forms of money-capital – notably the proliferation of secondary derivative markets – and deepened the separation of 'legal ownership' via shares and 'real possession and control' of capital assets by corporate managers. The market space for the realization of value-added has, in turn, transformed the retailing sector into monstrous big-box warehouses of commodities, and developed into new international networks of exchange, through trade and e-commerce. The international circulation of capital is now, moreover, not just of trade in commodities but equally of finance in all its forms, and the interlinking of international production networks. The implication of the deepening of the world market for national capitalisms is a point of central disputation.

These transformations in the circuits of capital have, as well, exposed the paradigmatic divisions over the trajectory of the institutionalized relations of capitalism. On the one side, globalization of exchange is posited as mandating a convergence in neoliberal policies and institutions, particularly liberalization of 'embedded' markets, reform of income security as the management of 'market risk', and marketization of state institutions. On the other side, persistent divergence of national models of capitalism – between

Anglo-American, East Asian, and European variations – is linked to differentiated 'extra-market' institutional capacities to shape competitive advantage and social adjustment in response to new market imperatives. But these abstracted empirical generalizations of systemic convergence or divergence can also be seen as aspects of the combined and uneven development of capitalism; that is, capitalist development is driven by encompassing competitive imperatives to adapt to the world market and the laws of accumulation, but it is also always differentiated by particular strategies of social actors, mediating institutions, and political conflicts. In this sense, it is the social logic and variations in the institutionalization of neoliberalism that needs to be conceptualized. It is to this division of interpretation of the 'new capitalism' within comparative political economy that this chapter now turns.

Neoliberal convergence

From Smith through to Hayek, neoliberal conceptions of capitalism have held that individualized exchange is the most general of human engagements. The post-war expansion of the Keynesian welfare state was, in this estimation, an inviable infringement on this natural process. The importance of Olson (1982) was, in part, to provide a neoliberal explanation of unexpected variations in growth processes, not easily correlated with the vast extension of collective actors: arguing, without irony or historical scrutiny, that more 'encompassing special interests' provided greater discipline and market-like behaviour than more fragmented ones which only served to create rigidities. It also made the neoliberal case for aggressively enforcing private property rights, liberalizing markets and extending exchange relations into new spheres. If social rigidities could be reversed, a new phase of capitalist growth could ensue. It is in this sense that the 'new capitalism' is not merely a quantitative extension of exchange relations through the global economic system, but is also a qualitative shift in their character. It is the qualitative shift in exchange relations that is requiring, for neoliberals, a convergence of socio-economic systems, and has given resonance to Fukuyama's (1992) claims to the 'end of history' with liberal capitalism.

Several features of this 'new economy', as neoliberals have often termed 'the current period', have most often been invoked. First, it is contended that the underlying production functions of capitalism have been transformed by the new technologies, as both industrial and service sector work can be subjected to systematic productivity advance. This has meant a qualitative shift upwards in the growth potential of the economy (Blinder and Yellen 2001; DeLong and Summers 2001). Second, new financial innovations have brought increased efficiency to capital markets as, for example, in improved capacities to assess and bear risk through venture capital, hedge funds, and derivative markets. Further, the loosening of ties between share ownership and active management of firms allows, on the one hand, financial markets to punish underperforming firms, and, on the other hand, enables tying CEO performance more closely to share valuations. The new financialization of corporate governance compels, in other words, confinement of management to the objective of producing profits and hence maximizing shareholder value (Jensen 2000). Third, the quantitative linking of markets around the world has, qualitatively, altered the economic calculus of the world market. Capital mobility, floating exchange rates, and flexible production systems have produced a 'borderless world' (Ohmae 1990) where price equilibration and profit maximization can be pursued with few organizational and transactional 'frictions'. States are thus compelled to discipline themselves and protect private market actors in line with the private property and laissez-faire governance regime being established by the International Monetary Fund (IMF) and the World Trade Organisation (WTO). Taken together, the extension of exchange relations into new sectors and areas of the world demarcates a new phase of capitalism.

These assessments cannot be easily dismissed, as has too often been the case in comparative political economy. They highlight many central features of the new imperatives shaping value-added production, and the importance of exchange relations and finance in the new configuration of power at the level of the firm and of the world market. In addition, there is a challenging thesis that financial capital must be theorized as more than just a 'rentier' interest. This is not because of the neoliberal case for the pure efficiency of capital markets in allocating the social surplus, a neoliberal proposition which can readily be dismissed as idealized nonsense, but because finance is an important disciplining agent on capital accumulation by unceasingly and coldly calculating to squeeze more profit out of existing investments. Derivatives and other secondary markets, moreover, are integral to capital accumulation, as a necessary sharing out of risk (the chance that investments will not be valorized in the future by appropriate sales) in the production and conservation of value, and thus operate as a particular form of money in capitalism. Finally, the neoliberal interpretation of the 'new capitalism' puts on the table, if indirectly, the quite Marxian notion that the quantitative developments in exchange may be registering underlying qualitative shifts in the social logic of this phase of capitalism.

While an endless number of Marxian objections to the neoliberal position have been raised, three will be signalled out as particularly important to conceptualizing the 'new capitalism'. First, while the relative dynamism of the US economy through the 1990s is clear enough, the consequences of the asymmetries in the American economy it has coincided with – rising debt levels in all sectors, budgetary and current account deficits, persistently high levels of poverty and labour reserves – and unevenness in growth in the world market has generated a blizzard of dissent and doubts. Henwood (2003), for instance, has raised serious empirical objections to casting the neoliberal phase as an exceptional period of productivity and growth performance; and in any case, such claims would have to be limited to the US since in other core countries, and certainly outside the core, stagnation seems to be more the general rule. What has occurred is an exceptional restoration of the relative strength of American capitalists. Moreover, as Brenner (2002a) and others (Harvey 2003; Pollin 2003) have argued, while liberalization of financial capital has indeed brought increasing discipline and competition, it has also marked an era of financial excesses and instabilities internal to the new models of corporate governance – excesses foremost seen in the American case with companies like Enron, but also evident in financial explosions in emerging economies, such as the Asian Crisis of 1997, Argentina, and Turkey. Hence global turbulence has marked the era of neoliberalism as much as anything else.

Second, neoliberal claims that globalization of exchange relations acts as an agent of equalization and modernizer of states are one-sided, if not simply facile. Arrighi (1994), for one, has pointed out that a continued hierarchy of states is being reproduced in the world market that has structural attributes characteristic of capitalism since its inception. Hence rather than conclude that the project of globalization, in setting new norms and rules for world economic governance institutions, has been levelling the playing field for all states, Marxian political economy has argued for the need to examine the 'new imperial challenge' (Panitch and Leys 2004). For example, Gowan (1999) has pointed out the enormous role played by the US in extending neoliberalism as an aspect of contesting European and Japanese claims for world leadership in economic and political matters. Panitch and Gindin claim, moreover, that rather than the extension of exchange relations simply occurring against states, states have been integral to advancing neoliberal policies. The American state in particular has extended its 'informal empire' and 'Americanization' across the world market. Thus the 'new capitalism' is also, in good part, American capitalism with its singular capacity to run massive current account deficits, gain seigniorage as the world's lead reserve currency, and use global military force and draw resources from the rest of the world.

Third, the structural role of American power in advancing neoliberalism raises a third point of Marxian critique. It is an entirely deterministic form of reasoning that liberalization of exchange relations would lead to convergence towards a singular model of neoliberal capitalism (Peck 2001). Neoliberal policies have been resisted and contested at every step of the way and at every level, from collective agreements to welfare policies to trade agreements, and thus existing social forces and institutions have mediated their implementation in many unexpected ways. Neoliberalism in North America, for example, has taken the form of 'punitive austerity', once key labour movements were defeated, while Sweden has tended towards 'shared austerity' in steadily negotiating neoliberal norms through neocorporatist structures of bargaining (Coates 2000: 233–44). The addition of institutions to context-ualize neoliberal propositions (North 1990) does not compensate for the failure of methodological individualist reasoning beginning from exchange to explain the inequalities of power and variations of development between states characteristic of the 'new capitalism' (Ingham 1996a; Fine 2002). The 'new capitalism' may well be neoliberalism, but with few of the virtues posited by the neoliberals.

Institutionalist divergences

Institutional political economy has always rejected the notion that pure market exchange can exist independently of extra-market social institutions. As the ideas and strategies that diverse social actors invest in these institu-tions are always contextually specific, it follows that variation is inherent in the very nature of capitalist markets (Hollingsworth 2000; Fligstein 2001). With the emergence of neoliberal globalization, the institutionalist project of stressing social variation and political choices has had special resonance. Indeed, reliance on market forms of adjustment alone in the context of the 'new capitalism' may well compound the hurdles of societal adjustment to new technological and organizational imperatives. Boyer, in particular, has argued that without non-market coordinating mechanisms 'every economy can be stuck into a specific local equilibrium . . . the transition to a superior institution can be blocked by all the sunk costs associated with the old insti-tutions' (Boyer 1996: 55).

The 'new capitalism' for institutional political economy is, then, quite distinct from the extension of exchange relations: it is the emergence of a qualitatively new socio-technical paradigm, a 'second industrial divide' as originally put by Piore and Sabel (1984). The nature of this divide has had innumerable conceptualizations, but the main features raised are easily put. First, computerization has allowed for more flexible production systems employing workers with more advanced skills, after the mass production systems and semi-skilled workers of the post-war system. Moreover, the new production system has allowed for a reorganization of capital assets as a whole, reversing the tendencies to horizontal and vertical integration, through more decentralized 'networked' – even 'weightless' or 'virtual' – corporations (Aoki 2001). These corporations are mobile, as systems of both property rights and productive assets, so that comparative advantages need to be constructed through 'untraded interdependencies', such as innovation zones, educational and training supports, even agreeable 'lifestyle' infra-structures, which keep capital in place (Storper 1997; Putnam 2002). These interdependencies imply that, for both capitalists and communities, corporate governance structures are no longer mere equity relations, but are questions of wider stake-holding interests in associative governance, over the usage of productive assets at the level of the firm, and over institutional coordination at the sectoral level (Hutton 1994). It is in a relationship to corporate entities and their competitive capacities that, in current institutionalist thinking, 'communities of fate' are now defined.

It follows, second, that the world market is essentially differentiated according to technological and competitive capacities formed, in good part, by comparative institutional capabilities. International competition hence ensues over occupying the limited space of the world market, as it is technology and organization and not exchange itself which produces wealth. This was Mills' case for 'infant industry' tariffs and of others for 'national policies'; and it is now the case for meeting the 'new competition' comprised of networked corporations endlessly competing over new product innovations (Best 1990; Whitley 2000).

Finally, the new context has provided the twofold challenge of sustaining competitive capacities to produce value and realize it in the world market, while remaking the variety of national governance and distributional bargains in line with the new competitive imperatives (Rhodes and Mény 1998; Esping-Andersen and Regini 2000). There has been no small amount of disagreement on how to proceed to re-embed capitalist markets in appropriate institutional supports, particularly over the scale of re-engineering foremost needed, between the global (Held 1995; Castells 2002), the national (Zysman 1994; Freeman 1997), and the regional–local (Scott 1998; Florida 2002). But these disagreements are, at the end of the day, policy disputes of relative emphasis, with the key issue still being the capacity of weak or strong states to take advantage of new market opportunities. As Hall and Soskice (2001: 60) observe: 'because of comparative institutional advantage, nations often prosper, not by becoming more similar, but by building on their institutional differences'. The qualitative break in the socio-technical paradigm of the 'new capitalism' has, however, been unevenly realized in its macroeconomic and societal aspects, as structural mismatches between the new productive capacities and institutional-distributional regimes remain. This is, for institutionalists, the enduring policy failure of neoliberalism (Stiglitz 2002; Wade 2003).

It clearly has always been a virtue of institutional political economy to demonstrate the salience of alternate institutional arrangements, and socio-technical evolution, for the variable ways that capitalist exchange relations are grafted into social formations. Thus the 'new capitalism' would not have – and has not – entailed a homogenous response to global competition. This has been the fundamentally important thesis that, against idealized deductive abstractions of featureless factors of production, 'place' and 'fixed capital' cannot be reduced to equilibration processes of monetary flows at the margin. And, in this sense, the new processes of adding value entailed a devaluation of one set of distributional relations and institutions (especially those of the old manufacturing sectors) and the valorization of another (especially those of the new service and computing sectors). This, too, is a quite Marxian conception, if conceived not as mere policy mismatches but as structural contradictions between new productive capacities and existing social relations.

The Marxian critique has exactly turned around the limitations of conceptualizing the 'new capitalism' as primarily a challenge of 'institutionalizing' capitalism and forming social solidarity for competitiveness. First, Harrison (1994), Huws (2003) and many others have pointed out that focussing on a technological break and possibilities for advancing national incomes misses the entire 'dark side' of the new labour market flexibility and technologies. Technological change is not being driven by supra-market processes of rationality, but by the imperatives of value production. This certainly means not only examining the new intensive accumulation in terms of the extent of yield of higher output per unit of labour input from the addition of new technologies to the capital stock, but also the squeezing of more surplus labour out of labour power in terms of the extension of work hours, work intensification, and the smaller share of new value-added being taken by workers. Explaining these developments as failures of institutional adjustment of training capacities, or collective bargaining demands, leaves unexplained the generality of the processes of austerity across different models of capitalism (Coates 1999). The 'new capitalism' is producing, in the Marxian view, new forms of poverty and wage compression alongside the production of new sectors of value-added.

Second, a similar critique of 'one-sidedness' has been levelled against the institutionalist conceptualization of the present form of competition in the world market. The world market is conceived, as with neoliberals, as tendentiously a homogenous space of exchange flows. But rather than always being a positive set of exchanges increasing the world division of labour, for institutionalists, the world market is a limited space to be occupied, a zone of 'head-to-head' competition. With the new technologies increasing the scale of market exchanges, international competition has become a necessary, if not always desired, central objective of economic policy. But Marxists have argued that this leaves two central problems. It leaves unaccounted the nature of power and hierarchy in the world market that has systematically reproduced differentiated competitive capacities, which requires a theory of the 'unequal exchanges' of value and power inherent in the world market even with 'rules-based' international trade (Carchedi 1991; Freeman 2001). Moreover, institutionalism posits that markets have become disembedded from states, when states have, in fact, been integral to the processes of neoliberal globalization, fostering the forms of international competition specific to this phase of capitalism, including reinforcing forms of 'competitive austerity' as all firms and states become increasingly export-oriented (Bryan 1995; Albo 1997).

This raises a third Marxian note of dissent with respect to the meaning of divergence in response to the convergent pressures of international competition. While there have been different emphases as between states (Weiss 1998) and industry (Hall and Soskice 2001) variables as to the key determinants of variation, the problem is that more 'co-ordinated market economies' have been pulled in their path of adjustment towards neoliberalism and not away from it (Radice 2000; Zuege 2000). There is no theoretical reason why the path-dependent evolution of different varieties of capitalism in space should preclude tracing out different routes of development within an alternate structural social logic in time. This is the Marxian point that the conditions of existence of specific institutions are the wider social structures that they mediate, rather than institutions being determinant relations unto themselves. In other words, institutions are always a consequence of the social actions that the agents of capitalist social relations undertake as a result of their strategies and rules of reproduction. Institutions – or the varieties of capitalism – are the specific contexts in which social agents act, and they are transformed by these actions. The strategies of capitalist agencies may well be neoliberal, as may be the unintended social logic which results from these actions; such that the social relations and structures that these institutions are mediating – even with the formal appearance of continuity in the institutions themselves – are no longer reproducing the same social positions that they once were. The formation of these structural imperatives and the social forms they take in specific contexts and class relations is, for Marxian political economy, what is to be investigated in different phases of capitalism. Without this investigation of structural imperatives, empirical investigation of the institutional variations of capitalism begins to look more like normative assertions and acts of policy advocacy than substantive social analysis. The 'new capitalism' has, indeed, many variations, but seldom does it look like 'post-Fordism', the 'networked society', the 'entrepreneurial city', or some other such imaginative stirring.

Marxian alternatives

In the Marxian conception of comparative political economy, capitalism develops – and transforms – within a world that is already differentiated into many complex social formations. Capitalism remakes a world not of its own choosing, and the combined and uneven development of the world market both further integrates and differentiates societies (Smith 1990).

The specificity of capitalism, as a historical mode of production, lies in the way capitalist social relations of production establish and reproduce processes of exploitation and appropriation, stratification and internationalization. The direct relations of exploitation and appropriation of surplus labour are always place-specific workplaces and communities (if universal in their abstract and simple characteristics). The social-property relations supported and legitimated by states are always particular in their characteristics (given the institutional and political mediations of class and social struggles); and the realization and pursuit of exchange-value knows no spatial boundaries (except the organizational capacity of capitalist agencies and the extent of the world market). The varieties of capitalism arise from the specificity of the social processes and places that are integrated as part of a wider social system, from the very strategies that social agents in these places undertake to expand their scale of action, thereby creating encompassing social structures that take the forms of the law of value and the imperatives of capital accumulation. Thus, national and local dynamics of capitalist development are always a process of combined and uneven development in the world market. Indeed, Marxian political economy suggests that as capitalism evolves and becomes increasingly complex in its social relations, both integration (tendencies to convergence) and differentiation (tendencies to divergence) can be expected to increase. As capitalist social relations become more generalized and the mass of capital to be valorized accumulates, the actions of social agents will tend to be progressively structured by market imperatives; but the increasing complexity of socio-economic processes will also mean that social agents are organized into evermore differentiated workplaces, territories, and state systems. Capitalist development, including its spatial organization into 'national models of capitalism', is fundamentally a contingent historical process as social actors struggle to transform their social conditions and institutional contexts and thus, in their very actions, transform capitalism itself (Lebowitz 2003). This is the central paradox of comparative political economy for Marxist theory: economic imperatives always spread and universalize certain features of development across the world market, but these features are never emulated or settle in exactly the same way in the differentiated spaces of capitalist social relations.

Marxian political economy provides, therefore, a unique methodological starting point and set of concepts for analysing the variations of the 'new capitalism'. This is based neither on the extension of exchange and markets nor on the evolution of technology and distribution in national capitalisms, but upon distinguishing phases of the internationalization of capital in the world market and the specific national dynamics of capitalist development in the system of states. From this premise, a number of features of the 'new capitalism' have been central to current Marxian research.

First, a great deal of attention has been paid to the labour process and the 'relations in production' that have been associated with the new technologies. The distinguishing Marxian thesis has been that the 'intensification' of capital from new technologies has not only increased the relative extraction of value from each worker, but has also expanded the capacity of managerial strategies of control over the workplace, including the length and intensity of the workday. This has extended across industrial employment as well as into new sectors of circulation and services where white-collar work predominates (Meiksins and Whalley 2002). These transformations have produced new stratifications within the international division of labour (Panitch *et al.* 2001).

A second focus has been new spatial patterns in the circulation of capital. This is partly the dispersion of industrial sector labour processes out of traditional manufacturing regions to greenfield sites, the subcontracting of specific tasks, and the extension of international production networks into new zones. But it is also the opposite movement of more highly concentrating financial, producer, and retail services in core 'city-regions' such as New York, London, Tokyo, and so on. Against the institutionalist view that the 'networked' firms are breaking up monopolies, Marxists have argued that the tendency of capitalism is still to intensify, concentrate and centralize capital even as global production processes become more spatially dispersed (Sayer and Walker 1992; Gereffi and Korzeniewicz 1994).

Third, the 'new capitalism' has seen an immense explosion in financial activities, encouraged by neoliberal policies of deregulation, with enormous consequences for capitalist dynamics. Marxian analysis has been singular in the proposition that financialization is at the same time a unique expansion of speculative capital staking out a cut of the surplus, and a disciplining of productive capital to be 'lean and mean' in the pursuit of profits and new ventures. Moreover, financialization has been central to the separation of ownership and possession in corporate governance structures, with finance capital re-emerging in the form of new ties between financial and industrial capitals (Altvater 2002; Carroll 2004). Together with the new capitalist sectors, this has suggested an important reconfiguration of the power bloc in each national state.

Fourth, in Marxian theory, the internationalization of capital is a constitutive aspect of capitalism. The 'new capitalism' has deepened the integration of the world market through the increased circulation of capital in all its forms as commodity, productive, money, and speculative capital. This has raised a number of theoretical paradoxes. International competition between places of production over markets is intensified, while the interpenetration and coordination of capitals also become more important. Furthermore, the internationalization of capital internalizes foreign capital as part of the power bloc of national states, while at the same time domestic capital seeks to internationalize and no longer single-mindedly acts like a 'national bourgeoisie' to protect the national economic space for itself (Bryan 1995; Albo 1997).

This pattern of internationalization tends to produce – and this is a fifth feature of the 'new capitalism' that has been a focus of Marxian research – state policies that mediate and support international competitiveness. Marxists have contended that this has been an integral component of the neoliberal reorganization of state institutions. The departments of the state have been reordered to augment the role of agencies dealing with economic internationalization and subordinate those dealing with welfare and labour policies. Similarly, a host of state functions concerned with economic matters, such as central banks, regulatory agencies, and special development projects, have been insulated from democratic structures by increasing their operational autonomy. As well, the entire state apparatus has been internally restructured through processes of marketization, privatization, and deregulation (Peck 2001; Panitch and Gindin 2004).

Finally, the adoption of these strategies has not only transformed the social relations and institutional contexts of national capitalisms, but it has also realigned the economic imperatives of the world market. This process captures an essential contradiction embedded in the self-expansion of capital that Marx returned to time and again, between the development of the social relations and material forces of production on the one hand, and the formation of an appropriate world market on the other (Harvey 1999). This has guided the Marxian position that global interdependence is not unique, but that rather neoliberal globalization is a historically distinct phase of capitalism, with particular patterns of competitive rivalry, conflict, and interdependence. The world market of the 'new capitalism' thus embeds distinct hierarchical relations between the imperial centres of the US, Europe, and Japan, and the rest of the state system, with the US attempting to re-assert its economic and political supremacy (Panitch and Leys 2004).

There has been no small amount of variation within Marxian political economy in interpreting these features in this phase of capitalism. Research agendas have differed over the method of analysing national dynamics of capitalism, but just as much over the political meaning and trajectory of neoliberalism. The 'regulation school' (Lipietz 1987; Jessop 2001) and the 'social structures of accumulation' approach (Bowles *et al.* 1990; Kotz *et al.* 1994), for example, have taken as their objective the periodization of capitalism, in terms of the evolution of institutional forms and their capacity to stabilize capital accumulation. This has entailed a research focus on the production and extraction of value in variant labour processes and hence accumulation regimes, such as post-war Fordism, and macroeconomic balance in terms of institutionalized national modes of regulation. Neoliberalism, in this view, increases the capacity to extract value from workers due to increased worker insecurity, but at the same time produces a 'monetarist catastrophe' in producing and realizing value because of its consequences on investment and effective demand. Neoliberalism represents a failure to discover a 'new institutional fix' matching regulatory modes with the new productive regime. Variations of models of capitalism are, therefore, so many possible trajectories blocked by the institutional discordance produced by the power relations of neoliberalism.

Rather than search for functional regulatory mechanisms that have failed to cohere under neoliberalism and kept post-Fordism at bay, the 'open Marxism' position has sought to explain the varieties of neoliberalism in terms of the political right's concerted efforts, and even successes, to resolve the economic crisis on terms favourable to capital from the 1980 onwards (Clarke 1988; Bonefeld and Holloway 1995). In this view, class relations are always reproduced through particular 'social forms', the institutionalized form of the social relations specific to capitalism. These social forms are themselves constituted by the actions and strategies by which social agents attempt to reproduce themselves. They are created in and through social conflict and thus always express the contradictions of capitalist society. Capitalism is a system of generalized commodity exchange, with both wage labour and private property control of capital assets, but general market exchange is specifically separated from the institutions of the liberal form of the state. Social relations are materially – but also artificially – separated into formally equal market actors and citizens that mask structural inequalities between workers and capitalists. This embeds a contradiction between the global character of capital accumulation and the national form of the state and class relations. For 'open Marxism', this relation is foremost mediated by money, as money under capitalism serves as an abstract form of labour. That is, labour that has been expended and that the world market has valorized as socially useful, and as a social form of power that the national state is committed to preserving. The institutions of the capitalist state are, therefore, inscribed with the rule of capital, even as they are at the same time juridically autonomous from particular interests and formed out of a plurality of national histories and struggles.

In the course of neoliberalism over the last two decades, the crucial problem has not been the lack of regulatory institutions, but the contradictory attempts by the state to stave off crises such as those that punctuated the world market in the 1990s – by credit expansion and increasing the rate of exploitation through austerity. State institutions are the terrain over which these contradictions have been disputed. In this sense, the variation of national struggles over neoliberalism has been struggles over its institutional form. Neoliberalism, for 'open Marxism', is a capitalist class response to an over-accumulation crisis, that is adding its own fuel of surging speculative investment and an asset-stripped public sector, and tendentiously leading to political crises and inter-imperial rivalries of its own making (Clarke 2001).

Neoliberalism as a particular class strategy to restore profitability has also been the viewpoint of more 'structural' Marxists, far less concerned with institutional forms and mediations. Indeed, these writers (Brenner 1998; Harvey 1999; Foster 2002; Dumenil and Levy 2003) have seen little in the way of a 'new capitalism' as opposed to continued crisis and stagnation relative to the post-war boom. Theoretically, this conclusion follows from their emphasis on the social logic of accumulation, or rules of reproduction in Robert Brenner's usage, specific to capitalism, on the one hand, and how these economic determinations are historically realized, on the other. Although explanations vary as to the specific dynamics causing overaccumulation, the continuing symptoms of crisis endure in relatively stagnant growth, overcapacity, mass labour reserves, perilous credit overhangs, and unprecedented international payments asymmetries, with only profitability showing some sustained – if still below peak levels – recovery. Neoliberalism, in this view, has dealt with some of the effects, particularly through attacks on workers and pillorying the public sector, but not overturned the causes of this long period of economic turbulence. Although capital may be differentiated into national contexts (or into David Harvey's socio-spatial fixes), these institutional variations and class relation are increasingly subordinated to the structural imperatives of competition under neoliberalism and a sharpening of inter-imperialist rivalry between the US, a German-led European Union, and Japan. From common economic imperatives to accumulate, and conjunctural constraints specific to this phase of capitalism, divergent institutions and class relations yield divergent responses: but the varieties of capitalism are, in this vision, so many varieties of an enduring crisis and stagnation.

Varied as these research agendas are, they demonstrate the fallacy of generalizing from already-determined institutional variations of individual capitalisms to make claims about comparative capitalisms, without grasping and beginning from the social logic of the whole. But they have also begged several questions. As capitalism has sustained two decades of real accumulation since the turning point of the early 1980s, why is this still a period of economic crisis? From the standpoint of capital, where is the crisis of social relations or power in the resurgent central zones of capitalism located? Why should neoliberalism be considered a mistaken mode of regulation or only a class ideology when it is systematically reproducing – across political regimes and 'national models of capitalism' of all types – forms of accumulation, institutions, and social relations favourable to the rule of capital?

These questions pose a more systematic break in the social forms of rule in this phase of capitalism that go beyond regulatory failures or an open-ended theorization of crisis, both of which begin to lose any temporal specificity and analytical weight, the longer they are invoked. This has been the theme of more 'agency-centred' Marxism (Hirsch 1999; Burkett and Hart-Landsberg 2000; Coates 2000; Saul 2001; Panitch and Gindin 2004; Greenfield 2005). In this view, the agencies of capitalist social relations act through, are constrained by, and transform institutions. Institutions are, in a very real sense, the 'crystallization' of power relations and class struggles of specific social formations; but institutional social forms are not reducible to class relations as their very materiality in terms of rules, norms and resources are quite distinct from class actors themselves. This conception carries two important implications. The social structures and economic imperatives that constrain and condition social agents are the unintended result of these same social agents acting through institutions, that is, they are relationally determined consequences produced by the actions of social agents and not by 'agent-less structures'. And although social agents are embedded in institutional contexts, their conflicting strategies for reproduction continually transform and reorder these institutions. It is in this dual sense that institutions may formally appear the same, but both the economic imperatives constraining and becoming embedded in them and their social form, in terms of the strategies and patterns of reproduction that social agents are adopting, may be substantively quite different. The varieties of specific social relations and class struggles – and hence institutions – fundamentally both mediate and transform the economic imperatives of the world market.

This Marxian conception radically shifts the understanding of neoliberalism today. Neoliberalism is no longer just a capitalist response to an economic crisis whose adequacy is measured by the appearances of profit and growth rates, debt loads, and current account imbalances. It is also a shift in strategy that transforms the institutional and economic contexts in which the crisis first appeared. This is the sense in which Panitch and Gindin's thesis that globalization has been authored by states, and in particular the American state, should be read: the pursuit of this strategy has transformed the nature of contemporary imperialism and compelled the emulation of the 'American model' in the world market, on terms favourable to the re-making of its 'informal empire'. In more abstract terms, the adoption of neoliberal strategies by capitalist social agents and the defeat of working-class strategies in the 1980s transformed the political terrain and economic imperatives, such that neoliberalism began to consolidate through the 1990s as a new social form of rule moulding the strategies of both capitalist and working-class agents and penetrating the common-sense of everyday life. Slower growth, unused capacity, and debt burdens may have the same appearance (or even have become accentuated), but they are now reproduced as part of the patterns of reproduction and contradictions internal to neoliberal globalization and societalization rather than as symptoms of economic crisis. Thus neoliberal strategies pursued by capitalist agencies have successfully reorganized the power bloc in terms of both the position of financial capital and the internalization of foreign capital, and restructured the hierarchy and modalities of state institutions that crystallize the new configuration of power. Neoliberal globalization is – and this is the radical point of departure from institutional political economy – a quite distinct historical phase of the capitalist world market. And as the strategies of capitalist social agents are forged in specific relations of exploitation and are legitimated in the institutional form of the national state in response to the transformed economic imperatives of the world market, there are many local and national variations and temporalities to be accounted for. For the study of comparative political economy today, the varieties of capitalism are varieties of neoliberalism.

Contesting the 'new capitalism'

There have been many ambitious efforts forwarded over the last number of years to theorize the socio-economic logic of the 'new capitalism'. The most prevalent thesis has come from the neoliberals. They have posited a new convergence towards liberalized markets and property rights enforcing states, as individualized exchange has been extended to encompass the globe. This essentialist and deterministic form of reasoning leaves completely unexplained enduring variations in the institutionalized relations of capitalism, and the persistent hierarchy in the relations between states in the world market. Institutionalists by contrast have insisted that, despite the market, technological and organizational imperatives of the 'new capitalism', there persist important politically determined variations in capitalist models between states. That is, 'globalization is in question' as a singular development path. But the institutionalist analysis reduces the persistent reproduction of the hierarchy of states within the world market to an array of technological and organizational capacities reinforced by strong, weak or failed states, seizing or failing to seize, market opportunities. The question of structural power in the world market is left to the side. Moreover, institutionalism reduces neoliberalism to a particular set of policy choices that may be voluntaristically rejected by selecting an alternate set of policies and models of capitalism to emulate. It fails to conceptualize the variations under which the social logic of neoliberalism has been incorporated into different social formations and national models. This is, indeed, a classic case of missing the forest for the trees.

Marxian political economy, in contrast, has contested that the search for a logic of convergence in exchange, or for empirical generalizations of ideal-typical institutional variations around technological-organizational poles of development, are limiting, if not besides-the-point, research programmes. In this view, capitalism has always been a social system driven by the encompassing accumulative imperatives of a world market, yet also differentiated by spatially specific processes of stratification and the particularities of the class relations necessary for the production of value. Marx captured this point in his comment that capitalism imposes 'one specific kind of production which predominates over the rest, whose relations thus assign rank and influence to the others. It is a general illumination which bathes all the other colours and modifies their particularity' (Marx 1973: 106–7). Capitalist development always spreads through imitation and emulation as competitive imperatives are incorporated into the strategies of social actors – the bourgeoisie fashioning a 'world after its own image' (Marx 1848: 40) – but always with commitments in their own institutional contexts, places, and class struggles.

Theorizing the variations of the 'new capitalism' is, then, a twofold project within Marxian political economy. On the one hand, the determinant patterns of exploitation, distribution, and reproduction need to be examined and theorized in their own right for this phase of capitalism. This is, in particular, a project of conceptualizing the social forms of rule under neoliberalism and the rivalries and interdependencies of the world market today. On the other hand, specific histories, places and class conflicts need to be explored as concrete cases of the modalities, social relations and class struggles of the 'new capitalism'. This is the project of mapping the varieties of neoliberalism, as institutionalized in states, in particular sectors and in specific workplaces and communities. It is, perhaps, where our knowledge is most lacking, after so much research effort has been spent on examining and advocating so many national models of 'progressive competitiveness', as failed policy recipes to be implemented by social democratic parties (Albo and Roberts 1999). Such research and conceptual clarification are necessary steps for contesting the 'new capitalism', in all its neoliberal variations, and to discern where paths towards more egalitarian and democratic social orders might reside.

Part II
The Approaches Applied

5

Economic Growth and the United States since 1870: A Quantitative Economic Analysis Incorporating Institutional Factors

Stephen Broadberry

Over the last century or so, there has undoubtedly been convergence of productivity and living standards among the advanced industrialised countries that are usually considered in the debate over the "varieties of capitalism" (Abramovitz 1986; Baumol 1986; Barro and Sala-i-Martin 1995). To understand these varieties using a quantitative economic approach, therefore, requires delving beneath the conventional aggregate economic indicators. This chapter takes a sectoral approach to economic growth, highlighting organisational and institutional differences, which underpin economic performance. Since institutions are slow to change, it is important to consider a long period, and we focus here on the period since 1870, for which reliable data are available. We consider Europe as a whole, which includes a number of countries that have remained relatively backwards as well as the key countries in the varieties of capitalism debate, and we also consider the US as the lead country during the twentieth century.

The sectoral analysis of economic growth in twentieth-century Europe yields a number of findings that help to shed light on the varieties of capitalism debates. First, structural change appears to be far more important than is allowed for in most economic models of growth. Indeed, the share of the labour force in agriculture is probably the best single predictor of per capita income that we have, and there has been an important North–South divide in the pattern of labour release from agriculture. Second, there has been rather less variation in comparative levels of productivity within industry than might have been expected, given the key role afforded to industry in most accounts of twentieth-century growth. Indeed, comparative levels of labour productivity within industry have been stationary in Northern Europe, although Southern Europe does display a catching-up pattern. Third, by contrast, services have played a more important role in changing patterns of comparative productivity levels overall than might have been expected.

These findings all point to a more important role for organisational and institutional factors than is normally allowed for in economic models of growth. Furthermore, by highlighting the "varieties of sector", they help to redress a bias towards manufacturing in much of the varieties of capitalism literature, a bias which is looking increasingly anachronistic in economies dominated by service sector activity.

The main sections of this chapter examine the empirical findings of growth and productivity performance at a sectoral level and provide an explanation of sectoral differences in comparative productivity performance, in a way that incorporates institutional factors. However, it is useful to first set out briefly in the next section some basic ideas from growth economics.

Ideas from growth economics

As we saw in Chapter 2, since 1950s until the early 1980s, the conventional economic analysis of growth relied upon the basic neoclassical growth model of Solow (1956) and its empirical offshoot, growth accounting. The Solow model starts with a production function linking output (Y) to inputs of capital (K), labour (L) and technology (A). It will be convenient to work with the Cobb–Douglas specification:

$$Y = AK^{\alpha}L^{(1-\alpha)} \tag{1}$$

Note that with $0 < \alpha < 1$, there are diminishing returns to capital, the accumulated input, i.e. as capital is increased, output increases but at a diminishing rate. Labour is assumed to grow in line with population at an exogenously given constant rate and capital increases with investment, which is financed out of savings, which are a constant proportion of income (which equals output). There is also an exogenously given rate of technological progress, and in equilibrium, per capita income grows at this steady state rate. Although an increase in the population growth rate can raise the growth rate of income, it does not affect the growth rate of income per capita in the steady state. So far the model does not contain any real surprises. However, the key result of the Solow model is less intuitive; an increase in the savings rate (and hence investment) does not raise the steady state growth rate. The reason for this is that the model assumes diminishing returns to capital. Hence, although there is a short-run increase in the growth rate of per capita income after an increase in the savings rate, in the long run it returns to the exogenously given rate of technological progress. In effect, the economy makes a transition to a new equilibrium with a higher capital–labour ratio and a higher *level* of income per capita, but with the same long-run growth rate.

The basic growth-accounting equation can be derived from the production function (Solow 1957). It is easy to show that the growth of output (g_Y) will depend on the growth of the inputs of capital (g_K) and labour (g_L), suitably weighted, and the growth of the technology shift factor (g_A):

$$g_Y = \alpha g_K + (1-\alpha)g_L + g_A \qquad (2)$$

Each factor is weighted according to its importance in production, which is usually measured by its share of national income. Hence, α is the share of profits and $(1-\alpha)$ is the share of wages in national income. As well as having an obvious intuitive appeal, this also turns out to be consistent with each factor receiving its marginal product under conditions of perfect competition. Since the growth of output, capital and labour, and the income shares of capital and labour are observed, the growth of the technology shift factor, usually known as total factor productivity (TFP), is obtained as a residual.

The empirical implementation of the growth-accounting approach from the late 1950s typically showed that the growth of TFP was the most important factor explaining growth, which Abramovitz (1956: 11) famously described as a "measure of our ignorance". This situation led Denison (1967) and others to seek to decompose the growth of TFP, often using rather *ad hoc* methods, which frequently conflicted with the assumptions underlying the identification of TFP in the first place.

This whole approach based on the Solow model and the basic growth-accounting equation was undermined in the 1980s by theoretical work on endogenous growth and the "new growth empirics" based on the convergence hypothesis. The pioneers of the theoretical work were Romer (1986) and Lucas (1988). Dissatisfied with the fact that the steady state growth rate was determined exogenously in the neoclassical model, these authors sought to endogenise the growth rate in various ways. Initially, the focus was on investment. The key result in the Solow model, that an increase in savings and investment does not affect the long-run growth rate, depends on the assumption that there are diminishing returns to capital. Hence, one way to endogenise the growth rate is to remove the assumption of diminishing returns to capital. Romer (1986) initially assumed that there was a positive externality associated with capital, hence raising the social returns to capital above the private returns, which determine the weight attached to capital in the growth-accounting equation. However, since the share of capital in national income is typically of the order of one-third, this requires an extraordinarily large external effect to raise the weight to unity, which is what is technically required to remove diminishing returns. Later work, therefore, tended to emphasise the importance of human capital, so that there could be non-diminishing returns to broad capital, consisting of both human and physical capital. Here, however, evidence of sufficiently large external effects also proved difficult to pin down, and a consensus emerged that the coefficient on broad capital was of the order of two-thirds (Mankiw *et al.* 1992). This was substantially above the one-third suggested by consideration of physical capital alone, but still substantially below the value of unity needed to remove diminishing returns to accumulated inputs. The other way to endogenise the growth rate was to endogenise technological progress rather than remove diminishing returns to accumulated inputs. This approach was pioneered by Romer (1990) and Aghion and Howitt (1992), and pointed, in particular, to a potential role for Research and Development (R&D) spending in raising the growth rate.

Accompanying these theoretical developments, there was an even more radical shift in the empirical analysis of growth, involving a consideration of levels as well as growth rates of per capita income. The two key papers here were by Abramovitz (1986) and Baumol (1986), which introduced the ideas of catching-up and convergence. For Abramovitz (1986), an important explanation of episodes of rapid growth, such as Japan after the Second World War, was the low level of technology and per capita income at the start of the process of catching-up. Since the technology did not have to be discovered by the catching-up country, but could be imported from abroad, the process of moving towards the technological frontier could occur much more rapidly than further pushing out the frontier by the leader. Baumol (1986) also pointed to the negative relationship between the starting level of per capita income and the subsequent growth rate over the period since 1870 in the sample of 16 countries of the Maddison data set. In a neoclassical growth model, a country with a low level of capital per worker should have a high marginal product of capital, attract a high rate of investment and converge on the same level of per capita income as the leader (but leaving the steady state growth rate unchanged).

Baumol's (1986) paper sparked off a huge literature on the convergence process. One important distinction is between unconditional and conditional convergence. Unconditional convergence is simply the straightforward notion that countries actually move towards the same level of per capita income. Conditional convergence is subtler, allowing for the possibility that there are forces propelling an economy towards the steady state level of productivity and steady state growth rate, but that steady states may differ between economies. In other words, there may be catching-up forces at work, but they may be offset by other effects keeping economies apart. Conditional convergence regressions may thus actually be more useful in establishing factors making for divergence than in establishing convergence.

It is possible to check for unconditional convergence by looking at the relationship between the initial level of per capita income (y_0) and the subsequent growth rate of per capita income (g_y):

$$g_y = \alpha - \beta y_0 \tag{3}$$

For unconditional convergence, there is a negative relationship between per capita income growth and the initial level of per capita income, and the parameter β determines the speed of the convergence process. For conditional convergence, allowance needs to be made for additional factors (Z), which may explain differences in steady states between countries:

$$g_y = \alpha - \beta y_0 + \gamma Z \tag{4}$$

Temple (1999) shows that a wide range of conditioning variables have been used, and that there is little consensus about the magnitudes of the effects of these variables. As well as using narrow economic variables, such as investment, human capital and R&D expenditure, economists have also experimented with wider social and political factors as conditioning variables. This provides an important link to the theoretical approach of Olson (1982), whose emphasis on the power of interest groups to block change acts as a useful counterweight to the simple idea that backwardness is good for growth, which seems at first sight to be the basic message of the convergence framework.

The above discussion of the convergence framework is restricted to forms of what is known in the literature as β-convergence. Barro and Sala-i-Martin (1991) also consider σ-convergence, which refers to a narrowing dispersion of per capita income levels over time, as measured by the standard deviation or coefficient of variation. Perhaps surprisingly at first sight, σ-convergence is not guaranteed by β-convergence. First, in a stochastic world, shocks which affect only some countries or all countries differentially (for example, wars or famines) may increase dispersion to offset any catching-up effects that are present. Second, Chatterji (1992) notes that the absolute difference in income levels between countries can grow, even as the poorer countries catch up proportionally. Third, Barro and Sala-i-Martin (1991) note the example of the ordinal rankings of teams in a sports league. Since the number of teams is fixed, the dispersion remains constant, i.e. there is no σ-convergence. However, it is still possible to discuss β-convergence in terms of how quickly the champions return to mediocrity. This is an example of Galton's fallacy, or the observation that heights of people in a family regressing to the mean across generations does not imply that the dispersion of heights across the population diminishes over time.

It is also useful to make a distinction between local and global convergence (Durlauf and Johnson 1995; Broadberry 1996). For global convergence, all economies must be converging to a single productivity path; i.e. in the limit productivity levels are equalised between all countries. For local convergence, however, a group of economies may be converging on a productivity path which remains below the path of another group, i.e. there may be more than one convergence club.

Empirical findings

Growth rates and levels of GDP per capita

Table 5.1 provides a bare quantitative summary of growth experience in 15 European countries and the US. Growth of Gross Domestic Product (GDP) per capita for a weighted average of the 15 European countries was 1.8 per cent per annum between 1890 and 1994. However, whilst Europe grew at roughly this secular rate before 1913 and after 1973, there was a period of

Table 5.1 Economic growth in Europe and the US, 1890–1994 (average annual rates of growth)

	European GDP	European population	European GDP per capita	US GDP per capita
1890–1994	2.4	0.6	1.8	1.8
1890–1913	2.2	0.7	1.4	2.0
1913–1950	1.4	0.5	0.9	1.4
1950–1973	4.8	0.8	4.0	2.9
1973–1994	2.1	0.4	1.7	1.4

Source: Feinstein, Temin and Toniolo (1997: 7, 9).

slower growth between 1913 and 1950, followed by a period of more rapid growth between 1950 and 1973. Although US growth also slowed between 1913 and 1950 and accelerated between 1950 and 1973, the deviations from the secular trend were clearly more pronounced in Europe. Feinstein *et al.* (1997) explain the slowdown between 1913 and 1950 largely by the impact of the two world wars and the intervening lack of economic cooperation. Furthermore, the greater impact on Europe is explained largely by the fact that the wars were fought mostly on European soil, with unprecedented severity. The acceleration between 1950 and 1973 is then seen largely as a return to the secular trend, with Europe's greater acceleration explained by the greater extent of the earlier slowdown.

In fact, the picture is a little more complicated than this, since it is usual to see Europe as catching-up on the US during the twentieth century. If Europe had simply returned to its pre-First World War secular growth path, then this catching up would not have occurred. Wars and the political settlements that followed, have clearly played an important part in shaping the growth experience of Europe. At the very least, then, this should alert us to the potential pitfalls of relying for our understanding of European growth on data sets beginning in 1950.

Let us turn now to the diversity of growth experience within Europe. In addition to the 12 West European and 4 non-European countries that make up Maddison's earlier sample of 16 industrialised countries, the Maddison (1995b) data set includes data on five South European countries (loosely defined to include Ireland) and 7 East European countries. The average annual growth rates in Table 5.2 are obtained from time series of GDP and population for each country, taken from historical national accounts sources. However, to obtain comparative levels of GDP per capita requires establishing benchmarks in a common currency, using price ratios adjusted for purchasing power parity. The figures in Table 5.3 are based on 1990 benchmarks, with extrapolation to other years, using the time series from historical national accounts sources.

Table 5.2   Growth of GDP per capita (% per annum)

	1870–1913	1913–1929	1929–1938	1938–1950	1950–1973	1973–2001
Twelve West European countries						
Austria	1.4	0.4	−0.4	0.3	4.8	2.1
Belgium	1.0	1.1	−0.5	1.0	3.5	2.0
Denmark	1.6	1.6	1.4	1.6	3.0	1.8
Finland	1.4	1.6	3.1	1.4	4.2	2.2
France	1.4	1.9	−0.6	1.4	3.9	1.7
Germany	1.6	0.8	1.9	−1.5	4.9	1.6
Italy	1.2	1.2	0.8	0.5	4.8	2.1
The Netherlands	1.5	2.1	−0.9	1.1	3.4	1.8
Norway	1.3	2.0	2.5	1.9	3.1	2.8
Sweden	1.4	1.4	2.2	3.0	3.0	1.5
Switzerland	1.5	2.5	0.1	2.9	3.0	0.7
UK	1.0	0.3	1.4	1.1	2.4	1.8
Five South European countries						
Greece		2.4	1.5	−2.8	6.0	1.8
Ireland	1.0	0.3	0.9	1.0	3.0	4.4
Portugal	0.5	0.8	1.2	1.9	5.5	2.5
Spain	1.1	1.7	−4.2	1.4	5.6	2.6
Turkey		−0.1	3.9	−0.4	3.2	2.0
Seven East European countries						
Bulgaria		−1.5	3.3	0.3	5.1	0.2
Czechoslovakia	1.4	2.3	−0.7	1.5	3.0	0.8
Hungary	1.2	1.0	0.8	−0.6	3.5	1.0
Poland			0.3	1.0	3.4	1.2
Romania			0.8	−0.4	4.7	−0.3
Russia	0.9	−0.4	4.9	2.3	3.3	−0.8
Yugoslavia		1.8	0.0	1.1	4.4	0.0
Four non-European countries						
Australia	0.9	−0.5	1.2	2.0	2.4	1.9
Canada	2.2	0.8	−1.2	4.1	2.9	1.7
USA	1.8	1.6	−1.3	3.7	2.4	1.9
Japan	1.4	2.4	2.1	−1.9	7.7	2.1

Source: Derived from Maddison (1995b, 2003).

The main trends in Tables 5.2 and 5.3 can be summarised as follows: (1) The UK had the highest per capita income in Western Europe in 1870, and can be seen as the European leader for much of the period. As predicted by the convergence hypothesis, the UK growth has been relatively slow, so that most West European countries had caught up by 1973; (2) Within Western Europe, only Switzerland had built up a sustained lead over the UK before the 1970s, and this is usually attributed to the special circumstances of war-time neutrality. (3) South European countries have remained a long way

Table 5.3   Comparative levels of GDP per capita (US = 100)

	1870	1913	1929	1938	1950	1973	2001
Twelve West European countries							
Austria	76	66	54	58	39	68	72
Belgium	107	78	72	77	56	72	75
Denmark	78	71	71	90	70	81	83
Finland	45	39	38	57	43	65	73
France	75	65	68	72	55	78	75
Germany	78	72	63	84	45	79	67
Italy	60	47	44	53	36	63	68
The Netherlands	107	74	80	84	61	77	78
Norway	53	43	46	64	52	62	88
Sweden	68	58	56	77	70	81	74
Switzerland	88	79	90	103	93	108	80
UK	133	95	76	98	72	72	72
Five South European countries							
Greece		31	35	44	20	47	45
Ireland	72	51	42	51	37	42	83
Portugal	44	26	22	28	22	46	51
Spain	56	42	43	33	25	53	56
Turkey		18	14	22	14	16	22
Seven East European countries							
Bulgaria		28	17	26	17	32	20
Czechoslovakia	47	39	44	47	37	42	32
Hungary	52	40	36	43	26	34	27
Poland			31	36	26	32	27
Romania			17	20	12	21	11
Russia	42	28	20	35	30	36	17
Yugoslavia		19	20	22	16	26	16
Four non-European countries							
Australia	155	104	74	92	75	75	78
Canada	66	79	69	70	74	82	80
USA	100	100	100	100	100	100	100
Japan	30	25	28	38	20	66	74

Source: Derived from Maddison (1995b, 2003).

behind Western Europe, despite the gains of the post-Second World War period. (4) East European countries have clearly failed to converge on West European levels of per capita income, and this is usually attributed to the adoption of socialist planning in the settlement after the Second World War and (5) By 2001, there was still a clear per capita income gap between most West European countries and the US. On a GDP per hour worked basis, however, a number of West European countries have caught up with the US.

These aggregate trends can be summarised using the language of the convergence framework, although as Prados de la Escosura *et al.* (1993) note, the convergence properties of the long-run European data set are not as strong as might be expected. Indeed, taking the trend in the unweighted cross-sectional coefficient of variation as a measure of unconditional σ-convergence in Table 5.4, we see that although there was clearly convergence among the West European countries both before the First World War and again more strongly after the Second World War, this was offset by growing dispersion among South and East European countries and between the various groups of countries. Hence, in Europe as a whole, there was no clear trend towards σ-convergence. Prados de la Escosura *et al.* (1993) also show that the finding of unconditional β-convergence is largely limited to the "core" West European countries after the Second World War. These core countries have featured prominently in debates over the varieties of capitalism, since their convergence in terms of per capita incomes implies that they all offer potential routes to success. Since they all look similar in terms of economic aggregates, we proceed to differentiate between countries on the basis of disaggregation by sector. The sectoral breakdown of GDP between agriculture, industry and services also sheds light on the differences between the core and the periphery.

Agriculture

Development economists and economic historians have always emphasised the importance of structural transformation as an integral part of the growth process (Lewis 1954; Fei and Ranis 1964). As late as the mid-nineteenth century, most European countries still had between half and three-quarters of

Table 5.4 Unconditional σ-convergence in Europe

	All Europe		Western Europe		Southern and Eastern Europe	
	N	σ	**N**	σ	**N**	σ
1870	18	0.33	12	0.30	6	0.18
1913	18	0.36	12	0.26	6	0.24
1929	18	0.40	12	0.25	6	0.32
1929	24	0.54	12	0.25	12	0.40
1938	24	0.49	12	0.21	12	0.31
1950	24	0.55	12	0.27	12	0.34
1973	24	0.47	12	0.15	12	0.33
2001	24	0.63	12	0.07	12	0.57

Notes: N = number of countries; σ = unweighted cross-sectional standard deviation of the log of per capita income.
Source: Derived from Maddison (1995b, 2003).

the labour force in agriculture, so that the key structural transformation during the following century and a half was the shift of labour from agriculture into industry and services. The countries that moved out of agriculture most rapidly also enjoyed the most rapid economic growth. Accordingly, we see a strong negative relationship between the level of GDP per capita and the percentage of the working population in agriculture across countries at any point of time, and also over time within a particular country. Table 5.5 reports a simple OLS regression of the log of GDP per capita, on the percentage of the working population in agriculture, which yields an R^2 of 0.795 and a negative slope coefficient that is highly statistically significant.

The time path of the release of labour from agriculture in the main regions of Europe can be seen in Table 5.6. While agriculture still accounted for almost half of the labour force in Western Europe in 1870, it accounted for substantially more than half in Southern Europe and more than two-thirds in Eastern Europe. By 1992, the proportions were down to about 5 per cent in Western Europe, a little more than 15 per cent in Southern Europe and still nearly 25 per cent in Eastern Europe. This pattern is suggestive of a "core", consisting of the West European countries and a "periphery" consisting of the South and East European countries, as noted by Prados de la Escosura *et al.* (1993).

Table 5.5   Regression analysis of the relationship between GDP per capita and the sectoral allocation of labour

	Agriculture	Industry	Services
Constant	9.47 (166.62)	7.10 (48.10)	6.72 (88.32)
Sectoral share of labour	−0.032 (−23.69)	0.041 (8.82)	0.047 (22.80)
R^2	0.795	0.349	0.782

Notes: The dependent variable is the log of GDP per capita in 1990 Geary-Khamis dollars. Figures in parentheses are *t*-statistics.

Table 5.6   Percentage of the working population in agriculture, 1870–1992

	1870	1913	1929	1938	1950	1973	1992
Western Europe	49.8	39.5	31.9	30.9	24.6	10.5	5.2
Southern Europe	57.3	51.6	52.5	50.7	46.2	30.3	16.1
Eastern Europe	69.8	65.4	65.6	65.2	61.8	55.5	23.4
All Europe	52.5	48.0	44.8	43.8	38.7	26.4	12.2

Note: Figures are unweighted country averages within each region.
Source: Derived from Mitchell (1998).

The South European lag is also visible in the data on productivity in agriculture provided by O'Brien and Prados de la Escosura (1992) and summarised here in Table 5.7. Output per worker has remained substantially lower in the South European countries, such as Italy and Spain, while the North European countries can be seen as converging on the UK levels of output per worker. It is interesting to note that the high levels of labour productivity achieved in the UK did not depend on high levels of land productivity. Indeed, output per hectare was substantially higher in the rest of Northern Europe, particularly the Netherlands, and did not even lag in most South European countries. The low labour productivity in South European agriculture thus appears to owe more to low levels of land per worker than to low levels of land productivity. This suggests a need to look at organisational and institutional factors to explain the slowness of the release of labour from agriculture in the European periphery.

Industry in the core and periphery

Development economists and economic historians have usually focused on the movement of resources out of agriculture into industry, particularly manufacturing. In fact, although the relationship between GDP per capita and the share of the labour force in industry is positive, as can be seen in Table 5.5, it is not particularly strong, with an R^2 of only 0.349. Furthermore, the pattern of comparative productivity levels in manufacturing is surprisingly

Table 5.7 Productivity in European agriculture, 1890–1980 (UK = 100)

	1890	1910	1930	1950	1970	1980
Output per worker						
UK	100	100	100	100	100	100
The Netherlands	82	90	94	94	92	124
Denmark	44	107	127	97	108	108
Germany	63	68	55	42	61	75
France	52	55	58	51	62	69
Italy	28	30	30	22	32	39
Spain	33	31	41	20	27	33
Output per hectare						
UK	100	100	100	100	100	100
The Netherlands	192	237	282	310	384	525
Denmark	140	202	270	228	217	188
Germany	148	205	218	176	208	194
France	128	136	153	111	128	127
Italy	146	161	180	134	156	151
Spain	58	55	61	46	59	70

Source: O'Brien and Prados de la Escosura (1992: 532).

stationary. Table 5.8 presents figures on comparative levels of output per employee in manufacturing for a sample of twelve countries, taken from Broadberry (1996, 1997a).

In Table 5.8, Britain is treated as the numeraire country. To facilitate comparisons between comparative productivity levels in manufacturing and the aggregate economy, Table 5.9 also provides figures on aggregate labour productivity with Britain rather than the US as numeraire country. Note that Table 5.9 is not quite the same as a rebased Table 5.3 because Table 5.9 uses the number of employees rather than the population as the denominator. Since participation rates have tended to move together in different countries, however, trends in comparative GDP per employee have been quite similar to trends in comparative GDP per capita. Taking account of international differences in hours worked per person employed, however, there are some more substantial differences between GDP per capita and GDP per hour worked. In particular, since the 1970s, there has been a more substantial fall in hours worked in much of Western Europe compared with the US, so that labour productivity on a per hour basis is now on a par with the US level. Long hours similarly make the Japanese productivity performance look rather less impressive.

If we compare Tables 5.8 and 5.9, we see some striking differences between manufacturing and the aggregate economy in both levels and trends of comparative labour productivity performance. First, as noted in Broadberry (1993), in manufacturing there has been no clear trend over the last 120 years or so in comparative labour productivity performance between the three major exporting nations of Britain, the US and Germany.

Table 5.8   Comparative levels of labour productivity in manufacturing (UK output per employee = 100)

	1870	1913	1929	1938	1950	1973	1989
UK	100	100	100	100	100	100	100
USA	204	213	250	192	263	215	177
Canada	88	153	170	145	151	153	123
Australia		138	102	101	96	86	81
Germany	100	119	105	107	96	119	105
The Netherlands			102	117	88	133	128
Norway		90	109	95	103	104	85
Sweden		102	94	100	118	128	121
Denmark			115	98	88	89	93
France		79	82	76	84	114	115
Italy		59	59	49	68	96	111
Japan		24	32	42	20	95	143

Source: Broadberry (1996, 1997a).

Table 5.9 Comparative labour productivity for the whole economy (UK GDP per employee = 100)

	1870	1913	1929	1938	1950	1973	1989
UK	100	100	100	100	100	100	100
USA	86	116	139	131	154	151	132
Canada	61	95	99	86	125	127	119
Australia	126	121	109	111	111	107	102
Germany	60	78	79	82	66	112	116
The Netherlands	89	91	113	103	93	124	111
Norway	41	49	62	67	74	90	99
Sweden	46	58	59	69	90	105	96
Denmark	57	76	91	88	94	103	98
France	52	64	75	73	72	117	129
Italy	38	46	51	54	56	93	103
Japan	18	23	33	38	29	85	103

Source: Derived from Maddison (1995b).

Output per employee in the US manufacturing has fluctuated around a level of approximately twice the British level, while output per employee in German manufacturing has fluctuated around a level broadly equal to the British level. This contrasts strikingly with the position at the whole economy level, where the US has pulled substantially ahead of Britain, having been slightly behind in the late nineteenth century, while Germany has come from a labour productivity level of about 60 per cent of the British level in 1870 to a sizeable labour productivity advantage over Britain. This means that the US forging ahead between 1870 and 1950 cannot be explained simply in terms of productivity growth in manufacturing, although given the scale of the Anglo-American productivity gap in this sector, there is some role for the expansion of the share of the labour force in the US manufacturing. Similarly, Germany's catching-up of Britain at the whole economy level cannot be explained by trends in manufacturing productivity, but must be attributed to trends in other sectors and sectoral reallocation of labour, particularly the reduction of the labour force in low productivity agriculture.

A second finding is that even within the set of countries that are normally seen as converging unconditionally at the whole economy level, it is possible to see a process of local convergence in manufacturing, with a number of separate convergence clubs. Broadberry (1997a) identifies and discusses different convergence paths in the New World, Northern Europe, Southern Europe and East Asia. Of particular interest, here is the difference between the North and South European convergence paths. In Northern Europe, we see that before the Second World War, despite the existence of a substantial labour productivity gap with Britain at the whole economy level, productivity in the manufacturing sector was already on a par with the British level. Catching-up at the whole economy level, then, depended not on catching-up in industry, so much as the structural shift out of low value-added agriculture and catching-up in services.

In Southern Europe, however, the productivity gaps at the whole economy level were matched by productivity gaps in manufacturing, so that catching-up at the whole economy level did require catching-up in industry. The difference between Northern and Southern Europe seems to be related to the greater importance of rural industry in the South, with productivity in urban-based factory industry being close to the British level in core and periphery alike. O'Brien and Keyder (1978: 152–3), for example, found labour productivity in France on a par with Britain in most branches of factory industry on the eve of the First World War. Even in Russia, where GDP per capita in 1913 was less than 30 per cent of the British level, output per worker in industries under factory inspection was more than three-quarters of the British level in 1908 (Flux 1924: 370). As in agriculture, we shall examine the role of organisational and institutional factors to explain these patterns of productivity performance in industry.

Services and the whole economy

Services have rarely received much attention from development economists or economic historians. It is perhaps more surprising that growth economists have also tended to neglect services, given that services now account for about three-quarters of employment in most Organization for Economic Cooperation and Development (OECD) countries. In this section, we note that there are good reasons for thinking that services have played a key role in explaining the different growth patterns within Europe since the late nineteenth century. First, returning to Table 5.5, we see that the relationship between GDP per capita and the share of the working population in services has been positive, and much stronger than the relationship between GDP per capita and the share of the working population in industry. It seems to have been more important for achieving high levels of per capita GDP to ensure that the labour released from agriculture was deployed productively in services than in industry. Second, and confirming this, it is worth noting that during the whole of the modern period, economic leadership overall has been associated with service sector leadership. This was as true of the Italian city-states of the Renaissance period and the Dutch Republic during the seventeenth century as it was of Britain during the Industrial Revolution and the US during the twentieth century (Kindleberger 1996; Sylla 2002). Industrial success alone does not seem to have been sufficient for overall economic leadership, as illustrated by the recent experience of Germany and Japan.

Again, we shall examine organisational and institutional factors to explain the pattern of productivity differences in services.

Explaining sectoral productivity differences

Agriculture and the release of labour

Over the period since 1870, the main contribution of agriculture has been the release of labour to other sectors of the economy. Countries that shifted labour out of agriculture early on achieved an early boost to GDP per capita, while countries that shifted labour out of agriculture later caught-up. Countries that have remained heavily dependent on agriculture have failed to catch-up. Understanding why some countries were able to shift labour out of agriculture early on, while other countries continued to employ a large share of the labour force in agriculture, is therefore crucial to understanding differences in growth performance.

We have seen in Table 5.7 that the low agricultural labour productivity of the European periphery owed more to low levels of land per worker than to low levels of land productivity. This, in turn, suggests the need to examine organisational and institutional factors underpinning the slow release of labour from agriculture. On organisation, O'Brien and Keyder (1978: 127–37) point to the importance of peasant proprietorship with family labour in underpinning relatively low land–labour ratios in France. By contrast, the system of large aristocratic landowners and their tenants is seen as underpinning relatively high land–labour ratios in Britain. On institutions, Broadberry (1997c) points to the contrast between agricultural protection in Germany and free trade in Britain, while O'Rourke (1997) analyses the different policy responses of European countries to the US grain invasion of the late nineteenth century.

Note that the strategic justification for protecting agriculture in peacetime so as to secure food supplies during war did not prove to be of much value during the twentieth century. As Olson (1963) points out, it was Germany, rather than Britain, that succumbed to blockade during the First and Second World Wars. Olson points to the ability of the British agricultural sector to expand output on the stored-up fertility of grasslands brought back into arable use compared with the inability of German agriculture to maintain output at full stretch in the face of wartime disruption. He also argues that a decisive factor was the flexibility of the large British service sector, which was able to draw on a wealth of experience in general administration as well as in distribution and finance.

Note also that the late release of labour from agriculture continued to exercise an important influence on the growth rate of many European countries until well after the Second World War. Kindleberger (1967) saw the release of labour from agriculture as an important factor explaining the high productivity growth of Western Europe after 1945, while Kaldor (1966) stressed the impossibility of further substantial labour transfers out of agriculture as a constraint on British growth. The importance of this factor in explaining differential productivity growth performance in post-war Europe has recently been emphasised by Temin (2002).

The productivity race in industry

For a nation to build a sustainable competitive advantage in manufacturing requires the development of technological capabilities that are not easily replicated elsewhere. This view underpins the "national systems" approach to industrial performance, which can be seen as lying at the heart of the "varieties of capitalism" literature (Hall and Soskice 2001). Here, we focus particularly on the absence of global convergence in manufacturing and, in particular, the persistent transatlantic productivity gap in manufacturing. Broadberry (1997a) sets out a model of technical choice to explain the persistence of the large transatlantic labour productivity gap in manufacturing identified earlier, and which can be seen very clearly in Figure 5.1. The central idea relies on the coexistence of two technological systems, geared around "mass production" and "flexible production". In mass production, special purpose machinery was substituted for skilled shopfloor labour to produce standardised products, while flexible production relied on skilled shopfloor

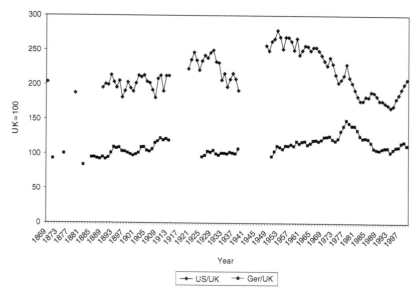

Figure 5.1 Comparative labour productivity in manufacturing

labour to produce customised output. Although it would be an over-simplification to identify American manufacturing with mass production and European manufacturing with flexible production, since in practice both systems coexisted on both sides of the Atlantic, mass production has been more prevalent in America and flexible production more prevalent in Europe.

The model is adapted from David (1975), which sought to provide an underpinning to Habakkuk's (1962) explanation of Anglo-American technological differences in terms of land abundance. Habakkuk (1962) saw this as leading to labour scarcity, substitution of capital for labour and hence higher labour productivity in the US manufacturing. In fact, however, Habakkuk's claim caused considerable controversy because in general, land abundance leads to capital scarcity as well as labour scarcity (Temin 1966, 1971). The issue was resolved by Ames and Rosenberg (1968), who pointed out that there was a complementarity between capital and natural resources, with which America was abundantly endowed. My model retains the complementarity between resources and capital, but distinguishes between two types of capital: human as well as physical capital.

America in the nineteenth century was well endowed with natural resources but faced shortages of skilled shopfloor labour. In Europe, relative factor endowments were the other way round, with an abundance of skilled labour and a shortage of natural resources. This meant that technology developed to suit American factor endowments could not be profitably employed in Europe because of relative factor price differences. This transatlantic difference was reinforced by the fact that American technology produced a more standardised product, suited to the rapidly growing, large and homogeneous American market, but less suited to the fragmented national markets of Europe, stratified by class differences (Rostas 1948; Frankel 1957; Chandler 1990). The greater standardisation in the US contributed to the higher labour productivity through scale economies associated with longer production runs, as well as through the greater machine intensity of production that this permitted.

Now consider what happens over time with technical progress. In a conventional neoclassical model, technologies might be expected to converge. However, David (1975) argues that initial factor proportions tend to be preserved over time, so long as technical progress can be characterised by "local learning". This can be thought of as a kind of trial-and-error process, or what Mokyr (1990) calls "micro inventions". The basic idea is that trial-and-error adaptations never stray too far from the original design. Note that once different techniques have been selected, in a way they are in competition with each other. Thus it is possible to have the coexistence of two techniques on the two sides of the Atlantic, perfectly rational in both countries, given their relative factor prices. As technical progress occurs in one country, the alternative technology in another country can remain viable so long as it can also be improved. There is thus "path dependence" in productivity performance, as an economy becomes "locked-in" to a particular technology (David 1985).

This model helps in understanding the long-run stationarity of the comparative productivity ratios in manufacturing noted earlier. When there were "macro inventions" in the US leading to the development of mass production technology, British craft-based flexible production methods were able to survive so long as they more or less matched the American productivity growth. To the extent that British methods were unable to keep up with US productivity improvements, however, those industries found their survival threatened, and indeed in some cases, such as cotton and shipbuilding, were effectively wiped out. For a sustained deterioration in British productivity performance to occur, however, it was necessary for the failing industries to be able to interfere with the operation of market forces, through, for example, protection or subsidies. Only then could those industries survive. Hence the retreat from free trade in the first half of the twentieth century was associated with a widening of the transatlantic productivity gap in manufacturing. When market forces were allowed to operate more or less freely, as in the 1980s, a return to the long-run productivity ratios occurred (O'Mahony and Wagner 1996).

Technology and organisation in services

Broadberry (1997b,c) provides an analysis of the US and German overtaking of Britain on a full sectoral basis, including international comparisons of productivity in services as well as in industry and agriculture for the period 1870–1990. In both the US/UK and Germany/UK cases, services played a key role in the change of overall productivity leadership (Broadberry 1998). Furthermore, this reflected trends in market services (transport and communications, distribution and finance) and not just composition effects arising from differential trends in the difficult-to-measure non-market services. Data on comparative productivity in services as a whole and in the key market service sectors are shown for the US/UK and Germany/UK cases in Table 5.10. Broadberry and Ghosal (2002) provide a framework of analysis for changing productivity leadership that is centred on services. This is useful in countering the manufacturing bias of much of the literature on the varieties of capitalism.

Britain was highly successful in commercial services during the nineteenth century, playing a key international role in shipping, distribution and finance. Britain still had a labour productivity lead over the US as well as over Germany in services as a whole in the late nineteenth century, as can be seen in Table 5.10. Similarly, British success in commercial services shows up in the balance of payments, with Imlah's (1958) figures on the net contribution of business services to the current account surplus amounting to £86.8 million in 1870, or about 8 per cent of national income. This British success was based on external rather than internal economies of scale. The City of London provided the largest agglomeration of commercial activity in the world, yet it consisted of a large number of small firms rather than

Table 5.10 Comparative labor productivity levels in services, 1869–1990 (UK = 100)

a. US/UK

	Total services	Transport and communications	Distribution	Finance, professional and personal services
1869/71	89.8	110.0	66.9	64.1
1889/91	94.1	167.1	97.0	53.2
1909/11	117.7	217.4	120.0	77.9
1919/20	133.3	250.6	109.0	103.6
1929	139.4	231.5	121.9	101.5
1937	132.6	283.4	119.8	96.1
1950	166.9	348.4	135.2	111.5
1973	152.3	303.3	149.6	118.0
1990	133.0	270.5	166.0	101.0

b. Germany/UK

	Total services	Transport and communications	Distribution and finance	Professional and personal services
1871	62.8	74.4	70.7	89.7
1891	64.4	113.5	45.9	77.0
1911	73.4	166.8	52.5	76.3
1925	76.5	140.0	47.1	86.7
1929	82.3	151.2	50.3	99.8
1935	85.7	132.4	54.3	105.6
1950	83.2	122.0	50.7	94.2
1973	120.1	119.5	88.0	98.4
1979	131.8	135.0	106.4	103.1
1990	134.9	125.7	111.2	120.5

Sources: Derived from Broadberry (1997b,c, 1998).

a small number of giant firms. The large scale of the overall activity facilitated specialisation, and each firm could benefit from proximity to other specialised firms in the classic way set out by Marshall (1890). Since asymmetric information was endemic in this type of activity, it was important to be able to deter opportunistic behaviour. As a result, trade often took place within networks of agents, who could be trusted (Greif 1989, 2000).

In 1870, although Britain still had a labour productivity lead over the US in services as a whole, the US had already caught up in transport and communications, as can be seen in Table 5.10. By the First World War, furthermore, the US had a substantial labour productivity lead over Britain in this sector. In distribution, the US had just overtaken Britain by the First World War, but Britain remained ahead in other services until the interwar period. In services as a whole, therefore, the US was already ahead by the

First World War and continued to forge ahead until the 1950s. Britain only narrowed the productivity gap with the US in services (and the economy as a whole) substantially from the 1970s.

Broadberry and Ghosal (2002) attribute this growing US superiority in services during the first three-quarters of the twentieth century to the spread of a standardised, high-volume, low-margin approach, based on hierarchical management and utilising technologies that improved communications and information processing, including the telegraph and telephone, calculating machines, typewriters, duplicators and vertical filing systems (Yates 1989; Cortada 1993). These technologies were slower to diffuse in Britain as a result of lower levels of education and strong labour force resistance to the intensification of the labour process that their efficient use required (Campbell-Kelly 1992, 1998; Broadberry and Ghosal 2002). This explanation is consistent with the observed pattern of comparative US/UK labour productivity levels, since these high-volume methods diffused rapidly in some sectors, but more slowly in others. These methods were first developed on the railways, then spread quickly to other parts of the transport and communications sector, including steamship lines, urban traction systems, and the telegraph and telephone systems (Chandler 1977: 189–203). However, in distribution, there were limits to the degree of centralisation and standardisation that consumers found acceptable, and there were also restraints on competition which acted to support small retail outlets (Hall *et al.* 1961: 131–8; Field 1996: 27; McCraw 1996). In banking and finance, there were obvious dangers in adopting a high-volume, impersonal, standardised approach, since asymmetric information and trust are very important in this sector, while regulations prevented the growth of inter-state banking (White 2000: 749).

Bakker's (2001) study of the entertainment sector is suggestive of how this approach can also be applied to other personal services, where output is often less well-measured in the national accounts. His use of the term "industrialisation of services" captures broadly the same phenomena as the shift to a standardised, high-volume, low-margin approach based on hierarchical management that is emphasised here.

In a complementary study, Broadberry (2003) examines the Anglo-German comparison. Although Britain began to fall behind the US in parts of the service sector from the late nineteenth century as a result of the adoption of high-volume methods using modern office technology, British productivity in most parts of the service sector remained higher than that in Germany until after the Second World War, as can be seen in Table 5.10. In sectors where Germany was able to adopt US methods (particularly in transport and communications), productivity was relatively high, but large parts of the German service sector remained too spread out in a predominantly rural society with a large agricultural sector. Britain's high level of urbanisation, together with an international orientation in much of the commercial service sector, generated external economies of scale which underpinned high levels of productivity.

German catching-up in most parts of the service sector occurred only after the Second World War, with the shrinking of the agricultural sector. The shift of labour from agriculture into services was accompanied by high levels of physical and human capital accumulation in Germany, associated with the institutional framework of the post-war settlement (Carlin 1996; Eichengreen 1996a). This underpinned the spread of vocational training from industry into services after the Second World War, coupled with high rates of investment in physical capital. As a result, Germany has achieved higher levels of productivity than Britain in most parts of the service sector since the 1970s.

Concluding remarks

This chapter has delved below the economic aggregates to shed light on the varieties of capitalism. The sectoral approach highlights the importance of organisational and institutional factors behind the different paths to high levels of aggregate productivity and living standards. An early release of labour from agriculture was important in allowing some countries to develop an overall productivity lead, by redeploying resources to higher value-added sectors. Organisational and institutional factors such as the land tenure system or protectionism, which retained labour in agriculture, delayed the catching-up process for other countries. In industry, there has been less change in comparative productivity than might be expected although the changing size of the industrial sector has played a role in changing comparative productivity performance overall. The persistence of productivity performance in manufacturing is explained by the path dependence of technology within a national system of industrial production. Change in comparative productivity performance in services has played a large role in overall change in productivity leadership. Again, organisational and institutional factors have been important, with the transition from customised, low-volume, high-margin business organised on the basis of networks to standardised, high-volume, low-margin business with hierarchical management playing a crucial role in the evolution of Anglo-American productivity differences in services.

6

Two Can Play at That Game...or Can They? Varieties of Capitalism, Varieties of Institutionalism

Colin Hay

The 'varieties of capitalism' (VoC) perspective, as it has come to be known, has been much lauded and rightly heralded as the newly ascendant paradigm in the comparative political economy of the advanced capitalist economies. As Howell has recently observed, comparative political economy 'has reached a moment of theoretical synthesis, similar to that which existed around the concept of neo-corporatism in the early 1980s, in which a series of discrete, incremental theoretical developments coalesced into a new theoretical paradigm' (2003a: 103). The rise to prominence of this new paradigm has been exceptionally rapid, aided greatly by the publication of Hall and Soskice's deeply influential edited collection, *Varieties of Capitalism: The Institutional Foundations of Comparative Advantage* and, in particular, their extensive theoretical introduction (2001). Yet, partly as a consequence of this, the VoC perspective has not given rise to as extensive a body of secondary literature – assessing and evaluating its core theoretical and substantive contributions – as have many far less influential perspectives (though see Blyth 2003; Goodin 2003; Howell 2003a; Watson 2003; and for a response to their critics Hall and Soskice 2003). A critical evaluation and assessment of this exceptionally influential body of literature is, then, long overdue and is a core aim of this book.

In this context the purpose of this chapter is more modest – to engage in a sympathetic and largely internal critique of the *institutionalism* of the VoC perspective. I argue that, ironically perhaps, despite its clear institutionalist pedigree, the VoC perspective is, in fact, insufficiently institutionalist to account adequately for the exhibited variation amongst capitalist economies; that, in its seeming preference for a micro-foundations-based rationalist variant of the new institutionalism, over other historical and sociological variants, it is insufficiently resourced conceptually to deal with issues of complex institutional change over time; and that, as a consequence, it tends both towards a rather agentless and apolitical conception of institutional adaptation to largely exogenous challenges and imperatives, and towards an overly mechanistic understanding of 'bifurcation' or 'dual convergence' amongst models of capitalism in response to globalisation.

Varieties of institutionalism

Operationalising capitalist institutional diversity

From the outset it is important to differentiate very clearly between the general analytical utility of the claim that capitalism comes in varieties (which I will seek to defend in what follows) and the specific analytical utility of the VoC perspective itself (which, to some extent, I will challenge). Whether the VoC approach is adequate analytically and methodologically depends on prior ontological assumptions about the nature of capitalism itself (on the general issue, see Hay 2002). It is important then that we ask ourselves whether capitalism does indeed come in varieties and, if so, whether the VoC perspective operationalises adequately that insight. Though these are independent issues, they are by no means unrelated. For, whilst an affirmative answer to the former is a condition of a similarly positive answer to the latter, it is certainly not a sufficient condition. In other words, one can defend the notion that capitalism comes in varieties without having to defend the VoC perspective of Peter Hall, Daniel Gingerich, David Soskice and their various co-authors (see especially Gingerich and Hall 2001; Hall and Soskice 2001). I start with this observation because there is a certain danger either that the VoC approach is seen as the only way to acknowledge capitalist institutionalist diversity (in which case the ontological claim that capitalism comes in varieties hangs or falls on the analytical utility of the VoC perspective) or conversely that any sceptical approach to the VoC perspective is seen to throw the baby out with the bathwater.

As this perhaps already indicates, it is potentially useful to consider the question of institutional variation within capitalism before turning to the more specific utility of the VoC perspective as a means to operationalise that institutional variation analytically. To be clear from the start, the present contribution arises from a deep intellectual affinity with the theoretical schemas – principally institutionalist – for which the claim that capitalism comes in varieties is ontological. Indeed, I would contend, it is only in analytical traditions that value parsimony over almost all other theoretical values that institutional variation amongst capitalist economies is seen as a distorting distraction. Moreover, to be fair to such largely orthodox rationalist and neoclassical perspectives, they rarely rest on ontological claims as to the institutional invariability of capitalism.

The defence of institutional insensitivity is more prosaic and pragmatic – it renders the (algebraic) modelling of political and economic conduct less and less possible (computationally) by degrees. This is an important point, to which we will return. For I will argue presently that the VoC literature, in drawing considerable inspiration from rational choice variants of the new institutionalism (which value analytical parsimony, if not to the same extent as their purist rationalist forebears), is in some danger of restricting its capacity to acknowledge and reflect theoretically the full extent of capitalist institutionalist diversity – between cases and over time.

Returning, for now, to the more general point, it would seem that the notion that capitalism comes in variant institutional forms is rather more widely accepted than one might first assume. Indeed, it strikes me that most commentators, whether they would choose to stress this or not, would accept the notion that capitalism comes in varieties which have some persistence over time and, moreover, that the characteristics of those varieties tend to cluster. In short, capitalism exhibits clustered variation which it is useful to map (empirically) and to conceptualise (theoretically).

That having been said, it is important to acknowledge the potential dangers that come from an unqualified emphasis upon institutional specificity and variation at the expense of an analysis of institutional commonalities. Four, in particular, might be identified and seen as potential pitfalls in *any* attempt to develop a VoC approach.

First, there is something of a tendency, widely recognised and much commented upon, to operationalise capitalist institutional variation in ways which serve to reify the national level. Though much of the broader VoC literature, within and beyond the Hall and Soskice framework, locates domestic political economies within a wider regional or global economic context, it does nonetheless tend to assume a high degree of institutional/ juridico-political closure and integrity at the national level. Whilst this is by no means an inevitable feature of the attempt to operationalise capitalist institutional diversity, it is characteristic of the path-dependence of this literature since the pioneering work of Shonfield and Gerschenkron. With the growing salience of transnational institutions, particularly at a regional level, in the transmission and reproduction of capitalist accumulation regimes, it is increasingly anachronistic. The limitations of such uniscalar approaches to capitalist variation are, of course, most cruelly exposed in contexts, like EU-Europe, where such regional-level institutions are most developed. It is then ironic that the majority of cases considered in the new VoC literature are drawn from EU member states.

Second, no less characteristic of attempts to operationalise capitalist institutional diversity has been a tendency to over-emphasise institutional path dependence and lock-in effects. It is hardly surprising that a heightened sensitivity to variations between (generally, national) cases tends to be reflected in a certain insensitivity to institutional variation *over time*. The result, again by no means logically entailed by the notion of capitalist variation but seemingly strongly selected for, has been a tendency to comparative statics – in which, say, the 'British political tradition' and the institutions through which it is instantiated, are contrasted to the 'French political tradition', as if both were essentially invariant over time. This, to be fair, is an occupational hazard not just of VoC perspectives but of institutionalism more generally. If institutions are regarded as contextual or structural, then institutionalism, almost by definition, is structuralist. This is a point to which we return presently, in considering the distinctive institutionalism of the VoC approach. Suffice it for now to note that this tendency to structuralism is not helped by the new institutionalism's reliance upon one of two principal social ontologies (Hall and Taylor 1996, 1998; Hay and Wincott 1998) – the 'calculus' approach (characteristic of rational choice institutionalism) and the 'cultural' approach (characteristic of sociological institutionalism). For each treats the behaviour of institutionally embedded actors effectively as a function of the institutional context in which they find themselves – with such actors either acting in a manner given by the bounded rationality, or the modes of conduct appropriate to the immediate institutional environment. Both sets of assumptions serve in essence to render actors as bearers of institutional logics, reinforcing the tendency to expect continuity rather than discontinuity. The result is a largely, and perhaps overly, incremental and path-dependent conception of institutional change, deviations from which can only be explained by appeal to exogenous shocks which either destabilise existing equilibria or call into question previously conventional modes of conduct.

This is, in turn, reflected in a third tendency – again characteristic if not logically entailed by any attempt to identify national or other models of capitalism. That tendency is towards political fatalism. If institutions and cultures impose non-negotiable lock in effects – if political actors in Britain are, in the end, confined to replicate and reinvent the British political tradition and the institutions which serve (and service) it ad nauseam – then there is little or no place for political dynamism. In a world of path-dependent lock-in effects and in the absence of destabilising exogenous shocks, institutionalists wedded to the notion of capitalist variation exhibited principally at the national level are likely to anticipate the replication of national distinctiveness over time, relegating political variables to a rather secondary role. Institutions tend to circumscribe the parameters of political choice, leaving political actors to fiddle at the margins with the specific, if not the general content of distinct policy-making styles and with the institutional settings within which they are assumed to have become embedded. In such a schema, like the weather in Britain, the best predictor of what things will be like tomorrow is what they were like today!

Fourth, a final occupational hazard, to which so much of the existing literature has fallen foul, is to over-emphasise the unit level (invariably the national) rather than the sector level or the system level. To be fair, in its attempt to bring the firm back into comparative political economy, the VoC approach provides something of a corrective to this tendency, though it is still perhaps insufficiently inclined to operationalise the notion of capitalist institutional diversity through a comparison of sectors, rather than national units. The failure to say much about the system level is altogether more pronounced. Indeed, it is sometimes difficult to tell that the objects of analysis are varieties of *capitalism* as distinct from varieties of exchange economy or, indeed, varieties of liberal democracy. Capitalism, as widely noted, is an empty vessel in much of this analysis.

It is important to remind ourselves that although these limitations are perhaps characteristic of attempts to differentiate between (invariably national) varieties of capitalism in general, none are inevitable or logically entailed by such a differentiation. They are perhaps best seen as occupational hazards that go with the terrain. As such, they provide a potentially useful benchmark against which to gauge the strengths, and indeed limitation, of the specific VoC perspective advanced by Hall and Soskice. But before attempting such an assessment, it is perhaps first important to establish the distinctiveness of the institutionalism of that approach.

Clustered variation: the distinctiveness of the 'varieties of capitalism' perspective

Much of the appeal of the VoC perspective, as outlined by Hall and Soskice, rests on its seeming ability to draw together and integrate disparate strands in the emergent new institutionalist literature on the comparative political economy of the OECD countries. In particular, though this is nowhere clearly articulated, it seems to offer a bridge between otherwise potentially antagonistic variants of the new institutionalism – especially between historical and rational choice institutionalism (for evidence that at least one of the principal authors is convinced of the possibility of such a rapprochement, see Hall and Taylor 1996). This impression is seemingly re-enforced by the range of rational choice and historical institutionalists brought together in Hall and Soskice (2001). Particularly notable, in this regard, are Thelen and Hall, as representative historical institutionalists, and Iversen and Soskice, as representative rational choice institutionalists.

A number of points might here be noted. First, it is remarkable that there has as yet been no explicit attempt of which I am aware to situate the VoC approach within the new institutionalism, either by its proponents or in the, albeit limited, secondary literature. Second, insofar as an implicit consensus might be identified on this issue, it would seem to suggest an acceptance of the notion that the VoC perspective is both intended as, and is largely successful, in constructing, a bridge between rational choice and historical variants of the new institutionalism. If I am correct both in discerning such an intention, and an acceptance in much of the secondary literature that this aim has been largely realised, then it is a view that I think must be challenged. It is the argument of this chapter that the VoC approach, at least as outlined by Hall and Soskice (2001) which bears the title of the approach, can only be seen as a variant of rational choice institutionalism. Moreover, this has a series of implications for the approach itself.

The rationalism of the VoC approach is perhaps most clearly exhibited in: (i) its quite explicitly stated preference for a formal, indeed micro-foundations-based, approach to the question of institutional interactions; (ii) its emphasis upon the (functional) role played by institutions and institutional clusters in resolving problems of coordination and collective action; (iii) its emphasis upon dynamic/homeostatic equilibrium; and (iv) its consequently largely deductive mode of analytical reasoning.[1] In short, wherever there is a choice to be made between a 'calculus' and a 'cultural' set of assumptions about institutionally embedded actors, a consistent preference is made for the former.

This has its advantages (elegance, parsimony and analytical clarity, for instance), but it also has its limitations. First, it suggests that it is perhaps somewhat disingenuous to present the VoC approach as actor-centred (Hall and Soskice 2001: 6), even if it is accurate to present it (theoretically, at least) as firm-centred.[2] On the face of it, this might seem like a contradictory statement, but the point is in fact a relatively simple one. A firm-centred approach to political economy which treats firms as rational and utility-maximising actors whose preference-functions, though potentially variable between institutional domains, are transitive, knowable in advance and non-specific to the firm in question, is in essence agentless. For it renders the (rational) behaviour of such actors in a given institutional context a product, purely and simply, of that context. Actors are, in effect, bearers of institutionally embedded rationalities. In this sense, the approach is not agent- or agency-centred but profoundly structuralist: it may be concerned with agents but it assumes their behaviour to be rendered entirely predictable, given a specific preference function, the assumption of rationality and knowledge of the institutional domain in which they find themselves. It is not difficult to see the attraction of such an approach in analytical terms, for it effectively sidesteps the indeterminacy otherwise injected into human affairs and social systems by agents capable of responding differently and unpredictably to common stimuli (see, more generally, Hay 2004a). It makes social and political systems far more predictable than they might otherwise be. Yet it comes at a price.

For the VoC perspective that price is the difficulty it has in dealing with complex institutional change over time. As Schmidt observes, the approach 'runs the risk of presenting reality as static, with the two varieties of capitalism maintaining a homeostatic equilibrium as they adjust to external economic pressures' (2002: 111). Much, though by no means all of this, is attributable to the choice of a rationalist micro-foundations-based approach to comparative political economy. For, at best, such an approach tends towards comparative statics. Indeed, one might go so far as to identify an innate difficulty in rational choice theory (institutionalist or otherwise) in accounting for, and even really in acknowledging theoretically, complex institutional change.[3] The reason for this is again simple. Rational choice institutionalism's preferred mode of analysis is the construction of stylised game-theoretic models at the micro level. In the case of the VoC perspective, such models reveal the emergence of coordinated solutions to collective action problems (viewed in firm-centred terms) under specific institutional conditions. Important though such deductive inferences are, however, they leave little space to operationalise macro-level change. Evolutionary games, of course, may extend the time frame in a limited way, but such extended game-theoretical scenarios are again conducted at the micro level and not at the level of the varieties of capitalism in question. More importantly, they generally fail either to anticipate or to be able to explain retrospectively any deviation from equilibrium once established. Consequently, they are rather better at explaining (or more accurately, perhaps, offering post hoc rationalisations for) stability than they are at accounting for change. It is perhaps not surprising then that the varieties of capitalism perspective places so much emphasis on exogenous factors – such as the intensification of competition between national models under conditions of presumed globalisation – in accounting for exhibited developmental trajectories. Yet even this is problematic. For where endogenously consistent equilibria are destabilised by exogenous shocks, as the above comments of Schmidt suggest, a rather functionalist set of premises tends to be invoked as, it is assumed, a bout of institutional adaptation and, possibly, innovation will serve to restore the homeostatic equilibrium (see also Watson 2003).

If the VoC perspective is to compensate for the seemingly inherent limitations which come from its theoretical privileging of a micro-foundations-based institutionalism then, ironically, it must emphasise rather more its historical institutionalist borrowings. For in rejecting the elegance and parsimony which comes from substituting the contingency of agency with a utility function, historical institutionalism is both rather more sensitive to and rather more able to deal with the possibility of significant institutional change. The social ontology of historical institutionalism, as Thelen and Steinmo have made very clear (1992; see also Hay and Wincott 1998), is one that does not seek to sidestep the inherent contingency and indeterminacy injected into human affairs by actors – refusing to depict actors as either prisoners of institutional convention (the 'cultural' approach) or as bearers of institutionally bound rationality (the 'calculus' approach). This allows for the possibility of an endogenised conception of complex institutional change, punctuated by crises and decisive interventions. The earlier works of Hall

(1986, 1993) are here exemplary. Moreover, it stands in some tension to the VoC perspective: (1) in its process-tracing approach; (2) in its seeming refusal to import a strong set of behavioural assumptions about given categories of actors; (3) in the case-specific nature of the chains of causality that it reveals; (4) in its emphasis upon cross-temporal variation within the same case; and (5) in the stress it places upon political dynamics and actors in the developmental trajectories of institutional complexes. Such a framework is, for my own purposes, inherently more attractive and more innately plausible in its conclusions than the elegance and stylised simplicity of the VoC perspective. Yet, it is incompatible with the high degree of analytical parsimony for which the VoC approach so clearly strives. Here, as is invariably the case, significant trade-offs are involved.

(Only) two can play at that game: liberal and coordinated market economies

Thus far, we have tended to focus our attentions on what might be seen as generic occupational hazards associated with the (not unfamiliar) claim that capitalism comes in varieties and the inherent limitations (whatever the compensating strengths) of a rationalist variant of the new institutionalism for taking forward such an insight. Yet it is equally important to consider the more specific problems which have, arguably, arisen from the manner in which the VoC approach has operationalised both the notion that capitalism comes in varieties and its chosen rationalist institutionalism.

Simply stated, it is my argument that the problems of the VoC perspective are less bound up with the notion that capitalism comes in varieties than they are with the manner in which this insight has been operationalised. Indeed, one might go further – a more consistently institutionalist perspective would be unlikely to fall into some of the traps laid theoretically by the VoC perspective. I will confine myself to a few brief observations designed to illuminate particular pathologies of the perspective itself.

Most important here, and much-commented upon in the emergent secondary literature (see, for instance, Blyth 2003; Goodin 2003; Howell 2003a) is the seemingly restrictive and dualistic distinction, for which the VoC perspective is perhaps best-known, between liberal and coordinated market economies (hereafter LMEs and CMEs respectively). A number of points might here be made.

First, the precise status of this distinction is not always clear. Sometimes, it seems, the distinction is little more than a heuristic device, a thought experiment, and a first cut at an initial ordering of what might otherwise appear as a potentially blistering diversity of capitalist varieties. Were this the case, there would be precious little here to concern us – though one might note in passing the potential dangers of reifying such a heuristic by limiting the analysis of capitalist variation to the LME/CME distinction. To reiterate, were the LME/CME distinction merely intended (and accepted by commentators) as a heuristic device, it is unlikely that it would have attracted the attention it has. Yet elsewhere, it seems, rather more is invested in this albeit self-confessedly ideal-typical distinction. At times, for instance, the LME/CME distinction is seemingly presented as the logical correlate of Hall and Soskice's micro-foundations-based institutionalism. Capitalism comes in varieties, each of which must resolve various collective action and coordination problems in order to prove tenable. Consequently, given Hall and Soskice's initial premises, it is merely a matter of logical deduction that capitalism comes not in many varieties, but in two liberal and coordinated varieties. Yet this is not the end of the confusion. For elsewhere, this deductive logic (quite consistent with a rational choice institutionalism) is replaced by a more inductive logic (Gingerich and Hall 2001). Here cluster analysis is used to establish, empirically, the validity of the LME/CME distinction. As alluded to above, this extremely elegant and highly persuasive statistical exercise might be seen as an empirical test of the deductively generated 'prediction' of a clear LME/CME distinction.[4] But, in the absence of a clear statement or analytical model of that process of deductive reasoning, indicating why capitalism should come in *two* varieties, why it should *only* come in two varieties and why it should only come in *these* two varieties, the confusion is perhaps understandable.

That confusion is only compounded by two further factors. First, as Hall and Soskice make very clear, their analytical enterprise is only confined to a consideration of the advanced capitalist economies. They note that there are possibilities for its extension and/or application beyond these countries (2001: 2, n.1), but they give no indication of the extent (if any) of the conceptual re-jigging that this would require. This leaves it very unclear whether the real claim that is being made is that capitalism comes in two varieties or that the political economic regimes of highly developed economies come in two varieties. These are very different claims. If, as I suspect to be the case, the answer to that question is the latter, then it places a certain onus on Hall and Soskice to indicate how their analytical assumptions reflect the specificity of the highly developed capitalist economies they privilege and, conversely, how those assumptions might be re-specified to consider capitalist institutional diversity amongst developing economies.

Second, presumably out of some respect, in particular, for the specificities of the French case that has been a consistent empirical referent for Hall, the possibility of a 'Mediterranean' institutional cluster is conceded (Hall and Soskice 2001: 21). This, needless to say, appears to violate the LME/CME distinction. Refreshingly candid though such a concession is, it raises further questions about the status of that distinction. If the distinction is merely heuristic, then the concession is of no great consequence; yet if the distinction is indeed a logical correlate of the micro-foundation-based approach to capitalist variety, then it presumably calls into question other parts of that framework. Moreover, it suggests the salience of looking for geographical clusters. If the Mediterranean deserves to be treated as a separate and distinctive geographical cluster, then might not the continental-European economies, the Nordic countries, the Antipodean countries and so on? Most of these potential varieties would seem to be at least as tightly clustered as, arguably more than, the Mediterranean variety. In accepting the possibility of a Mediterranean variety of capitalism, then, there would seem to be a certain danger in opening the floodgates to an inductive (as opposed to deductive) approach to geographical clusters.

This does not exhaust the limitations of the dualistic LME/CME distinction. Ironically, the central problem here is not so much a product of the perspective's natural affinities with the generic institutionalist claim that capitalism comes in varieties, but its lack of affinity with such a claim. Quite simply, in restricting itself to a dualistic schema, it limits its ability to acknowledge, let alone dissect and interrogate, institutional diversity. In particular, such a schema can only fail to capture adequately the distinctive, and often case-specific, institutional interactions which the perspective otherwise suggests are crucial to the operation of capitalist economies. This is a problem of inconsistency as much as anything else. For, as argued elsewhere,

> Hall and Soskice are surely right to argue for the incorporation ... of the – almost by definition – case-specific 'strategic interaction' between particular sets of institutions at the national level. The dualistic counterposing of LMEs and CMEs ... – and the associated tendency to attribute poor economic performance to 'inconsistency' with respect to such ideal-types – can only serve to hide precisely such case-specific institutional interactions. (Hay 2004b: 12)

Moreover, the at times rather clichéd and timeless depiction of Germany and the USA as archetypal varieties (Blyth 2003) tends to lend itself towards a conception of LMEs as institution-light and CMEs as institution-dense (see also Howell 2003a). As Thelen herself notes, there is something of a danger here that 'liberal market economies become a residual category ... mostly characterised in negative terms ... rather than analysed in terms of the alternative logic that animates them' (2001: 73). This is unfortunate, for as Hall and Soskice themselves note, LMEs are not uncoordinated, just coordinated in different ways – by markets (2001: 8 n.6). Yet even this is problematic. For markets are by no means self-regulating or self-equilibrating and, partly as a consequence, the commodification and marketisation that is often associated with (stylised) LMEs is frequently a product itself of the institutionalisation of market-like incentives and rationalities. Institutional interactions are, then, no less significant in LMEs than they are in CMEs.

The depiction of LMEs as institution-light and CMEs as institution-dense may also result in an (albeit inadvertent) tendency to present CMEs as rather more fragile than their LME counterparts (see, especially, Goodin 2003). If

Table 6.1   Accounting for change within the VoC approach

---

1.   The emergence of a new variety of capitalism (from two to three varieties)*
2.   The subsumption of one variety by the other (from two varieties to one)
3.   Variety switching – in which specific capitalisms move from one cluster to the other
4.   Greater or lesser variation amongst the total set of capitalist economies
5.   Convergence or divergence between the two VoC
6.   Convergence or divergence within the two VoC

---

* Of course, as indicated earlier, whether this is even a theoretical possibility depends on the status of the LME/CME distinction which remains rather ambiguous in the literature at present.

institutional interactions are presented as the key to the viability of the 'coordinated' [*sic*] variety of capitalism, then any challenge to specific institutions (endogenous or exogenous) may serve to undermine the institutional complementarities on which good economic performance is seen to rest. Interestingly, in response to criticism, Hall and Soskice (2003: 246) suggest that they do not regard the CMEs to be as fragile as is often assumed. What they fail to acknowledge, however, is the extent to which their critics in this respect are essentially playing devil's advocate – exploring the implications of assuming institutional interactions to be the key to the comparative institutional advantage of CMEs whilst presenting LMEs as less institutionally dense.

This brings me to a final observation. In voluntarily restricting itself to the categories LME and CME, the VoC perspective does not arm itself well with concepts which might register and reflect the complexity of capitalist institutional development. The point is perhaps an obvious one. Restricting itself to a dualistic depiction of capitalist institutional clustering leaves the VoC approach with only a limited number of ways of describing any exhibited developmental tendencies (see Table 6.1).

Of course, the first three options in Table 6.1 are largely dismissed from the outset, the fourth is not really discussed to any extent and the fifth is effectively discounted. This leaves the sixth potential description and it is here that the key empirical contribution of the variety of capitalism perspective is made – the perspective being closely associated with the influential 'dual' or 'co-convergence' thesis. It is to the issues that this raises that we now turn (Hay 2004b).

The dual convergence thesis

Empirically, the VoC perspective has provided the theoretical context for many of the most systematic attempts to date to explore, expose and detail the institutional mechanisms involved in the process(es) of convergence and divergence. It is concerned essentially with the dynamic relationship between political-economic regimes at the national level and the international/ global context in which they are increasingly embedded and, more specifically, with the viability of institutionally and culturally distinct 'models' and/or 'varieties' of capitalism under conditions of globalisation. The dual convergence thesis spans a range of authors with, in fact, quite diverse and at times divergent views. What follows is an attempt merely to outline the thesis' core contentions and to gauge its overall contribution.

Within this VoC perspective globalisation is assumed to present political-economic regimes at the national level with a series of common pressures. Yet, in opposition to more orthodox accounts, the dual convergence theorists posit a series of institutional mediations which may serve to channel common inputs and pressures in different directions.

Amongst these, four in particular stand out. The identification of common pressures or inputs associated with globalisation is insufficient to ensure convergence, since: (i) there is differential exposure to such pressures; (ii) common pressures reinforce or erode patterns of 'comparative institutional advantage' and disadvantage, to different degrees; (iii) different interpretations may be reached of common experiences of common pressures to inform different responses; and (iv) even where common understandings of similar pressures are reached, substantive responses are likely to reflect different strategic and institutional capacities and modes of economic intervention and corporate governance.

Yet if the identification of such complex mediations would seem to point to the contingency of the process of convergence or divergence, we should recall that this is nonetheless a *dual* convergence thesis. In other words, whatever contingency is injected into proceedings by these four mediations, it is insufficient to ensure any deviation from the twin paths of dual convergence. Herein lies a tension. For, the compound institutional mediations, (rightly) identified in this literature, are suggestive of no mechanism capable of chan-nelling patterns of convergence and divergence to produce this exhibited 'bifurcation' (Hall and Soskice 2001: 58) – besides, that is, a rather vague sense of heightened inter-institutional competition, lubricated by capital mobility, aligned to a rather functionalist appeal to an adaptive evolutionary logic and assuming capitalism to come in only two variant forms.

Arguably, the identification of *dual* convergence owes much to the distinc-tive counterposing of *liberal* and *coordinated* market economies as varieties of capitalism (Hall and Soskice 2001) – or, by extension, *social democratic corpo-ratism* (SDC) and *market liberalism* (ML) as varieties of partisanship (Garrett 1998). It is surely tempting to suggest that, had a greater number of initial clusters been identified, a rather more complex pattern of convergence, diver-sity and/or divergence might also have been identified. If dual varieties of capitalism (or partisanship) lead to dual convergence, then might not triple varieties of capitalism lead to threefold convergence, quadruple varieties of capitalism to fourfold convergence and so forth?

In taking the argument a little further, it is worth considering the seminal contribution of Garrett, whose work on the persistence of partisan politics, in the context of globalisation, is both broadly representative of this strand in literature and an early intervention in the debate.[5]

Garrett (1998) is presented as a profound and devastating attack on the prevailing orthodoxy on globalisation. His controversial conclusion is simply stated and is broadly similar to that reached by other exponents of the dual convergence thesis. Insofar as globalisation can be seen to 'select' certain varieties of partisanship/capitalism over others, it rewards 'coherence' in matters of economic policy. Thus, consistently, social democratic and corporatist modes of economic governance and coordination are rewarded just as much as the consistent pursuit of market-conforming neoliberalism. In the increasingly frenetic search for havens of good economic performance, under conditions of heightened capital mobility, and following a significant intensification in the competition between nations, then, there are at least two Pareto optima. There *is*, in short, an alternative to neoliberalism's logic of economic compulsion – at least for those economies with the institutional architecture and political culture required to pursue a consistent programme of social democratic corporatist governance. Where the political will and the encompassing labour-market institutions persist, so does the possibility of social democratic corporatism under conditions of globalisation.

Despite its laudable attempt to dispel the 'logic of no alternative' with which globalisation has come to be associated, Garrett's account is characterised by a series of tensions, ambiguities and contradictions, many of which speak to broader problems with the dual convergence thesis. A number of specific and more general comments might here be made. For present purposes I confine my observations to those which might credibly be generalised to the dual convergence thesis and hence the VoC perspective with which it is synonymous.

First, it is by no means clear that Garrett's work does serve significantly to temper the 'logic of no alternative', with which more obviously conventional accounts of globalisation have in recent years become intimately associated. If, as he at times seems only too anxious to concede (see, for instance, 1998: 48; though cf. 1998: 131, 155–7), there are strong institutional and political/cultural preconditions for the pursuit of social democratic corporatism and, as a range of commentators have noted, such institutional factors are increasingly difficult to sustain in the context of European monetary union, then the prospects for a social democratic corporatist alternative to an otherwise-rampant neoliberalism outside of an ever more residual Nordic enclave look bleak indeed. For aspirant social democrats in Britain, France or even Germany, there is little solace to be gained from Garrett's attempt to resuscitate social democratic optimism. For these cases, lacking as they do the institutional preconditions for social democratic corporatism, the only inference to draw from Garrett's work would seem to be that neoliberalism is the best and only way.

Second, in one sense, the above comment is specific to the analysis that Garrett presents. Nonetheless, if its logic is accepted, it has potentially important implications for the dual convergence thesis more generally. It suggests at minimum the need for a rather more exhaustive analysis of the extent to which EU-European economies in particular have been subjected to a process of globalisation over recent decades. If, as much recent scholarship suggests (for instance, Kleinknecht and ter Wengel 1998; Hirst and Thompson 1999; Hay 2004b), the story has in fact been one of EU-isation rather than of globalisation, then the implications one might draw from conclusions of dual convergence may also be in need of revision. If, for instance, it is the institutional architecture of European Monetary Union (EMU) combined with the economic reality of deepening European economic integration that has conspired to make social democratic corporatist solutions more difficult to export beyond a Nordic enclave, then there may be good political reasons for revisiting that institutional architecture. Talk of globalisation may merely serve to divert attention from the pressing political task at hand.

Third, if the logic of the dual convergence thesis is that market liberal and social democratic corporatist regimes (or LMEs and CMEs) are, *ceteris paribus*, good (if not necessarily nice) places to be under conditions of globalisation and it is conceded that the institutional preconditions of the latter are ever more difficult to secure, then it is also important that we examine, in a rather more exhaustive fashion, the supposedly diminishing returns to all other regime types within contemporary Europe. Garrett, along with other proponents of the dual convergence thesis, may be rather too hasty in dismissing the advantages of 'incoherent' regime types. Here, it must be noted, the terms in which the debate is conducted are extremely unhelpful. What we see, once again, is an unfortunate and, presumably, unintended consequence of the dualistic counterposing of LMEs and CMEs, SDC and ML. For there is, on a more sustained reflection, nothing especially 'incoherent' about, for instance, either the German or Dutch regime type(s), save other than the fact that they do not closely approximate a Scandinavian or Anglo-Saxon ideal type. Indeed, both have been presented as models to be emulated albeit in other contexts.[6] The point is that it is only with respect to social democratic corporatism and market liberalism as ideal-types that Garrett's 'incoherent' regime type appears incoherent at all. Moreover, in the postscript to Garrett's book, in which he eventually considers the data for the 1990s, it is the incoherent regime type which, in fact, performs rather better than either its social democratic or its market liberal counterparts, certainly with respect to economic growth and unemployment (see, for instance, Garrett 1998: Table 6.4). In short, there are many ways to coordinate economic governance and it is not at all clear from the evidence that Garrett (and others) present, that open economy conditions (if that is indeed the contemporary European experience) can only sustain social democratic corporatist and market liberal modes of coordination. What this in turn suggests is the need to dispense with dualistic distinctions, such as those between LMEs and CMEs and SDC and ML.

The above discussion is not intended to detract from the considerable potential and significant insight offered by the co-convergence thesis – a perspective whose theoretical sophistication, methodological rigour and empirical breadth stands in marked contrast to much of the literature on globalisation. Yet, the rather arbitrary and dualistic manner in which the boundaries between the distinctive varieties of capitalism/partisanship it identifies are drawn becomes a hindrance to its further development. Partly as a consequence, the VoC perspective arguably compromises the very institutionalism which ostensibly informs it, and out of which it arises, in failing to give adequate consideration to the complex institutional and ideational mediation of pressures for convergence.

As this suggests, it is both possible and, arguably, desirable to differentiate between the (generic) institutionalism which animates this perspective and the substantive content of the specific dual convergence thesis it has increasingly come to advance. Yet it may also be, as argued above, that the choice of a micro-foundational-based rational choice institutionalism is part of the problem here, serving to lessen the approach's sensitivity to institutional and ideational mediations.

Either way, it is my contention that an (historical or ideational) institutionalism more sensitive to the mechanisms involved in the translation of common pressures into convergent, divergent or merely diverse outcomes should be incapable of settling for the parsimony of the dual convergence thesis, or for the LME/CME distinction on which it rests.

Conclusion

The argument of this chapter though, I imagine, controversial is nonetheless relatively simply stated. Perversely, the VoC perspective is insufficiently institutionalist to account adequately for the exhibited variation amongst capitalist economies. Moreover, in its seeming preference for a micro-foundations-based rationalist variant of the new institutionalism over other historical, ideational and sociological variants, it is insufficiently resourced conceptually to deal with issues of complex institutional change over time. Consequently, it tends towards both a rather agentless and apolitical conception of institutional adaptation to largely exogenous challenges and imperatives and an overly mechanistic understanding of 'bifurcation' or 'dual convergence' amongst models of capitalism in response to globalisation.

Yet this should not lead us to abandon the analytical enterprise that the VoC perspective has set out for itself; quite the contrary. The VoC perspective poses the right question and starts from the correct premise – the institutional variation amongst capitalist economies. What it shows us is not the futility of institutionalist political economy, but that if that utility is to be maximised we must dispense with the dualistic counterposing of LMEs and CMEs, with the parsimony of the dual convergence thesis and, preferably, with a micro-foundations-based approach to the question of institutional diversity and development.

Notes

1. Gingerich and Hall's eloquent attempt to demonstrate inductively and empirically (through cluster analysis) the validity of the dualistic classification of VoC for which the perspective it perhaps best-known (and to which we return) might be seen as an exception to this (2002). However, is might just as easily be seen as an attempt to evaluate and test, retrospectively, the deductively inferred prediction that capitalism comes in two variety clusters – namely, liberal and coordinated market economies. As such it hardly violates the designation of the VoC perspective as rational choice theoretical its in core analytical assumptions and inspiration.
2. The extent to which the theoretical advocacy of a 'firm-centred approach' to comparative political economy is consistently operationalised in the more applied and substantive chapters of the collection might also be questioned, but in seeking to evaluate and characterise the theoretical content of the perspective, that is not the principal issue at stake here.
3. Rational choice does, of course, have other compensating advantages. As I have elsewhere suggested, all political analysis involves trade-offs and rational choice is particularly distinctive in this regard, in valuing parsimony over complexity when it comes to analytical assumptions. Arguably this makes it more adept at dealing with equilibrium rather than disequilibrium scenarios.
4. It is perhaps important at this point to qualify this statement. For in many respects, the cluster analysis presented by Hall and Gingerich does not really test the core claim of the VoC perspective. That claim, as I understand it, is that VoC cluster in terms of the institutional complementaries their political economies exhibit. The good performance that characterises the CMEs, for instance, is accounted for in terms of the existence of a series of specific institutional interactions. Convincing though Hall and Gingerich certainly are in revealing two clusters, they do not demonstrate that these clusters are characterised by the presence of these specific institutional interactions.
5. There is one respect, however, in which Garrett's work is unrepresentative of the VoC perspective. His concern with the persistence of partisan politics leads him to a conceptual schema, cast not in terms of varieties of *capitalism* per se but varieties of *partisanship*. Although Garrett is keen at times to emphasise the institutional preconditions of partisanship in a manner suggestive of the links between varieties of partisanship and varieties of capitalism, this theme is never fully explored. In this context it is interesting that Garrett should identify a Scandinavian archetype (social democratic corporatism) rather than a German archetype (the coordinated market economy) as the counterpoint to ML/the LME. As a consequence, Garrett's 'incoherent' regime type (Germany) is in fact Hall and Soskice's archetype.
6. The irony, of course, is that Germany, the most significant example of Garrett's 'incoherent' regime type, is one of Hall and Soskice's archetypes.

7

The Politics of a Miracle: Class Interests and State Power in Korean Developmentalism

Vivek Chibber

Of all the success stories of post-war economic history, perhaps none is as remarkable as Korea's extraordinary ascent in the world economy. Its success is all the more remarkable, in that, as recently as 1960, the country was on the verge of being abandoned by international experts and policy advisors as an irredeemable basket-case. Less than two decades after, it was already becoming an object of intense scrutiny, only now as a shining success story in Third World development. Not surprisingly, given that its entrance into academic debates came around the time of the debt crisis and the turn toward neoliberal orthodoxy in the West, the Korean experience was initially appropriated as a vindication of free-market orthodoxy (Chen 1979; Lal 1983; Linder 1986). But within a few years the neoliberal interpretation was subjected to withering critiques. A new, revisionist interpretation of the Korean 'miracle' was offered, based on intensive empirical examination of actual policy, and buttressed by an impressive battery of case studies at the level of sector and firm. Led by such scholars as Amsden, Wade, Woo, Rodrik, and others, a counter-orthodoxy emerged. Against the neoliberal insistence that Korean success was based on an adherence to free market principles, revisionists adduced evidence of a massive reliance on state intervention, in virtually every sphere of economic activity. Far from trusting the operation of an unfettered market, it turns out that Korean success was built on one of the most ambitious and far-reaching attempts at capitalist planning we have yet seen. And after two decades of trench warfare in the academic badlands, the revisionists can comfortably claim to have shifted the received interpretation of the Korean 'miracle' away from what Coates referred to in Chapter 1 as a market-centered analysis.

Naturally, the emphasis on state intervention has required that revisionists offer some arguments as to how Korean planners were able to achieve their success – especially when these scholars acknowledge that efforts at capitalist planning so often met with failure in other settings. It is in their answer to this question that the weaknesses of this scholarship emerge. For what the revisionists have done, in successfully displacing neoliberal *market*-centered analyses, is to offer an alternative that is implausibly *state*-centered. The implausibility of their position does not lie in their descriptions of what the Korean state *did*. On this matter, I believe that they make their case very well – the central measure on which the Korean state succeeded, where other states trying capitalist planning failed, was that of imposing discipline on local firms (Amsden 1989). Elsewhere, in similar attempts at rapid industrialization, planning efforts were far less successful in disciplining investors, falling prey, instead, to rent-seeking and corruption. In these other, less-fortunate cases, subsidies and financial favors, which were meant to spur investment were, instead, used to line the pockets of local industrialists, or plowed into lines with low social returns (albeit high private returns). In Korea, revisionists correctly argue, planners were able to successfully direct local conglomerates into appropriate lines, and then insure that public monies allocated for investment were turned into best-practice production.

Hence, the problem with the state-centrism of this argument does not lie in the description of what the state did: that is discipline its domestic capitalists. It lies, rather, in the explanation of how it was *able* to impose this discipline – which has been allowed to pass with surprisingly little comment. The statist explanation is the following: the Korean state's ability to discipline local firms issued from *its general domination of the capitalist class as a whole*. In other words, Korean planners were ensconced in a state that, because of it dominance over local capital, was free from the pressures that normally issue from powerful capitalists – individually, and as a class. And in wresting free from these pressures, *the state was able to achieve more or less complete autonomy from its capitalist class for close to a quarter of a century* (the period of 'high developmentalism'). Hence, Kim's verdict that, after 1961, 'the state was *clearly the dominant partner*, with capital under its control and with an expanded and reformed economic bureaucracy' (Kim 1997: 117). And in their authoritative study of the country's political economy, Jones and Sakong summarize the state–capital relation as one in which '*the dominant partner is unequivocally the government*... [In Korea], *the government's wishes are tantamount to commands*, and business dare not take them lightly' (Jones and Sakong 1980: 67) and so on. It is no surprise that the state was able to impose discipline on capital, since capital had no recourse but to follow orders.

It is remarkable that such claims have not elicited closer scrutiny. Perhaps we can forgive this of neoliberals, to whom this would only seem one among many fantastic claims about the abilities of planners, bureaucrats, and other motley characters. But among those who are working in more heterodox traditions, or in fields where the state is taken more seriously as a potential actor, these arguments ought to have raised some eyebrows. For they seem to posit a state in a capitalist economy that is not constrained by the latter's structural constraints. One possible reason is that, to those who sympathize with the revisionist critique, the picture of the state that they paint is a pleasing one in some respects. What the Korean case seems to show is that the state can, under appropriate conditions, play a critical role in transforming domestic structures, and can do so away from the direction that would be taken by the spontaneous functioning of markets. In so stressing the role of political institutions, the analyses offer an alternative to the bleak determinism of market-centered analyses of development. In an era of unrelenting attack on the state by conservatives, Left academics obviously feel that this is an idea worth defending. While the Korean state in its developmentalist phase was by no means an exemplar of progressive governance, it does show the possibility of successfully 'governing the market'. Another reason might be that, over the past two decades, a kind of neo-Weberian strand of theorizing has become quite prominent among political scientists and sociologists, which views the state in capitalism as far more autonomous from class constraints than Marxist theory would seem to allow. This more Weberian wing of radical state theory has served to create an intellectual space for the claims made by Korean experts. Arguments about the exceptional character of the Korean state are thus both politically pleasing, and theoretically plausible.

In this chapter, I will suggest that the urge to accept this picture of the Korean state, while understandable, is mistaken. And in so doing, I hope to show that the basic claims of Marxian theory – for the constrained position of states in capitalist economies – are valid for the Korean case as well. I proceed in two basic steps. First, we will examine the mechanisms which, according to statists, allowed Korean state managers to so thoroughly dominate local capitalists. The mechanisms that supposedly gave the Korean state its dominance over local capitalists can be assimilated along two dimensions: an *intrinsic* and an *extrinsic*. Whereas the first made it possible to shield planners from the instrumental control or pressure of capitalists, the second made the state impervious to capital's structural power.

On the intrinsic dimension, the salient feature was the inheritance of a healthy bureaucratic tradition, which was bolstered by the creation of a cohesive and clearly structured policy apparatus among economic agencies. Whereas so many other late developers were saddled with state apparatuses which were porous and susceptible to capture by local industrialists, the Koreans were able to wield a leviathan which, at least in its economic policy agencies, maintained its integrity. This transformation was critical for allowing planners the institutional space and power to not only design development plans but also to wield a policy apparatus which, they could be reasonably sure, would actually implement them.

The increased state autonomy generated by internal reforms was important for increasing the state's instrumental autonomy from capital. But it is aspects relevant to the second, extrinsic, dimension, which are really taken to be fundamental to Korean exceptionalism. It is these aspects that are taken to have endowed the state with the holy grail of policymaking – autonomy from the *structural* power of the capitalist class, which issues from their control over investment. There are two institutional facts that are typically presented as responsible for this remarkable hiatus from structural constraints: the small size of the domestic capitalist class and the state's control of the national banking system. These facts allow planners to go beyond simple insulation from bourgeois political pressure or lobbying; they enable the planners to, through the state, actually dominate the class as a whole. And in Korea, after 1961, it was supposedly this power that enabled the regime to impose an entirely new accumulation model onto local firms, that of export-led industrialization (ELI), with little regard for whether or not industrialists themselves approved of such a model – for what, after all, could they do, if they were powerless to resist?

I will argue that none of these factors can bear the weight that statists place upon them, and the conclusions they draw ought to therefore be rejected. I will then offer an alternative analysis of the Korean political economy, and of the relation between the state and local capitalists, which can also account for the state's remarkable ability to discipline local firms. Finally, I will trace how the relations between the actors changed over time, so that, by the late 1980s, the basis for Korean developmentalism had eroded.

The statist argument: a critique and reformulation

The heart of the statist account, it should be clear, is the claims made about the extrinsic sources of state dominance – the small size of the domestic business class and the effects of state control over finance. In particular, it is the latter that is most commonly pointed to as critical. In what follows, I shall question both claims, and in particular, show that the argument regarding the effects of state control over finance cannot stand scrutiny. This is not to say that they are without any merit whatsoever. It is certainly not the case that the control of credit and finance is irrelevant to state autonomy, or that they did not play a crucial role in the state's ability to discipline capital. They were in fact very important. But their importance lay in their enhancement of the state's capacity to discipline individual *firms*, not the class *as a whole*. In fact, even with state-owned banks, it will be a condition for the ability to discipline individual firms, that the state maintains an alliance with the broader class. If this is true, then it follows that what set Korea apart was not that the state was able to force capitalists to accept an accumulation model, but that it was able to secure an alliance around this model, and it was a feature of the model that state disciplining of particular firms did not threaten the ongoing alliance with the broader class of capitalists. And if this is true, then the exceptionalism of the Korean variant of capitalism did not reside in the state's ability to stand apart from class constraints, but rather in the manner that it was able to negotiate those constraints. I now proceed to the critique and reformulation.

The scope of state power

There is much in the statist argument that I will not dispute. To start, the account of the Korean state's intrinsic sources of success – its internal cohesiveness, bureaucratic rationality, and strategic flexibility – is indisputable. And it does serve, on its own, to set Korea apart from many other late developers, in which business classes were able to penetrate the state, or where the state itself was unable to forge the internal cohesiveness necessary for development strategy. In what follows, I take for granted the validity of this component of the statist argument. In fact, as I will argue, Park Chung Hee's seriousness about building a strong and cohesive state – able to perform crucial functions for firms, which included a brutal repression of labor – was critical to cementing the alliance with the chaebol around the accumulation model. So on this issue, there is a complete convergence between my analysis and that of the statists.

It is on the second, extrinsic dimension, that the problems arise. Let us take first the matter of the size of the Korean capitalist class during the early 1960s, when Park Chung Hee embarked on the model of ELI. It is certainly true that domestic capital did not occupy the position in the economy that their counterparts did in advanced industrial countries. But on what basis is it possible to say that they were too small to have their preferences matter? Clearly, we need a non-arbitrary measure of what counts as 'too small'. One obvious method is to find other developing countries where local capitalists were able to exert their weight, and then compare their relative position in the economy to that of the Koreans. Table 7.1 shows the relative weight of the industrial sector in selected developing countries at the time that they embarked on, or were in the midst of, their state-led development programs. India began its planning era around 1950, Brazil in the Kubitchek administration, Mexico in the Camacho-Aleman decade, Argentina during the first Peron administration, Turkey after the coup of 1960, and Korea after the

Table 7.1   The share of industry in GDP in select countries

	Korea (Park)	India (Nehru)	Brazil (Kubitchek)	Mexico (Aleman)	Argentina (Peron)	Turkey
Manufacturing	20.2% (1962)	16.1% (1950)	23% (1955)	19% (1950)	24% (1950)	21% (1960)

Sources: For India, Goldsmith 1977: Table 3.2; for Korea, Mason *et al.* 1980: Table 13; for Brazil, Mexico, Peru and Colombia, Bethell 1998: Table 3.4; for Turkey, Richards and Waterbury 1990: Table 3.6.

ascension of Park in 1961. As should be clear, the Korean economy harbored an industrial sector of roughly the same size as other late industrializers embarking on state-led development. If the share of industry in the economy is an indicator of the 'size' of the capitalist class – and there is every reason to take it as one, albeit not the only one – then there is nothing to convince us that the Korean state could have had qualitatively greater power over its industrialists when it launched its state-building program than did other states over their respective classes. Even more, it is widely recognized that ownership in Korean manufacturing was highly concentrated, more so than in most other developers, making it even easier for capitalists to engage in collective action.

The size or concentration of the local business elite could not, therefore, have allowed the Korean state a power over its fortunes that was of a different order than that of other states in late developers. We turn then to the second possible mechanism, the control over finance. As I explained earlier, this is the real heart of the statist position. The new Park regime nationalized banks soon after acquiring power in 1961. And having secured control over banks, scholars committed to state-centrism argue that the regime was able to more or less coerce the class as a whole to accept a new development model – ELI. Thus, Fields says that, 'from this *position of dominance* and institutional capacity, the Park regime *engineered* Korea's export-oriented industrialization with the private chaebol as the chosen instruments to carry out this strategy' (1995: 48). H-J Chang in his otherwise excellent article on Korean industrial policy, repeats the importance of state control over finance, adding that after these reforms, the business community were like 'criminals on parole on condition that they "serve the nation through enterprise" and, economically, a paper tiger *with little power to make investment decisions* – the ultimate capitalist prerogative' (1993: 152; also 1994).

But does this really follow? There is no doubt that control over finance considerably increases the state's power over capitalists. But it is not clear how this power could be sufficient to render state managers indifferent to the latter's reactions to policy changes. For a typical capitalist state, the fundamental constraint on policy options is the need to attend, more or less closely, to maintaining a healthy investment climate. If policies trigger a decline in business confidence, leading to a downturn in new investment, the immediate impact is a shortfall in government revenue as tax receipts shrink, and an increase in unemployment, creating problems of legitimacy for political elites. States incurring such a reaction face a shrinking resources base, as well as the potential for greater instability. The common denominator to any set of choices, therefore, will be their orientation to nurturing a healthy rate of accumulation. Now, for the statist argument to work, it must be the case that control over finance frees state managers of this constraint, so that business confidence is no longer a concern.

In fact, and *pace* the statists, publicly controlled finance works as a lever only against the backdrop of healthy business confidence. Finance works as a lever only so long as it is in demand by capitalists; obviously, it will be in demand only so long as firms are of the view that it makes sense to make investments of the kind that planners are calling for. If they do not hold such a view, if they consider the changes being imposed to be disastrous, how will the lever work? Consider the likely scenario if the state tries to unilaterally impose a series of new regulations or a new accumulation strategy – like export-led development – on the domestic bourgeoisie. If there is a widespread sentiment among firms that the new policy will be harmful to their profits or their rates growth, the most probable reaction will be a cascading decline in business confidence, as firms become unsure of future returns. If this does happen, the tangible result will be a decline in the *demand* for finance, since firms will be slowing down the pace of investment. Now, if the demand for finance is itself in decline, it is difficult to see how the state's *control* over finance can be an effective weapon over the capitalist class. Control over an input cannot work if demand for that input disappears. Trying to use finance as a lever in this situation will be, to use Keynes' memorable phrase, like pushing on a string.

Nationalizing banks in a capitalist economy cannot, then, free planners from the normal constraints that bind capitalist states. No doubt it does increase the state's power, but only against the backdrop of a healthy rate of accumulation – which means that in these settings, just as in the others, states must attend to the maintenance of business confidence. This being the case, it is hard to imagine how the Park regime could have foisted a new accumulation model – ELI – on its local capitalist class, being impervious to the latter's reactions. The latter seems to have been comparable in size to its counterparts elsewhere, as shown in Table 7.1, and the control over finance cannot have garnered for Park a complete autonomy from structural constraints. In its basic structural relation to local capital, the Korean state was not in a position qualitatively different from that of its counterparts. Hence, for the new accumulation model to be stable, it had to have garnered the support of local firms.

Of course, *once the new strategy was settled upon* – in the sense that large sections of the business class had agreed to switch their investment patterns accordingly – then there is no doubt that the control over finance was an effective weapon for disciplining *individual firms*. So long as business confidence remained high, the threat of withholding credit from recalcitrant firms could serve as a very effective weapon. The targeted business would face a real opportunity cost as the restriction in credit hampered its rate of growth, or resulted in closure. For state elites, imposing such sanctions would not entail great risk since, given that business confidence was high, it could be expected that other firms would pick up the slack generated by the targeted firm being punished. Hence, against a background of a buoyant investment climate, a state with adequate institutional coherence and capacity could effectively impose discipline on particular firms.

What this amounts to, then, is the following: securing control over finance certainly does enhance the state's ability to demand compliance from producers. But the power extends only over particular firms, not over the class as a whole. In fact, since states are extremely sensitive to maintaining an acceptable level of business confidence, any move to punish or reign in particular firms will be taken only if there is ample indication that it will not trigger a downturn in the investment climate, as other firms feel threatened. That is to say, the imposition of discipline can occur against the backdrop of a sturdy *alliance* between the state and capital. Hence, far from having a power over capitalists as a whole, the Korean state, like any other state, was in the position of needing an alliance with the class. Where it differed was in its exceptional ability to actually monitor firms and extract compliance from them, *once that broader alliance was in place*, and for that, there is no doubt at all that its internal cohesiveness and its control over finance was of critical importance. The statists are therefore correct in pointing to the importance of these factors in endowing the state with its remarkable developmental capacity. Where they err is in their assessment of this power's scope.

The politics of export-led industrialization

How, then, did the turn to ELI come about? For the Park regime, the turn to exports made good sense for obvious reasons. All developing countries run up large import bills as they have to purchase capital goods and raw material from abroad, and also because of the burden of repaying foreign debt. But in Korea of 1963, a failure of the First Five Year Plan had saddled the regime with a particularly harsh payments crisis on the external front, which only made the general concern for export success more pointed. As the regime started work on the Second Plan, the need to boost exports was therefore at the forefront of all considerations.

For Korean industrialists, the turn to exports was acceptable because of a series of developments which combined to make success in foreign markets highly likely. Starting in 1960, Japanese companies had been coming to Korea and establishing links with Korean firms, to set up joint operations for exporting light manufacturing goods to the US markets. Through joint ventures, Korean firms could potentially gain access to Japanese know-how and finance, while the Japanese could find partners who knew how to 'work' the local bureaucracy and handle local labor. Just as importantly, local partners would provide a market for Japanese capital goods. Along with joint ventures, the Japanese arrived in the form of their giant trading companies, the Sogo Sosha, which held the promise of providing Korean firms with two critical resources for export success: cheap commercial loans to buy raw material and (Japanese) capital goods, as well as access to their marketing and sales networks in the US (Castley 1997: 144). The new political regime and domestic business thus formed an alliance around ELI.

Now, the foregoing account raises an important question. I have accepted that the Korean state did wield a remarkable ability to discipline domestic firms; but I have stipulated that this could only be possible if the wider class of industrialists did not revolt against the idea of granting the state this kind of interventionist power. But if capitalists have the power and the ability to rebuff such state-building agendas, why would they ever countenance such power on the part of planners? Why, in other words, would a business class enter into an alliance, the main result of which would be that the state would accumulate the power to routinely intervene directly into their most-prized domain – the discretionary power over investment? Why, in addition to ELI, did capitalists also accept a developmental state? The answer, I submit, lies in the demands made by ELI on firms based in a developing economy. Put briefly, *this was an accumulation model which, because of its demands on firms, made it rational for them to accept a state with the power to discipline them.*

To appreciate why ELI would generate an interest on the part of capitalists to accept a developmental state, consider how it affected their environment for accumulation. In ELI, firms committed to manufacturing goods headed for external markets, centrally to those of the advanced industrial world. But the conditions of these markets would be fundamentally different than those which obtained at home. Whereas home markets were underdeveloped, easily dominated by local firms (under high tariffs), and protected from foreign competition, export markets were highly competitive, with well ensconced incumbent firms, which had access to massive pools of finance and the latest technology. Further yet, in many of the sectors which late developers typically entered – textiles, apparel, and so on – the absence of well-developed sales networks acted as a prohibitive barrier to entry. If local firms could not be expected to withstand international competition at home, they hardly stood a chance as exporters to the markets of the industrialized countries. Indeed, the difficulty of entry and survival there would be even greater. First, they would have to secure funds to make the minimum scales of investment individually; but a more important obstacle was that these investments would have to be in technologies with which the firms had no experience and training; and worse yet, any given investment would typically require complementary investment by other firms, either upstream or downstream, if it was to bear fruit.

In addition to these obstacles related to investment, there was also the overhead cost of establishing marketing and sales networks in countries where the firms had no history of success, a barrier which, as Gereffi and others have pointed out, is perhaps the most important for producers in textiles and other light industry – precisely those lines in which less developed countries (LDCs) first enter as exporters (Lall 1991; Gereffi 1996). Success thus involved overcoming the paucity of funds, acquiring and mastering new technology, solving the problem of investment coordination, and gathering the information and contacts needed for marketing. Now, these are problems that are present in any capitalist market, whether local or external. What made it pressing and forbidding for exporters, however, was that these conditions had to be secured in a context of intense competition with producers who had access to far greater funds, who not only had experience with new technology but had, in fact, *developed* it, and who had a massive advantage in sales networks. This placed severe pressure on exporting firms to not only solve the problems just outlined but to do so rapidly, and on a continuing basis.

The severity of these conditions generates the basis for a fast alliance with the state around its developmental agenda. Surviving in highly competitive markets, *as long as firms are trying to move up the value chain*, requires strategies which cannot but be dependent on state support. Hence, state managers now have far greater leverage against firms, since the latter must depend on the former to solve many of the problems just mentioned. So long as firms are willing to hazard the export market, and hence must survive in that market, they have to depend on the state to provide a steady stream of finance, help acquire and unpack technology and its attendant supports, establish sales and marketing networks, and perhaps most importantly, to coordinate investment in complementary lines. This gives state managers the bargaining power to make demands on firms in return for the subsidization and support that they provide. But just as crucial is a second aspect of the state-business relation: under ELI, not only does the state's role assume greater importance, but there is a greater incentive for firms to *comply* with state manager's demands for performance. When firms have to perform in the highly competitive external markets, there is a direct incentive to adhere to the state's demands for increasing the efficiency of production in a line because the firm's survival in that line depends in steadily increasing its productivity.

Since firms benefit enormously from strategic state intervention and coordination, they have an interest in having a state that has the capacity to effectively coordinate and monitor investment, in order to more ably assist their expansion into external markets. The more stringent competitive conditions, greater uncertainty, tenuous relations with customers, and so on, decrease the margin for error that firms can take for granted in safer domestic markets. While slow and maladroit coordination of investment may not be a serious problem in protected domestic markets, where firms do not face strong competitive threats, it poses a considerable threat in export markets, where firms have to be able to respond rapidly to new entrants, new technologies, and the like. Further, matters such as quality standards, which are almost a non-issue in monopolistic domestic markets, become exceedingly important under more competitive conditions. Here too, state monitoring and imposition of such standards is not only unlikely to elicit firms' objections, but is in fact more likely to be welcomed. The upshot is that in export-led strategies, capitalists have no reason to oppose the project of building a disciplinary developmental state; indeed, they have good reason to support it – so long as such a state is a precondition for export success.

We see, then, how ELI made it possible for the state to forge an alliance with domestic capital – an alliance, moreover, in which it was rational for firms to accept a state with the power to discipline firms. As long as the chaebol needed the state to solve coordination and collective action problems, and as long as this broad partnership reaped dividends, the occasional slap on the wrist of a firm, or even more severe measures, would not pose a political problem because capitalists willing to take the place of the malcontent could always be found. The state could, therefore, impose discipline without fear of triggering an investor panic. And that, I would submit, was the secret of the Korean state's apparently miraculous power over local industrialists. What set the Korean state apart was not that it was able to escape the normal constraints of a capitalist political economy; its secret lay in the manner that it was able to negotiate them. The nationalization of the banking system did not, and cannot, therefore, provide a panacea for ambitious state managers. Even with this resource at hand, the penultimate control over the investment decision leaves capitalists with the effective veto power over state strategy. The road to state-building, in the absence of a mass movement or some other source of state autonomy, goes through, and not around, the capitalist class.

The demise of ELI and the state-capital alliance

With the development model in place, and the developmental alliance between the state and the chaebol secure around the model, the industrial policy regime was able to scale extraordinary heights during the next quarter century. The chaebol penetrated the US market at an extraordinary rate, initially filling the niches hitherto occupied by the Japanese, and then expanding into new, high-tech lines. During this transition, the state played a critical role in the movement up the value chain: in coordinating firms' investment decisions (Rodrik 1995), assisting in the acquisition and unpacking of technology (Kim 1997), providing cheap credit (Woo 1991) and helping generate an extensive sales and marketing network. The spectacular growth of the chaebol, which resulted from this alliance, made the issue of discipline fairly unproblematic for planners, as the enormous growth possibilities acted as an irresistible magnet to new entrants to the market. For any incumbent firm, there were ten others willing to take its place if it fell out of favor with planners.

Why, then, did the terms of the alliance begin to fracture in the late 1980s, and eventually fall apart in the following decade? The reason has to do with two basic elements of the ELI model itself, which, over time, dynamically undermined the terms of the state-capital alliance. These were: first, the fact that the chaebol had an interest in supporting a developmental state only as long as they had to rely on it for their success; the second was that, in hitching their wagon to the massive American market, the Korean economic planners were also vulnerable, over time, to American pressure to liberalize their own policies. Over time, as the chaebol grew in size and power, their need for state coordination decreased, and their toleration of discipline only followed in train; by the 1990s, they could therefore join the constant US pressure to dismantle the state apparatus of the previous decades. These aspects of ELI thus made the model dynamically unstable after a given period of time. Let us see how this worked itself out.

The chaebol joined in the state-building process in the 1960s out of their own self-interest. ELI generates this interest in the early stages of industrialization. Although firms may recoil at the prospect of having the state acquire its considerable monitoring and coordinating capacity – which always carries the threat of being turned against bourgeois interests – they abide by it because without it, success in foreign markets does not appear possible. Lacking the means to acquire the inputs and the coordination called for by the highly competitive markets in industrialized countries, firms find it rational to accept the state's accretion of power to impose discipline. So long as firms lack the experience, the managerial skills, channels for technology acquisition, and financial resources that approximate those of their competitors, the alliance with a developmental state should be expected to hold. And this was the case through the first twenty-five years or so after Park's ascension to power. But as firms grow in size and resources, and the need to rely on the state for survival recedes, so should the rationale for tolerating the overweening power of a disciplinary planning apparatus. Once local industrialists develop the means to acquire, without assistance, the inputs that they need for export success, planners lose the leverage to impose conditions in exchange for their subsidies. Businesses thus are able to demand that state managers scale back the apparatus of regulations and controls which formed the teeth of the developmental state...without fear of immediate losses in performance. This does not mean that firms will cease to ask for subsidization. It only means that they will now be in a position to demand that subsidies be more or less unconditional.

If we turn now to the facts of the Korean case, the changes which led to the chaebol's defection from the developmental alliance are quite apparent. The critical period, as most commentators agree, was the second half of the 1970s, the years of the Heavy and Chemical Industrialization drive. By the time of its completion, the chaebol's position in the economy had become considerably stronger than in the 1970s (Kang 1996). Their increasing control of large swathes of the economy is pointed to by scholars as the basis for their new-found power against the state. But for our purposes, this is an issue of secondary importance, since I have argued that they were sufficiently powerful to give Park pause even in the 1960s. Of far greater importance are the *qualitative* changes that came about as part of the industrialization process, which made firms more self-sufficient than before. In other words, it is not the increasing dependence of the state on capital – emphasized by so much of the literature – that merits attention, but rather, the decreasing dependence of capital on the state.

And in this regard, at least three developments are noteworthy. First, the reliance on the state for research and technological upgrading declined by the 1980s. In 1970, the public sector accounted for 97 per cent of all Research and Development (R&D) expenditures in the economy – not surprising, since there was but one corporate center for R&D in 1971! By 1980, the private sector's share of total expenditure had increased to 36 per cent, and in 1990 it vastly overshadowed the public sector, accounting for 81 per cent of the total, while the share of R&D in the economy had risen from 0.38 per cent of the GNP to almost 2 per cent. The number of corporate research centers in the country, meanwhile, had risen to almost one thousand (Kim, L. 1997: 54–5). All this reflected the fact that the biggest Korean firms had been frantically mastering and improving upon foreign technology during the Park years, often under pressure from Park himself, who appears to have put a high priority on forcing industrialists to set up independent research centers.

Second, most of the biggest chaebol were able to acquire control over independent sources of finance. By the mid-1980s, eight of the ten biggest conglomerates owned at least one non-banking financial institution (NBFI), making them far less reliant on the state for cheap finance (Kim 1997: 189). Further, even though the chaebol were still heavily leveraged, the system of industrial finance had undergone significant restructuring. Whereas bank loans accounted for around one-third of external finance in the late 1960s, by the early 1990s they hovered around 15–16 per cent; and while loans from NBFIs and the sale of securities comprised less than a quarter of the external funds borrowed in the late 1960s, by the early 1990s they accounted for almost two-thirds of it (Jang 2000: 275). Hence the source of indebtedness had shifted from state-owned banks to private sources, making firms more independent of planners.

Third, the chaebol had spread into altogether new sectors of the economy, especially upstream lines, enabling them to reduce the problem of coordination with other firms. In purely quantitative terms, the average number of subsidiaries under each chaebol rose from 4.2 in 1970 to 17.9 in 1990, and 22.3 in 1996. The numbers were even more impressive for the top five conglomerates (Hyundai, Samsung, Daewoo, Lucky-Goldstar, and Sunkyung), which, in 1994, controlled 210 affiliates between them, for an average of 42

(Jang 2000: 352). Perhaps even more important was that this rise was accompanied by a diversification into new sectors: the average number of industries in which each conglomerate owned subsidiaries rose from 7.7 in 1970 to 14 in 1989, and was at 18.8 in 1996 (Jang 2000: 294). Although much of this diversification was horizontal, spreading into other, unrelated industries, for many of the top chaebol it was also an index of greater vertical integration. This development had the effect of making much of the needed coordination between firms an affair internal to a conglomerate, rather than something which had to be arranged between conglomerates by economic planners.

These changes were of considerable significance for the stability of the developmental alliance between the state and capitalists. At the new level of resources and expertise that the chaebol wielded, the need for assistance in acquiring inputs and in inter-firm coordination was far less than it had been at the outset of ELI. This meant that the state, in turn, began losing the leverage over domestic capitalists which it once possessed. The threat of withholding assistance, or access to cheap inputs, no longer carried the grave consequences it did during the pervious two decades. Hence, by the late 1980s, Korean capitalists were in a position to start pushing back against the state, demanding a curtailment of its power over their investment and sales activities. And as many students of the Korean political economy have noted, the turn against the state at this point was made all the more potent because of the increased economic weight of the chaebol in the economy.

From the other side, the US had been pressing since the early 1980s for Korea to liberalize its trade regime and financial markets. In a dynamic not unlike that which Japan encountered, the very success of Korean exports created a backlash in the US against the asymmetry of the equation: access to the American market for Korean firms, with no reciprocity on the trade front by Korea. This was a tolerable state of affairs for the US during the height of the Cold War, since Korea did reciprocate by allowing a massive American military presence in the north. But as the intensity of the Cold War receded, so did the toleration of the Korean trade regime. This was made all the more pressing as American trade and fiscal deficits soared in the 1980s, and access to Korean markets became pressing for economic policymakers. As long as the domestic alliance was secure in Korea, American pressure could be handled with some degree of dexterity. But as the basis for the alliance between the state and the chaebol was itself dissolving, the pairings in the triangle began to shift, and the chaebol joined in the pressure to initiate a change in development strategy.

By the early 1990s, the chaebol were calling fairly consistently for the state to scale back its regulatory apparatus, in tandem with the calls for liberalization by the US. The attack was led, of course, by the biggest of the chaebol, who were becoming increasingly impatient with the panoply of regulations and limitations under which they had to labor. Bolstering this lobbying was a massive ideological blitz by newly established research institutes, many of which were established by the chaebol themselves or by their umbrella group, the Federation of Korean Industries (FKI). Thus, for example, the 1990s witnessed the establishment of the Korean Economic Research Institute (sponsored by the FKI), the Center for Free Enterprises (also FKI), and individual research institutes such as the Daewoo Economic Institute and its counterparts set-up by Hyundai and Samsung – all dedicated to a more liberalized economy and all tirelessly spinning out position papers commending it. In this respect, the Korean bourgeoisie learned well from its US counterpart, which had also put into place an enormous thicket of think-tanks in the 1970s and 1980s to trigger an ideological shift in the country (Judis 2000). Indeed, the US was relevant in another respect as well. Since the middle of the 1980s, each administration had exerted tremendous pressure on Korea to liberalize its external economic management. But the real change came in 1992–1993, when Korea lobbied to join the OECD. Now the US was able to extract a commitment from Roh Tae Woo and, following him, from Kim Youn Sam, to initiate a dismantling of the control regime, as a condition of membership into the OECD.

Already, before the ascension of Kim to the Presidency, Roh Tae Woo had begun to loosen the industrial policy regime (Chang *et al.* 1998: 740). But the real changes began with Kim's Presidency, who released almost immediately upon taking office his '100-day plan for the new economy' – a clear cut promise to liberalize the economy. Interestingly, Kim's commitment to liberalization was not a simple plan to hand things over to the chaebol. In fact, the 100-day Plan came along with another initiative, to streamline the massive conglomerates, reduce their indebtedness, and increase economic competition. The centerpiece of this plan was called the 'core business line' drive which was designed to induce the biggest chaebol – with the usual mix of sticks and carrots – to pare down their operations to a few core sectors. The plan had been introduced by Roh in 1991, but was carried over by Kim in his Presidency. This is worth mentioning because the plan embodies many of the same principles that were put into effect after the 1997 crisis, but with very different results. Alongside this initiative were also other elements intended to put up some semblance of an orderly transition to a more liberal economy. Central to this was a plan to increase the restrictions on chaebol entry into the financial sector and a reform of the taxation system. The overall thrust of these reforms, therefore, was to induce the chaebol to greater efficiency, while at the same time putting mechanisms in place to prevent their usurping control over the crucial levers of finance.

Within a short period of his announcing this program, Kim found himself face to face with a revolt by the chaebol. Not only did they cavil at the program, but the business groups demanded an acceleration of the liberalization and privatization program. Concomitant to this, and perhaps as a consequence, the rate of investment in the economy plummeted in the winter and spring of 1993, driving down the rate of growth. The shaken Kim immediately began to backpedal, and arranged for a long series of one-on-one meetings with the heads of the biggest chaebol at the Blue House through the Spring and Summer. By the Fall of the year, it became clear that the industrialists' demands had made an impression. Kim announced a series of privatizations (December), loosened control over bank loans to chaebol (January 1994), and further loosened the barriers to entry in the financial sector – in other words he went exactly in the opposite direction from his initial program! These economic reforms were complemented in the policy sphere by the abolition of the legendary Economic Planning Board in December 1994, and in April 1995, industrial licensing for the chaebol was also abolished (Jang 2000: 338–9). Thus began the wholesale dismemberment of the Korean developmental state. In 1995, regulations on bank loans to chaebol were abolished; regulations on Foreign Direct Investment (FDI) were liberalized, as was the capital account; and crucially, in mid-1995, foreign borrowings were allowed under some very loose criteria. By late 1995, one could say with some confidence that the state's ability to steer and coordinate investment was crippled beyond repair.

Conclusion

Korea's exceptionalism did not reside in its possession of a state that could simply dominate the local business class. In its relation to the class as a whole, there is no evidence that the Korean state possessed a kind of power that its counterparts elsewhere lacked. What was exceptional about the country was the co-occurrence of two conditions, each of which was necessary, and neither sufficient, for the construction of a highly effective developmental state: first, an alliance between the political elite and local capital around an accumulation project – one which made it rational for firms to accept a developmental state; and second, the presence of a stratum of state managers almost fanatically committed to building the kind of state that could successfully manage the economic ascent. Without the underlying alliance, there is no reason to think that Korean capitalists would have accepted a state with such powers to manage and control *private* investment decisions. As I have shown elsewhere, an attempt to build a state with the same sorts of powers failed in India because of opposition by local industrialists (Chibber 2003). But the alliance, in turn, would have been frittered away, had there not been a political leadership with the talents and the will to transform state institutions in a developmental direction. The fact that effective developmental states were so rare in the post-war world reflected the rarity of the co-occurrence of these conditions.

The chapter is intended to argue for a return-to-class analysis in studies of the developmental state. But it should also have some appeal to practitioners of the 'Varieties of Capitalism' approach (henceforth VoC). As Soskice describes the approach, it 'analyzes the way in which micro-agents of capitalist systems – companies, customers, employees, owners of capital – organize and structure their interrelationships, within a framework of incentives and constraints or "rules of the game" set by a range of market-related institutions in which the microagents are embedded' (Soskice 1999). Note that the basic approach is structuralist, in that it examines the effects of social structures on the choices of agents embedded in them; and it has affinities with class analysis, in that the central structures are what Marxists would describe as inter- and intra-class relations. Now, although work in the VoC frame has tended to focus on how institutional differences generate distinct economic dynamics, there is no reason that this basic approach cannot be extended to studies of state forms. Huber and Stephens (2001) have recently attempted to link production regimes with forms of the welfare state, in just such an effort. The guiding theoretical premise is that kinds of production regimes enjoy a selective affinity with different state forms. Huber and Stephens do not draw out the causal processes linking the two, but it is easy to surmise that the links would operate in the manner suggested by Soskice: as underlying dynamics of the production regime change, so firms' choices with respect to state institutions would also change, generating pressures for changes in state form. This is not all that distant from a class analysis of the state. The notion that 'aspects of the welfare state and production regimes "fit" each other in a mutually support-ive or enabling way' (Huber and Stephens 2001: 104) is reminiscent of some structuralist arguments, like those developed by Jessop and his colleagues, that argue for a link between state forms and accumulation models (Jessop 1990). And it would therefore also be compatible with my argument, that the adoption a particular kind of accumulation model (or production regime) – ELI – made it rational for capitalists to accept a developmental state.

It is not clear whether practitioners of the VoC approach would want to see their framework interpreted in this fashion, nor can we assume that they will develop it with a clearer conceptualization of their agents (firms, employees, owners of capital) as class actors. But there is no getting away from the fact that, if taken at its word, the VoC approach steers to the same kind of structuralism that characterizes class analysis. In principle, therefore, there ought to be the possibility of a healthy debate between the two approaches.

8
Euro-Capitalism and American Empire

Leo Panitch and Sam Gindin

For some two decades now, progressive American, British and Canadian intellectuals, determined to resist neoliberalism's 'there-is-no-alternative' mantra, have looked to continental Europe for an alternative model. One virtue of this academic and political project – which within the field of comparative political economy has now come to be known as the 'varieties of capitalism' or VoC approach – has been that it challenged the notion that capitalist globalization inevitably needed to take the form it has, apparently entailing, as so many of its proponents imagined, the growing impotence of nation states and the increasing homogenization of social formations. The insistence on variety among states has meant trying to refocus attention on the continuing salience of institutional arrangements and social relations specific to particular social formations and their histories, the very dimensions largely ignored in the equations of neoclassical economics and the policy prescriptions of the International Monetary Fund (IMF). Above all, this approach has suggested that whether and how societies adapt themselves to global competition remains an open and important question.

There are, however, a number of analytic problems with the VoC approach, which must give us pause. We argue in this chapter that apart from an inadequate and misleading conceptualization of the relationship between state and market in the era of globalization, the most severe problem with this approach is its tendency to treat all the advanced capitalist states as equal units of analysis. This occludes the overwhelming power – and above all the penetrative capacity – of the American state and capital *vis-à-vis* even the other leading capitalist states in the world. On the basis of this critique, we go on to make the case for the need for European capitalism to be theorized within the framework of American neo-imperialism today. This then leads us, in the second part of this chapter, to present historical and empirical evidence that challenges the presumption (constantly lurking in the VoC approach) that the material base for the maintenance of American hegemony has eroded. That this is not in fact the case does not mean that the contradictions of the American imperium and neoliberal globalization have vanished. But it does mean, as we will show, that strategic advance for the Left in this context will have to entail far more than defending or extolling existing European models of capitalism.

Rethinking 'varieties of capitalism' in relation to neo-imperialism

One major strain in the VoC literature (Evans 1997; Weiss 1998; Hirst and Thompson 1999) has attempted to counter the nostrums of neoliberalism by extolling the ideal of the state, thereby reflecting a certain neo-Hegelianism on the left today (Panitch 2002). Some proponents of this approach downplay the significance of globalization, but in any case all emphasize the continuing viability of state-led economic development and competitiveness strategies. Apart from the fact that many of the states they look to in this respect hardly qualify as progressive, there has always been an other-worldly quality to the categories of 'weak' and 'strong' states employed by this approach. This especially applies to the designation of the American state as 'weak' solely on the basis of the limited scope of its domestic industrial and social policies, while states that are puny players in the setting of the global neoliberal policy framework are considered 'strong' on the basis of domestic economic interventions alone. This all too often ignores the role of the American state in the post-war era in reconstructing the very states considered 'strong' domestically, and it occludes any clear view of the domestic and international strength of the American state as revealed through its sponsorship of neoliberal globalization in the subsequent era. It also ignores how Japan – once the apple of the neo-Hegelian statists' eye – floundered through the 1990s; and it is unable to account for why the American Treasury dictated the terms of adjustment – right in the Japanese state's own regional backyard – during the East Asian crisis of 1997–1998 (Panitch 2000).

There are those in the VoC school (Hall and Soskice 2001) who put more emphasis on firms, rather than states, pointing in particular to the linkages between banks and industry and, to a lesser extent, to certain corporatist relations between unions and employers associations, as the key to the difference between European 'coordinated market economies' (CMEs) and Anglo-American 'liberal market economies' (LMEs). They thereby avoid some of the statist idealism discussed above, but it must be said that the expectation that LMEs can be brought to emulate CMEs on industrial and social policy looks suspiciously voluntarist in light of the widespread deployment throughout the whole approach of notions of institutional sedimentation and path-dependency. Indeed, Hall and Soskice themselves admit that actors with 'little experience of such coordination to underpin requisite common knowledge will find it difficult to develop non-market coordination'. In fact, they go so far as to suggest that emulation can only go the other way: because 'market relations do not demand the same level of common knowledge...there is no such constraint on CMEs deregulating to become more like LMEs' (Hall and Soskice 2001: 62). In the light of this, it would appear that the policy implications of the VoC analysis can only relate to helping CMEs adjust to neoliberalism in a way that involves conserving the core institutional arrangements that have heretofore allegedly given them 'comparative advantage'. This has been the basic point of Albo's long-standing critique of 'progressive competitiveness' (Albo 1994, 1997).

It is sometimes claimed that greater recognition in the Anglo-American LMEs of the existence and success of the CMEs would have 'radical implications for policy making' in the former countries (Hall and Soskice 2001: vi). But far from offering a strategy for radical change against neoliberal globalization, what is in fact being advanced here is at best a limited and defensive strategy. Trying to convince policymakers in the state and business communities in the Anglo-American countries to pay more attention to following the European example by improving the coordinating capacities of firms with other actors, and convincing them that social policies could improve the operations of markets rather than impede them, does not amount to a radical strategy. On the contrary, to make its case, this approach adopts a mode of analysis that embraces not only the competitive criteria of success and failure of neoclassical economists, but even their categories of analysis to the extent that it is mainly oriented to demonstrating that state intervention, collective bargaining and inter-firm collaboration do *not* necessarily distort market efficiency. The categories of analysis (states, firms and markets) are the same; only their ideal values are inverted. Nor can the consequences of competitiveness in material terms be averted. As Bryan has put it:

With the rise of the competitiveness agenda as the rationale for national economic policy, there is a conceptual merger of a theoretical discourse from a microeconomic framework (the individual firm's performance in open markets) with claims of benefit in a macroeconomic framework (the national gains of competitiveness)...The notion that [benefits] accrue throughout the nation is but a hypothetical possibility, with no clear mechanisms for realization, certainly none of the conventional Keynesian mechanisms of national redistribution...A predictable policy consequence is to shift onto labour the costs involved in the pursuit of national competitiveness...Although the advocates of competitiveness extol the possibilities of high wages associated with working for high profit companies in high productivity industries...benefits accrue to labour only for relative productivity...for it is only productivity converted into profitability that supports wages growth. Hence the prospect is that penalties in the form of wage cuts and/or work intensification are the likely dominant outcome of global competition for most of the world's workers. National policies of competitiveness for collective gain thereby secure the complicity of labour in a policy program in which the gains are private, and the collectivism is a rhetorical construction based on statistical aggregation. (Bryan 2001: 70–1)

Even more problematic in the VoC approach is the manner in which it posits no relationships among national economies at all, apart from competition among them. The strategic and analytic problems of the VoC approach are rooted in how it conceives the nation state, and the actors within it, in relation to capitalist globalization. In this approach, globalization – and its economic expression as competitive market pressures – is merely seen as an external constraint to which states and domestic firms and social forces must adjust. The only difference with the conventional account of globalization is that the VoC approach argues that one of the ways in which states can successfully cope is by paying special attention to adapting or restoring, under the new conditions created by globalization, the national institutional structures making for economic coordination.

What is obscured here is the extent to which globalization is a development, not external to states but internal to them. Recognition of the active role of nation states and domestic capitalist forces in constituting the more liberal international trade and financial regime associated with capitalist globalization and carrying responsibility for its expanded reproduction is hardly a new discovery (Gill 1992; Panitch 1994). Trying to understand why and how even CME states have come to play this role cannot be left out of the analytic focus of any serious comparative political economy.

This must involve an examination of the role played by foreign capital, as a social force within each nation state, as well as that of the increasing transnational orientation to accumulation on the part of domestic capital. It must also not ignore the responsibility that states have increasingly taken for ensuring that their national policies contribute to the stability of, or at least do not disrupt the functioning of, the global economy. This is what Cox (1987) meant by 'the internationalization of the state'. And especially for those who take political institutions seriously, the study of the relationship of the state to globalization also needs to involve, as Cox insisted, the examination of the restructuring of states in terms of shifts in the hierarchy of state apparatuses away from those agencies concerned with domestic social forces and issues, such as labour or welfare departments, to those, like central banks, more directly concerned with and closely linked to the social forces and international institutions associated with globalization. Moreover, this analysis must remain open to the recognition that departments of labour and welfare often seek to retain their status amidst globalization by redefining their main role as that of developing policies to make the domestic labour force contribute more to facilitating international competitiveness.

It should be evident that reconceptualizing the state's relationship to globalization in this fashion is a very different exercise than that engaged in by those who practice the VoC approach. It is rather strange that social scientists, of a decidedly institutionalist bent, should largely leave out modes of coordination (and institutional capacities for coordination) among states, let alone ones that reflect asymmetric power, and that indicate *which* states and *which* capitals and *which* modes of coordination are most salient in the process of globalization. What is needed is a new approach to comparative political economy that examines the diverse ways in which states have been involved in the constitution of both capitalist globalization and American empire, and that encourages analysis of the way in which a wide variety of national institutional forms can be reproduced and articulated within them. Conceived in this way, such an approach can link up with the VoC literature, but go beyond it by paying attention in addition to a comparative understanding of the role that capitalist states play in the reproduction of global capitalism. This must today involve attempting to comprehend the nature of the American state's pre-eminent role in this respect, and therefore appreciating that the role of other nation states can only be understood in the context of their relationship to the American state and capital. But it will also be necessary to conceive this relationship as not simply a matter of external, one-way imposition. Indeed, a crucial dimension of any theorization of what might be called 'neo-imperialism in the era of globalization', must be the explanation of why the penetration by the American state and capital into other social formations has so often been welcomed as contributing to the strengthening of the host state, to the expanded reproduction of domestic economic and social relations, and to the possibility of influence on American policy-making.

At the core of this neo-imperialism is the relationship between the American state and the other developed capitalist states. It is here, not with the capitalist peripheries, that imperial penetration is densest and institutional linkages and coordination most developed. It is the implicit recognition of this that makes the VoC literature's relative neglect of the Third World capitalisms plausible; but a literature that blithely ignores the global pre-eminence of the American state and treats the USA only as one of many LMEs against which to contrast CMEs must be seen as impoverished. What is missing from the VoC literature is any systematic study of how international financial institutions, and the US Treasury and Federal Reserve through them, set limits to the economic policy-making autonomy of other states. In general, comparative political economy rooted in the Marxist tradition has been more sensitive to this, but only insofar as its practitioners have broken with the classical conceptions of imperialism. Exemplary in this regard was Poulantzas's understanding that the entry into Europe of American multinationals meant that a powerful new social force had been established within the European social formations, with the consequence that the European bourgeoisies – even at the height of the dollar crisis in the late 1960s and early 1970s – no longer had any interest in challenging American hegemony (Poulantzas 1975). This did not mean that European states were by-passed or rendered irrelevant; on the contrary, they became responsible for coordinating a more complex set of domestic class relationships, which still remained distinctively specific to each social formation. Yet Poulantzas's admirable concern to demonstrate that globalization was *not about* 'the virtual disappearance of national state power' in Europe led him to consider American capital primarily in terms of its effects on European social formations and states. He did not examine in any detail the forces within the American economy that were impelling foreign direct investment (FDI) in Europe and the contradictions this represented for American capitalism. Even more crucially, he also failed to examine the modalities and mechanisms of American neo-imperialism, as it was expressed in and through the apparatuses of the American state and the international institutions it dominated. Gowan has done much to fill this gap although it is arguable that the European states are treated as too passive agents in his account of the transition to neoliberalism (Gowan 1999).

What still needs attending to, however, is a more detailed examination of the distinctive institutional make-up of American state power, and its institutional capacity to act as the global state that global capitalism needs, to keep order, to manage crises, and to close contradictions among the world nation states and the diverse social forces that compose them. For it is our view, and here we would go beyond the arguments of writers such as Strange (1989), Shaw (2000) and Hardt and Negri (2000), that the new American empire that evolved after the Second World War was not dismantled in the wake of the crisis of the Golden Age in the 1970s, and the development of greater trade competitiveness and capital mobility that accompanied it, but rather has been refashioned through the era of neoliberal globalization over the past two decades. None of this means, of course, that homogeneity of state and economic structures – or indeed the absence of divergence in many policy areas – characterizes the new imperialism. Nor is there any reason to assume that contradiction and conflict do not enter into the asymmetric power relationships within it, as they do in any other. Rather we locate those contradictions not so much in the relationships between states, as *within* states as they try to manage their internal processes of accumulation, legitimation and class struggle, and especially in the American state's ability to do this while also managing and containing the complexities of neo-imperial globalization. Assessing this, however, requires sober and careful analysis. It is to this that we now turn.

American hegemony beyond the crisis of the golden age

The American state's ability to maintain its hegemonic authority and capacity, to act on behalf of global capital, is conditional on its capacity to reproduce the material base of American capital. What has often been common to both Marxian and non-Marxian analyses, whatever the analytical and political differences between them, is their belief that this capacity has been undermined; and they see this as central to the crisis that ended the post-war 'golden age' (Kennedy 1988; Petras and Morley 1992; Arrighi 1994). Attempts at resolving the crisis – the accelerated internationalization summarized as 'globalization' and the turn to social regulation through markets summarized as 'neo-liberalism' – are, in this perspective, generally seen as having failed, simply causing new problems and new instabilities, or postponing old ones. The American spurt in the last half of the nineties must thus have been a last hurrah, and the piercing of the bubble is a confirmation of this.

We take issue with this interpretation. It seems to us to be too pat a reading of the dynamics – and dynamism – of capitalism since the seventies, and too casual a treatment of the depth of American hegemony. The American boom of the latter nineties, and therefore the current potential of the American economy, cannot be so easily dismissed. There remains an underlying strength in American capital and the American state, a strength that is the cumulative consequence of the economic and social restructuring that took place since 'the Volcker shock' over two decades ago. All this does not, of course, imply that there may not be new crises, but it does suggest that such crises must be analysed in a new context, not as a postponed outcome of the early seventies. And it means that, whatever our moral judgment of the American-led model, our political agendas cannot rely on a protagonist in decay.

In what follows, we first attempt to clarify the special historical status of the period called the 'golden age' – the quarter century after the Second World War. We then argue that the crisis of the 1970s needs to be understood as a turning point, a decade during which capitalist states and bourgeoisies stumbled through strategic confusions as well as class and international conflicts. Those theorists who see the period since that time through the lens of the 1970s – portraying the past quarter century in terms of the working out of the crisis that began in that decade – are, we contend, wrong. We argue that a new period begins with Reaganism and Thatcherism, and above all with the Volcker shock applied to the American economy (and through it to the world economy) at the beginning of the 1980s. During this period, we argue, the economic as well as the ideological and military underpinnings of American imperial hegemony were re-established.

By way of presaging our overall argument, it may be useful to begin with an even longer historical overview, which affords some perspective on why it is that establishing the post-1945 golden age as the standard – especially in defining 'crises' – sets the bar too high (Gindin and Panitch 2002). When people point to the slower growth of the last quarter century in contrast with the previous quarter century as indicative of a capitalist crisis characterizing the whole period, we must remind ourselves that it was the earlier and not the later period that was historically unique. In fact, as Table 8.1 indicates, the growth of the post-73 period is rather respectable when placed within the sweep of capitalism's longer trajectory.

Table 8.1 Annual growth in real GDP per capita

	US (%)	Europe (%)	World (%)
1820–1870	1.34	0.95	0.53
1870–1913	1.82	1.32	1.30
1913–1950	1.61	0.76	0.91
1950–1973	2.45	4.08	2.93
1973–1998	1.99	1.78	1.33

Source: Maddison, *The World Economy, A Millennial Perspective* (OECD 2001: 265).

In terms of our own periodization, which separates the decade of the 1970s from the two subsequent ones, what is especially worth noting is that the growth in American real GDP per capita in the period that followed the Volcker turning point (1982–2001) was 2.4 per cent – not as high as the 3 per cent of the booming 1960s, but hardly suggesting stagnation. And though productivity growth as measured by overall output per hour declined significantly in the US, if we concentrate on manufacturing, where data are also more reliable, the productivity growth since 1982 is actually higher than in the golden age: annual manufacturing output per hour increased from an average of 2.6 per cent in the period 1950–1973, to 3.5 per cent in the period 1982–2000.

Let us now take a closer look at the twists and turns of the past half-century. The economic dimensions of the post-1945 world order were not designated as 'globalization' until well after the economic slowdown, but the project of moving towards a seamless, single world economy was initiated at the end of the Second World War, in reaction to the catastrophic failure of a pre-First World War international capitalism that was fragmented into rival imperialisms and separated spheres of influence. International accumulation had actually been relatively thin within each imperial block in the pre-First World War era. The global division of labour then was largely complementary rather than competitive (manufacturing in one country and resources in another, rather than, as at present, a two-way flow of similar products), and capital flow was largely arms-length portfolio investment. From the Second World War on, however, FDI, with its deeper impact on economic and social structures, had a much larger role to play. The fact that the term 'globalization' did not become part of our lexicon until the late 1980s/early 1990s was not because it was not already pervasive – international trade, production and finance had already been growing much faster than domestic economies by the mid-sixties – but because its later combination with neoliberalism accelerated those international trends and the process seemed to take on a life of its own.

In the immediate postwar period, rebuilding economies and social relations implied a bias in the process of accumulation towards structures that emphasized the mobilization of resources. This did not set aside competitive pressures, but it did limit some of its dimensions: for example, capital markets were generally subordinated (domestically and internationally) to the needs of reconstruction. This period was, however, transitional both in its underlying goal of moving towards an international liberal order, and its inherent logic. Its successes tended to subvert its institutional foundations. The rebuilding of Europe brought American direct investment; and that investment, along with the expansion of trade, undermined capital controls. Capital mobility undermined pegged exchange rates. Rising standards of living meant larger pools of savings and increased competition within the financial sector, just as rising inflation undermined existing forms of financial regulation and corporatist integration. Steady growth raised worker expectations at the same time as the exhaustion of the singular conditions existing in the postwar years eroded the system's ability to continue to deliver economic security and rapid growth at the same pace as before.

A key economic dimension of the challenge faced by capitalism by the late 1960s and early 1970s took the form of a falling rate of profit. The well-known productivity slowdown at this time was due in large part to the growing relative size in the economy of low-productivity service sectors, which lowered average productivity growth for the economy as a whole. Manufacturing represented over 30 per cent of US non-agricultural employment in 1966: by 1978 this was under 24 per cent, and by late 2000 it was under 14 per cent. But while the lower productivity rates showed up primarily in sectors outside manufacturing (sectors which were growing in relative weight), this did not negate potential problems for accumulation within manufacturing. Sustaining the productivity growth in manufacturing required relatively more capital inputs at the same time as worker militancy was resisting any downward pressures in wages. This led to the familiar decline in the rate of profit.

In Marxist terms, one would see this in terms of the organic composition of capital rising while the rate of exploitation remained relatively stable, causing a decline in the rate of surplus extraction (Webber and Rigby 1996; Dumenil and Levy 2003). But the debate, in this context, about whether or not the cause of falling profits lay with technical conditions of production, or a profit squeeze rooted in labour's strength, is largely beside the point. Even if the 'original' cause was technical, from capital's perspective, the restoration of profit rates was being frustrated by the relative strength of labour (relative, that is, to capital's capabilities and needs through the sixties and seventies).

Brenner (1998, 2002a) has correctly emphasized that the strength of labour, in itself, does not explain a sustained crisis (Brenner 1998, 2002a). What needs illumination is why the profit-led downturn was not self-correcting through the normal process of the devaluation of a portion of capital, the consequent concentration of capital in the most dynamic firms, and the accompanying weakening of labour through this restructuring. Brenner's intriguing explanation was that increased international competition increased entry while the concentration of capital and the large sunk investments of corporations decreased exit. This led to excess capacity and a profit squeeze independent of the relative strength of labour. There seem to us to be two fundamental problems with this rather elegant response. First, while Brenner is quite right to point to the limits on competition as being a condition of the crisis – that is, to restrictions on the logic of capitalist competition working itself out – he is wrong on the source of those limits. Second, Brenner incorrectly generalized the contradictions of the late 1960s and 1970s into a permanent feature of capitalism.

To grasp what was in fact happening, we have to integrate the state into the discussion, and pay special attention to the role of the American state (Gindin 2001). With the end of the circumstances that made the golden age possible, capitalism inevitably had to confront anew the question of from where its new source of vitality would come. Because this issue emerged in the form of slower growth and intensified competition, there was some inclination on the part of national states to both extend the competitive capacity within their own social formations and limit the negative outcomes of competition domestically. No western state was really prepared to go so far with this as to impose the kind of trade and capital restrictions that would undermine international economic integration; but their initial domestic response at least blocked, in the 1970s, the kind of intensive restructuring of capitalism necessary for capital's revival, and it was only unblocked when the American state itself accepted the need for competitive discipline at home (expressed in the Volcker shock of 1980). It was only with the consequent generalization of such discipline internationally that capitalism's vigour seemed to return.

Through the 1960s and into the 1970s, all states, facing pressures at home, were reluctant to let the market declare – at least to the degree necessary to resolve global excess capacity – that domestic facilities were redundant. The American state, in particular, was not about to let this process work itself out according to market criteria, and in the seventies it moved erratically from import surcharges to periodic bouts of economic stimulus, from supply side incentives to some degree of manipulation of exchange rates. This was not just a matter of imperial arrogance, or even a reflection of the fact that the destruction of global excess capacity would fall disproportionately on the domestic US economy. It is important to recognize that, for the American state, the 'crisis' went beyond the immediate economics of profit rates to the more general issue of controlling and reproducing the empire. At home, the American state was confronting a civil rights movement and a youth rebellion that included sections of the working class. Abroad, it was now facing extensive trade competition from Europe and Japan, and a Third World restless and frustrated with its position within global capitalism. The unpopular war in Vietnam directly limited the immediate possibility of any American acceptance of, or active leadership in, the kind of economic and social restructuring necessary to restore its relative competitive strength. During the seventies, the American state was in no position to take on the risks associated with a reconstruction of its economic base.

The historic significance of the Volcker shock was that it came to grips with the American reluctance to firmly take the lead and restructure itself as well as the world order along neoliberal lines. Just as the American state initially blocked the outcome of competition and thereby reinforced the continuation of the stagnation through the seventies, the American state now reversed itself on this and – contrary to Brenner's argument – accelerated the closing of facilities after the early eighties in spite of sunk costs. In 1961, the business failure rate in the US was 64 per 10,000 existing firms; this rate steadily declined and by the late seventies, it had fallen (in line with Brenner's argument) to well under half the 1961 rate. In the 1980s, however, the business failure rate rose dramatically, reaching 120 by 1986 – almost double the rate at the start of the sixties (see Figure 8.1) and it remained well above the earlier rate right through the 1990s. This was subsequently reinforced by the further liberalization of capital movements across regions and countries.

The official intent of Volcker's money targets, the decisive event introducing neoliberalism, was to break the back of inflation, which was threatening the American financial system, the Federal Reserve's control over monetary policy, and the credibility of the American dollar. The problem was not an American problem, since the earlier move to flexible exchange rates had, by eroding pressures for internal discipline, reinforced global inflationary pressures. And as Rude (1999) has shown, in studying the institutional capacity

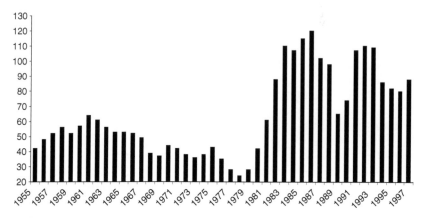

Figure 8.1   Failure rate of business (failures/10,000)
Source: *Economic Report of the President* (2002: Table B-96).

and balance of class forces that allowed Volcker to act when he did, the Federal Reserve was not so much addressing a technical problem as a political one (Rude 1999). Behind the concern with inflation lay the need to reconstitute American capital at home and American-led restructuring globally. The solution that emerged was based on the conclusion that the crisis could only be resolved with 'more capitalism': that is, by building on the structural power of capital to reorganize and discipline both labour and capital.

It is important to emphasize that the passing of the golden age had also raised questions about internal (domestic) forms of accumulation and institutional arrangements in every other state, which were then compounded by the question of how to influence the reconstitution of the American-led international order. The two could not be separated: the reconstitution of the American-led economic order was neither an abstraction happening 'out there' nor simply an American project occurring against other nation states. By its very nature, it included mutual problems that had emerged, through the golden age, within each of their own social formations. Although the economic gap between the US and Europe/Japan narrowed through the fifties and sixties, no serious challenge to American hegemony was ever on the agenda. At most, the growing confidence of Europe and Japan led to hopes of renegotiating certain aspects of American dominance. This was not only because hegemony involved more than economics. Nor was it only that American economic dominance remained intact, as can be seen if we look beyond trade figures and consider American leadership in technology and the relative scale and depth of American finance and foreign investment. What was central was the degree of economic, military, ideological, cultural and political integration that had already taken place in the quarter century after the war. That integration may not have been strong enough to avoid tensions once the slowdown came, but it was strong enough to block the possibility of that tension leading to direct challenges to, or withdrawals from, the liberal world order that had been jointly constructed under American leadership.

It is quite wrong, therefore, to see the transition to neoliberalism in terms of the Americans prevailing against (what were always quite tepid in any case) European or Japanese proposals for extending capital controls in the 1970s in the context of the crisis of Bretton Woods and the American state's delinking the dollar from gold. Rather, what prevailed was the emerging common understanding amongst the American, European and Japanese elites that, in the new integrated international environment already in place by the late 1960s, capital controls now implied much broader restrictions on economic activity, and would have to go much further than they were prepared to have them go. For example, FDI, by then starting to flow both ways, also carried with it pressures to liberalize international finance and involved growing levels of intra-firm trade. It was on this cascading process of economic and social integration that neoliberal globalization was eventually built. This was reinforced by the project of European integration, through which the EU would become an agency of neoliberal discipline, however much social policy and human rights were also on its agenda.

By the 1980s, a twofold project of domestic and international reconstitution evolved in all G7 states under American leadership and this created the conditions for renewed national and global accumulation. After a decade of indecisive and stumbling attempts to escape the persistent economic malaise, the new project was given coherence as neoliberalism took the form of state-led economic restructuring oriented to removing, through the expansion and deepening of markets, democratically imposed barriers to accumulation (earlier concessions on the part of capital that once reflected capitalism's munificence now resurfaced as problems that demanded reversal).

That solution was presaged by the degree of economic integration that had already taken place, and the growing influence and capacities of finance at both home and abroad. While the increased mobility of capital threatened the role of the American dollar, emphasizing the priority of investor credibility, it also represented new opportunities. The structural power of American finance could potentially contribute to mobilizing global savings for use within the US, and the neoliberal emphasis on discipline could find no better friend than a section of capital ready to move where returns were highest. On this latter point, it is important to see that this was not a matter of the opposition between production and finance. With the exhaustion of Keynesianism (broadly defined) and no alternative focus for regeneration, productive capital readily accepted a new more aggressive role for finance as being functional to its own interests.

In the period after the Volcker shock, the rates of growth in GDP, profits and productivity in the USA began their slow climb back to earlier levels – and investment soon followed, albeit with a lag (see Figures 8.2, 8.3 and 8.4).

As neoliberalism gained in coherence and confidence, its ideology became more pervasive and its institutional drive more comprehensive. Labour everywhere suffered a major defeat. At the same time, the new digitalized economy brought, however unevenly and apparently irrationally, significant new technological potentials; and finance – in spite of speculative excesses and scandals – proved to be functional to real capital accumulation and economic growth. The rate of growth in the USA from 1983 to 2002 was greater than in all the other G7 countries (see Figure 8.5). And by the end of the nineties, the real GDP of the US was some 20 per cent higher than the total of the largest dozen economies of Western Europe – a gap impressive enough compared to the approximate equality that existed in 1982, but especially striking given that the gap at the beginning of the golden age, in 1950, was only 13 per cent (see Figure 8.6). For Germany, France and Italy the gap was smaller in 1998 than it was in 1950; collectively, they were 55 per cent behind the US in 1950, and narrowed this to 37 per cent by 1982, but the gap rose back to 51 per cent by 1998.

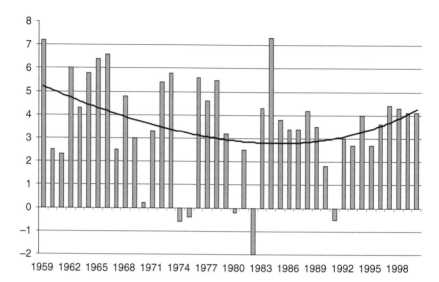

Figure 8.2   Real growth in US GDP
Source: *Economic Report of the President* (2002: Table B-4).

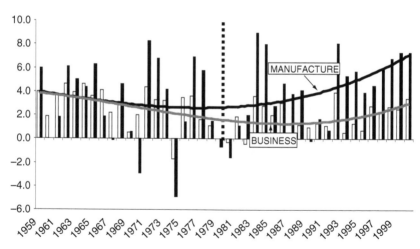

Figure 8.3   Annual change in output/HR
Source: US Bureau of Labour Statistics (2003).

To be sure, the defeat of the American labour movement, crystallized in the restructuring of state agencies like the National Labour Relations Board, was reflected in the historically unprecedented stagnation in real wages: private sector hourly earnings, in 1982 dollars, were $8.40 in 1978 and

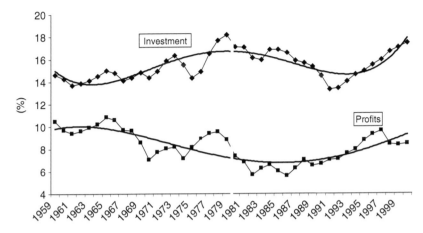

Figure 8.4 Investment and profits: % of GDP
Source: Economic Report of the President (2002: Tables B-1, 18, 90).

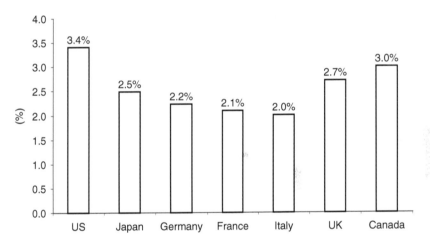

Figure 8.5 INTL comparisons: average growth in GDP 1983–2001
Source: Economic Report of the President, (2002: Table B-112).

only $8.00 in 2000. But this did not lead to a corresponding stagnation in consumption. Rather, debt dependence expanded (with all its individualizing and disciplining repercussions) and overall hours of work increased dramatically. While Europe experienced a 12 per cent decrease in hours of work per capita in the last quarter of the twentieth century, the US saw a 12 per cent increase (Maddison 2001: 352–5). This ability to extract more labour per capita (more family members working, more hours per worker, more intensity of

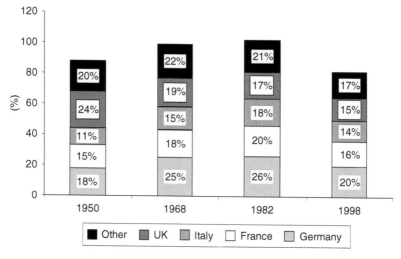

Figure 8.6   Post-war Europe (12): GDP as % of US
Source: Maddison (2001: 272–5).

work per hour) was one expression of American dominance and goes a long way in explaining the increase in the US–European GDP gap cited above (especially if we note that until recently, productivity as measured by GDP/ hour was actually growing faster in Europe).

The recent collapse of the 'new economy' has provided ample ammunition to those originally sceptical of its hype. But leaving aside the exaggerated claims originally made for the new technology, and acknowledging the excess capacity and shady deals that were part of this, two facts remain. First of all, it was in the US that the new technological innovations emerged rather than anywhere else, and there was everywhere a race to imitate and catch-up to the American innovations on this terrain. Even Hall and Soskice recognize this American comparative advantage in explaining why companies from the CMEs of Europe moved to the USA 'to secure access to institutional support for radical innovation...Nissan locates design facilities in California, Deutsche Bank acquires subsidiaries in Chicago...and German pharmaceutical firms open research labs in the United States' (Hall and Soskice 2001: 57). Second, the significance of the new digitized technology is not confined to its own sectors. Of greater importance is its potential dissemination to other sectors (traditional sectors such as auto as well as both old and new services) and, alongside this, the potential integration of these technologies with broader managerial strategies that combine centralization and decentralization within each sector (from design to sales, from accounting to outsourcing). To date, this potential has only been scratched.

There is a similar scepticism about the role of finance. But here again, whatever moral objections one can raise, the fact is that finance has been more than a speculative drain on the 'real' economy. It has provided needed overall liquidity at a time of 'competitive austerity' and, through the depth of American financial markets, was especially important in delivering the venture capital that accelerated the development of the new digitized technology (as well as being a source itself for the development and application of that technology). The deepening and spreading of financial markets has been crucial to managing the risk inherent in a globalized economy of flexible exchange rates – even as it itself was one cause of that risk. In its role in enforcing productive discipline, finance also reallocated capital across sectors, contributing to the process of correcting the previous decline in overall capital productivity.

The globalization of financial markets, combined with the broader structural power of the American economy, was part of the mechanism that brought global savings to the US. This created the space for the American state to bridge its role in stabilizing the international economy (via the imports of American consumers and businesses) while strengthening the American economy as the core material base for American neoimperialism (through the additional investments generated by the capital imports). Where trade deficits were signs of weakness and panic in the late 1960s and early 1970s, in the post-Volcker world – with its renewed confidence in the political power of the American state domestically as well as internationally – we witnessed two decades of repeated trade deficits with little or no international alarm until very recently. And even the sharp and possibly unsustainable growth in the trade deficit since the latter 1990s signals the relative success of the US economy as much as any decline. The deficit paradoxically reflects more rapid growth in the latter 1990s; the attraction of the US for investors in good times and bad; and the failure of Europe and Japan to restructure fast enough to lower the American deficit through their own growth.

The last two decades of the twentieth century, in short, highlighted American-led capitalism's stunning proficiency in reshaping labour markets, revolutionizing the forces of production and communication, integrating the world spatially, commodifying more aspects of daily life, and generally restructuring the world 'after its own image'. Where specific breakdowns occurred, they have thus far been impressively contained. That is, they have been localized, limited in their duration, and so far managed to the extent that, as Gowan (1999) has argued, such crises have so far become functional to demands for expanded reproduction of the global system. And all this has been achieved while lowering the expectations of its citizens and containing democratic opposition to a degree most of us would never have thought possible. Can we really deny the remarkable (if objectionable) dynamism capitalism revealed?

Sassoon has written that 'how to achieve the European version of the American society was the real political issue of the 1950s' (1997: 207). So was it of the 1990s, we would argue, at least in terms of emulation of the US economic policies, flexible labour markets and shareholder values. As before, remaking the world in the American image, while it did not mean homogeneity or anything like complete convergence, *did* mean accommodation and emulation; and American financial and management practices have been very widely adopted within European industrial and financial firms (Carpenter and Jefferys 2000; Lutz 2000). In this context, it may be noted once again that even Hall and Soskice were obliged to acknowledge that 'the internationalization of finance put pressure on the institutions of CMEs', citing one American financial and corporate practice after another in terms of their impact on German firms 'extending all the way down to production regimes' (Hall and Soskice 2001: 60–2). Their assertion that the pace of change also allows German firms to 'maintain many aspects of their long-standing strategies' (the only example offered being the retention of works councils) hardly qualifies the main point.

For all the talk of America's economic problems today, the immediate stagnation in the global economy has more to do with the inability of Japan and Germany to resolve their own sluggish development – a weakness that raises anew the question of exactly what we mean by 'weak' and 'strong' states. Their limited capability to match the American economy's ability to restructure has left Europe and Japan unable to carry the weight of added international stimulus, and consequently play a role in any constructive correction of the American trade deficit. Any real alternative to American capitalism on their part would mean a radical break with global capitalism and neo-imperialism – an alternative not currently on their radar screen, and inconceivable, in fact, without a fundamental change in class relations and state structures in those societies.

Political conclusions

Any alternative politics cannot rely on the current tarnishing of the 'American model' and the imminent decline of American hegemony (even though recessions and new instabilities will of course recur). The rejection of this model will have to be based on a collective condemnation of its relationship to human potentials, even when it is doing 'well' in its own terms. Political openings and contradictions will have to be found within capitalism's strengths and 'successes' and not only within its weaknesses and 'crises'. Such openings/contradictions will emerge, inside the USA and elsewhere, we believe, out of the impact of globalization on domestic class relations.

For example, capitalism's success in restructuring states to more closely serve the demands of global accumulation comes at the expense of the legitimation capacity of states. Where states could once promise linear material progress and democratic relevance to national political institutions, the promise of material well-being, ecological sustainability and democratic participation is increasingly hollow for large numbers of people in all countries. Similarly, the drive to constitutionalize property rights internationally (through international agreements like the North American Free Trade Agreement (NAFTA) and institutions like the World Trade Organization (WTO)) suffers from the social distance of international institutions and their lack of authority to legitimate such rights. This stage in the development of capitalist property rights consequently highlights and exposes – much like the original 'tragedy of the commons' – property rights as coming at the expense of popular rights. The current corporate scandals in the US, reflecting an arrogance that comes with success and a system that has not yet matched new circumstances to new forms of regulation, enhance at least the conjunctural possibilities for ideologically challenging the competence and authority of those who manage what are ultimately society's resources and wealth.

To take another example: as globalization internationalizes domestic capitalist classes – in the sense of shifting their orientation towards global accumulation – it affects the relative roles of domestic classes in national economic development. In the Third World, it undermines the base for domestic bourgeoisies to create the national economic coherence that is fundamental to capitalist development. While the strength of global neo-liberalism comes from its pressures to restructure existing capitalist institutions (political, legal, cultural as well as economic) in the CMEs of Europe and Japan into even more responsive vehicles for accumulation, it is rather ineffective when confronting the absence of such institutions in most of the world's states. Globalization consequently carries no general solution for third world development. The implications of this particular failure in the third world are, however, not self-evident. They will depend on the extent to which resistance within the third world brings this failure into the first world – either through its unmanageable impact on integrated financial markets, or via the costs to the American state and its junior partners of having to suppress the resistances (and perhaps even of being pushed to do something genuinely redistributive to cope with them).

Recent tensions between Europe and the US revolve around the role of the American state as acting on behalf of the particular interests of American capital as opposed to acting in the interests of global capital; and, in broader terms, acting as the embodiment of an all-too-often chauvinist definition of American national interests as opposed to the larger neo-imperial interest. While universal global rules therefore become essential, the American state needs and demands the flexibility *vis-à-vis* any rules to reproduce its hegemony and that of American capital. The line between measures necessary for that continued hegemony, as opposed to measures that are simply reflective of particular American interests is, as we see with Bush, often blurred and therefore a source of ongoing international strains even with the other leading capitalist states, which are junior partners in the American empire. This provides certain openings for oppositional forces (Gowan 2003). We should have no illusions, however, that the transformations in European class and state structure would have to be other than very fundamental indeed before these strains become ruptures. European bourgeoisies have even less interest and intention today of challenging American hegemony than they did in the 1970s. This is evident when the head of Bertelsman proudly and publicly proclaims that his investments in the USA should not be seen as foreign since he sees himself as 'an American with a German passport'; and it is no less evident when Daimler's takeover of Chrysler feeds back into German politics, in the form of a demand from its CEO that the German government restrain its criticism of the Administration's warmongering towards Iraq.

That said, it is by no means impossible that their very integration with the American imperium may lead to a domestic loss of legitimacy on the part of such bourgeoisies, and on the part of states insufficiently autonomous from them and the American state. And if and when this happens, the consequences are incalculable precisely because the imperium, even if it has military bases everywhere, cannot rule except with and through states. As Wood has put it:

> National states implement and enforce the global economy, and they remain the most effective means of intervening in it. This means that the state is also the point at which global capital is most vulnerable, both as a target of opposition in the dominant economies and as a lever of resistance elsewhere. It also means that now more than ever, much depends on the particular class forces embodied in the state, and that now more than ever, there is scope, as well as need, for class struggle. (Wood 2002: 29)

This is precisely why a comparative political economy that actually *does* take institutions seriously is so badly needed if we are to really understand the state and globalization today. Of course, whether we adopt a Weberian or Marxist analytic perspective will obviously have practical strategic implications, affecting how we think about state 'autonomy' as well as how we approach the issue of building the political capacities to resist or modify the main trajectories of globalization. But what is clear is that the integration of capital across borders means that the strategic political issue can no longer be merely expressed as responding nationally to external competition. Since national formations now include foreign capital *inside* each state, and since domestic capital is increasingly *outside*-oriented, it is vital that those oriented to progressive politics more rigorously clarify the nature of national political projects based on 'national' capital. At the same time, the fact that discrete economies and states are such an integrated part of a coherent whole means that significant change – and perhaps minor changes as well – requires developing the popular political confidence and capacities to transform the capitalist state into an alternative democratic state that is capable of a degree of de-linking from the neoimperial international economic order, and from the logic of competition as the arbiter of what is possible.

None of this would make any sense if all differences between states have been eradicated. Not only institutional sedimentation but also uneven class and economic development and contingent new institution-building will mean the continuation of difference. The point rather is that this variety remains part of the construction of the whole, and therefore incorporates the limits of that whole. The issue is not convergence *versus* divergence, but the scope for substantive variety within a global capitalist totality that is still antithetical to the full and universal development of human potentials.

Part III
The Approaches Evaluated

9
Varieties and Commonalities of Capitalism

Jonas Pontusson

This chapter critically examines the analytical foundations and some of the empirical claims of the Varieties-of-Capitalism (VoC) School of comparative political economy. Virtually, the entire field of comparative economy subscribes to the idea that capitalism takes on different institutional forms and, furthermore, that the institutional arrangements of real-existing capitalist political economies vary according to some kind of systematic logic, so that it is possible to speak of a limited number of more or less coherent types of capitalism. In recent years, however, the term 'Varieties of Capitalism' has been successfully claimed by advocates of a particular approach to comparative political economy, pioneered by Soskice in various writings and articulated most comprehensively by Hall and Soskice in their introduction to *Varieties of Capitalism* (2001). The questions raised by this chapter pertain not to the existence of varieties of capitalism per se, but rather to the adequacy of the VoC framework elaborated by Soskice and Hall for understanding the diversity and dynamics of contemporary capitalism.

Relative to other comparative political economy traditions, the VoC approach is strikingly single-minded. The approach is 'single-minded' in that it conceives the field of comparative political economy in terms of a single, overriding question: do firms and other political-economic actors have the capacity to coordinate amongst themselves, so as to be able to overcome collective action problems and engage in mutually beneficial cooperation?[1] The VoC literature posits, and to some extent demonstrates that coordinating capacities depend on institutional arrangements and that there exist institutional complementarities across different spheres of the political economy (labor relations, training and innovation systems, labor relations, corporate finance and governance, and so on). As a result, the answer to the core question is unambiguously 'yes' for one set of countries – the coordinated market economies (CMEs) – and unambiguously 'no' for another set of countries – the liberal market economies (LMEs). Whatever the specific outcomes to be explained might be, the explanations offered by VoC scholars invariably involve the claim that CMEs and LMEs operate according to fundamentally different logics.

Let me state at the outset that I consider the VoC approach to be an important advance on previous institutionalist approaches to comparative political economy. The central role that the Hall–Soskice framework assigns to the firm stands in sharp contrast to the analytical primacy traditionally assigned to political institutions by political scientists working in the field of comparative political economy (cf. Pontusson 1995a). In my view, the relational view of the firm at the core of the VoC literature provides a more solid political-economy foundation for institutional analysis. Relative to previous literature in the institutionalist tradition, the VoC framework also provides a more satisfactory micro-foundational account of how institutional arrangements alter the behavior of individuals, firms and collective actors, and how institutional equilibria are reproduced. At the same time, however, the VoC approach partakes in certain limitations or blind spots of the institutionalist tradition.

In the end, my critique of the VoC approach boils down to two complaints. First, the VoC approach focuses almost exclusively on the nature and sources of variation among advanced capitalist political economies, ignoring what these political economies have in common. Put differently, the VoC literature has a great deal to say about 'varieties', but surprisingly little to say about 'capitalism'. Second, the VoC approach theoretically privileges considerations pertaining to efficiency and coordination at the expense of considerations pertaining to conflicts of interest and the exercise of power. The latter complaint is directly related to the former to the extent that conflict between labor and capital constitutes a common feature of all capitalist political economies.[2]

The case studies that make up the empirical bulk of the VoC literature commonly recognize conflicts of interest among collective actors and discuss the relative power of these actors, be they 'labor' and 'capital' or fractions of these broad aggregates. To clarify, my complaint is that empirical observations along these lines have a taken-for-granted quality and largely go under-theorized, while the core theoretical claims of the VoC approach seem oblivious to or, indeed, downplay the significance of the distribution of power among socio-economic groups. More or less explicitly, VoC scholars postulate that the capacity of actors, with common interests to coordinate, is a crucial precondition for cooperation and compromise among actors with different interests. This postulate strikes me as eminently sensible. And yet the distribution of power among political-economic actors remains, in my view, an important variable that cannot be reduced to a function of the coordinating capacities of the actors involved. Moreover, coordination should be seen, I think, as a necessary but not sufficient condition for cooperation and compromise. We must also attend to the substantive interests of the actors involved and the extent to which economic conditions allow for the reconciliation of conflicting interests.

I do not mean to argue that the VoC literature is wrong and should be rejected. My point is rather that the VoC approach, as currently constituted, does not represent an adequate framework for the comparative study of capitalist political economies. I hasten to clarify that this claim very much depends on a certain idea of what are the core questions in comparative political economy. In my view, the Hall–Soskice framework provides a solid foundation for exploring the institutional sources of comparative advantage, but leaves a great deal to be desired if we want to explain distributive labor-market outcomes or understand the politics of welfare-state restructuring in the current era. A more comprehensive and inclusive framework might be built by treating efficiency/coordination and distribution/power as interrelated but separate, equally important analytical dimensions. Put differently, I want to argue for a synthetic perspective that integrates the insights of the VoC approach with insights from more 'power-oriented' approaches to comparative political economy.

I am inclined to think of the 'power dimension' of political economy in terms of class conflict and class compromise, but I do not wish to insist on this particular understanding of what the power dimension is about. Certainly, 'labor' and 'capital' are not unitary actors whose interests can be derived from some abstract understanding of capitalism. Each of these categories can and should be disaggregated. Also, as Swenson (2002) and others remind us, 'cross-class alliances', based on common interests between particular categories of workers and employers, are a ubiquitous feature of modern capitalism. To my mind, the salience of class interests, relative to sectoral or occupational interests, as the basis for distributive conflict and for policy or institutional preferences is an empirical question.

Conflicts of interest enable us to understand why institutional equilibria might come undone, and the power balance among political-economic actors provides the most obvious point of departure for an explanation of why institutions or policies change in a particular direction. Thus, I want to argue that attending to conflicts of interest and the distribution of power enables us to tackle the problem of explaining changes in contemporary capitalist political economies. Though VoC scholars have become increasingly attentive to issues of change, this remains, I think, a fundamental weakness of the VoC approach. I hasten to add that interests and power are also relevant to the 'comparative statics' of the VoC literature. This brings me to another theme to be developed below: the distinction between LMEs and CMEs fails to capture many important differences among advanced capitalist political economies. I shall argue that the distribution of power among class actors and the way class conflict has been institutionalized provides the basis for a second, orthogonal dimension along which the OECD countries can and should be distinguished.

One additional theme in the following discussion should be noted at the outset. Like other institutionalists, VoC scholars typically pose the question of change in terms of institutional convergence between individual countries or clusters of countries. For VoC scholars, the crucial issue about 'globalization' becomes whether or not the CMEs are becoming more like the LMEs as a result of increased trade, intensified international competition and capital mobility. This formulation misses the question of whether or not globalization has had effects, in terms of government policies or economic outcomes, that can be observed in LMEs as well as CMEs, but do not entail institutional convergence between LMEs and CMEs. As political economists, we ought to be interested in explaining common trends as well as cross-national differences (cf. Pontusson 1995b).

The following discussion is divided into two parts. The first part elaborates on the general critique of the VoC approach sketched above. The second part, in turn, engages a series of specific claims about labor-market dynamics and welfare states advanced by Estevez-Abe *et al.* in their contribution to *Varieties of Capitalism* (2001). Billed as 'a reinterpretation of the welfare state', the piece by Estevez-Abe *et al.* represents an important extension of the VoC approach, bringing it into direct contention with the emphasis placed on conflicts of interest, working-class mobilization, and government partisanship by much of the comparative welfare-state literature. In the second part of the chapter, I try to show concretely that there are important trends that are common to the advanced capitalist countries, and that the VoC approach fails to account for these trends. The problem is more serious, goes deeper, than this formulation suggests: not only does the VoC approach fail to account for these common trends, it directs our attention away from them.

Critique of the varieties-of-capitalism approach

Mapping varieties of capitalism

To reiterate, the VoC approach pivots on the distinction between CMEs and LMEs. Indeed, it is hard to identify any theory in the VoC literature that might be evaluated separately from evaluating the adequacy of the CME/LME distinction as the basis for deriving varieties (types) of capitalism from the diversity that we observe as we survey the OECD countries. Two preliminary remarks are in order before I try to articulate my reservations about this dimension of the VoC enterprise. First, it should be noted that the CME and LME labels are not entirely accurate. As Hall and Soskice (2001: 8–9) state clearly, markets serve to coordinate economic activities. What distinguishes the 'CMEs' is not coordination per se, but rather the prevalence of 'non-market modes of coordination' or, alternatively, in the words of Gingerich and Hall (2002), 'strategic coordination'. It should also be noted that VoC scholars recognize that a number countries do not fit either ideal type.[3] It is commonplace in the VoC literature (e.g. Hall 2001) to classify France, Italy, and other Southern European countries as 'mixed' or 'hybrid' cases.

The failure to generate a clearer conceptualization of political economies that do not fit the CME and LME ideal-types, that is, to specify additional varieties of capitalism, represents an important limitation of the VoC approach. To my mind, however, the more serious problem with the VoC typology has to do with variation among countries that get coded as either CMEs or LMEs. Most obviously, does it really make sense to treat Japan as a variant of the same political-economy type as Germany and Sweden? At issue here is the analytical importance of 'institutionalized class compromise' for our understanding of varieties of capitalism. On an economy-wide basis, Japanese unions are weak by comparison to their Northern European counterparts. Also, the Japanese labor movement has not been an influential political actor – at least, political parties purporting to represent the interests of organized labor and/or the 'class interests' of workers have traditionally been, and remain effectively, marginalized. From the perspective of 'labor-centered corporatism', it is not surprising that the Japan ranks at the very bottom of the OECD league on public provision of social welfare (as a percent of GDP).

The VoC response to these objections would seem to run roughly as follows. First, Japanese unions are really quite strong at the firm level. Second, lifetime employment and corporate welfare systems represent the functional equivalent of European-style employment regulation and public provision of social welfare. Third, as far as wage formation is concerned, the important issue is the ability of employers to coordinate their behavior and Japanese employers are just as able to do so as German or Swedish employers. And fourth, as far as corporate governance and inter-firm relations are concerned, the Japanese and European CMEs operate according to the same logic.

I do not mean to suggest that Japan should be categorized as an 'LME'. My point is that it does not follow from Japan's 'non-LMEness' that Japan belongs in the same category as Germany and Sweden.[4] Lifetime employment and other corporate practices provide certain categories of Japanese workers with considerably more 'social protection' than American workers enjoy, but the distributive implications and political dynamics of these arrangements are very different from those of the European CMEs (cf. Streeck 1996). Similarly, the question of whether or not industrial unions play a central role in coordinating the process of wage formation may not matter for overall wage growth (wage restraint), but it is likely to matter greatly to the distribution of wage increases (Rueda and Pontusson 2000). For certain purposes, the CME–LME distinction may be a perfectly adequate typological device, but something important seems to be lost if we settle for a typology of advanced capitalist political economies that is based on this distinction alone.[5]

The degree to which post-war political economies were organized around the incorporation of the labor at the national level or, in other words, around some form of 'class compromise', also serves to distinguish among the LMEs.[6] At least to some degree, the 'UK problem' represents the LME equivalent to the 'Japan problem'. Though the prominence of financial markets and the absence of strong business associations indicate that the post-war British political economy belongs with the US in the liberal camp, this coding ignores the size and universalistic cast of the Beveridgean welfare state as well as the formidable powers of trade-unions, and the centrality of incomes policy and other corporatist practices prior to the Thatcher era. To be sure, British 'collectivism' was deeply flawed, but it did play an important role in regulating the economy, especially labor markets, and should be seen, I believe, as a manifestation of the power of the British labor movement.

These considerations suggest that a more broadly applicable typology of advanced capitalist political economies might be constructed by treating 'business coordination' and 'class compromise' as independent, orthogonal dimensions of cross-national variation. The crude version of such a typology is the 2×2 table shown in Figure 9.1. Based on the British experience, one might perhaps argue that the lower-left box in this table represents an inherently unstable combination or, in other words, that sustained class compromise presupposes business capacities to coordinate, more broadly, the institutional infrastructure characteristic of CMEs. In some of Soskice's (1999) formulations, entrenched unions and public welfare provisions do indeed appear as dysfunctional elements that weakened the competitiveness of Britain's LME and had to be shed in the face of accelerating globalization (cf. also Fioretos 2001). One may well object to the functionalist overtones of this interpretation of Thatcherism. Moreover, one might well invoke episodes in the history of European CMEs to suggest that causality sometimes

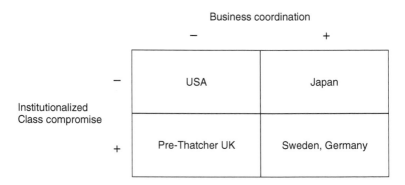

Figure 9.1   Alternative typology

runs in the opposite direction, for example, that labor militancy stimulates employers to develop coordinating capacities. In any case, the proposition that class compromise presupposes business coordination is an empirical claim, not something to be resolved at the level of classification. Also, it should be noted that there is no obvious reason to think that the upper-right hand box in Figure 9.1 represents a combination that is inherently unstable.

The two-dimensional typology illustrated in Figure 9.1 obviously allows us to capture more of the diversity of advanced capitalist political economies than the coordination-based typology of the VoC approach. This typology also brings the question of institutional change into focus. At least over the last two decades, we observe more movement on the class-compromise dimension than on the coordination dimension.[7]

Economic growth and production profiles

One of the most compelling things about the VoC approach is the thesis that there are multiple paths to economic success. In Hall and Soskice's (2001: 21) words, 'both liberal and coordinated market economies seem capable of providing satisfactory levels of long-run economic performance'. Very sensibly, Hall and Soskice thus shift the terms of the debate between proponents of laissez-faire and social partnership away from economic growth rates, pointing to the need to deploy other 'performance indicators' in assessing the relative merits of the two types of capitalism. On closer inspection, the VoC literature actually encompasses two distinct versions of the multiple-paths-to-success thesis. One version focuses on institutional coherence while the other focuses on comparative institutional advantage. In this section, I want to elaborate briefly on each of these arguments and point out how they raise questions that take us beyond the analytical framework of the VoC approach. (Note that I am not claiming that the two arguments are inconsistent with each other.)

Gingerich and Hall (2002) develop and test the argument about institutional coherence most systematically. Gingerich and Hall proceed from a theoretical model in which firm-specific investments by management and labor enhance micro-economic efficiency and, by extension, improve aggregate economic performance. The returns that such investments bring to each actor depend on the other actor making analogous investments and the equilibrium levels of firm-specific investments chosen by management and labor in turn depend on two variables: (a) the intensity of financial market pressures on firms for maintaining continuously high profitability; and (b) the ability of management and labor to engage in strategic coordination with each other over wages. Gingerich and Hall's model hinges on the interaction of these two variables. Strategic coordination in labor relations does not benefit growth in the presence of financial pressure for continuous profitability, nor does the insulation of corporate management from financial markets benefit growth in the presence of fragmented and adversarial labor relations, but strategic coordination in corporate governance and labor relations jointly produce higher rates of economic growth.

Empirically, Gingerich and Hall measure 'strategic coordination' in corporate governance and labor relations as continuous variables. In a series of pooled cross-section time-series regressions, the interaction term for these two variables consistently turns out to have a significant positive effect on the growth rate of GDP per capita. In addition, Gingerich and Hall create a composite overall coordination index, and demonstrate that this index has a U-shaped association with economic growth. In general, countries with low and high values on the composite coordination index have tended to grow more rapidly than countries with medium values.

Gingerich and Hall's analysis provides strong support for the idea of institutional complementarities across spheres of the political economy and the concomitant proposition that more coherent political economies have an efficiency advantage over less coherent political economies.[8] The analysis also raises an important puzzle: what accounts for the persistence of 'incoherent' political economies in the face of institutional complementarities?[9] While Gingerich and Hall pose this question in their concluding discussion, they do not provide us much, if any, guidance as to how we might go about answering it. Efficiency considerations alone clearly do not provide a satisfactory explanation of institutional choice (or evolution). Arguably, the key to explaining the persistence of incoherence is to identify powerful actors with an interest in maintaining certain institutional arrangements, regardless of whether or not they serve to maximize aggregate economic performance. In this sense, Gingerich and Hall's empirical analysis can be read as an invitation to go beyond the analytical framework of the VoC literature.

The other version of the multiple-paths-to-success thesis is the argument about comparative institutional advantages developed by Soskice (1999) and replicated by a number of contributors to *Varieties of Capitalism* (notably Fioretos 2001; Vitols 2001). In essence, the argument holds that the institutional infrastructure of CMEs provides firms with a comparative advantage in diversified quality production (DQP), while the institutional infrastructure of LMEs favors radical innovation and enables innovative firms/sectors to grow more quickly. (Note that this is an argument about the sectoral composition of national economies as well as an argument about firm strategies within any particular sector.)

To recapitulate very briefly, CME institutions provide both workers and firms with the incentives to invest in the firm- or industry-specific skills required for the successful pursuit of DQP strategies, which involve incremental process innovation, continuous quality improvement, and some degree of customization of mass-market products. According to the standard VoC formulation, cooperative labor relations and supplier relations as well as patient owners and insulation from financial markets also facilitate DQP strategies.[10] On the other hand, Soskice (1999: 117–118) argues that the corporate governance arrangements characteristic of LMEs facilitate radical innovation by providing for strong and effective control by top management. In addition, vibrant markets in corporate government enable firms to buy and sell subsidiaries readily, while deregulated labor markets enable firms to hire and give the necessary incentives to employees with skills in new areas. For reasons that are not articulated quite as clearly, LMEs are also said to have a comparative advantage in internationally competitive service industries (Soskice 1999: 113–114).

For Soskice and other VoC scholars, the bottom line is that these alternative corporate strategies are, at least in principle, equally viable. What distinguishes CMEs and LMEs from each other is not whether they can compete, but rather how they compete in world markets. From this perspective, there is no 'best-practice model', and intensified international competition does not in any way undermine the viability of the CMEs. Quite the contrary, Soskice argues that globalization encourages firms and national economies to specialize in areas where they enjoy comparative advantage, and thus serves to sharpen the contrast between CMEs and LMEs. Not only does specialization give national firms a stronger stake in the maintenance of existing institutional arrangements, but multinational corporations also seek out the comparative advantages offered by different national systems and portfolio investors operating on a global scale manage risk by investing in different types of firms and national economies. Thus, Soskice rejects the notion that 'global capital' has an interest in imposing LME arrangements on the CMEs.

The logic of this argument about comparative institutional advantage is compelling, but the way in which the argument is marshalled by Soskice and other VoC scholars ignores the question of differential growth rates across markets in which LMEs and CMEs enjoy comparative advantages. This question may not be relevant from the point of view of individual firms, but it is surely relevant from the point of view of national economies (and hence governments). As Streeck (1997: 42) points out in discussing recent challenges to the German model, 'worldwide product markets for quality-competitive goods must be large enough to sustain full employment in an economy that has barred itself from serving price-competitive markets'. Clearly, this represents a potential problem for the CMEs as a group. To return to my discussion of Gingerich and Hall's analysis, we should not expect a slowdown of economic growth relative to LMEs to translate directly into institutional change in CMEs, but we might very well expect slow growth to be associated with intensified distributive conflict. In any case, to evaluate the plausibility of Soskice's argument about comparative institutional advantage as a source of institutional stability, we clearly need a better understanding of the dynamics of the world economy than the VoC literature provides.

Institutional dynamics

It is commonplace to fault the VoC literature for failing to explain how the institutional equilibria that it delineates arose in the first place and for its lack of attention to the question of institutional change. The response of VoC scholars to this line of criticism is ambivalent. Proponents of the VoC approach take the position that explaining how currently existing political economies work does not require an explanation of how they came to be configured in the way that they are configured. In other words, these are considered to be separate explanatory projects. As we have seen, proponents of the VoC approach also argue quite vehemently against the idea of convergence between CMEs and LMEs as a result of globalization or, for that matter, as a result of any other trends.[11]

The argument against convergence could be read as a denial that explaining institutional change is an important challenge for comparative political economy. At the same time, however, VoC scholars clearly do aspire to go beyond 'comparative statics'. In Hall and Soskice's (2001: 62) words, the VoC approach offers a 'dynamic conception of national political economies in the sense that it anticipates change in them and contains specific propositions about the processes through which it will occur'. The notion of path dependence provides the most obvious way to reconcile Hall and Soskice's emphasis on dynamics with the argument against convergence. By this interpretation, Hall and Soskice (and other VoC scholars) seem to be saying that both CMEs and LMEs are indeed changing in important ways, but they change according to their distinctive logics.

Exactly how does the VoC approach provide a 'dynamic conception of national political economies'? Hall and Soskice's (2001: 62-4) general discussion begins with the observation that change occurs in response to 'external shocks emanating from a world economy in which technologies, products, and tastes change continuously'. Hall and Soskice then proceed to make three arguments about the dynamics of institutional change that have a more distinctive 'VoC flavor' (cf. also Soskice 1999: 125-32). First, they argue that adjustment to external shocks will be 'oriented to the institutional recreation of comparative advantage' at the national level as well as the firm level. In CMEs, producer groups and voters, with substantial interests in strategic coordination, will pressure governments to maintain (or restore) existing institutions. Second, Hall and Soskice point out that the importance of 'common knowledge' to successful strategic interaction entails an asymmetry between LMEs and CMEs: while the creation of CME conditions is a long and slow process, there are no 'common knowledge' constraints on CMEs deregulating to become more like LMEs. Third, they stress the ambiguous role of institutional complementarities, which discourage radical change, but also raise the prospects that 'institutional reform in one sphere could snowball into changes in other spheres as well'.

The arguments about asymmetry and snowballing open up the possibility of convergence on Anglo-American capitalism (cf. Goodin 2003), but, again, virtually all contributors to the VoC literature deny the existence of any tendency towards such convergence between CMEs and LMEs. In the end, the argument about production regimes and the interests of CME employers (as well as labor) in the maintenance of existing institutions seems to trump the arguments about asymmetry and snowballing, and it is not clear that the latter arguments have an important role to play in the VoC approach to institutional dynamics.

Hall and Soskice's observation that efforts by firms and governments to maintain or restore competitive advantages 'may entail changes to existing institutions or practices in the economy' (2001: 63) also deserves to be noted. In this passage, Hall and Soskice seem to recognize that we might miss important changes in institutional practices and outcomes by focusing on the question of convergence between CMEs and LMEs or, more precisely, on the question of whether or not CMEs remain a viable alternative to Anglo-American capitalism. However, the brevity and vagueness of Hall and Soskice's treatment of this issue is striking. To advance our understanding of institutional dynamics, comparative political economists clearly need to articulate more precise expectations about the kinds of changes that are necessary to maintain different kinds of competitive advantages under new economic conditions. So far, much of what the VoC approach has to say on this topic seems to boil down to the rather uncontroversial claim that reforming CMEs involve negotiations among powerful collective actors and tends to be an incremental process.[12]

As Hall and Soskice's discussion makes very clear, the sources of change are essentially external to the analytical framework of the VoC literature. Intensified competition, globalization, and new technologies are commonly invoked to explain change, but these forces are never the subject of sustained analysis, and VoC scholars devote surprisingly little attention to specifying the mechanisms whereby they generate change, or at least contestation, around existing institutions and practices. A satisfactory political-economy approach to politics of change – policy change as well as institutional change – must surely involve an account of how these 'external' forces alter the options and/or interests of economic actors.[13]

Most obviously, it seems quite plausible to attribute a number of recent institutional reforms and policy changes to the fact that 'globalization' increases the exit options of firms as well as investors and thus alters the balance of power between labor and capital. Increased exit options for capital do not necessarily translate into union membership losses or any major change in the institutional framework of industrial relations and collective bargaining (let alone convergence between CMEs and LMEs).[14] The point is rather that capital mobility alters the parameters of bargaining, in the political arena as well as the industrial arena, in favor of capital. So far as I can tell, none of the empirical contributions to the volume edited by Hall and Soskice seriously engage this line of argument.[15]

Labor markets and welfare states

Social protection

In this section and the next, I will challenge some of the empirical claims about trends in labor-market regulation and labor-market outcomes made by Estevez-Abe *et al.* (2001). Following Soskice (1999), Estevez-Abe *et al.* (2001) proceed from the observation that CME firms rely more heavily on firm-specific and industry-specific skills than LME firms. In CMEs, vocational training systems subsidize the acquisition of firm-specific and industry-specific skills, but the acquisition such skills still involves significant investments by individual workers (cf. also Soskice 1994). Investment in firm and industry-specific skills entails greater risks than investment in general skills. In the case of firm-specific skills, workers must feel reasonably sure that they will work for the same employer over an extended period of time in these kinds of skills. In the case of industry-specific skills, they need assurance of good long-term employment prospects within the same industry and temporary income support during possible unemployment spells.

For Estevez-Abe *et al.* (2001), then, employment protection (restrictions on the ability of employers to fire workers) and unemployment compensation (income support for the unemployed) should first and foremost be seen as a form of risk insurance, creating incentives for workers to invest in firm and industry-specific skills. The implication of this interpretation is that employers who rely on such skills have a strong interest in the creation and maintenance of social protection. Echoing Swenson's (2002) emphasis on cross-class coalitions in the making of post-war welfare states, Estevez-Abe *et al.* (2001) thus explain the apparent resilience of the welfare state in the European CMEs in terms of the existence of a 'strong alliance between skilled workers and their employers in favor of social protection' (2001: 147). In support of this argument, they observe that

> from the 1970s to the 1980s and 1990s, unemployment benefits remained stable or rose in most continental European countries, but they were cut in Ireland and all the Anglo-Saxon countries with the exception of Australia. Moreover, whereas labor markets have become even more deregulated in the latter countries, employment protection has remained high in the former. (2001: 176)

Are social protection arrangements really as well ensconced in the European CMEs as Estevez-Abe *et al.* (2001) claim? There can be little doubt that employment protection and unemployment compensation became more contentious issues in the European CMEs over the last two decades. At least some employer groups seem to have played a leading role in calling into question such 'labor market rigidities' (e.g. Kinderman 2003), but maybe these employers engaged in rhetorical excess for strategic reasons? Let us stick to 'hard evidence'. The most commonly used OECD index of employment protection legislation (EPL) refers to the strictness of protection against dismissals for regular employees. The OECD (1999: 57) reports score on this index for the late 1980s and the late 1990s. As Estevez-Abe *et al.* (2001: 164) point out, the country scores for these two periods are almost perfectly correlated ($r=0.99$). Estevez-Abe *et al.* (2001) are surely correct to say that employment protection has remained high in the European CMEs, but it should also be noted that the OECD employment protection index does not capture any deregulation of labor markets in the LMEs. As measured by the OECD, the strictness of protection of regular employment changed in only two of the standard eighteen countries over the 1990s (increasing slightly in Germany, declining substantially in Finland).

In passing, Estevez-Abe *et al.* (2001) observe that some European CMEs 'have seen a notable relaxation in the protection of temporary employment' (2001: 176). According to the OECD's measures, the strictness of government regulation of temporary employment was significantly reduced in six of the nine European CMEs from the late 1980s to the late 1990s. As Figure 9.2 illustrates, plotting change over time against the strictness of regulation in the late 1980s produces a picture that suggests some convergence among the advanced capitalist countries in this regard.[16]

Judging by OECD indices, the European CMEs have accommodated pressures for employment flexibility by relaxing restrictions on temporary employment while maintaining restrictions on dismissals of regular employees. The analytical framework developed by Estevez-Abe *et al.* (2001) provides a compelling explanation of the latter part of this observation, but it does not provide any clues as to how we should think about the former part. By the logic of Estevez-Abe *et al.* (2001), it is difficult to imagine that an expansion of the market for temporary employment does not have long-term implications for skill formation in CMEs. Arguably, the relaxation of restrictions on temporary employment represents a wedge, which will gradually alter the conditions of regular employment. Alternatively, the expansion of temporary employment can be interpreted as an increase of labor-market dualism.[17] Either way, it would appear to represent an important alteration in the way that CME labor markets operate.

Turning to unemployment compensation, Table 9.1 summarizes recent changes in net income replacement provided by public unemployment insurance schemes, drawn from a recent paper by Allan and Scrugge (2002).[18] Contrary to what Estevez-Abe *et al.* (2001) assert, we observe some reduction of unemployment compensation in every one of the European

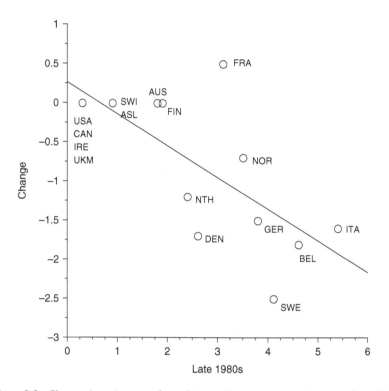

Figure 9.2   Change in strictness of regulation of temporary employment from late 1980s to late 1990s versus strictness of regulation in late 1980s
Note: R-square = 0.56 (0.72 without France).
Source: OECD (1999: 63).

CMEs since the early 1980s. Measuring change from the peak year to 1999, Allen and Scrugge's data indicate that LMEs have cut unemployment compensation far more extensively than European CMEs, but this discrepancy is entirely due to early and unusually large cuts in the Irish and British cases. Leaving the Irish case aside, European CMEs averaged cuts that were larger than those of the LMEs over the period 1985–1999. As Figure 9.3 illustrates, moreover, Allan and Scruggs' data point to some convergence among the OECD countries: irrespective of political economy type, countries with more generous unemployment compensation provisions have tended to cut back more than countries with less generous provisions. I do not wish to oversell this evidence for convergence. Again, the important point is that cutbacks in unemployment compensation represent a common trend across the OECD countries. In seeking to explain this trend, we must go outside the VoC framework.

Table 9.1 Net income replacement rates of unemployment insurance

	1999	Change since 1985	Change since peak
European CMEs			
Austria	64	−1	−2 (87)
Belgium	62	−11	−12 (83)
Denmark	79	−16	−21 (83)
Finland	65	−6	−6 (85)
Germany	66	0	−3 (83)
The Netherlands	76	−12	−14 (78)
Norway	70	−1	−1 (85)
Sweden	73	−10	−14 (88)
Switzerland	77	−1	−2 (95)
LMEs			
Australia	46	+3	−6 (89)
Canada	66	−3	−3 (85)
Ireland	43	−22	−29 (79)
New Zealand	43	−9	−14 (86)
UK	32	−3	−31 (75)
USA	58	−9	−10 (84)
France	71	−2	−5 (87)
Italy	47	+38	0 (99)
Japan	56	+1	0 (99)

Note: Average net income replacement for (a) a fully insured single worker earning the average production worker (APW) wage; and (b) a fully insured couple with a single APW wage and two children.
Source: Allan and Scrugge (2002).

Labor market inequality

Estevez-Abe *et al.* (2001) also link wage-distributive outcomes to skill formation. Establishing that there is a close cross-national association between the incidence of vocational training and levels of wage inequality, they argue that 'because specific skills systems generate high demand for workers with good vocational training, young people who are not academically inclined have career opportunities that are largely missing in general skills systems' (2001: 177). The causal logic implied by this statement is not entirely clear. Why (or how) do vocational careers for those who are not academically gifted or motivated translate into a more compressed distribution of earnings? On the assumption that vocational training increases the productivity of low-paid workers, it seems equally, if not more plausible, to suppose that causality runs in the opposite direction: that is, that wage compression increases employer support for vocational training.

More persuasively, Estevez-Abe *et al.* (2001) argue that coordinated wage-bargaining provides for stability in the distribution of earnings across

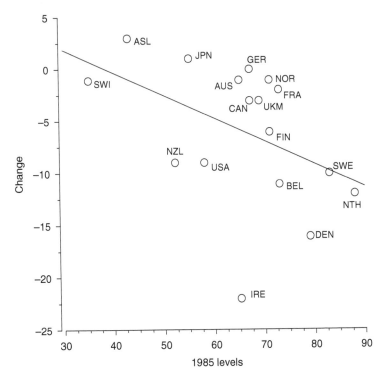

Figure 9.3   Change in unemployment compensation 1985–1999 versus levels of unemployment compensation in 1985
Note: *R-square* = 0.20 (0.33 without Ireland).
Source: Table 9.1.

occupations, protecting the relative wages of workers who invest in specific skills and, again, creating a skills-based incentive for CME employers to support the maintenance of existing wage-bargaining institutions. Though they do not present any empirical evidence on this score, Estevez-Abe *et al.* (2001) expect 'stable distributions of earnings across occupations' in CMEs (2001: 154).

Based on the OECD's dataset on relative earnings among full-time employees, Table 9.2 shows annualized percentage changes in 90–10 wage ratios from the earliest post-1979 observation to the most recent observation available. Looking at the data for both men and women (first column), we observe very significant increases of wage inequality in all the LMEs (particularly large in New Zealand and the US). Among the European CMEs, the Netherlands and Sweden stand out as the two countries in which wage inequality increased substantially. In five out of eight European CMEs, both-gender wage inequality actually declined. The same basic pattern of

Table 9.2 Average annual percentage change in 90–10 wage ratios for full-time employees

	Men and women	Men only
European CMEs		
Belgium 1986–1994	–0.86	
Denmark 1980–1990	0.14	
Finland 1980–1998	–0.11	0.22
Germany 1984–1995	–0.43	0.21
The Netherlands 1980–1997	0.64	1.51*
Norway 1980–1991	–0.40	
Sweden 1980–1997	0.50	0.63
Switzerland 1991–1998	–0.48	–0.10
LMEs		
Australia 1980–1999	0.31	0.84
Canada 1981–1994	0.28	0.62
New Zealand 1984–1997	1.27	2.05
UK 1980–2000	0.66	1.23
USA 1980–1999	0.93	1.47
Italy 1986–1996	0.74	1.55
Japan 1980–1998	–0.04	0.31

Note: *1985–1997.
Source: OECD Directorate for Education, Employment, Labour and Social Affairs.

cross-national variation appears in the data on relative earnings for men only (second column), but in every single country wage inequality among men increased more or declined less than wage inequality among men and women combined. In most countries, continued compression of between-gender differentials offset growing within-gender inequality over this period. Disregarding between-gender differentials, there is clearly a common trend for wage inequality to rise in the advanced capitalist countries.[19] Consistent with the argumentation of Estevez-Abe *et al.* (2001), this trend has been most pronounced in LMEs.

I hasten to point out that the OECD dataset on relative wages fails to take account of the distributive effects of part-time employment as well as unemployment and labor-force exit. In all the OECD countries, part-time employees earn considerably less than full-time employees on an hourly basis, and in most countries, the incidence of part-time employment increased significantly from the early 1980s to the late 1990s.[20] The figures in Table 9.2 thus tend to understate the growth of wage inequality. The failure to take account of the distributive impact of employment losses renders comparative assessments of CME and LME performance, based on the figures in Table 9.2, particularly precarious. To the extent that employers hang on to skilled, well-paid employees while shedding unskilled, low-paid workers during an economic downturn, an increase of unemployment automatically reduces inequality among employed workers. To some extent, then, slower growth of wage inequality in CMEs relative to LMEs might be a reflection of the fact that unemployment rose more rapidly in CMEs than LMEs over the period in question.

To capture the employment dimension of labor market inequality, Kenworthy and Pontusson (2004) use data from the Luxembourg Income Study (LIS) to calculate Gini coefficients for gross earnings of households headed by working-age individuals (25–69 years of age). Showing annualized percentage changes in Gini coefficients from the early 1980s to most recent observations available (the late 1990s for most countries), Table 9.3 conveys a picture that is strikingly different from that conveyed by Table 9.2. To begin with, inegalitarian labor market trends are more pronounced in the LIS data.[21] More importantly, we no longer observe a clear contrast between CMEs and LMEs in these data. The UK stands out as the country that has experienced the greatest increase of gross earnings inequality among working-age households, but following the UK we find Finland, Sweden, Denmark and Germany with inequality growth above one percent per year.

As illustrated by Figure 9.4, plotting annual change in gross earnings inequality against initial levels again suggests some degree of convergence among the OECD countries. In the more inegalitarian LMEs, low-income households appear to have compensated themselves for rising returns to education and skills by increasing their employment relative to high-income households (in terms of hours worked as well as the number of working household members). In the more egalitarian European CMEs, by contrast,

Table 9.3 Average annual percentage change in Gini coefficients for gross earnings of working-age households

European CMEs	
Denmark 1987–1997	1.20
Finland 1987–2000	1.36
Germany 1981–2000	1.03
The Netherlnds 1983–1994	−0.46
Norway 1979–2000	0.54
Sweden 1981–2000	1.24
Switzerland 1982–1992	0.37
LMEs	
Australia 1981–1994	0.04
Canada 1981–1998	0.99
UK 1979–1999	1.60
USA 1979–2000	0.95

Source: Kenworthy and Pontusson (2004).

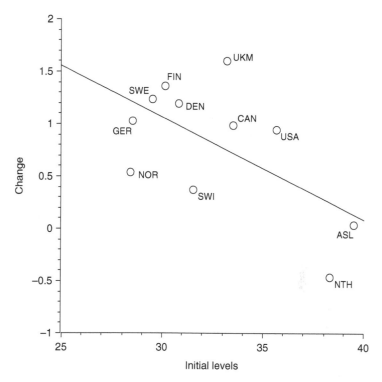

Figure 9.4 Average annual change in Gini coefficients for gross household earnings versus initial Gini coefficients

Note: R-square = 0.362.

low-income households appear to have lost employment relative to high-income households, presumably because of weak relative demand for the kind of labor that low-income households can offer.[22]

Taking access to employment into account, labor markets in all the advanced capitalist countries have become more inegalitarian since the early 1980s, but the dynamics of labor market inequality are distinctly different in LMEs and CMEs, much as the VoC literature would lead us to expect. The specific line of argument advanced by Estevez-Abe *et al.* (2001), emphasizing the interests of CME employers in stable wage relativities, to shore up the supply of firm- and industry-specific skills, does indeed constitute a plausible explanation of the fact that the growth of wage inequality has been more muted in CMEs than LMEs. However, the Estevez-Abe *et al.* analysis sheds little or no light on the underlying forces generating more inequality. Technological change, capital mobility, trade with low-wage countries, immigration and public-sector retrenchment surely figure among these underlying forces. Most importantly for my present purposes, Figure 9.5 indicates that changes in wage inequality are rather closely associated with changes in union density on a cross-national basis.

Pooling time series and cross-sectional data, Rueda and Pontusson's (2000) analysis of wage inequality among full-time employees shows that the egalitarian effects of union density hold up when we control a range of other relevant variables. Estimating the effects of union density separately for LMEs and European CMEs, Rueda and Pontusson find that these effects are essentially the same in both political-economy types. To explain distributive labor-market outcomes, we must attend to market forces and power relations as well as the institutional arrangements and production strategies captured by the distinction between CMEs and LMEs.

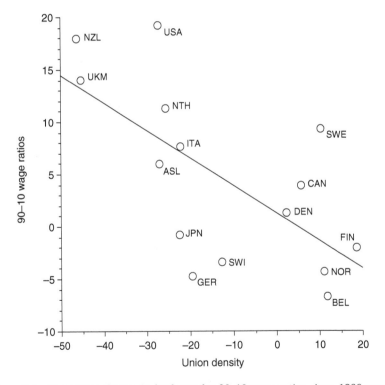

Figure 9.5   Percentage change in both-gender 90–10 wage ratios since 1980 versus percentage change in net union density 1980–1995
Note: R-square = 0.43 (0.55 without Sweden).
Sources: Table 9.1; OECD (1997: 71); Waddington and Hoffmann (2000: 54).

Class conflict and government partisanship

While Hall and Soskice (2001: 51) observe that 'governments introduce social legislation for many reasons, some of them conditioned by partisan competition and the demands of labor', the VoC approach to the comparative study of the welfare state and the politics of welfare state retrenchment strongly emphasizes common interests embedded in production regimes that vary across countries. This analytical orientation stands in sharp contrast to the power-resources approach, which emphasizes the causal significance of cross-national variation in the distribution of political power among political-economic actors with divergent distributive interests (e.g. Huber and Stephens 2001; Korpi and Palme 2003).

In an important twist, Hall and Soskice's (2001: 57–8) discussion of the political dynamics suggests that the power-resources perspective is more relevant to LMEs than CMEs, at least in the current era:

> In the face of more intense international competition, business interests in LMEs are likely to pressure governments for deregulation, since firms that coordinate their endeavors primarily through the market can improve their competencies by sharpening its edges. The government is likely to be sympathetic because the comparative advantage of the economy as a whole rests on the effectiveness of market mechanisms. Organized labor will put up some resistance, resulting in *mild forms of class conflict*. But, because international liberalization enhances the exit options of firms in LMEs ... the balance of power is likely to tilt toward business ... In coordinated market economies, however ... governments should be less sympathetic to deregulation because it threatens the nation's comparative institutional advantages. Although there will be some calls for deregulation even in such settings, the business community is likely to provide less support for it ... In these economies, firms and workers have common interests to defend because they have invested in many co-specific assets, such as industry-specific skills. Thus, the political dynamic inspired by globalization in these countries is likely to entail *less class conflict* and to center around the formation of cross-class coalitions ... [emphases added].[23]

To the extent that parties of the Left and the Right represent different class interests, the implication of Hall and Soskice's argumentation is that we should have observed increasing effects of government partisanship in LMEs over the last couple of decades, while partisan effects in CMEs should have remained stable. The rhetoric of Reaganism and Thatcherism lends some plausibility to this expectation, but does it in fact hold up in a more rigorous analysis of policy outcomes?

Pooling time series and cross-national data, Kwon and Pontusson (2003) explore time-varying effects on the rate of social spending growth by means of 'moving windows'.[24] With a battery of control variables and with different measures of government partisanship, we find that the effects of government partisanship on social spending growth increased markedly in the European CMEs from the mid-1970s through the first half of the 1990s. Governments dominated by Left parties became more distinctly 'pro-welfare' while governments dominated by Right parties became more distinctly 'anti-welfare'. In the LMEs, by contrast, partisan effects fell from the early 1960s through the early 1980s, increased sharply in the late 1980s, and then fell again in the mid-1990s. (For most 15-year periods, the effects of government partisanship are statistically insignificant for the LMEs.)

My work with Kwon not only fails to confirm the expectation that CME conditions attenuate partisan conflict over social; but the results also indicate that CME conditions actually accentuate partisan conflict in the face of globalization. Why might this be so? There are three plausible (and complementary) explanations of the LME–CME contrast that ought to be explored. First, preliminary analyses indicate that there is an interaction effect between government partisanship and economic growth: that is, partisan differences with respect to social spending are more pronounced during economic downturns. Since the mid-1970s, economic growth in CMEs has decelerated not only absolutely but also relative to LMEs, and this might explain why partisan conflict has become more pronounced in CMEs.

Second, it seems plausible to argue that the extent to which globalization generates partisan conflict over social spending depends on the extent to which social spending undermines market dynamics. When the OECD countries are ranked by Esping-Andersen's index of welfare-state decommodification, using data for 1980, the six LMEs included in our analysis occupy the bottom six positions while the European CMEs hold the top positions (Esping-Andersen 1990: 52). Arguably, well-organized employers with a strong interest in curtailing social spending have pulled Right parties away from the median voter, towards a more anti-welfare position, in European CMEs. In contrast to the VoC approach, this argument posits a common employer interest in 'market conformity' across varieties of capitalism.

The third explanation instead proceeds from the idea that unions pull Left parties away from the median voter, towards a more pro-welfare position. Union density declined sharply in most LMEs over the period 1975–1995. The membership losses suffered by unions in some European CMEs were small by comparison, and union density actually increased in other European CMEs.[25] The divergent fortunes of unions thus might also explain why we observe increasing effects of government partisanship in CMEs but not LMEs. Again, further empirical analysis is needed to ascertain whether these arguments explain time-varying patterns of partisan effects on social spending in CMEs and LMEs. My point here is simply to illustrate what I have in mind in arguing for an approach that builds on, but goes beyond the analytical framework of the VoC literature.

Conclusion

Clearly, there is a great deal of institutional diversity among advanced capitalist political economies. There is also a great deal of change to be observed as we survey the experience of the advanced capitalist political economies over the last couple of decades. Whatever the particular map of the varieties of capitalism that we employ – say, Esping-Andersen's threefold typology of 'welfare regimes' or Hall and Soskice's twofold typology – we do not observe many instances of fundamental 'regime change', but we do observe many instances of a specific institutions being reformed or realigned. Equally important, relatively stable institutional configurations seem to be generating new policy outputs and socioeconomic outcomes.

The extent to which firms and workers have the capacity to coordinate to overcome collective action problems and to engage in mutually beneficial cooperation represents an important analytical dimension for mapping varieties of capitalism, but we must also attend to the distribution of power among collective actors. To clarify, distributive conflict is a common feature of capitalist political economies, but the distribution of power is a source of variation among them. The distribution of power is also a source of variation over time. Power relations among collective actors are embedded in institutions and clearly do not change overnight. Yet power relations among collective actors are fundamentally dynamic, reflecting changes in underlying economic structures as well as cyclical changes in market conditions.

There are common dynamics at work in the advanced capitalist countries in the current era, having to do with globalization, deindustrialization and technological change. As the VoC literature emphasizes, the effects of these 'system-wide' changes are mediated by national-level institutions, but the analytical concerns of comparative political economy ought not be confined to the study of 'institutional mediation'. We need a more nuanced understanding of 'globalization', conceived as a political-economic process, and its implications for the interests and (strategic) behavior of collective actors within nationally defined arenas of interaction. Obviously, the dynamics of European integration also need to be taken into account as we grapple with reconfigurations of European political economies. The institutionalism of the VoC approach is too confining not only on account of its focus on coordination, but also on account of its focus on the nation state as the unit of analysis.

Notes

1. This formulation implies that (non-market) coordination yields superior outcomes. As we shall see, Hall and Soskice argue that this is not the case as far as economic growth is concerned, that coordinated economies are distinguished by different sectoral growth patterns rather than higher rates of growth. Though never stated quite so explicitly, however, the VoC literature clearly treats coordinated market economies as superior to liberal market economies across a range of other outcomes (quality of jobs, employment security, income distribution).

2. Howell (2003a,b) also criticizes the VoC literature for its de-emphasis of conflict and power, and his commentaries inform a number of my formulations in the following pages.

3. Space does not allow me to sort out the thorny issue of whether or not the VoC literature actually deploys 'ideal types' in the Weberian sense. Suffice it to say that this literature commonly presents Germany and the US (sometimes also Japan and the UK) as if each of these (real) cases were a more or less perfect representation of the two types of capitalism.

4. Cf. Streeck's (2001) characterization of Germany and Japan as cases of 'non-liberal capitalism.'

5. To capture differences between Japanese and European CMEs, Hall and Soskice (2001) make a secondary distinction between 'group-based' and 'sectorally-based' coordination (the former category referring to Japan's infamous keiretsu networks). In a similar vein, Soskice (1999) distinguishes between the 'centralized egalitarian' model of coordination characteristic of the Nordic countries and the 'flexibly coordinated' model characteristic of Germany and other continental CMEs. The VoC approach thus allows for at least three CME sub-types, but this differentiation among CMEs pertains to the forms that coordination takes, and does not directly speak to the balance of power among different economic actors.

6. To clarify, I use the term 'class compromise' to refer to some form of national-level incorporation of labor, as distinct from 'firm-level corporatism' (particularly prominent in Japan, of course). Put differently, 'class compromise' presupposes that workers are organized as a class at the national level.

7. The conflation of Nordic and continental CMEs (Sweden and Germany) in Figure 9.1 and the preceding discussion are not entirely satisfactory (cf. Pontusson 1997, also Streeck 1997). To capture the important differences between these political economies with regard to wage solidarity, welfare state redistribution, immigration and female labor force participation, a third dimension could be added to Figure 9.1. Tentatively, this dimension might be labeled 'inclusive egalitarianism.'

8. While I am sympathetic to the idea of institutional complementaries, I want to make one cautionary remark (which I owe to Erik Olin Wright): we ought not assume that 'homologous' institutions necessarily complement each other. For instance, it need not be the case that market-oriented social policies represent the best complement to market-oriented corporate governance arrangements.

9. The same question might be asked of Alvarez *et al.* (1991) path-breaking analysis of the effects of government partisanship and labor organization on macroeconomic performance. (As Gingerich and Hall note, their argument and analysis bears a strong resemblance to that of Alvarez, Garrett and Lange.)

10. The argument about the 'institutional requisites' of DQP originates with Streeck (1991).

11. It should perhaps be noted that the VoC approach is quite open to the idea of convergence among CMEs and LMEs (i.e. within the CME and LME camps). As Soskice suggests, the Thatcher experience might be interpreted as Britain converging on the (purer) American version of the liberal market economy. Similarly, Sweden might be said to have converged on the German model in the 1980s (Pontusson 1997). On 'dual convergence' or 'co-convergence,' see Kitschelt *et al.* (1999) and Iversen and Pontusson (2000).

12. The concomitant claim that LME conditions are conducive to Thatcher-style radical reform is problematic on two counts. First, it is not clear whether this is really an argument about the institutional structure of the political economy rather than an argument about the institutions of government. The US experience suggests that the success of radical reform in the UK and New Zealand has more to do with institutions of government. Second, as the VoC framework makes clear, these 'radical' reform experiments went with (not against) the grain of the institutional configuration of the political economy.

13. Pontusson and Swenson (1996) attempt to provide such an account of decentralization of wage bargaining in Sweden.

14. As Hall and Soskice (2001: 59) show, union density and bargaining centralization generally held up quite well in the CMEs in the 1980s and early 1990s. It should be noted, however, that the group averages presented by Hall and Soskice hide divergent union density trends among CMEs since 1980: significant declines in Austria, Germany, Japan, the Netherlands and Switzerland have been offset by increases in Belgium, Denmark, Norway and Sweden. This pattern emerges even more clearly in Waddington and Hoffmann's (2000: 54) data.

15. Exit options for capital do feature in at least one passage in Hall and Soskice's introduction (see below). Parallel with globalization, the emergence of the private service sector as the principal engine of employment growth represents another important common trend in CMEs and LMEs alike over the last two decades. Space does not allow me to explore the implications of the coherence of national 'regimes' of regulating capitalism. Suffice it to note that there is a rather strong 'manufacturing bias' to the way that the VoC literature conceptualizes such regimes and classifies individual countries (a bias that this literature shares with most other research traditions in comparative political economy).

16. To clarify, Canada, Ireland, the UK and the US occupy the same data point in Figure 9.1.

17. Temporary jobs are not necessarily 'junk jobs,' but one thing seems clear: workers on fixed-term contract are less likely to be (active) union members than workers on indefinite contracts.

18. Korpi and Palme (2003) report very similar trends in unemployment replacement rates (but do not report any levels data).

19. The tendency for wage inequality to rise in the 1980s and 1990s represents a reversal of the egalitarian tendency shown in Rowthorn's inter-industry data for 1973–1985 (1992: 92).

20. Denmark, Norway, Sweden and the US are the exceptions to the latter generalization. See Pontusson (2003) for evidence and further discussion.

21. The exceptions to this trend are Australia and especially the Netherlands. It is noteworthy that we lack observations for the late 1990s for both these countries (and also for Switzerland).

22. Arguably, high 'reservation wages' (i.e. public income support) has also made it less imperative for low-income households to compensate themselves by working

more in the European CMEs. As Kenworthy and Pontusson (2004) show, taxes and government transfers compensated for some of the growth of household earnings inequality in all the advanced capitalist countries in the 1980s and 1990s.

23. In a footnote, Hall and Soskice clarify that they use the term 'deregulation' as shorthand to refer to 'policies that remove regulations limiting competition, expand the role of markets in the allocation of resources, or sharpen market incentives.'

24. Simply put, we re-estimate the same regression model for 20 consecutive 15-year periods from 1963–1978 through 1983–1998.

25. See note 14 and Figure 9.5.

This essay is the product of an ongoing dialogue with the proponents of the varieties-of-capitalism approach. I would like to thank Peter Hall and David Soskice for encouraging me to write it and for comments on previous drafts. For comments on previous drafts, I would also like to thank David Coates, Joe Foudy, Chris Howell, David Rueda, Kathleen Thelen and, most of all, Mary O'Sullivan.

10
The United States in the Post-war Global Political Economy: Another Look at the Brenner Debate

Martijn Konings

Over the past decades, mainstream comparative and international political economy has displayed a renewed concern with the role of institutions and political agency. The rise to intellectual prominence of institutionalist themes is best understood against the background of the crisis of the post-war period. During the first decades after the war, marked as they were by economic growth and political stability, there had been little reason to theoretically problematize institutions as distinct from the economic or social system. This assumption was dented when the post-war economic dynamic began to taper off towards the end of the 1960s, and became increasingly anachronistic as the downturn began to envelop broader social processes and political arrangements during the 1970s and 1980s. Institutions were back in the scholarly limelight, and with the benefit of hindsight, the immediate post-war period could be explained as a function of the integrative capacities of international regimes and national institutional arrangements.

While institutionalism flourished, Marxist political economy went through more troubled times. Although there has been no shortage of historical materialist explanations of the crisis of the 1970s, it is probably fair to say that the tension existing between Marxism's commitment to the ontological primacy of economic structures and the need to take into account such things as the renewed importance of political agency, institutions and ideology has all too often resulted in a somewhat uncomfortable importation of Weberian and institutionalist concepts to be grafted onto the still-functioning laws of capitalist production (an intellectual direction epitomized by regulation theory).

This situation certainly accounts for much of the excitement and commotion stirred up in Marxist circles by the appearance of Brenner's 'Uneven development and the long downturn', a comprehensive account of the post-war period (Brenner 1998). There can be little doubt about the enormous contribution this work has made. Nevertheless, it has generated plenty of heated criticism too. Almost all major Left periodicals have devoted articles to it, and the debate that took place on the pages of *Historical Materialism* has even come to be known as 'the Brenner debate II'. Unfortunately, most authors participating in especially the latter debate seem to have seized on the opportunity to (re)assert their orthodox credentials. This chapter, by contrast, will argue that whatever weaknesses Brenner's work has are a result not of his alleged abandonment of Marxist theory, but, instead, of his continued adherence to a structuralist mode of explanation.

Brenner's argument

Brenner's work is cast as a critique of 'supply-side explanations', which interpret the crisis as a crisis of profitability caused by the deteriorating relation between wage growth and productivity: when, towards the end of the 1960s, labour began to use its accumulated market and institutional power to secure higher wage increases and stepped-up labour militancy put downward pressure on productivity growth, wages began to outrun productivity, leading to a squeeze on profits (e.g. Glyn and Sutcliffe 1972). According to Brenner, this supply-side perspective cannot account for the length, intensity or universality of the crisis. While labour militancy and the bargaining strength of unions may cause local reductions in profitability, in such cases, capital will shift investments to lower-wage localities in order to restore profitability. This theoretical argument is allied to the empirical observation that class militancy did not precede but followed the decline in productivity and profit rates.

The alternative explanation of the crisis that Brenner proposes does not centre on the 'vertical' relations between capitalists and workers, but on the 'horizontal' relations of market competition between capitals. In a neoclassical world, where information is perfect and all change incremental, competition pursued by means of technological change naturally results in a higher profit rate. However, in the real world, relations of inter-capitalist competition are anarchic: since investment typically does not occur in small coordinated chunks according to the extension and contraction of the market but 'tends to take place in waves and be embodied in large, technically interrelated, developmental blocks' Brenner (1998: 30), cost-cutting producers will seek to capture market share, beyond what is vacated, by lowering output prices. The higher-cost producers, however, although they are unable to recover the costs of their fixed ('sunk') capital, will stay in business as long as they can make at least the average rate of profit on their circulating capital. The result of this failure to exit is overcapacity and a lower average rate of profit. The fall in productivity growth or the decline in the rate of investment, then, should be viewed as the consequence of capitalists' inability to mark up sufficiently over costs and the concomitant reduction of incentives to make new investments.

This conceptual framework yields a historical narrative for the post-war period that goes roughly along the following lines (drawing on Brenner 1998, 2000, 2002a,b, 2003). For reasons that will become clear, I will focus my account on the US.

The US had already experienced a good decade of rapid economic growth when Germany and Japan embarked on their program of post-war reconstruction. The latter, highly export-dependent economies were thus set for a classic phase of 'catch-up', which would come at least partially at the expense of the long-term health of the American manufacturing sector, as manifested in a loss in productivity growth, deterioration of the trade balance and a decline of the dollar. A brief US economic revival occurred during the period 1958–1965 (owing to an assault on labour by US employers), but this did nothing to eliminate the root cause of US stagnation, that is overcapacity in the manufacturing sector in a context of intensified international competition.

This became all too clear after 1965, when increasingly competitive German and Japanese manufacturers were able to capture large shares of the international market, thus preventing US manufacturers from marking up sufficiently over costs and exposing the overcapacity that had built up in that sector. Many US firms failed to exit their overcrowded lines of production and as a result the profit rate dropped sharply between 1965 and 1973. Due to the sheer weight of the US manufacturing sector in world production, this trend of falling profits soon engulfed the other advanced industrial countries as well. The upshot of this situation was that while the Germans and Japanese enjoyed ever-larger current account surpluses, the US was faced with mounting deficits. Under speculative pressure, the US suspended convertibility of the dollar into gold, which was followed by several major devaluations.

The modest revival of US fortunes that followed was entirely bought at the expense of its rivals: the fundamental problems of overcapacity and insufficient exit remained intact. Japanese and German producers turned out to be equally unwilling to fold their businesses, and were aided in this by the continuation of (especially US) Keynesian fiscal and monetary policies that boosted demand and so forestalled the kind of large-scale industrial rationalization that could only lay the basis for a new upturn.

The turn to monetarism of 1979–1982 represented a reversal of these policies. The sudden restriction of credit reduced aggregate demand and pushed up interest rates and the exchange rate, and so sparked a massive shake-out of uncompetitive manufacturers. However, at the same time, these policies severely depressed aggregate demand and so prevented a new secular boom. The economic revival of the 1980s was thus almost entirely a product of the massive program of Keynesian deficit spending, initiated by the Reagan administration in 1982. It was not driven by a new investment boom, and the world market was still a zero-sum game. The US subsidy to world demand facilitated the expansion of Japanese and German exports, which resulted in ever-higher US trade deficits. In addition, the early 1980s saw the rise of the East Asian economies, which rapidly penetrated the American market. The US manufacturing sector went into major decline, and the overvalued dollar became unsustainable.

In the Plaza Accord of 1985, the advanced industrial nations undertook to devalue the dollar, shifting the burden of global overcapacity onto Germany and Japan. Although the competitive position of the US improved, productivity growth and investment remained low, and the decline of the manufacturing sector continued. It was only by the early to mid-1990s that higher profit rates, deriving from the steady rise of exports since 1985, began to translate into a certain regeneration of American manufacturing: exports and investment shot up, which led to a rise in productivity. On the basis of this revival, the service sector experienced increased productivity growth, and finance, which had already begun its recovery after the recession of 1990–1991, now received a new impetus.

However, at the very moment that the US economy looked poised to escape from the zero-sum logic that had held it captive for over three decades, the rise of the dollar, consequent on the Reverse Plaza Accord, began to weaken the competitive position of the US manufacturing sector. At the same time, these developments produced a large inflow of financial capital into the US, buying government debt and pushing up the stock market. This flood of funds greatly expanded the availability of credit, dramatically boosting corporate and household debt as well as aggregate demand. The stock-market bubble thus enabled 'the American economic expansion to accelerate on the basis of rising shares, increasing debt and runaway consumption' (Brenner 2000: 16). The wealth effect fuelled not only consumption but, substituting for profitability, also investment (especially in the high-tech sector), which seriously exacerbated the underlying situation of overcapacity. Then came the Asian crisis (1998), which was only prevented from engulfing the US economy by the Fed's interventions in and signals to the financial markets. The result was a further rise of the stock market and increased reliance on debt. While exports and profits declined and the trade deficit reached new heights, the largest financial bubble in history was taking shape.

Had debt-based US consumption substantially promoted exports from Germany and Japan, in turn causing demands for US goods to increase, and thus sustaining profits, manufacturing investment and productivity growth, the American economy might have been able to move out of its highly unstable predicament. The global and systemic situation of overcapacity, however, prevented any such symbiotic process of growing exports from materializing. Instead, by mid-2000, several years of falling profitability were taking their toll, as one major company after the other (especially in the high-tech sector) got into trouble and share prices dropped sharply. As corporations experienced a negative wealth effect they began to cut back on investments, thus exposing the massive overcapacity that had built up over the previous years and putting further downward pressure on profits. Through declining US imports, these developments have tended to drag down the entire world economy, which has in turn resulted in lower US exports and has sent the trade deficit soaring. Throughout all this, the main prop of the economy has been the continued increase in household consumption and borrowing, spurred on by a series of cuts in interest rates. Given the massive imbalance between the economy's dependence on high levels of indebtedness and a (deflated but still substantial) stock market bubble on the one hand and its ever poorer performance on such fundamentals as profitability, manufacturing investments and the trade balance on the other, the US economy is becoming ever more vulnerable to the possibility of capital flight, and a complete melt down in the near future seems a distinct possibility.

Too little orthodoxy?

While there is no space in this chapter to do justice to the many critiques that Brenner's work has provoked, we can discern a particular line of argument that has dominated these. This argument (put forward by authors such as Bonefeld [1999], Callinicos [1999], Clarke [1999], and Lebowitz [1999]) states that Brenner's contribution is problematic due to his excessive reliance on the 'horizontal' relations of competition between capitals: his analysis is couched in terms of the formal manifestations of the capitalist economy, rather than the structural processes of value creation and exploitation that underlie these ideological appearances. This does not allow him to locate an objective foundation for the tendency for the rate of profit to fall in the relations of production, and leads him to attribute this tendency to certain contingent and subjective aspects of the competitive relations between capitalists. In other words, Brenner has abandoned a distinctively Marxist point of view for a bourgeois conception of market competition. None of these critiques simply insist on the primacy of vertical *vis-à-vis* horizontal relations or seek to merely rehabilitate the profit squeeze approach. Instead, they emphasize the importance of understanding competition as the medium through which the ontologically prior law of capitalist production appears. That is, the relation between capital and labour is not to be conceived in a narrow sense, but as the foundation of the process of capital as a whole.

However, these arguments are fraught with problems that become apparent when they need to be worked out in more concrete terms. For what needs to be identified is a mechanism that functions at the level of the relation between capital and labour, without the mediations of competition, and that is then merely imposed through market competition. None of the critics manage to effectively square this circle. Even Clarke's highly sophisticated theoretical framework is unable to identify a dynamic of over-accumulation, without having recourse to the level of exchange relations: the pressure to increase investment and productivity is imposed by the actions of other capitalists, and it is the limited extent of the market that turns accumulation into *over*accumulation. In the final analysis, Clarke (1999: 65) is forced to simply posit that the tendency to overaccumulation is subject to its own laws and is not constitutively affected by capitalist competition. All in all, the critiques discussed in the above reproduce too many of the problems traditionally associated with the Marxist search for deep-structural laws of production and principles of accumulation.

It may therefore be worth entertaining the possibility that market competition is not accidental but *essential* to any conception of overaccumulation. The object of the critics' denunciations may then well turn out to be an effective escape from a longstanding problem in Marxism. In order to see this, it should be understood that anything can potentially affect the rate of profit – oil shocks, labour resistance, earthquakes and so on. These occurrences, however, are clearly not logical or necessary conditions of the process of capital accumulation. Brenner's theory precisely aims to show what it is in the *very nature* of the capitalist process of accumulation that turns it into overaccumulation and tends to lower the average rate of profit. So, the foundation for the tendency for the rate of profit to fall needs to be located in the modalities of capitalist investment itself. What Brenner, and before him Reuten (1991), note, is that the need for capital to tie itself down in the form of long-term fixed investments implies that, given a positive rate of technological progress, these capitals will exist in a hierarchical relation. And the fact that less competitive producers have incentives to stay in business – even though this may appear unwarranted, given the rate of profit in the branch as a whole, or even that on their own capital taken as a whole – means that they drag down the average rate of profit.

The more important question, then, would seem to be how far this theoretical innovation takes us in explaining the post-war period. We could note that there seems to exist a certain tension between Brenner's theorization of the falling rate of profit in terms of 'sunk' blocks of fixed capital on the one hand, and his claim that labour strength and militancy could have nothing more than a localized and fleeting impact on profits, on the other. The latter argument rests on an assumption about the mobility of capital that the former seems to negate. Brenner's conceptualization of the tendency for the rate of profit to fall is correct on a systemic level, that is within a given extent of the market. However, one of the most important developments of the post-war period was the extension of capital's playing-field to include large parts of the Third World. The fact that, despite this, the rate of profit in the Western world (the object of Brenner's analysis) has continued to fall would seem to point to other factors contributing to this decline, one obvious candidate being the strength of labour.[1]

Moreover, Brenner seems rather quick to write off the relevance of labour's strength, as regards other than strictly economic developments. As Arrighi (2003) and Gindin (2001) point out, it is hard to imagine that the major turmoil caused by workers during the 1960s and 1970s should have had no constitutive impact on the global political economy. So, what is perhaps missing in Brenner's account is not the capital–labour relation as the structural, objective foundation of the process of capitalist accumulation as a whole, but rather class as *agency*. Broadening this point, we could say that Brenner's mode of explanation, far from being too voluntarist, is still too structuralist, too rooted in the tradition of classical Marxism. Given the fact that Brenner set himself the task to explain the great turbulence of the global post-war political economy, his account is somewhat mechanical and one-dimensional, paying scant attention to such things as the role of state institutions, political agency and social struggles and financial developments – all prominent features of the post-war period. Even if they are no longer posited at the level of production, Brenner is still looking for economic laws of capitalist development that explain to us how agents behave.

But if my concerns with Brenner's work clearly echo certain themes that have always figured prominently in the institutionalist critique of orthodox and structuralist Marxism, my argument is not simply that he should have imported more elements of an institutionalist 'varieties of capitalism' analysis in order to do justice to the role of institutions and political agency. In fact, Brenner fully acknowledges the role of domestic institutions in the construction of the differential growth patterns of national economies. At the same time, one of his main strengths is precisely to recast this question in terms of the competition between national capitalisms, in the context of the imperatives emanating from the world market (which tend to be downplayed in most institutionalist analyses). In other words, Brenner's work pays attention to the effects of national institutions as well as global economic structures, and as such both incorporates and goes beyond institutionalist insights. Rather, then, my concerns relate to the fact that Brenner construes the role of institutions in rather narrow terms and does not seem to appreciate their constitutive impact to the fullest possible extent: he understands institutions as ultimately at the mercy of, and subordinate to, the structural determinations of the global market economy, and what receives scant attention is the role of institutions in the formation of those very economic imperatives. Institutionalists and Brenner's Marxism tend to converge around an understanding of institutions that limits their role to the construction of national competitiveness *vis-à-vis* given economic structures (even if they differ profoundly in their conception of the nature and efficacy of these economic structures, and even if this in turn has far-reaching implications for their views on the capacity of national institutional configurations to construct coherent, durable and non-contradictory trajectories of growth); both are much less-minded to show how institutions help shape those economic structures in the first place. Both, that is, tend to separate economic developments and institutional dynamics.

In the next section, I will work this argument out in historical terms, offering a reading of the post-war period that differs in emphasis from Brenner's. In the fifth section, I will return to some of the broader theoretical points that can be drawn from this discussion and place my critique in the context of the overarching theme of this book: that is the relation between economic structures and political institutions and the merits of historical materialism and institutionalism in explaining this relation.

An alternative reading of the post-war period

Re-interpreting the role of the US in the post-war political economy

As a point of departure, we may observe that this tendency to separate institutional and economic developments leads Brenner's analysis to reproduce certain problems normally associated with mainstream political economy. Interestingly, Brenner's understanding of the position of the US in the long downturn fits in quite well with the mainstream literature on the decline of American hegemony. According to this perspective, the growth of international economic interdependence since the late 1960s undermined the economic position of the US, and dwindling economic fortunes translated into a reduced capacity to function as world hegemon (e.g. Gilpin 1987).[2] Institutionalism has its own literature on declinism, which sees decline as the typical fate of economically and technologically advanced nations whose states fail to maintain their developmental capacities. The criteria that these theorists use for arriving at their diagnosis of hegemonic decline are very similar to the ones used by Brenner to assess the strength of American capital.

This mainstream perspective ignores the fact that the institutions of American power during the first decades after the post-war period were not just grafted onto a pre-constituted, generically conceived international economy, but were themselves constitutive of, and had a transformative impact on, this order. According to both mainstream international political economy and institutionalism, the role of states during the first decades of the post-war period was based on the doctrine of embedded liberalism, prescribing a Polanyian embedding of the pre-existing international market economy in national political and social institutions. The prevalence of embedded liberalism itself is seen as an expression of US hegemony. By contrast, I would like to suggest that (although certain Polanyian qualities and Keynesian policies were definitely part of their repertoire) the role of states was much more salient in the deepening and entrenchment of a specific kind of capitalist dynamic. This argument can be made in two steps. First, as Lacher (1999) has argued, the institutions of the post-war period, far from embedding the market, in fact, presided over its expansion and the far-going commodification of social life. Globalization began much earlier than mainstream international political economy would have it (as Brenner would agree). However, while I am sympathetic to this argument, I believe it still does not go far enough: what marked the post-war period was not just the quantitative extension of the capitalist market economy, but the expansion of a very specific kind of economic dynamic. The post-war period has witnessed not just the expansion of free trade and markets 'overseen' by the US, but the projection into the international arena of social, economic and political forms that were specifically American in origin. These observations lead to an interpretation of globalization that is broadened to encompass not only the integration of product markets, but also movements of direct investment, finance and the transformation of state structures. While broader, it is also more specific: it does not understand globalization as a natural tendency of capitalism, but instead as something shaped and promoted by the US state.

Such a perspective would begin by revaluing the salience of the Bretton Woods system (Gindin 2001). Rather than the main pillar of a premeditated form of US hegemony, based on a regime of embedded liberalism, it is perhaps better viewed as a set of international institutions that different states subscribed to in the interest of reconstruction in the context of great power imbalances (Burnham 1990). This is, of course, not to downplay the import of Bretton Woods. Instead, it is merely to suggest, first, that there was no automatic transmission mechanism for US hegemony and that American power could only work through other states; and, second, that the period is perhaps better seen as the construction phase than as the pinnacle of US power.

Bretton Woods cannot be understood solely in terms of the balance between the longer-term movement towards free trade and the opening up of markets on the one hand, and capital controls and embedded finance on the other. For one thing, the opening up of the world market was much more immediately to the advantage of Germany and Japan than it was to that of the US, which rapidly began to suffer the consequences of increased German and Japanese competitiveness. So the more important trade-off was one of ensuring European prosperity by allowing these countries to regulate their own market as well as access to the American market in return for the role of the dollar as international reserve currency, the overseas expansion of US corporations and banks, and more generally US influence in the reconstruction of Europe. Part of this is noted by Brenner (e.g. 1998: 47), but it remains unclear what exactly happens with the latter side of the bargain after the 1950s.

Panitch and Gindin have argued that the first decades of the post-war period saw the penetration of Europe and Japan by American companies, who brought in their wake not only American banks, but also a range of institutions and practices that would serve to bind the reproduction of capitalism in these countries to the reproduction and expansion of American capitalism (Panitch 2000; Gindin 2001; Panitch and Gindin 2004). As Panitch argues, quoting Poulantzas, this resulted in 'a new type of non-territorial imperialism, implanted and maintained not through direct rule by the metropolis, nor even through political subordination of a neocolonial type, but rather through the "induced reproduction of the form of the dominant imperial power within each national formation and its state"' (2000: 9). Drawing on a broader conception of globalization than Brenner, Panitch and Gindin do not see globalization as undermining the position of the US, but instead as the vehicle for US imperialist expansion.

For instance, Brenner does occasionally note that over the course of the post-war period, American corporations began to invest increasingly more abroad, but he seems to relate this almost exclusively to the fall in the rate of profit and the lack of adequate investment opportunities at home. While the reduced profit rates will certainly have played an important role in companies' decisions, it does not account for the fact that the US state had been promoting such overseas expansion from early on in the post-war period. In other words, it is misleading to present the process as a kind of 'capital flight'. Clearly, to some extent, the migration of companies from the US to Europe was part of a state project, or a capitalist strategy, rather than an expression of competitive weakness.

With respect to Brenner's treatment of finance, we may note that his account pays scant attention to certain kinds of financial developments. My point here is not so much that exchange rate movements consequent on changes in relative competitiveness may be amplified by speculation (a criticism made by McNally 1999), but rather that Brenner tends to ignore certain aspects of financial relations that cannot be so straightforwardly reduced to economic fundamentals, but need to be seen in a very different light, *as the result of distinctive strategies and as possessing their own institutional framework*. Actors may have a wide range of reasons for holding specific types of assets that cannot be explained in terms of exchange rates and the competitive position of a country's manufacturing sector. More specifically, Brenner's work fails to take into account the following two aspects of financial relations. First, in addition to its *exchange* function, the dollar possesses a *liquidity* function, deriving from its status as world reserve currency (Odell 1982). Second, the US credit system has not just been one credit system amongst others, but has played an increasingly central role in bolstering the economic position of the US. Especially, the interaction between these two elements has been important.

These considerations yield a picture of the post-war period that is rather different from that painted by Brenner. Let us have a closer look at some of the defining moments, episodes and turning-points in that period.

Bretton Woods...

During the Bretton Woods negotiations, Keynes objected to the establishment of the dollar as a numeraire currency because he feared it would favour rentier interests. Under US pressure, the dollar became the reserve currency after all, and this greatly aided the international expansion of American banks and corporations: US banks' international flexibility and privileged position, deriving from their unique ability to issue dollar-denominated debt, greatly facilitated the expansion of US corporations in Europe, which in turn promoted the expansion of US finance. Moreover, the expansion of the Euromarket during the late 1950s and 1960s, facilitated by the international role of the dollar, signified an important shift towards financial innovation and the bypassing of traditional financial intermediaries, which promoted not only the extension of US financial relations abroad, but also the deepening of the domestic financial market (Seabrooke 2001).

As the post-war period wore on, the reserve function of the dollar came increasingly into conflict with its role as medium of exchange. The dollar glut (a result of a large capital outflows) undermined international confidence in the dollar's gold value, which led to speculative pressures on the dollar. A range of measures was proposed – devaluation, the creation of a new source of international liquidity, discouraging Foreign Direct Investment (FDI) – but little in the way of decisive policy shifts materialized (Odell 1982). The uncertainties associated with the default policy of 'benign neglect' offered US banks even further opportunities for financial innovation, thereby furthering the internationalization of US finance, as well as adding to pressure on the dollar. Thus, by the late 1960s, the US was not only experiencing problems with its balance of payments, but had also developed a highly integrated and liquid financial structure (both domestically and internationally). The latter element would prove stronger than the former.

...and its demise

Whereas Brenner understands the crumbling of Bretton Woods as a purely defensive reaction to the crisis, other authors see the events of the early 1970s as the beginning of an attempt by the US to break out of what had become the restrictive arrangements of the post-war order. Brenner evaluates the American break-up of the Bretton Woods system, exclusively in terms of the consequences for the exchange rate of the dollar and the competitiveness of the manufacturing sector. Although the devaluations were undoubtedly of great importance, what is perhaps more significant from a longer-term historical perspective is the transition from a dollar-exchange standard to a pure dollar standard: that is the fact that the US had acquired the extraordinary capacity to take its currency off gold, and still have it function as the world's reserve currency. The basis of the international monetary system from then on would be the pieces of paper bearing the imprint of the US state.

Gowan (1999, 2001) has emphasized the consequences of the end of Bretton Woods that cannot be captured in terms of the position of the American manufacturing sector. According to him, it was a crucial moment in the qualitative reconstruction of the rules of the world economy. One result was that the US would henceforth be much less vulnerable to the disciplinary pressures of international finance. The Eurodollar market, which had earlier been the source of more than a little concern for the US government, now appeared as a market where the US could exercise unlimited seigniorage privileges – a dynamic further bolstered by US measures to liberalize capital markets. More generally, the new role of the dollar had the effect of reinforcing the role of US financial markets: given the dominant position of the dollar, 'the great majority of states would want to hold the great bulk of their foreign currency reserves in dollars, placing them with the American financial system' (Gowan 1999: 24). The sheer growth in the size, depth and liquidity of American financial markets itself became a good reason for investing in these markets, which in turn strengthened the dollar. Gowan has labelled this dynamic the Dollar-Wall Street Regime.

What has been far more important in the financing of the US trade deficit than attempts to improve manufacturing competitiveness has been the development of an extraordinary capacity to sell US debt. The liberalization and globalization of financial markets has not rendered the US vulnerable to the same disciplinary pressures as in other countries, but instead largely freed it from the balance of payments constraint. Globalization, while it may have contributed to the decline of US manufacturing competitiveness through the integration of product markets, has been much more important in other respects.

However, it is important to appreciate that all this is better understood as a process of the US state seeking to loosen some external constraints, and in the process, becoming aware of the leeway and structural power it commanded, than as the implementation of a grand imperial design. Nor was the American reconstruction of international capitalism in any way completed during the 1970s: the Euromarkets and the hikes in oil prices were not just functional but also posed contradictions for the US state, as attested to by a crisis of confidence in the dollar. Similarly, the disciplinary pressures of international financial markets on other states offered no guarantee that these states would effectively internalize these pressures: Keynesian policies continued, and the working classes remained restive. 'Induced reproduction', in other words, remained far from perfect. It is against this background that the turn towards monetarism should be viewed.

The rise of monetarism

In Brenner's analysis, it remains rather unclear why the monetarist revolution occurred at the moment that it did. Indeed, if often seems as if Brenner views the monetarist shock of 1979–1982 as nothing but a failed set of policies (e.g. 1998: 153): although monetarist policies did force uncompetitive producers out of business, due to its generally depressing impact on the economy it also prevented sustained investment in new lines of production. It was Keynesian deficit-spending that was in the end responsible for the partial recovery of the 1980s. Even these policies turned out mostly to the advantage of Germany and Japan, and did little to reverse the decline of US manufacturing.

This is a rather one-sided interpretation of the events of 1979–1982. It is beyond dispute that monetarism, taken by itself, did little to revive the fortunes of the American manufacturing sector. But it remains an open question whether the industrial shake-out that followed the squeeze on credit was a necessary (if certainly not sufficient) condition for the US economy to experience the relative revival that it did from the beginning of the 1990s.[3] More importantly, however, we should perhaps seek the significance of monetarism in something other than its impact on the manufacturing sector. The Volcker shock, a reaction to the intractability of domestic inflation, produced high interest rates that not only choked off manufacturing activity but also led to a massive inflow of financial capital. Three years later, the Reagan administration, in addition to pursuing a program of massive tax cuts and a program of military Keynesianism, complemented tight money policies with a high dollar policy and a further deregulation of the financial sector (Gowan 1999: 40) – which, as Kapstein puts it, had the effect of at least partly bringing the Euromarket back home (Kapstein 1994: 52).

Brenner sees the decline of the manufacturing sector 'as a symptom of economic crisis', and does not really entertain the possibility that it should prompt him to question 'the relevance and validity of his focus on manufacturing' (Arrighi 2003: 47). In other words, is it possible that the trend towards de-industrialization indicates the diminished salience of manufacturing compared to other processes of capital accumulation, not that it is as important as ever but in crisis? Relatedly, Brenner sees the trend towards accumulation through other, notably financial channels very much as a recent occurrence rather than as a long-term development. This means that he fails to accord due importance to financial developments before the 1990s, and that financialization is easily characterized as nothing but a bubble bound to burst sooner rather than later.[4] If, however, the trend towards financialization is placed in a somewhat longer-term perspective, such conceptions seem to stand in need of reconsideration.

Not properly incorporated into Brenner's account is the fact that, especially from the 1970s onwards, an important response to the crisis had been the diversion of funds into financial assets. As Arrighi observes, the dominant response of manufacturing producers to the heightened pressures of competition and overaccumulation was not the 'strenuous defence of their sunk capital', but rather the diversion of 'a growing proportion of their incoming cash flows from investment in fixed capital and commodities to liquidity and accumulation through financial channels' (2003: 49). This greatly promoted financialization on a global scale. At the same time it gave an impetus to the deepening of the US financial markets, a process additionally furthered by deregulation and flexible exchange rates as well as increased participation by the public in financial markets (what Seabrooke [2001] calls the 'socialization of high finance') (not least as a result of pressures on commercial banks to diversify their traditional activities in the direction of debt and equity markets). All this greatly enhanced the structural capacity of US intermediaries to raise capital.

It is in this context that the significance of the Volcker shock needs to be located. Although the policies of the 1970s still failed to draw in sufficient financial capital, the US had already developed the financial capacities that would allow it to become the main beneficiary of a shake-up of the global financial system. The Volcker shock could not have been undertaken by other countries with very different financial systems, and it would not have been so successful had the US financial system not already been marked by a great degree of liquidity. The rapid innovation in financing techniques and the enhanced capacity of US intermediaries to raise capital then put serious pressure on other advanced countries to liberalize their financial sectors, which reinforced the dynamic.

This, then, laid the foundation for the financing of the budget deficits of the Reagan administration. Brenner notes that all recoveries since the late 1960s have been dependent on Keynesian deficit spending and the stimulation of demand. However, the fact that there is a longstanding pattern here should perhaps prompt us to not dismiss it as mere demand-generated recoveries that fail to develop into new long upturns sustained by investment,[5] but to enquire into the conditions that allow the US to finance, on an almost permanent basis, the kind of deficits that for any other country would result in a massive flight of capital. Instead of seeing the extraordinary levels of indebtedness that resulted from the double deficit merely as signs of the US weakness, we should perhaps pay attention to the fact that, against the laws of economics, *the US has been able to transform its indebtedness from a liability into an asset* (so to speak)[6] – that is, US indebtedness has made other countries more, not less, vulnerable to the vagaries of the US financial system and the dollar. The US has developed an extraordinary degree of leverage over its creditors.

The US economic revival

Whether one understands monetarism as a set of failed policies or as a crucial moment in the reconstitution of the international economy has major implications for one's interpretation of the development of the US and world economy during the 1980s and 1990s. Brenner ascribes great significance to the devaluation of the dollar consequent on the Plaza Accord of 1985 and the revaluation following the Reverse Plaza Accord of 1995 because of their effects on the manufacturing sector. However, I tend to concur with Arrighi's claim that these events need to be situated in the context of the much more important monetarist revolution. What to me stands out about the period after the Volcker shock is that the strategies of both the US public and private actors for dealing with the indebtedness associated with the 'double deficit' became *themselves* increasingly of a financial nature. To evaluate the period primarily in terms of the regeneration of manufacturing may therefore well be to impose a rather ahistorical standard on history.

According to Brenner, although the dollar devaluation consequent on the Plaza Accord had the effect of pushing up exports and so profit rates, investment and productivity growth remained stagnant until well into the 1990s. The expansion of the service sector occurred entirely over the back of the ailing manufacturing sector, and on the basis of unprecedentedly low wage growth. Similarly, finance languished until manufacturing took off. Just when manufacturing showed signs of life (investment picked up, productivity and exports grew), the Reverse Plaza Accord aborted this incipient expansionary dynamic. Although its immediate consequence was a rise in the stock market that fuelled demand and so boosted the US (and the world) economy, its more fundamental significance was to be found in the resumption of the secular decline of the manufacturing sector.

However, we can here pose the same question as in the above: does the shrinking of the manufacturing base and the growth of the service sector indicate crisis or the diminished salience of industrial accumulation *vis-à-vis* other process of capitalist accumulation? With regard to the financial sector, we might note that Brenner exaggerates the recency and uniqueness of its expansion, and as a result entirely pre-empts the question of how (un)sustainable debt-based demand and demand-based expansion are.[7] However, the US position in international finance has a longer history, elements of which have been discussed in the above. Similarly, in arguing that it was only the suddenly increased liquidity of US financial markets as a result of foreign investment that was responsible for the increased indebtedness of corporation and households, Brenner ignores the fact that corporate and household indebtedness were by no means new phenomena but date back to much earlier in the post-war period (Seabrooke 2001). The wealth effect might, therefore, be less ephemeral than supposed by Brenner.

Brenner seems to view the Reverse Plaza Accord primarily as an attempt to bail out the Japanese manufacturing sector, the collapse of which would have destabilized the entire world economy. Other interpretations have argued that, far from the US being caught between having to choose between suffering the consequences of a Japanese crisis or revaluating its currency and accepting intensified competitive pressures on its only recently revived manufacturing sector, the Reverse Plaza Accord was a much more offensive attempt to destabilize the East Asian economies, which were heavily dependent on exports and had their currencies linked to the dollar

(Gowan 1999; Burke 2001). In other words, it was part of a pattern of attempts by the US to manufacture localized crises in the expectation that these will result in huge flows of financial capital into the US.

How feasible is it to argue that the US economy was fundamentally weakened by a crisis that the US itself orchestrated? Ultimately, Brenner does not really offer an argument for why the lack of investment in the manufacturing sector should be assigned so much more weight than the inflow of financial capital, low interest rates, and higher levels of demand, and why the latter should be inherently unsustainable. And even if there is a strong element of instability about the wealth effect, there still remains the distinct possibility that a meltdown of the stock market will be offset by drastic fiscal expansion. Over the past decades, the US has shown a tremendous willingness to fuel demand through deficit spending, and an extraordinary capacity to finance these deficits; there is, then, no necessary reason why a return to Keynesian policies through public deficits – if necessary supported by something like a second Volcker shock – is impossible if private demand falters (see Grahl 2001: 46). In fact, it does not require much imagination to read such a scenario into the current direction of American policy under the Bush Administration (which is in complex ways allied to a vigorous renewal of a commitment to geopolitics and warfare). To dismiss this, as Brenner (2003) does, as nothing but an attempt to reinflate the bubble is to miss much of what makes these policies more than incoherent last-ditch attempts to deal with a fundamentally hopeless situation. This is not meant to deny that these policies are still dependent on the US's continuing ability to attract finance – which Brenner sees as highly precarious, given declining competitiveness and an ever-growing trade deficit – but rather to draw attention to the fact that predictions about the unsustainable nature of the trade deficit have been made, and disproved, for several decades now; investors' decisions to hold the US assets are clearly affected by rather different considerations than the state of the current account or the manufacturing sector. The capacity of the US state to flout 'economic fundamentals', far from being akin to attempts to defy gravity, is deeply embedded in the structures of the world economy. To say that the 'unprecedented increase in the acquisition of US assets by the rest of the world' as a consequence of the debt- and deficit-driven boom has left 'the American economy theoretically vulnerable to the same sort of flight of capital, asset depreciation and downward pressure on the currency that wrecked East Asia' (2000: 6) is to miss something essential about the different positions in the international economy occupied by the US and East Asia.

Marxism, institutionalism and social theory

The (all too brief) sketch of an alternative reading of the post-war period offered in the previous section pays, I believe, more attention to institutional characteristics than does Brenner's account. At the same time, however, my narrative is not framed in terms of different varieties or models of capitalism, and the analysis has retained a strongly Marxist affinity in its focus on the formation and impact of global economic processes. That is to say, I have neither concentrated on the diverging responses of different states to changing economic realities nor tried to criticize such a perspective by underscoring the causal primacy of the global market economy *vis-à-vis* national institutions. Instead, I have sought to show how global economic imperatives are themselves the product of dynamics engendered within specific – and, given the fact that the nation state still forms the main locus of political authority, predominantly national – configurations of institutions, above all the specific institutional arrangements of the US state.[8] These issues concerning the relation between national institutional configurations (foregrounded in the institutionalist 'varieties of capitalism' literature), and more structural and global economic processes (on which Marxist analyses tend to concentrate) are, of course, at the heart of this book. While there is much to be said for the idea that each of these perspectives captures part of the truth, and that they should therefore be combined, there is a danger that such theoretical pluralism could fall prey to an eclecticism that does little to remedy the problem common to each of these approaches: that is, the tendency to separate economic and institutional developments. I hope that in the above I have highlighted enough problematic implications of this tendency as to at least have piqued the reader's curiosity concerning the possibility of a qualitatively different articulation of economics and institutions.[9]

As a starting point, we may note that this separation of institutions from economic developments manifests itself in a certain tendency for both Marxist and institutionalist explanations to assume a certain degree of :tructuralism and determinism. Although a critique of orthodox Marxism's economic determinism has traditionally formed an important background to the formulation of the institutionalist perspective, it is by no means clear that the latter escapes very similar charges – even if the determining instances have now been displaced from the economic onto the political. As Hay and Wincott (1998) argue, the institutionalist literature inclines towards a structuralism of its own – which Coates, in his chapter in this volume, has tried to capture with the concept of 'institutional determinism'.[10] Common to Marxist and institutionalist analyses, then, is a commitment to structural explanations: to explain social dynamics and interaction is to find a causal mechanism that (at least partly) determines them. Whereas Marxism locates such a structure at the economic level, institutionalism looks to social and political institutions. Now, while I believe that institutionalism's insistence on the central importance of institutions is entirely apposite, I would like to suggest that their structuring effects are better grasped if we break with a conception of structures as exerting causally determining effects of their own and instead adopt a 'softer', less active conception of structure: that is, a conception of structures that is less material and causal than cognitive and mediating.

Institutionalists tend to conceive of institutions as causal structures that govern the behaviour of actors within a particular sphere of society. The complexity and diversity of human agency is then accounted for in terms of the large variety of social and political institutions that structure social life. While such pluralism introduces an openness to the variety and open-endedness characteristic of human interaction that is often absent from more mono-causal approaches, there still seems something awkward about this combination of structuralist and pluralist modes of explanation. So, instead of trying to first clinch the relation between institutions and agency, and then allowing for the multiplication of institutions, we should perhaps try to introduce such pluralism into the very relation between institutions and agency. This would mean to strip institutions of their causal status and to conceptualize them more as structures in Giddens' sense: that is, as the rules and resources that actors draw upon, formal rules and public conventions that do not have an existence independent of the ways in which they are invested by agents (Giddens 1979). Institutions, then, do not, in any meaningful way, causally govern the behaviour of agents; instead, they form the shared conventions around which individuals develop their strategies, and so serve to provide agents with a somewhat stable sense of their environment. It is not institutions that govern agency, but agents that invoke, act on and in the process transform or reproduce ('instantiate', in Giddens' terminology) institutions. Try as we might, we will never be able to specify a way in which a given institutional framework forces us into a specific course of action. The constitutive role of institutions, then, has more to do with how they mediate the way in which certain actors position themselves *vis-à-vis* other actors than with any determining powers.

However, this relativization of the autonomous causal powers of institutional structures and concomitant shift of emphasis towards agency should not be taken as a rejection of the obvious fact that individuals experience their own agency as subject to a range of constraints, pressures and incentives. The point, rather, is that the latter are not produced by institutions themselves, but by the ways in which other agents use these institutions to pursue their own interests. Social pressures are not causal determinations emanating from institutions, but precisely the effects of strategies pursued by actors on the basis of the public rules and conventions available to them.

Institutionalism has difficulty accounting for this mediating function of institutions: a conception of human interaction as governed by the institutions within which it is situated entails a Weberian understanding of power as predominantly direct and overt – for the way power functions is defined by, and can therefore be read off from, the institution in question. As Roy (1997: 13–14) argues, this tends to downplay the extent to which relations of power are indirect: that is, constituted by the way in which agents, by practically investing institutional forms, shape the context in which other agents act. Agents are only ever constrained by other agents, but this never occurs in a direct way, and that – that is, in their mediating role – is where institutions matter. What Roy calls 'structural power' is power that is indirect and not defined by or formally lodged in institutions, that works through 'setting up the choices the actor faces and the consequences of any particular action' (1997: 13–14). Power relations are not, in Weberian fashion, determined by the institutions 'within' which they are situated, but are formed *through* institutions. Agency always has spillover effects, so to speak; its social meaning and ramifications are never fully contained in a given institution (al) framework. To a certain extent, social interaction always eludes the formal qualities of institutions.

These insights allow us to articulate an understanding of the role of institutions that takes its cue from the Marxist unease with the formalism of institutionalist analyses, yet does not succumb to a structuralism of its own. What Marxists tend to view as socio-economic structures underlying and pre-existing institutions and agency are nothing but the effects of our actions as mediated by institutions: economic structures do not exist independently from and prior to political institutions, but are the result of how people use and invest the social conventions, public meanings and political institutions they find before them. In this sense, the orthodox Marxist wish to define capitalism in terms of an economic logic can be deeply misleading – as are attempts to grasp the essential qualities of the current phase of capitalist development in terms of the 'disembedding' of the market economy from its institutional framework. No economic dynamic is autonomous or immune from the mediations of state institutions, and even in an era of globalization, economic action is as much situated and embedded in social institutions as it ever was – even if people certainly act differently within these institutions and produce very different effects with a much greater (indeed global) reach that are ever less encapsulated by the formal qualities of (national) institutions themselves.

Two points emerge from this discussion. First, it should serve to caution against excessive reliance on a rigid notion of laws of capitalist accumulation, seen as existing prior to and defined in abstraction from the interaction of strategies and institutions, and instil greater appreciation for the dramatically different social dynamics that agents can produce within a given institutional framework (which is, of course, not to preclude the possibility of those institutional frameworks themselves too being subject to transformation). As I hope to have shown in the previous section, one thing Brenner's analysis lacks is an appreciation of the qualitative novelty of, and the potential coherence and contradictions *internal* to, the economic dynamics generated by actors adjusting their strategies in response to the declining efficacy of their old strategies. To evaluate new practices and the economic dynamics they generate, in terms of their degree of correspondence to a pre-given definition of capitalist accumulation, means therefore to risk obscuring precisely those aspects that set them apart from the old practices and dynamics.

Second, to explicitly relate this discussion to the global level at which Brenner's narrative is cast: given the fact that it is still the nation state that constitutes the main institutional nexus of social relations, there is no international economy apart from the interactions of agents operating from within different national contexts. This is certainly not to suggest that there is no such thing as a relatively unified international economy, but rather that its exact nature bears the imprint of the dynamics generated by the interaction of agents within national institutional configurations. To merely say that at any given time certain countries will occupy a stronger position within the international economy than others still betrays a conception of economic structures and states as ready-made entities. And within such a logic, institutions can be 'matched onto' economic structures and we can trace the differential capacities of institutional configurations in shaping national responses to a set of pre-existing economic constraints (as both Brenner and the 'varieties of capitalism' literature do), but we will never be able to do justice to the constitutive effects of state institutions on the nature of international economic processes themselves. That is, we will be unable to account for the fact that different countries participate to different degrees and in qualitatively different ways in the shaping of the global economy, occupy structurally different positions in it, and are differentially affected by the pressures emanating from it. It is this element of constitutive asymmetry and in-built bias at the heart of the world economy (as opposed to countries' uneven development in a given global economic structure) that is lost in Brenner's account of the post-war period.

Concluding remarks

For Brenner, the long downturn continues unabated. Capitalism as a system has run out of steam, and the only solution is the massive devaluation or destruction of capital, as occurred during the 1930s and the Second World War. Those aspects of the contemporary economy that many hail as the harbingers of a new economy or a new accumulation regime, Brenner sees as more or less spasmodic attempts to avert an inevitable fate. The remarks in this chapter should not be read as an argument for the stability and solidity of the current phase of American capitalism – indeed, developments in recent years have certainly demonstrated that the US does not possess a magic wand to keep the world economy turning over. Like all social and economic rationalities, financialization and debt-based demand will be marked by contradictions of their own. But the point is precisely that these will be *new* contradictions, the result of distinctive strategies pursued in specific institutional settings, that cannot be pre-judged by measuring them against an ideal-typical notion of how capitalist accumulation is supposed to proceed. My remarks in this chapter are, then, meant as a plea for entertaining greater openness to the many ways in which agents use and manipulate the institutional structures they find before them. *That* should and could be the contribution of Marxist theory, a project that remains very much incomplete.

Acknowledgements

I would like to thank Robert Brenner, David Coates, Sam Gindin, Samuel Knafo and Leo Panitch for their very helpful comments on earlier drafts of this chapter.

Notes

1. This can clearly only hold for the period up to the late 1970s, after which labour in the West was decisively weakened. But whereas Brenner adduces the fact that no new upturn has ensued in spite of this onslaught on labour in support of his interpretation of the crisis in terms of the competitive relations between capitalists, other authors (such as Panitch and Gindin and Arrighi) have a much more favourable interpretation of economic development since especially the early 1990s, and locate the major turning-point in the rise of neoliberalism, which was responsible for the clampdown on labour. The question of how we assess the strength and defeat of labour is therefore closely linked to how we assess the revival of the world economy since the early 1990s, that is whether we view it as based on nothing but financial bubbles or as a more stable kind of expansion (based in part on the defeat of labour world-wide). This issue will be addressed (although by no means resolved) in the section on 'Concluding remarks'.
2. The decline thesis has come under attack from more radical IPE scholars who claim that it overlooks the fact that American power has been transformed from state-based to market-based, structural power (e.g. Gill, Strange). However, this conception of structural power continues to rely on a conception of state institutions and economic structures as distinct entities. Although the idea is very fruitful within the bounds of the discipline, it is not worked out very well: it remains very unclear what the operative mechanisms and relations are, and it often seems an almost rhetorical device designed to come to terms with the anomalous fact of enduring US dominance. Although this paper engages Brenner's work rather than critical IPE, it can be read as working out a conception of structural power that does not fall prey to these problems.
3. See Panitch and Gindin in this book, Figure 8.4 for figures that suggest a more optimistic interpretation than Brenner's.
4. Brenner makes no efforts to provide arguments for his understanding of financial developments as necessarily 'bubbleish' and unsustainable. Ultimately, it seems to derive from a certain faith in the tangible nature of manufacturing as opposed to the fictitious character of financial titles (as illustrated by Brenner's likening financial speculation to a cartoon character running over a cliff, only able to keep on running because he refuses to see that the ground beneath his feet has disappeared [2002b: 18]).
5. At times, Brenner almost appears to conceive of Keynesian deficit spending as 'not playing by the rules'.

6. 'One of the US's impressive feats from its promotion of direct financing and extension of structural power was to transform indebtedness into a strength rather than a weakness' (Seabrooke 2001: 199).

7. It should be noted that Brenner gives rather different indications as to at what point he sees the financial sector taking off. In Brenner (1998), it is claimed that the condition of the financial sector began to improve well before 1990, with the share of FIRE of total investment having doubled by 1990 compared to 1975. Brenner (2000) argues that finance took off after the 1990–1991 recession, whereas Brenner (2002b) states that the rise in the stock market was wholly warranted by the recovery of profitability right up until 1995.

8. It does so on an admittedly superficial level. I believe that a convincing account of the post-war period will have to dig much deeper into the domestic dynamics of the state that has been the main driving force behind the post-war international political economy than has so far been done, but a political sociology of the US state is clearly not something I am able to take up in this chapter.

9. For an elaborated version of the argument that follows, see Konings (2005) forthcoming.

10. Given the space available, a certain degree of caricature is inevitable, and I would like to emphasize that I am trying to draw out a tension within institutionalist thought rather than passing a blanket judgement. Especially the article by Hay and Wincott offers a sophisticated conceptualization of the relation between institutional structures and agency that is still formulated within the parameters of an institutionalist analytical framework and in many ways comes close to the considerations offered here.

11
The Capitalist Economy, 1945–2000: A Reply to Konings and to Panitch and Gindin

Robert Brenner

Konings pursues two closely interrelated lines of argument in offering a critique of and an alternative to my understanding of post-war economic evolution, one methodological, the other substantive. His purpose is to undermine structure in favor of agency, in order to give pride of place to state power, class struggle, and the initiatives of capitalists, and, in this way, to found a particular interpretation of the evolution of the post-war order, which can be briefly summarized in the following way. The American state was the unshaped shaper of the post-war international economic order and imposed rules of the game designed to open the way for the penetration, and domination, of the European and Japanese economies by US multinationals and banks. Working-class resistance, along with the rise of social movements, put an end to the great post-war boom by making for a major fall in the rate of profit from the mid-1960s through the mid-1970s, against the background of a crisis of productivity. During the 1970s, the US government could not mount the will to impose the needed stabilization policies, largely for fear of the political consequences. Capitulating to a wide range of social forces, it sought to keep the economy turning over through Keynesian deficits, but these brought runaway inflation and a declining dollar, very much exacerbating the crisis. At the start of the decade, the US did put in place the first key pre-condition for American recovery by junking the Bretton Wood system of fixed exchange rates and dollar convertibility and taking the world to a dollar-dollar standard. But the turning point came only in 1979–1980, when led by Fed Chair Paul Volcker, the US state re-assumed its hegemonic responsibility for revitalizing the world capitalist order by imposing structural adjustment on the American economy itself. This opened the way to not only the destruction of the working-class resistance at the root of the crisis, but also to the necessary shakeout of high-cost, low-profit means of production, as well as the impetuous ascent of finance. Henceforth, by means of a rationalization and renovation of American industry made possible by the financers, as well as the expansion of the financial sector itself, the US economy steadily recovered, regaining its former heights in terms of the main indicators of economic performance.

In advancing this argument, Konings closely aligns himself with the view of Panitch and Gindin. The latter, for their part, construct their interpretation of post-war economic development, and their criticisms of the Varieties of Capitalism approach, to a not inconsiderable degree by means of a critique of my own approach. So, my response to Konings must be, at least in part, simultaneously a response to them.

Structuralism: the profitability constraint

Konings's methodological bottom line is that 'what Marxists tend to view as socio-economic structures underlying and pre-existing institutions and agency are nothing but the effects of our actions as mediated by institutions' and 'do not in any meaningful way causally govern the behaviour of agents' (p. 206). But this is a misleading point of departure, to say the least. For, as we know, in the presence of a framework of capitalist social-property relations – quasi-universal throughout today's advanced economies – economic agents, unlike economic agents in any pre-capitalist economy, will obsessively seek to maximize their profits, no matter what the extant agents, institutions, or states. Konings contends that 'try as we might, we will never be able to specify a way in which a given institutional framework forces a specific course of action' (p. 206). But, how could it be more clear that capitalist economic agents go after the highest returns because, separated as they are from their means of subsistence, they must do so in order to survive under the constraint of competition? And how could it be more evident that they can also be counted on to systematically specialize, apply their surpluses to adding plant and equipment and expanding their labor force, bring in the latest innovations, and move from line to line in response to demand, precisely because these strategies or rules for reproduction are requisite to maintain competitiveness? Because capitalist economic actors are obliged to adopt capitalist rules for reproduction, we can expect, as we cannot in the presence of any pre-capitalist system of social property relations, the growth of labor productivity, the increase in size of the labor force, the rise in relative surplus value leading to increasing real wages – all of which, taken together, make for economic growth.

The consequences are multiple, not least for the issues of the exercise of power and the forging of innovation that so concern Konings. Because the rate of profit expresses the size of the surplus that capitalists can derive from a given amount of capital stock, and constitutes the best available predictor of future profits, it is the key determinant of the increase of investment and employment, thus economic growth. High profitability makes for high growth, low profitability, low growth. Because not just economic but also non-economic agents depend on economic growth as a condition for the realization of their own goals, and because economic growth requires investment and employment growth that are themselves predicated on capitalists' making profits, virtually all can be counted on, in their own interest, to pursue strategies that prioritize the requirements of profit-making. This means that under capitalism – unlike in pre-capitalist societies where growth is slow or non-existent and zero-sum conditions thus prevail – states, classes, and other sorts of social groups are strictly limited in the degree to which they can sensibly pursue redistributive strategies at the expense of the dominant class. By the same token, all will tend to benefit, with or without redistribution, when profitability is high and economic growth is proceeding well but will find it correspondingly difficult to oppose the re-distributive claims of capital when profitability has fallen in order to revive the economic health.

It follows that processes of innovation – not only in production itself, but also in political and economic institution building, government policymaking, and even, to an important degree, class warfare – will generally take account of, and in any case find themselves powerfully constrained by, the needs of competitiveness and profit maximization. To improve profits, firms must seek new technologies and create new forms of organization that improve their ability to compete. To increase their tax revenue, raise employment and wages, guarantee social stability, and secure re-election, governments are obliged to devise macro- and micro-policies that speak to the profit-making requirements of the corporations. Meanwhile, in constructing their strategies toward their employees, employers will compare the apparent potential for profit-making through smooth capital accumulation that can often be insured by adopting accommodating forms of labor relations, with those that might be secured through planned assaults on labor, despite the disruptions of production that are inevitably entailed. Workers, for their part, will, sooner or later, be obliged to take into account the profitability of 'their' firms, if they are not to so squeeze competitiveness and discourage those firms' investment or encourage the expansion of production elsewhere where labor resistance is lower (at least to the extent that transforming the social-property relations is off the agenda, as it has been through most of the post-war epoch).

Konings claims that 'one thing [my] analysis lacks is an appreciation of the qualitative novelty...of the economic dynamics generated by actors adjusting their strategies in the response to the declining efficacy of their old strategies' (p. 207). But I hope it will be evident in what follows that, on the contrary, I attempt, more or less systematically, to understand the fashioning of new approaches on the part of governments, capitalists, workers, and others, precisely in terms of the 'the declining efficacy of their old strategies'. It should go without saying that such transformations cannot be directly derived, or read off, from the needs of economic reproduction, and require historical analysis in their own terms. But the fact remains that 'the declining efficacy of old strategies' is manifested and measured precisely in terms of their declining ability to sustain profit-making, while new approaches that arise to replace them will succeed in maintaining themselves only if they themselves do secure stable capital accumulation.

It is with the foregoing strictures in mind that I have made the point of departure of my work on the post-war capitalist development, the evolution of the profit rate. In the remainder of this text, I hope to vindicate that approach.

Posing the problem: explaining the long boom and the long downturn

From just after the end of World War II to the end of the twentieth century, the history of the advanced capitalist economies in general, and the US economy in particular, naturally divides into two roughly equal parts, each about a quarter century in length – a long boom from the later 1940s to 1973 and a long downturn from 1973 onward. The fundamental aim of my work has been to account for the long post-war prosperity, for the transition from boom to downturn, and for the reduced dynamism that then came to characterize the economy. In the first instance, my interpretation is straightforward, and, speaking most generally, in keeping with the results of a number of others in the Marxist tradition (e.g. Armstrong *et al.* 1991; Dumenil and Levy 2003). What made possible the inauguration and long perpetuation of the post-war boom in the US, Europe, and Japan was the achievement in the late 1940s of elevated rates of profit and their maintenance for the next two decades. What brought the post-war boom to an end was a sharp fall in aggregate profitability between 1965 and 1973, beginning in the US and extending to Western Europe and Japan. The reason that, as of 2000, there had been no clear revival for the global economy or its US component is that there had been no recovery of profitability.

Panitch and Gindin have sought to undermine this basic picture, by calling into question the reality of the long downturn. The post-war golden age, they aver, was unprecedentedly, indeed uniquely, dynamic, so that employing it as the standard to judge the economy's health 'sets the bar too high' (p. 145). 'A longer historical perspective clearly shows that the post-1973 period was not unusual in terms of growth' (Gindin and Panitch 2002: 35). In their view, the downturn that gripped the economy in the wake of the fall in profitability was confined to the 1970s, and was transcended immediately thereafter. According to Panitch and Gindin, '[i]n the period after the Volcker shock...the rates of growth in GDP, profits, and productivity in the USA began their slow climb back to earlier levels' (p. 151). Because they believe that the problems that set off the long downturn have been long overcome, with the consequence that the economy's dynamism has been successfully restored, it is their conclusion that '[t]hose theorists who... [portray] the past quarter century in terms of the working out of the crisis that began in [the 1970s]...are...wrong' (Panitch and Gindin: p. 145). But, it seems to me that every one of these contentions is controverted by the evidence.

As I pointed out in Brenner (1998: 39), the post-war boom of the *economy of the US* – which is the focus of the work both of Konings and of Panitch and Gindin – was unquestionably powerful, but not in a league of its own. The growth of labor productivity, per capita income, and real wages was higher in the post-World War II golden age than in the comparable period of growth before World War I, but not by all that much. On the other hand, the growth of GDP and of investment proceeded as rapidly or more so in the latter period than the former. The boom from 1950 through 1973 thus surpassed the expansion from 1890 through 1913, but it remains reasonable to group them together (see Table 11.1).

Because the pre-World War I and post-World War II expansions are in the same ballpark, even though the former clearly lagged the latter, economic performance during the long downturn after 1973 looks weak, not only when compared to that of the post-war golden age, but also, *pace* Panitch and Gindin, when juxtaposed to the long boom between 1890 and 1913. It thus fell palpably short of both expansions with respect to virtually all of the main macro-economic indicators: the growth of labor productivity, of GDP, of GDP per person, of real wages, and of the growth of investment (see Tables 11.1 and 11.2).

Nor is it the case that, from the time of the Volcker shock the economy got steadily better, so as to come 'back to earlier levels'. Economic performance during the post-Volcker business cycles from 1979 through 2000 failed even

Table 11.1 Comparing long booms: 1890–1913 versus 1950–1973 (average percent change)

	1890–1913	1950–1973	1973–1996
GDP	4	4	2.9
GDP/hour	2.2	2.6	1.2
GDP/capita	2.1	2.5	1.8
Real wage (mfgr)	1.6	2.2	0
Gross capital stock	5.4	3.2	n/a
Gross capital stock/hour	3.4	1.7	n/a

Sources: Maddison, A. (1991), *Dynamic Forces in Economic Development*, pp. 71, 140, 142; Maddison, A. (2003), *The World Economy: Historical Statistics*, Table 2b, pp. 84–6; Table 2c, pp. 87–9; Bureau of Economic Analysis, *National Income and Product Accounts*, Table 7.1; Rees, A. (1969), *Real Wages in Manufacturing, 1890–1914*, p. 120; Bureau of Labor Statistics, *Hourly Earnings of Production and Non-Supervisory Workers* (BLS website); Bureau of Labor Statistics, Consumer Price Index-U (1982–1984) (BLS website) (wages are for manufacturing instead of whole economy, as wages outside of manufacturing are unavailable for earlier period).

to approach that during the golden age business cycles from 1948 through 1969. It was less good in the decade of the 1980s than that of the 1970s, not to mention the 1950s and 1960s. During the first half of the 1990s, it was *worse than in any other five-year period during the whole post-war era.* The unquestionable boom of the second half of the 1990s did raise performance for the decade as a whole above that of the 1980s, but was itself obliged to depend in large part on the enormous fillip to both consumption and investment provided by the historic and ill-fated stock market bubble of those years (Brenner 2002a: 188–217). Even then, the US economy did no better in the supposedly dynamic 1990s than in the ostensibly crisis-bound 1970s (see Tables 11.1 and 11.2).

Panitch and Gindin make much of the ostensibly impressive GDP per capita growth achieved in the post-Volcker period. But, in light of the unquestionably dismal growth of GDP per hour (labor productivity) in this era, it is clear that the GDP per capita numbers were made possible only by virtue of the big increase in the hours worked per person per annum and the simultaneous sharp rise in the proportion of the population in the labor force, which resulted largely from women's increased need and ability to take up employment in these years. Panitch and Gindin inexplicably see 'this ability to extract more labor per capita' as 'an expression of American dominance' *vis-à-vis* their international rivals (p. 154). But it was obviously a manifestation of something very different – that is the dominance of US capital over US labor. Panitch and Gindin's reference to American capitalism's 'stunning proficiency in revolutionizing the forces of production and communication' (p. 155) must therefore be taken with a large grain of salt. In fact, the average annual growth of labor productivity (GDP/hour) from 1979 through 2000, at a mere 1.4 percent (1.5 percent for 1990–2000), was barely half that from 1948 through 1969, at 2.65 percent, and more than 20 percent below that of the 1970s. Indeed, *it was almost 40 percent below the average for the entire 90-year period between 1890 and 1980, at 2.3 percent.* Not surprisingly, average annual real wage growth for the private economy for the same twenty-year period was a flat *zero.* The 'remarkable dynamism of capitalism revealed', according to Panitch and Gindin (p. 155), in the two decades following the Volcker shock thus expressed itself in by far the worst productivity and real wage performances for any comparable period during the entire twentieth century! (Maddison 1991: 71; US Bureau of Labor Statistics 2004).

The reason that US economic performance from the time of the Volcker shock through 2000 failed to surpass that of the 1970s, let alone that of the 1950s and 1960s or the 1890s and 1900s, is that, *contra* the contentions of Panitch and Gindin, the fundamental problem that first manifested itself between 1965 and 1973 and propelled the economy from boom to downturn in those years did not come to an end with the end of the 1970s, but perpetuated itself through the end of the century. That problem was the fall,

Table 11.2 Long boom versus long downturn (percent change)

	1948–1959	1959–1969	1948–1969*	1969–1979	1979–1990	1990–2000	1979–2000*
GDP	3.7	4.6	4.15	3.3	2.9	3.2	3.05
GDP/hour	2.9	2.4	2.65	1.8	1.3	1.5	1.4
GDP/capita	1.95	3.04	2.5	2.18	1.97	2.04	2
Real wage (manufacturing)	3.4	1.6	2.5	0.8	−0.4	0.4	0
New capital stock (private economy)	3	3.9	3.45	3.8	3	2.9	2.95

Notes: Intervals correspond roughly to business cycles, sometimes grouped together, peak to peak: 1949–1959 inclusive; 1960–1969 inclusive; 1970–1979 inclusive; 1980–1990 inclusive; 1991–2000 inclusive.

Sources: Bureau of Labor Statistics, *Industry Analytical Ratios and Basic Industry Data for the Total Economy*, folder, 6 May 2004; *For profit rates, see R. Brenner, 'Profit Rates and Productivity Growth: Definitions and Sources,' in *The Boom and the Bubble. The US in the World Economy*, 2002, Appendix 1; BLS, 'Hourly Earnings of Production Workers in Manufacturing' (BLS website); BLS, CPI-U (1982–1984).

and failure to recover, of the rate of profit. In the wake of Volcker's harsh medicine, profitability in the non-farm economy for the 1980s business cycles was the lowest for any comparable period during the post-war epoch, and lower in 1989 than in 1979. Despite the major revival of the US profit rate between 1985 and 1995, during the comparable long business cycle of the 'roaring 90s', average profitability failed to rise above the level sustained during that of the 1970s and remained about 17 percent below that of the entire long boom between 1948 and 1969.

I would emphasize that the drop-off in economic performance has not been confined to the US, but has been even more striking throughout Western Europe and Japan, where the major macro-economic indicators have continually deteriorated, decade by decade, since the 1960s. Put another way, the US economic performance weakened in absolute terms, but less so than that of Western Europe and Japan (Brenner 2002a: 47). Even so, pace Panitch and Gindin, it should not be thought that in the recent period the US has outperformed Europe. By the end of the century, a number of West European economies, including France and Italy, had succeeded in closing the once-enormous productivity gap between the US and themselves, the *level* of their output per hour having climbed higher than that of the US. During the past decade (1993–2003), moreover, the *growth* of productivity in Euroland as a whole has been a bit higher than in the US,[1] while the increase of GDP/capita has been virtually the same[2] (Daly 2004: 1–3). The slowdown of the last quarter of the twentieth century was thus generalized, reflecting the profound interdependence of the system's parts, and resulted from the system-wide failure of profitability to recover, not only in the US, but across the advanced capitalist economies as a whole. The central problem that I have, therefore, sought to confront is what was responsible for the high profit rates in the advanced capitalist economies in general and the US in particular, that underpinned the long boom and what caused the generalized decline and failure of recovery of the profit rate that was the source of the long downturn through 2000 (Table 11.3).

Table 11.3   Net profit rate for the US non-farm economy, 1948–2000 (percent)

	1948–1959	1959–1969	1948–1969	1969–1979	1979–1990	1990–2000
Net profit rate (non-farm economy)	13.53	14.21	13.87	11.47	9.89	11.85
Net profit rate (corporate)	12.12	13.57	12.845	9.99	9.02	10.65
Net profit rate (non-financial corporate)	11.62	13.14	12.38	9.59	8.8	9.7

The US power and the post-war boom: the potentials and limits of hegemony

What lay behind the continuing high rates of profit that sustained the post-war boom for at least two decades was, I have argued, a dynamic process of uneven development. This was itself made possible by a powerful, if conflictual and self-undermining, symbiosis, underwritten by the US state, between an earlier developing bloc of capital in the US – characterized by technological leadership, more advanced socio-economic evolution, and the hegemonic position of the state and dominant class – and later developing blocs of capital in Western Europe and Japan – marked by technological followership, retarded socio-economic evolution, and the hegemonized position of the associated states and ruling classes.

As a consequence of the US economy's earlier development, especially the extended period of capital accumulation during the decade of the 1940s, its leading industrial corporations faced relatively high, and rising costs, and the relatively restricted growth of domestic demand. The huge buildup of fixed sunk capital embodying the latest techniques discouraged new entrants, thus new investment and productivity growth. The parallel shrinking of the 'surplus army of unemployed' in declining agricultural and small business sectors weakened the supply response to the increased demand for labor, provoked by rapid capital accumulation. A residually powerful labor movement was well positioned to exploit tight labor markets, so as to secure large wage increases. Still, those same corporations that were so constrained at home enjoyed unchallenged technological superiority and unmatched financial strength on a world scale, and were therefore fully prepared to invade the most promising international markets, especially through foreign direct investment that allowed them to combine the most advanced techniques with relatively skilled lower-waged labor.

By contrast, as a consequence of their later development, West European and Japanese firms enjoyed historically unprecedented prospects for keeping down costs and thereby sustaining high rates of profit, even while responding to the rapid growth of demand by sustaining high rates of capital accumulation. Due to their position as technological followers and later developers, European and Japanese producers were not only relatively little burdened by sunk fixed capital embodying obsolescent technology, but enjoyed huge possibilities for catch-up – to cut costs by adopting cheap but advanced US technology, as well as through innovating by way of the learning by doing and the economies of scale that naturally accompanied the rapid build-up of new plant and equipment. Due to their relative socio-economic backwardness, European and Japanese producers could also take advantage of the huge pools of underemployed workers that populated their still relatively large rural and small business sectors, so as to keep wage growth relatively low compared to productivity growth, as they ramped up investment and employment.

Meanwhile, impelled, as a question of survival, to stand up to competition on the world market from the first-comers – the UK, then the US – they had evolved a series of institutional forms that specially fitted them to hothouse technical change and accelerate the growth of productivity in the interest of lower costs – in particular, by constituting close relationships between the great manufacturing corporations and great banks who financed them over the long run, as well as by participating in various forms of vertical and horizontal networks, which made possible greater inter-firm coordination and cooperation and thereby allowed for greater planning, reduced input costs, and more secure markets. Finally, highly interventionist, mercantilist states were ready to 'repress finance' so as to impel the allocation of funds to domestic manufacturing – and away from international lending speculation, and (in the case of Japan) domestic consumption – while providing the protection and subsidies required to enhance the capacity of domestic business to conquer world export markets.

In this situation, the most powerful forces in the US economy, bent on globalization, turned out to have an overriding interest in the regeneration of the national economies of their nascent rivals in Western Europe and Japan. The US multinational corporations, along with the banks that helped to finance them, seeking to expand beyond the relatively slow-growing domestic market, needed profitable fields abroad for their overseas direct investment. Domestically based manufacturers, needing to increase exports, required fast-growing overseas demand for their goods. An imperial US government, aiming to contain communism and keep the world safe for free enterprise, sought economic success for its allies and rivals as the indispensable foundation for the political stability of the post-war capitalist order. This meant, counter-intuitively, that the dominant elements in the US economy had come to depend for their own prosperity upon nurturing the capacity of their allies and rivals to realize their economic potentials via the achievement of rapid investment- and export-oriented growth, focused on their manufacturing sectors. In the event, a hegemonic US state was ultimately willing to tolerate the erection by their prospective rivals of protective barriers to their domestic markets, restricted mobility of capital, undervalued exchange rates, the repression of finance, and relatively easy access to the US market, in aid of their more rapid capital accumulation and overseas sales. Meanwhile, it imposed a high dollar and subsidized its own foreign direct investment through tax breaks and the like, so as to promote the globalization of its multinationals and banks, while demanding of its allies and rivals that they not cash in their dollars for gold, despite the USs ever-mounting balance of payments deficits. Based on the interdependence of European and Japanese domestic manufacturers, who prospered especially by seizing great chunks of the world export market from their US competitors, and US multinationals corporations and commercial banks, who thrived especially through massive direct foreign investment, especially in manufacturing, there followed the greatest boom in world history... characterized, as a consequence of its unbalanced foundations, by unprecedented growth for Western Europe and the relative decline of the US domestic economy (Brenner 1998: 39–48, 2002a: 9–15).

Konings appears to accept the foregoing picture, so far as it goes. He finds it, however, wanting in one, very fundamental, respect: its insufficient appreciation of the creative role of US imperial power. What Konings wishes to bring out is how the US state constituted a framework of international institutions that shaped, rather than being shaped by, system-wide economic imperatives. He wants to elucidate, in turn, how that framework spoke, for this reason, to the interests of US capital in particular; the way in which this framework thus induced the construction of national capitalisms in Europe and Japan profoundly subordinate to, irrevocably bound to, and incapable of challenging that of the US; and why it is therefore incongruous to understand this framework as leading to the weakening of the US economy.

Konings is thus willing to accept my understanding of the contrasting politico-cum-institutional configurations of the earlier developing versus later developing national capitalisms in terms of their divergent relationships to the competitive pressures of the world market. He nevertheless sees it as 'ultimately flawed by its failure to grasp the role of institutions in the formation of those very [system-wide] economic imperatives', or competitive constraints. 'What marked the postwar period', he asserts, 'was not just the quantitative extension of the capitalist market economy, but the expansion of a very specific kind of economic dynamic'; and this was because 'institutions of American power were not just grafted on to a pre-constituted generically conceived international economy, but were themselves constitutive of, and had a transformative impact on, this order' (p. 196). 'It is', he proclaims, 'this element of constitutive asymmetry and in-built bias at the heart of the world economy (as opposed to countries' uneven development in a given global economic structure) that is lost in Brenner's account of the post-war period' (p. 201).

In fact, of course, Konings notwithstanding, the 'element of constitutive asymmetry and in-built bias' that defined the US hegemonic position, along with its technological leadership and advanced socio-economic structure, is at the very core of my characterization of the earlier-developing US economic bloc, and therefore a defining and determining element in the process of the uneven post-war development that I attempt to chart. Indeed, as should be evident, Koning's own formulation mirrors my own view (above) of the foundational role of the US hegemon in fashioning the post-war international economic order. Nevertheless, the conception that Konings wishes to derive from this – of the US state as unmoved mover of the international system, unlimited in its initiatives by the pre-existing economy – is unsustainable. This is because the exercise of US power in forming and reproducing the institutions of the global economic order was itself, despite Konings'

contentions to the contrary, decisively constrained precisely by the requirements for the economic reproduction of the capitalist system as a whole,
thus of the requisites for profit-making of its constituent parts. It was also
consistently plagued by the conflicting needs and interests of the different
sections of its own national capital: multinational versus domestic, manufacturing versus finance, and so forth. As it would throughout the entire
post-war epoch, the US retained from the start the initiative in shaping and
reshaping the international political economy. But it was never able to
escape the contradictory pressures that derived from either its own reliance
on the health of its rivals and competitors that derived from economic
interdependence, or the built-in conflicts of interest of its capitalist constit-
uency.

On the morrow of World War II, the US state dominated the capitalist
world economically and politically to an extent without historical precedent.
Free to dictate terms in the interest of the leading sections of its own capitalist
class, it initially sought to put in place, via the Bretton Woods agreement,
the famous 'multilateral world order', also known as 'the imperialism of free
trade and investment'. This constituted an 'equal playing field', to which all
would have equal access by virtue of the unfettered movement of commodities
and capital, smoothed by currency convertibility. Not coincidentally, under
such free market conditions, both US manufacturers and financiers could be
expected to dominate the world economy by virtue of their overwhelming
competitive advantage. Nevertheless, the fact remains that the Bretton
Woods perspective for international economic policy and institutions, vig-
orously pursued by the US government between 1945 and 1947 with the
enthusiastic support of the leading US industrial corporations and banks,
turned out to be profoundly counter-productive for US capital, even
though essentially imposed by the US government. A huge 'dollar gap'
quickly opened up, manifesting enormous trade and payments deficits for
the European and Japanese economies, resulting from their inability to
compete with American capitalists in either commodity or capital markets.
This drove overseas governments, aiming to reduce their deficits so as to
gain control of their economies, toward a variety of protectionist and bilateral
trade arrangements that threatened, in turn, to drive the world economy
back toward the collapse into autarchy that had accompanied the inter-war
depression, while opening the way to left-wing perspectives both domestically
and internationally...not to mention the further maturation of working-class
resistance.

The upshot was that the untrammeled exercise of US power in its own
immediate interest, without regard to the imperatives of systemic economic
reproduction, threatened to undermine the very overseas markets that all of the
different sections of the US capital required in order to themselves develop.
In this situation, the US had little choice but to back off and accept, on
a long-term basis, the protectionist barriers, the statist policies, the organized

capitalism, the repression of finance, and the undervalued exchange rates that, as already explained, made it possible for the European and Japanese economies to pursue their export-oriented paths to prosperity. This did enable the US's greatest industrial corporations and banks to thrive by taking the road to globalization. But, in the process it disadvantaged its own domestically based manufacturers on the world market, ultimately including the US itself. As a consequence of the US acceptance of capital controls and a quite delayed move to currency convertibility, it also clipped the wings for the time being of its greatest financiers. Contrary to Konings' assertions, the international institutions and policies that could feasibly be imposed by the US were indeed 'ultimately at the mercy of and subordinate to the structural determinations of the global market economy', including the US itself (p. 195 *emphasis added*) (Block 1977: 43–91; Eichengreen 1996a: 93–133; Brenner 1999: 72).

Because the US was in the end obliged, in the interests of its own leading capitalists and its state, to accept politico-institutional arrangements required by its allies and rivals in order to better compete with US companies on the world market, the claim of Konings, following Panitch and Gindin, who themselves follow Poulantzas, that 'a new type of non-territorial imperialism, [was] implanted and maintained ... through the "induced reproduction of the form of the dominant imperial power within each national formation and its state"' (p. 198; Panitch 2000: 9) is misleading. Despite the penetration of the US multinationals and banks into the heart of Europe and (to a much lesser extent) Japan, the statist, organized capitalisms, through which West European and Japanese economies developed with America's blessing, diverged sharply in form from that of the US, despite adopting much American technology and management technique. Far from opening the way to US economic takeover, they served to found a powerful challenge by West European and Japanese corporations to the dominant position of American firms on the world market.

Against this background, the idea of Konings and of Panitch and Gindin that, by imposing the post-war institutional order, and thereby facilitating the penetration of US industrial and financial capital into Europe, the US 'bound' the capitalisms of Western Europe and Japan to itself is extraneous. The manufacturing-cum-banking capitals of these economies saw international economic integration as their highest priority, for they understood with crystal clarity that their fate was tied to that of the US, not only because they relied so heavily for their expansion on access to the US domestic market, but also because they depended so greatly for their technical progress and capital accumulation on access to US capital goods imports and US finance. Panitch and Gindin, again following Poulantzas, attribute the failure of the West European or Japanese to challenge US hegemony, even at the height of the economic/financial crisis at the end of the 1960s, to the penetration of US multinationals and banks, as a result of which 'domestic capital tended to be "dis-articulated" and no longer represented by a coherent and independent national bourgeoisie' (Panitch and Gindin 2004: 19). In fact, the West European and Japanese governments, and the capitalist classes they represented, continued to acquiesce in a world economic order constituted and reproduced by the US hegemony not because the implantation of US multinationals prevented them from acting coherently in their own interest, but because this was by far their best option, as is confirmed by the fact that the Japanese went along no less than did the West Europeans, even though the penetration of the US multinationals into Japan was minimal.

Konings finds particularly objectionable my argument that the powerful trend toward the ever-faster increase of investment overseas by US manufacturers compared to that at home – which is a central component of my account of the US economic trajectory during the post-war boom (Brenner 1998: 55–6, 62–3) – responded to the relatively higher costs of production and the relatively slower growth of demand in the US, compared to Western Europe and Japan, as well as to elevated protectionist barriers in these places. Far from 'capital flight', argues Konings, the 'migration of companies from the US was part of a state project [and] capitalist strategy, rather than an expression of competitive weakness [of production based in the US]' (p. 198). In fact, the fundamental reason that US multinational corporations made the penetration of Western Europe and (to a much lesser extent Japan) such a high priority, and that the US government sought to frame post-war international economic institutions to facilitate this, was precisely because returns from foreign direct investment in manufacturing promised, and turned out, to be so relatively high. *Pace* Konings, this did indeed amount to capital flight, undercutting the US domestic economy, even though it represented not the weakness but strength of US multinationals.

The decline in the rate of profit, 1965–1973: manufacturing overcapacity or class struggle?

In the end, it is hard to see how Konings can persist in denying, *a la* Panitch and Gindin, that the operation of the US-sponsored post-war international economic order, in general and the internationalization of the US economy in particular, undercut the US, in view of the fact that it was precisely the intensification of international competition from the US's leading partners and rivals, leading to system-wide overcapacity in manufacturing, that set off the dramatic fall in the rate of profit in the US that brought to an end the long post-war boom. Beginning in the mid-1960s, the extension, and accentuation of the very same processes of uneven development that had made for unprecedented, though mal-distributed, economic expansion, within a US-dominated framework of international economic institutions, began to undermine it. Manufacturers based in the later-developing economic blocs – most notably in Japan and Germany – were able to combine relatively advanced techniques and relatively low wages to sharply reduce relative costs *vis-à-vis* those required to produce the same goods in the earlier developing US. On this basis, and with the help of increasingly undervalued exchange rates, they not only succeeded in imposing their relatively low prices on the world market so as to dramatically swell their shares of that market, but were also simultaneously able, precisely by virtue of their relatively reduced costs, to maintain their old rates of profit. The US producers thus found themselves facing slower-growing prices for their output, but were caught with inflexible costs as a result of their being lumbered with plant and equipment that embodied production methods that had been rendered too costly, as well as relatively high wage levels that could not quickly be squeezed downward. Those capitals that could no longer make the prevailing average rate of profit, even on their variable capital alone, had to shed productive capital and/or reduce capacity utilization. Others, in order to hold on to their markets, had little choice but to swallow significantly reduced rates of profit on their fixed capital, since they could not raise prices above costs as much as they had previously.

As a consequence of the unexpected irruption of lower-priced products on the world market, US manufacturers turned out to have over-invested, and were prevented from raising prices in line with labor and capital costs. The overall outcome was that, while the lower-cost and lower-price manufacturers of the later-developing economies succeeded in maintaining their profit rates, US manufacturers were unable to avoid very sharply reduced rates of return. This made for a declining aggregate rate of profit in the international manufacturing sector of about 25 percent in the G-7 economies taken in aggregate, which was manifested in system-wide overcapacity, and was the inexorable result. This decline came to be more evenly shared-out when the dollar was sharply devalued, and the yen and mark sharply revalued, between 1969 and 1973, and German and Japanese manufacturers came to shoulder much of the burden previously carried solely by their US counterparts.

The decisive role of intensified international competition leading to manufacturing overcapacity in forcing down profit rates was evidenced by the striking fact that the decline in the rate of profit was largely confined to the manufacturing sector, composed mostly of tradables and therefore vulnerable to international competition, while barely affecting the non-manufacturing sector, composed mostly of non-tradables and therefore largely protected from international competition. Whereas manufacturing profitability fell by 43.5 percent in the US between 1965 and 1973, non-manufacturing profitability fell by only 13.9 percent in the same period (9 percent, if no adjustment is made for the indirect business taxes that cut increasingly into non-manufacturing profits, but not manufacturing profits). This was the case even though labor productivity grew much faster and real wages grew significantly less rapidly in manufacturing than in non-manufacturing, so that *overall production costs increased much more slowly in manufacturing than in non-manufacturing* (Brenner 1998: 93–107).

Panitch and Gindin and Konings, though failing to come to grips with the foregoing argument, attempt to transcend it by advancing a version of the view that the fall in the rate of profit that drove the world economy from boom to crisis resulted from the strength of the working class, and by arguing – implicitly in the case of Panitch and Gindin and explicitly in the case of Konings – that I am able to maintain my own interpretation only by ignoring class struggle or treating it in mechanical terms, neglecting 'class as agency' (p. 195). According to Panitch and Gindin, '[s]teady growth raised workers expectations at the same time as the exhaustion of the singular conditions existing in the post-war years eroded the system's ability to continue to deliver.' (p. 147). The onset of 'the well-known productivity slowdown....at the same time as worker militancy was resisting any downward pressures in wages' thus made for a wages-productivity squeeze on profits that was ultimately 'rooted in the strength of labor (relative to capital's capabilities)' (p. 197).

But, as I have argued at length elsewhere, this interpretation has fatal problems, not least because its theorization, in terms of technological difficulties and workers' power, prevents it from explaining why the crisis of profitability was largely focused on manufacturing and only lightly touched non-manufacturing. Doubts are heightened, when it is realized that there is evidence neither of 'the well-known productivity slowdown', nor of the operation of either of the two possible causes of it advanced by Panitch and Gindin – the using up of technological potential or of a rising share of output in non-manufacturing where productivity growth was ostensibly slower than in manufacturing. Between 1938 and 1965, productivity growth outside manufacturing was just as fast as within it, so there can be no presumption that a shift to non-manufacturing makes for productivity slowdown. Moreover, between 1965 and 1973, when profitability fell, both labor and capital productivity in the non-farm economy as a whole continued to grow at almost exactly the same pace as between 1950 and 1965 (Brenner 1998: 241, 2002a: 24).

The fact is, as Panitch and Gindin realize, labor productivity growth in the manufacturing sector, where most of the decline of profitability took place, actually increased as the rate of profit fell. As a result, they are obliged to contend that 'sustaining productivity growth in manufacturing required relatively more capital inputs than hitherto' (p. 147),...which is another way of saying that a drop-off in capital productivity that more than offsets the rise in labor productivity was behind the fall in the manufacturing rate of profit. Nevertheless, the fact remains that there was no fall to speak of in manufacturing capital productivity – by which is meant the *real* (price adjusted) output–capital ratio – in the relevant period, thus no manufacturing productivity problem whatsoever. The *nominal* output–capital ratio did fall sharply in manufacturing and played a major role in reducing the manufacturing profit rate. This was no reflection of declining productivity growth, but was attributable instead to the downward pressure on prices that plagued manufacturing as a consequence of international competition and overcapacity. Non-manufacturers experienced about the same rate of growth of their real output–capital ratio (capital productivity) as did manufacturers, but were able for the most part to avoid a decline in their nominal output–capital ratio by raising output prices in a way manufacturers could not precisely because they were sheltered from the world market (Brenner 1998: 95–108, 2002a: 16–24).

What about wage growth and the power of and pressure from labor? The reality runs directly counter to the assertions of Konings and Panitch and Gindin. From the end of the 1950s, and again from the middle of the 1960s, it was not workers but employers, mainly in the manufacturing sector, who initiated the step-up in class conflict, introducing in the process major innovations with regard to both strategy and organization for fighting labor. They did so, in each case – pace Konings, who may regard this explanation as 'mechanical' – in response to the onset of intensifying international competition and sharp downward pressure on the manufacturing rate of profit: initially after the mid 1950s, again from the mid-1960s. The outcome was that, over the course of the period, employers were able to achieve much success in weakening labor organization, as is indicated by major declines in the proportion unionized and of the percentage of National Labor Relations Board (NLRB) union representation elections won, as well as the gap between wage gains won in the unionized versus non-unionized sectors of the economy (Brenner 1998: 58–62, 108–11). It should not then be surprising that, contrary to what Panitch and Gindin contend, workers' resistance was unable to prevent manufacturers employers from securing major *reductions* in the growth of wages during the 1960s and early 1970s, as manufacturing real wage increase between 1965 and 1973 was more than a third lower than that between 1948 and 1965. This did not, of course, prevent the sharp fall in the manufacturing rate of profit, as decreased upward pressure on wages was far more than compensated by increased downward pressure on prices.

That neither 'productivity crisis' nor workers' resistance had much to do with the fall in the rate of profit between 1965 and 1973 is confirmed by the fact that non-manufacturers were hit with real wage increases that were more than 40 percent *higher* than were manufacturers, while having to satisfy themselves with labor productivity growth that was almost a third *lower*, yet experienced only a minimal fall in the rate of profit. Despite sustaining a growth of unit labor costs that was 50 percent higher than in manufacturing, non-manufacturers escaped largely unscathed because, immune as they were from the sort of international competitive pressure and overcapacity that plagued their counterparts in manufacturing, they were able to raise prices to compensate for rising costs with relatively little restraint (see Table 11.4).

Table 11.4   The growth of profitability, prices, and costs, 1965–1973 US manufacturing versus non-manufacturing (average annual percent change)

	Manufacturing	Non-manufacturing
Net profit rate	–5.5	–3
Real wage	1.9	2.7
Labor productivity	3.3	2.35
Capital productivity (real output–capital ratio)	–0.4	0
Capital–output ratio	–3.2	–1.1
Unit labor costs	3.05	4.7

Profitability fell least where pressure on costs was greatest, most where it was weakest.

The response to falling profits in the 1970s: employers' offensive, US counter-attack, and Keynesian deficits

The system-wide fall in profitability, focused on the international manufacturing sector, brought about an enormous transformation in the modus operandi of capitalists and their states. With their survival depending on it, corporations backed up by their governments, had little choice but to turn their every effort to revive their rates of return. The near uniformity of their responses all across the advanced capitalist world, stage by stage and period by period – an ever-deepening employers' offensive against labor, accompanied by Keynesianism in the 1970s, monetarism in the 1980s, and budget balancing in the 1990s – resulted from extended processes of trial and error, and constitutes a decisive demonstration, if any further were needed, of the power of the structural constraints, operating on an international system-wide basis, about which Konings expresses such doubt.

Employers' offensive and Keynesian deficits

Above all, employers in every advanced capitalist country, without exception, quite suddenly abandoned their *relatively* accommodating attitude of the previous two decades toward the growth of wages, direct and indirect, which had been conditioned by high profit rates and record economic growth. Launching an ever-more implacable assault upon workers that was designed to revive their reduced profitability, they succeeded virtually overnight in radically reducing the increase of salaries and benefits, as well as of government social spending... and were ever more successful as time went on in extinguishing it. Indeed, one of the most telling demonstrations of the overriding constraint on government policy represented by the requirements of profitability and capital accumulation is the virtual termination, by the 1980s, of the growth of social spending across all the capitalist economies,

Table 11.5 Employers offensive: the growth of real wages and social expenditures

	RW 1960–1973	SE 1960–1975	RW 1973–1979	SE 1975–1980	RW 1979–1990	SE 1980–1985
US	2.8	6.5	0.3	2	0.4	2.7
Japan	7.7	8.5	2.8	8.2	1.6	3.2
Germany	5.4	4.8	2.5	2	1	2.7
EU-11	5.6	7.6	2.8	4.2	0.9	2.6

Sources: 'Statistic Annex,' *European Economy*, no. 71, 2001, Table 31; OECD, *Social Expenditures 1960–1989*, Paris, Table 31; *Social Expenditures 1989*, Paris, p. 28; OECD, *The Future of Social Protection*, Paris, 1988, p. 11.

whether they had social democratic or conservative governments or coordinated or liberal capitalisms, and whatever the relative strength of labor. Put another way, the variation *over time* in the growth of the welfare state, as the profitability crisis and economic stagnation became ever-more pressing from 1973, is far greater than the variation *over space*, across the advanced capitalist countries (Table 11.5).

Simultaneously, again with near unanimity, governments turned to deficit spending and super-low interest rates in an effort to keep the economy turning over. Contra Panitch and Gindin this was not, for the most part – and least of all in the US – out of fear of resistance from workers or social movements... although no administration seeking re-election wished to be associated with austerity and recession if it could help it. Keynesianism was the near universal first choice of the authorities because it was their soft option, expressing the elite consensus that the downturn would be easily reversed, and above all the desire of the ruling class to avoid the huge costs to capital, in terms of profits and bankruptcies that would have been – and eventually were – entailed by the alternative policy of structural adjustment. The pain of monetarism would not be imposed until it became unavoidable.

Failure of profitability to recover

Despite the extraordinary success of the employers' offensive in *immediately* bringing about a sharp reduction in the growth of direct and indirect wage costs, neither the advanced capitalist countries in general, nor the US in particular, succeeded to the slightest degree in reviving profit rates over the course of the 1970s. This persistence of reduced profitability, in the face of workers' inability to prevent *further* very major reductions in their pay, demonstrates that, despite the claims of Panitch, Gindin and Konings, there is no more to the idea that labor perpetuated the crisis than that it initiated it. But it also raises questions concerning my own argument. If overcapacity in manufacturing, stemming from intensified international competition, was the initial source of the fall of the rate of profit, why wasn't the problem soon transcended through the standard market mechanism of reallocation of resources? Specifically, why did not corporations redirect investment out of over-subscribed low-profit lines sufficiently to bring about the restoration of the rate of return?

The answer to the foregoing question seems to me to be threefold. Leading manufacturing corporations, in possession of proprietary capital in the form of technological knowledge, as well as networks of customers and suppliers, believed they had a better chance to prosper by remaining in their own field and fighting via cost-cutting to increase market share than by switching to a new line with which they were unfamiliar. At the same time, the ongoing process of uneven development opened the way for producers in parts of the developing world, above all East Asia, to profit handsomely from entering even oversubscribed industries by combining the most advanced technology with low wages. Meanwhile, governments across the advanced capitalist world made it possible for both incumbents and new entrants to add capacity to already over-supplied lines without plunging the economy into recession, by subsidizing demand through increased public borrowing. The upshot was that the initial problem of overcapacity leading to reduced profit rates remained unresolved: profitability in 1978–1979 was no higher than in 1973 (Brenner 1998: 147–52).

Konings expresses skepticism concerning this account. Asserting that I fail to grasp how early came the shift to finance, he asserts that manufacturers' primary response to falling profits was not to fall back on their manufacturing prowess, but to move into consumer lending and the like – 'a diversion of a growing proportion of their income and cash flows from investment in fixed capital and commodities and accumulation through financial channels' (p. 201). But this ignores the economy's fundamental trends and basic contours.

Even after they had absorbed a reduction in their rate of return of more than 40 percent between 1965 and 1973, US manufacturers, between 1973 and 1979, maintained the growth of their investment at just about the same high rates as at the height of the boom, while continuing to provide about 25 percent of the economy's total non-residential investment in this period, compared to the mere 6–7 percent provided by the financial sector. It could hardly be clearer that US manufacturers sought to invest their way out of their profitability and competitiveness problems, and that their refusal to reduce the rate of growth of their capital stock vastly exacerbated the international overcapacity that underpinned the crisis (Brenner 1998: 161–4).

As earlier developer and hegemon, the post-war US distinguished itself from its later developing rivals by the powerful and relatively free position of its financial sector in international markets. Throughout the 1940s and 1950s, the US government sought to open the world for its banks to the most profitable investment opportunities. Though largely frustrated for a time by the highly regulated character of the post-war political economy of its competitors and partners, its efforts were crowned by the establishment of the Eurodollar market as an unregulated center of international financial activity in the early to mid-1960s, undoubtedly the turning point in the freeing-up of international finance. But the fact remains that, despite Konings contention to the contrary, even in the US, the decisive shift toward finance failed to take place in response to the initial fall in the rate of profit. With its top priority being the restoration of manufacturing competitiveness and profitability, as well as macro-economic stability, the US government adopted expansionary policies that issued in high inflation, negative real interest rates, and a plummeting dollar – conditions that could hardly have proved more discouraging to financial sector profit-making and expansion (Brenner 1999: 73, 2002a: 81).

Konings also wonders why the rise of industry in the Less Developed Countries (LDCs) did not provide the markets needed to absorb manufacturing over-supply. It could of course have had that effect, had rising LDC output proved mainly complementary to that of the advanced capitalist economies. But, as is well understood, the rationale for the establishment of new manu-facturing capacity, especially in East Asia, was – by means of emulation via technological borrowing from the advanced economies (rather than new inventions) – to provide goods already being produced in the core with equal efficiency but lower wage costs, so as to seize market share by forcing down prices. As a result, the entry of the NICs, and LDCs more generally, had the effect not so much of expanding markets as for depressing profitability in the core economies, and provoking increasingly aggressive protectionist responses.

The US counter-attack

Against the background of continuing systemic overcapacity and reduced profitability in manufacturing, the US government made great efforts to assist domestic producers to respond to international manufacturing competition and shift the weight of the profitability fall to their rivals overseas, while offering enhanced support to the US financial sector. Its pivotal step in this direction was to abandon the Bretton Woods system between 1968 and 1973, refusing any longer to honor its pledge to convert dollars held overseas into gold or to redeem foreign currencies at a fixed rate. The turn to floating exchange rates enabled the US to save the dollar as key currency, yet avoid the resort to tight credit and recession that would otherwise have been required in order to sustain its value by erasing current account deficits. It thereby freed successive administrations to implement a host of interrelated policies that would have been unfeasible under the old system: to sustain Keynesian public deficits and negative real interest rates so as to keep the economy turning over; to bring down the exchange rate of the dollar so as to increase international competitiveness by welcoming the current account deficits that were the inevitable concomitant of those public deficits; to reduce by the same means the value of the 'overhang' of dollars held by partners and rivals overseas; and, especially in the wake of the government's moves to end capital controls in 1973–1974, to open up the vast new field of the trading and hedging of floating currencies for its highly competitive financial sector (Brenner 2002a: 26–30). Konings, inexplicably, complains that I fail to see the 'crumbling of Bretton Woods' as 'the beginning of an attempt by the US to break out of the what had become the restrictive arrangements of the post-war order' (p. 199), when it should be self-evident that that is precisely what I argue.

Konings argues that the break from the constraints of the Bretton Woods order enabled the US government and the US capitalists to not only adopt a series of new strategies that would have been ruled out under the old system, but also free itself from the contradictions inherent in these new departures. Due to the continuation of the dollar as key currency, in the context of floating rates and ever-freer capital markets, the US economy could now, according to Konings, 'exercise unlimited seignorage privilege', 'be much less vulnerable to the disciplinary pressures of international finance', and 'largely freed...from the balance of payments constraint' (p. 200). But, the illusion that the dollar-dollar standard rendered the US somehow immune from the economic laws of gravity was demolished before the decade was out, and would be again and again over the next two decades. The US could run exploding current account deficits, but only so long as rising asset prices attracted foreign funds to finance it. But the rising dollar that could not but accompany such influxes from overseas inevitably undermined domestic competitiveness. This would further amplify current account deficits, while raising doubts about both their ability to be financed and of the dollar to retain its value...leading to the decline of both asset prices and the dollar, tending to restore both competitiveness and the current account.

Thus, as the 1970s wore on, US policies for economic expansion and currency devaluation proved themselves decreasingly capable of restoring profitability or vitality, and issued instead in record-breaking current account deficits and runaway inflation. As a result, they ended up endangering the dollar's very position as key currency, upon which those very policies, not to mention the international financial system, were predicated. With the current account deficit rising, the demand for dollars with respect to other currencies continued to fall, and the demand for US financial assets at a time in which real interest rates had fallen below zero was unable to compensate. There ensued a series of ever-more devastating runs on the dollar, and these made it simply impossible to continue with deficit-driven expansion (Brenner 2002a: 34–5). Bluntly put, precisely the de-regulated global financial markets and dollar-dollar system that, in Konings' view, allowed the dollar to exploit without limit its role as key currency, provided the basis upon which international financiers imposed the discipline, from which the US was supposedly invulnerable, in order to enforce the balance of payments constraint from which the US was supposedly free. As a result, US capitalism was obliged to submit to precisely the sort of structural adjustment program from which its privileged place in the international financial order ostensibly protected it.

The turn to monetarism and neoliberalism: no miracle of the market

Konings contends that 'my analysis remains unclear as to why the monetarist revolution occurred at the moment that it did' (p. 200). But I could hardly have been more explicit that the Volcker shock and its sequels represented the adoption of radically transformed state and corporate strategies, in order to confront the same fundamental but still unresolved problem of sharply reduced profitability leading to economic stagnation that had initially provoked the adoption of Keynesianism. It took place as a consequence of the fact that 'the attempt of US manufacturers during the 1970s to invest their way out of their problems with the help of the government's deficit spending, cheap money, and dollar devaluation policies had failed dismally' (Brenner 2002a: 48). As a result, by the end of the decade, unprecedented inflation and historic current account deficits were, as just noted, precipitating runs on the dollar that demanded decisive action if the dollar's status as key currency was to be preserved. Totally reversing the expansionary trends of the previous decade, the shift to Reaganomics constituted a major turning point in post-war economic evolution by bringing in ultra-tight credit, a super-high dollar, tax breaks to the corporations, and major steps toward financial de-regulation. It was intended, most generally, to push up unemployment so as to further reduce wage pressure all across the economy. But it also aimed to restructure the economy: to counter overcapacity by shaking out the huge ledge of high-cost low-profit means of production that still held down manufacturing profitability; to directly redistribute income from labor to capital; to reduce inflation in the interest of manufacturing competitiveness and profits on lending; and to speed up the reallocation of resources into the US financial sector from both domestic and overseas sources, while buttressing its profitability (Brenner 2002a: 35–6).

Konings, like Panitch and Gindin, believes that I fail to sufficiently appreciate the contributions of monetarist austerity, and the ensuing ascent of finance, to US economic recovery. I do believe it was a mixed bag. As I go out of my way to emphasize and document – despite inexplicable assertions to the contrary by Panitch and Gindin – the titanic shakeout precipitated by the Volcker interest rate shock and the resulting run-up of the dollar did constitute the 'necessary pre-conditions for the recovery of international competitiveness and of profitability' (Brenner 2002a: 50) by eliminating great masses of high-cost low-profit means of production and initiating the revival of manufacturing productivity, as well as by detonating an extended period of stagnating or declining wages (Brenner 1998: 156, 183, 190, 197, 199, 2002a: 37, 50–2, 59). But the accompanying blow to both investment and consumer demand discouraged the laying down of new plant and equipment and held back growth more generally for an extended period. Moreover, *contra* Konings, I see the accompanying state-led and corporate-led financial expansions of Reagan's 'decade of deals' as doing little for the US economic recovery, while driving the economy from one impasse to another and leaving it by the turn of the decade in the greatest debt crisis of the post-war epoch.

Contradictions of Reaganomics

Konings is impressed by what he believes to have been the unique capacity of the US to pull off the Volcker shock and to finance, partly from abroad, the ensuing record build-up of government deficits. He seems to forget that the UK successfully accomplished a parallel shift to tight money and industrial shakeout slightly before the US, while Germany sustained its own tight credit regime further into the 1980s than did the US. As to the huge flow of funds to cover the skyrocketing government debt, this responded not so much to the country's 'extraordinary capacity to sell US debt' (p. 200), as to the most elevated real interest rates of the twentieth century, thus historically unprecedented returns on lending to the government. Even then, as Volcker himself observed, the public deficits were able to be financed without provoking a financial crunch only because the Japanese government incited a massive flood of Japanese money into US Treasuries in a politically – not profitability-driven – effort by Japanese financiers to keep the dollar up (and the yen down), so that Japanese export-oriented growth could continue (Brenner 1998: 183–84, 193, 193 n.3). It is hard to see what was accomplished by this record run-up of public debt and the accompanying inflow of foreign money, aside from the transfer of a true mountain of wealth from US working class taxpayers to America's – and the rest of the world's – very rich.

In any case, Konings' belief in US immunity from the discipline of international financial markets notwithstanding, by early 1985, the balance of payments constraint was once again asserting itself. As a consequence of the skyrocketing dollar that accompanied the inflooding of foreign funds, the current account deficit, made up almost entirely by the surplus of manufacturing imports over exports, was smashing all records, with the result that an accelerating sell-off of the dollar began to depress the value of the currency, just as in the later 1970s. The Reagan administration's attempt to make the US the 'investment capital of the world' had thus brought devastation to the US industrial sector, still, by far, the economy's most important source of profits and capital accumulation. It therefore had little choice but to relinquish its policy of attracting foreign funds through an elevated currency, in favor of manufacturing revival via dollar devaluation. Following the G5's agreement to the Plaza Accord of 1985, the dollar plunged, ceding a third of its value in less than two years (Brenner 2002a: 81–4).

But this abrupt shift came with contradictions of its own. As the US interest rates and the currency declined, the value of dollar-denominated assets plunged, and investors disowned them just as they had embraced them at the start of the decade. The resulting flight of capital opened the way to the crash of the US stock market in October 1987, which might have proved a good deal more serious had the Japanese government not once again come to the rescue (Brenner 2002a: 84–5). Meanwhile, Konings' ostensibly autonomous and self-propelling US current account deficit had proved anything but immune, falling from its record level of 1986 to zero in less than five years. Far from rendering the US and its currency invulnerable, the operation of deep and freed-up US financial markets, in association with the floating dollar-dollar standard, made for massive currency instability and serial crisis.

Lurch to finance and crisis

The US financial sector faced a major problem in this era. The government's moves toward financial de-regulation did, as I have previously emphasized, open the way for capital to lurch sharply in that direction. But how could lenders and speculators make a killing from firms and households in a situation in which non-financial corporations were producing such sharply reduced surpluses with respect to their capital stock and wage earners were so hard-pressed? The difficulty of profiting in a period of powerful downward pressure on profits in international manufacturing had already been forcefully brought home in the course of the 1970s, when commercial banks, facing the drying up of opportunities in the core economies, piled into lending to newly industrializing countries, and ultimately precipitated the catastrophic LDC debt crisis of the early 1980s. The flooding of US Savings and Loan institutions into commercial real estate followed a similar pattern, leading inexorably to bubble and collapse by the end of the decade (Brenner 2002a: 85–6).

Nor did the leveraged buyout craze turn out very differently. The financial engineers in charge did, at the start, manage to net higher returns by means of massive layoffs, refusing to invest, and running down the capital stock of non-financial corporations, while breaking contracts with unions and cutting off long standing relationships with suppliers. This is the grain of truth in the Konings-Panitch-Gindin perspective. But the resulting gains via once-and-for-all productivity improvements and reductions in input costs were soon wiped out, as more people tried to get in on the action, as stock prices rose ever higher, and as the cost of buyouts rose correspondingly, while corporate debt skyrocketed (Long and Ravenscraft 1993). *Contra* Panitch and Gindin, there was little evidence that 'finance had reallocated capital across sectors' from unprofitable to profitable lines. Instead it had made possible an unheard of level of corporate borrowing to enable an orgy of speculation. By the time the decade was over, the non-farm and non-financial corporate sectors faced rates of profit that had failed to rise above their level at the end of the 1970s, as well as paralyzing levels of debt without remote historical precedent. Meanwhile, commercial banks, which had sought a way out by financing the mergers and acquisitions and commercial estate booms found themselves in their worst condition of the post-war epoch, experiencing sharply reduced returns on equity and the greatest wave of bank failures since the Great Depression (White 1992: 13). Despite its enormous expansion, the financial sector's profits as a percentage of total corporate profits were scarcely higher during the 1980s than in the 1970s and its rate of return fell sharply. A decade of monetarism, neoliberal deregulation, and further defeat for labor had, *contra* Konings and Panitch and Gindin, left both non-financial and financial sectors in a weakened condition (Brenner 1998: 193, 2002a: 88–91).

Finally, *pace* Konings (p. 201), I see no reason to alter my characterization of the huge growth of the non-manufacturing sector that took place over the course of the 1980s as expressing economic decline. This is because the growth of non-manufacturing productivity in these years fell to its lowest level for any comparable period during the whole of the twentieth century, while non-manufacturing real wages fell by no less than 10 percent. Had US employers been obliged to operate under the regulations imposed by unions and the state throughout most of Western Europe, which simply rule out the terribly low-paying service sector jobs that dominated the US employment expansion, the US economy would have experienced skyrocketing joblessness, not job creation (Brenner 1998: 204–6).

The US economic revival: the central place of manufacturing

The huge shakeout of high-cost, low-profit means of production that resulted from the imposition of high interest rates and the high dollar constituted a necessary, but far from sufficient, condition for US economic recovery; for, by 1985, US industry was in its worst condition of the post-war epoch. What made possible the major revival that took place during the subsequent decade was a huge, 70 percent increase in the rate of profit in the manufacturing sector, which brought about, *by itself*, a dramatic rise in the overall private (non-farm) rate of profit above its level of 1973 for the first time in a quarter century. In the wake of the rise of profitability, GDP, investment, and productivity all began to increase rapidly from 1992–3. The ascent of the manufacturing rate of profit was attributable in the first place to a huge re-distribution of income from labor to capital, made possible by preventing any increase in the manufacturing real wage for the entire decade, as well as major tax breaks for the corporations. It resulted secondly from a profound devaluation of the dollar, which allowed US producers to impose lower prices and thereby increase profitability, while seizing market share from their competitors. It was the consequence finally of a fall in long-term real interest rates, which derived from a slowdown in inflation that was itself attributable to the deep recessions of the first half of the 1980s and the early 1990s (Brenner 2002a: 48–93).

Konings rejects my focus on the manufacturing sector in explaining the US economic revival. In view of 'the shrinking of the manufacturing base and the growth of the service sector' and what he believes to be the 'diminished salience of industrial accumulation' (p. 201), it is his contention that to evaluate the period primarily in terms of the regeneration of manufacturing is to impose a rather ahistorical standard on history. But this is to ignore the reasons I adduced to justify my argument. While the proportion of manufacturing output and employment in the total certainly fell significantly over the course of the long downturn, the salience of manufacturing in capitalist accumulation hardly declined. As I went out of my way to emphasize, even as late as the middle 1990s, manufacturing was by far the major source of profits for the corporate economy, generating in 1995 no less than 48 percent of total corporate profits – that is profits *gross of interest*. This was almost double that generated by finance at that point. With this in mind, it is easy to see how the variations in manufacturing profitability could have accounted, to such a large extent, for the variations in overall profitability over the course of the long downturn. Since the rate of profit outside manufacturing did not fall very much at any point, it was, as emphasized, the decline and failure to recover of the manufacturing rate of profit that largely accounted for the fall of profitability in the private (non-farm) economy as a whole that lay behind slowed growth. Since, by the same token, the non-manufacturing profit rate failed to rise at all between 1985 and 1995, it was the increase in the manufacturing rate of profit that was totally responsible for the dramatic rise in the private (non-farm) rate of profit that took place in that period, and underpinned the ensuing recovery of the US economy (Brenner 2002a: 71).

On the basis, in the first instance, of the recovery of profitability and the ensuing expansion, the financial sector was finally able to take off, and continued a virtiginous ascent right through the end of the decade. Every major trend ran in its favor. Non-financial corporations boomed, and stepped up their borrowing. Inflation was suppressed, especially as the dollar soared after mid-decade. The Clinton administration pushed banking de-regulation to its logical conclusion, opening the way to the rise of huge commercial banking, investment banking, and insurance conglomerates. The stock market bubble offered historically unmatched opportunities to rake in fees and profits for superintending share issues and mergers and acquisitions, while simultaneously managing the explosion of household and corporate borrowing. Finally, as the decade neared its end, the nascent run-up in

Table 11.6   Financial profits as a percentage of total corporate profits

1948–1959	1959–1969	1969–1979	1979–1990	1990–2000
14	16.7	22.25	24.4	38.5

housing offered still another huge field for raking in profits. Between 1994 and 2000, financial sector profits net of interest doubled, and, because non-financial corporate profits net of interest swooned after 1997, accounted for a stunning 75 percent of the *increase* in total corporate profits net of interest accrued in these years. Having already accounted for 38 percent of total corporate profits net of interest by 1997, financial profits net of interest accounted for 50 percent in 2000! (Table 11.6).

Boom, bubble, bust: limitations of the US recovery

The US economic recovery could not, in the end, sustain itself because, contra Panitch and Gindin and Konings, the fundamental problem that initially precipitated the long downturn – that is, reduced profitability resulting from manufacturing overcapacity on a system-wide basis – had still to be transcended. This was manifested in the fact that, during this era, it was impossible for one major national economy to gain without others losing. The US revival of profitability, occurring as it did by means of currency devaluation and very slow wage growth in both absolute and relative terms – and accompanied as it was by a major slowdown in the growth of the US market – thus came heavily at the expense of the US's leading competitors in Germany and Japan, who experienced their worst recessions of the post-war epoch during the first half of the 1990s (Brenner 2002a: 94–6 ff.). The upshot was that the US government, just shocked by the Mexican crisis and bailout, was obliged to come to their aid in much the same way as they had been required to rescue the US a decade earlier – by way of a major revaluation of the currency. But, just as the yen and mark revaluations following the Plaza Accord had placed major downward economic pressure on the German and Japanese economies, the rise of the dollar in the wake of the Reverse Plaza Accord of 1995 threw the US economic revival far off course.

First and foremost, the rising dollar, in the context of persistent system-wide manufacturing overcapacity, put an end to the long rise of the US manufacturing profitability and after 1997 played the central part – along with the Asian crisis, which was also rooted in international overcapacity in manufacturing – in driving it downward. The new decline in profitability was the underlying force that put an end to the boom. Along with a flood of money from Japan and East Asia into US Treasury bills that rapidly reduced the cost of borrowing, the dollar revaluation also set off a precipitous run-up of equity prices, in stark defiance of the declining trend in profitability. Finally, the enormous splurge of borrowing that was made possible by the apparent increase in collateral that was derived from rising equity prices – the so-called wealth effect – enabled rapid investment growth to continue, in the face of, and very much exacerbating, manufacturing overcapacity. Panitch and Gindin notwithstanding, far from disciplining capital so as to enforce a movement of resources out of low-profit into high-profit lines, the freed-up financial sector had, as in the 1980s, made possible a titanic mis-allocation of funds... opening the way once again to equity price collapse and new cyclical downturn (Brenner 2002a: 154–217).

Accelerated capital accumulation and record high price-equity ratios could not, of course, long persist in the face of declining profitability, and by the end of 2000, the stock market was crashing, trillions of dollars in assets were vanishing, and the economy was plunging into one of the worst recessions of the post-war period. The central role of manufacturing over-capacity in determining the economy's trajectory could hardly have been more decisively demonstrated. The fall in the rate of profit that drove the economy into the recession of 2001 occurred *entirely* in the manufacturing sector. The record-breaking loss of jobs that was the key factor in forcing down demand and perpetuating the downturn was likewise accounted for *in toto* by manufacturing disemployment.

What next?

In the recovery from the recession of 2001, one of the worst of the post-war epoch in terms of GDP, the US economy has pursued an extraordinarily contradictory path, which can only very briefly be outlined here.

Employers in the non-financial sector have achieved an extraordinarily rapid recovery of profitability, largely through job reductions that totally smashed all post-war records and the accompanying massive speedup, as well as a stunning reduction in wage growth.[3] Demonstrating for still another time that US capital's main trump card is its domination of labor – one mani-festation of which is its ability to redistribute income from workers – non-financial corporations had, already by the first quarter of 2004, raised their rate of profit very close to its post-1973 peak, achieved in 1997. Benefiting, meanwhile, from the continuing boom in housing, as well as the Federal Reserve's explicit commitment to keep short-term interest rates at rock bottom levels in the face of much higher long-term borrowing costs, the financial sector continued the extraordinary expansion that had begun as far back as the beginning of the 1990s. If prevailing rates of return can be sustained, the economy, having achieved a huge shakeout of labor and perhaps means of production as well,[4] has secured the potential basis for a sustained recovery.

On the other hand, the unprecedented hemorrhaging of jobs, the sustained stagnation of wages, the disappearance of investment growth – all of which persisted into the second half of 2003 or beyond – delivered a titanic shock to demand, which, all else equal, would have sent the economy into deep and extended recession. What enabled the economy to avoid this fate and launch a so-far halting recovery was a historic run-up of debt – household, governmental, financial, and, to a lesser extent, non-financial corporate. In particular, consumer spending, based on money raised through borrowing against residential housing, drove the economy. Indeed, taken together, mortgage refinancings, cash-outs through home sales, and second mortgages, along with residential investment spending and purchases of home furnishings, were responsible for no less than two thirds of the total growth of GDP between 2000 and the first half of 2003. But the fact remains that the rock-bottom interest rates that have founded the recovery – keeping consumption growing and the financial sector prospering – have been sustained only by the stunning intervention of East Asian governments intent on keeping the dollar high *vis-à-vis* their own currencies. Especially in the wake of the stock market crash and corporate scandals, *private overseas investors* have distanced themselves from US assets, above all equities but also US treasuries. But the Chinese and Japanese governments have more than made up for their declining interest through massive interventions in the US financial markets. Without their gigantic purchases of US government bonds – East Asian governments now hold around $2 trillion in US assets – it would have been impossible for the Fed to keep interest rates down and the recovery would have aborted. Nevertheless, the outcome has been a stunning series of distortions and imbalances – a new run-up of equity prices that has far outdistanced the growth of profits, the record-breaking ascent of housing debt, a new explosion of financial sector debt, and the continuing, unprecedented run-up of the current account deficit, resulting from the continuing takeover of world and US manufacturing markets by the East Asians. These raise serious questions about the sustainability of the recovery. Will the desired, more rapid expansion lead to higher borrowing costs that undercut it, by wreaking havoc with over-extended households and financial institutions? Will it not also exacerbate the current account deficit, ultimately making for a destructive sell-off of an already declining dollar, with devastating consequences for financial assets of all sorts? Can the economy continue to advance by way of the expansion of a service sector catering mainly to consumption, when manufacturing remains weighed down by overcapacity and ever-more potent East Asian competition? Can the financial sector continue to accrue such stunning returns once the housing boom is exhausted and the Fed ends its commitment to keep short-term interest rates artificially low? Can East Asia continue to save the day?

Notes

1. Panitch and Gindin rightly emphasize the acceleration of US manufacturing prod-uctivity growth in the 1980s and especially the 1990s. But, even between 1990 and 2000, it did not clearly outdistance that of its leading rivals: US: 3.9 percent; France: 4.1 percent; Japan: 3.7 percent; West Germany: 3.2 percent. (US Bureau of Labor Statistics 2003, Table 1).
2. In this context, it is unclear what Panitch and Gindin think they are demonstrating in showing that US GDP growth and GDP levels have been higher than that of the other G7 countries. As they are well aware, to the extent that US GDP numbers have been higher, this simply reflects the faster growth and higher level of US population, labor force participation, and annual hours worked per person.
3. The resulting huge increases in output per hour has been labeled productivity increase, but, given that even by 2003 investment had yet to return to its level of 2000, it is evident that what was responsible was increased labor inputs per hour than greater efficiency.
4. Data on bankruptcies are no longer kept.

12
Disparate Models, Desperate Measures: The Convergence of Limits

Travis Fast

In the wake of the 'long downturn' that began in the early 1970s, the relative positions occupied by a number of advanced capitalist economies in the various league tables that measure economic performance began to slide. As they did so, an international search began for an appropriate 'model of capitalism' which in whole or part might correct this slippage. Japan, Sweden and Germany quickly became frontrunners for emulation – seemingly capable of generating relatively low unemployment and inflation, coupled with high productivity and growth – but by the early 1990s, Japan, and Sweden had fallen out of the running and even the shine of post-unification Germany had begun to dull. The relative reversal in the fortunes of the emulative models of the 1980s then brought about a temporary lull in the debate over emulation during the mid-1990s. For a while, not only was there seemingly a lack of emulative models, but there was also a recognition among scholars of the general impossibility of grafting institutions from one national social formation onto another. However, the question of emulation is once again back on the table. This time it is the once-derided Anglo-American models – the US and the UK, and the miraculously 'cured' Dutch patient – that are now widely proffered as the new economies to copy.

The object of this chapter is to track developments in what may be termed the 'comparative political economy of exploitation' in these favoured economies: the US, the UK, the Netherlands, Sweden, Germany and Japan. The central argument to be made in this chapter is that, in truth, there is not much to emulate here. On the contrary, those advanced capitalist countries – in particular the UK, the Netherlands and Sweden – which managed to meet or exceed US performance over the latter half of the 1990s, did so only by reinforcing extra-economic forms of exploitation which they already deployed, and by devising new strategies of exploitation that circumvented existing 'bottlenecks' of resistance to flexibility. For, what is perhaps most interesting about the case for the new emulative models is that it is not being made on their capacity to generate egalitarian outcomes from a fundamentally inegalitarian economic system. Rather, it is being made on their capacity to restructure their political economy in such a way as to re-enforce the coercive inegalitarian outcomes generated by capitalist markets, with only some limited measure of *ex post facto* distribution. In this sense, the chapter will argue that it is less productive to talk about the 'success' of the new emulative models than it is to speak of the exhaustion in the capitalist boom of the post-war era as a pole of adjustment to which the new emulative models of the 1990s and their attendant electoral parties have successfully adapted.

The ascendancy and decline of the emulative cases

This section critically interrogates the widely held opinion that the macroeconomic performance of the new emulative models of the 1990s was superior to the old emulative models of the 1980s.

Domestic macroeconomic comparisons

Table 12.1 presents comparative cross-national GDP per capita data for the six model cases. The left column (L) measures GDP per capita relative to the US and the right column (R) indicates a simple ratio of each country's average GDP per capita growth rates relative to the US.[1] By these measures the common cleaving of the model cases into two distinct groupings – one of the old model cases of the 1980s and the other of the new model cases of the 1990s – is given some credence. Clearly, over the 1990s, the Japanese and German models fell on tough times, although in the case of Germany, this weakness began to show during the latter half of the 1980s. The Swedish case is an outlier in that it does not fall neatly into the periodization suggested. In fact, Swedish weakness began to appear in the latter half of the

Table 12.1 GDP per capita relative to the US

	71–75		76–80		81–85		86–90		91–95		96–01	
	L	R	L	R	L	R	L	R	L	R	L	R
JPN	69	1.9	71	1.3	76	1.2	79	1.9	85	0.9	79	0.5
DEU	84	1.2	86	1.3	86	0.6	84	1.2	78	–1.0	73	0.7
SWE	84	1.4	80	0.4	81	0.8	79	0.9	74	0.0	73	1.4
NDL	80	1.4	79	0.7	76	0.4	73	1.1	76	1.1	76	1.4
GBR	67	1.1	66	0.7	65	0.9	67	1.3	66	1.1	67	1.3
USA*		1.6		2.5		2.1		2.2		1.3		2

*US figures are not expressed as a ratio but rather as real GDP per capita growth in 1995 PPPs.
Note: L denotes level GDP per capita relative to the US; R denotes the ratio of GDP per capita growth to the US (less than 1 represents a decline relative to the US). All figures calculated based on constant 1995 PPPs.
Source: GDP authors own calculations based on Source OECD, *Economic Outlook No. 73*; population series taken directly from World Bank, *WDI Online*.

1970s and did not manage an appreciable reversal until the latter half of the 1990s. By these measures, Dutch performance was actually better than that of Sweden over the two decade-long slowdown beginning in the mid-1970s, with an appreciable reversal not taking place until the second half of the 1990s. The UK case is interesting because, if we average out its performance over each decade, what is remarkable is the degree to which UK performance closely tracks that of the US. Moreover, if the data is examined for the last half of the 1980s and 1990s, which roughly corresponds to the peak of each business cycle, it is clear that the relative performance of the UK economy to the US has been no better under the 'tutelage' of New Labour, than it was earlier under the 'yoke' of Margaret Thatcher's Conservatives. Decade averages for the US reveal that the performance of the American economy did not improve over the 1990s, when it was still performing under its 1970s levels, and well under its 1980s levels. Hence, it is tempting to conclude that what made the American economy seem so strong through the 1990s was partially an artefact of the comparative decline in the performance of its chief emulative rivals.

One of the problems in using GDP per capita growth to measure economic performance in this way is that it does not reveal very much about the path of productivity. Nor does it reveal much about other important macroeconomic variables such as unemployment and inflation: all three of which are key measures when assessing the relative decline and ascendancy of the model cases. So Table 12.2 presents three additional measures of macroeconomic performance. Unlike the measures presented in Table 12.1, the averages presented in Table 12.2 have been cyclically adjusted, so as to provide a comparison of the macroeconomic performances of each case over

Table 12.2   Productivity, unemployment, and inflation rates: cyclically adjusted

	Labour productivity		Unemployment rate		CPI	
	1980s	1990s	1980s	1990s	1980s	1990s
JPN	3.1%	2.1%	2.5%	3.6%	1.7%	0.4%
DEU	0.8%	0.9%	5.1%	8.1%	2.8%	2.3%
SWE	1.3%	1.8%	2.7%	6.9%	7.6%	3.0%
NLD	2.6%	1.4%	9.3%	5.3%	2.9%	2.6%
GBR	2.0%	1.9%	10.0%	7.4%	7.4%	3.7%
USA	1.2%	1.6%	7.0%	5.6%	4.1%	2.8%
AVDEV	0.72	0.32	2.67	1.32	2.06	0.74

Note: Labour productivity is measured as output per hour worked.
Source: Productivity and unemployment figures based on data from SourceOECD, *Economic Outlook No. 73: Annual and Semi-annual data*; Consumer Price Index (CPI) taken directly from World Bank, *WDI Online*.

the entirety of their business cycles. On these measures, a somewhat different picture of the relative strength and weakness of the model cases emerges.

In terms of labour productivity performance, the top three were Japan, the UK and Sweden respectively. Note that two out of the top three performances occurred in the models held to be in relative decline. In terms of open rates of unemployment, the superiority of the new model cases is more apparent, with the Netherlands and the US rounding out the top three. Even so, their reduction in open unemployment rates still takes them nowhere near what was conventionally understood as full employment prior to 1973. (To the extent that either the Netherlands or the US can be considered to have achieved full-employment over the 1990s, it can only be understood as a functional level of unemployment, of which more is said in the next section.) For all the cases, inflation trended lower over the cycle of the 1990s, with the strongest reductions occurring in Sweden and the UK.

Two points are worth highlighting. Once again, American strength over the cycle of the 1990s was as much a function of the poorer performance of its rivals over the two cycles, as it was a function of the US prowess in terms of labour productivity growth and open unemployment rates. Second, while the data presented here contradict the impression left by the GDP per capita figures presented in Table 12.1 with regards to Japan, they do confirm the pervasive decline of the German case.

International macroeconomic comparisons

The final set of measures that need to be taken into account when assessing the relative macroeconomic performances of the emulative cases are those which provide some indication of the overall competitiveness of each case *vis-à-vis* its emulative rivals. Table 12.3 presents three measures, which simultaneously provide an indication of export effort and competitiveness. By the first two measures, it is clear that Japan and Germany saw an erosion of their market share from the 1980s to the 1990s. In the German case, the trend is particularly troubling, given that by 2000 and despite an increase in export effort (exports as a per cent of GDP) the German share of high-income OECD trade remained well below its 1980s level. In the case of Sweden and the Netherlands, despite a substantial increase in export effort over the 1980s and 1990s, the two economies only managed to retain existing market share. This is significant because it demonstrates the effort that small countries need to make simply to maintain existing market shares. For the UK, a minimal increase in export effort has been matched by a slight decrease in export shares – certainly not the hallmarks of a rejuvenated export sector. Alternatively, the US increased its export effort and captured a larger share of high-income OECD trade over the 1980s and 1990s. Thus, on these two measures, only in one of three new emulative cases has there been an appreciable improvement in international competitiveness.

Table 12.3   Comparative measures of export effort

	Exports						High-technology		
	% GDP			% Hinc OECD			% Manufacturing exports		
	1980s	1990s	2000	1980s	1990s	2000	1989	1990s	2000
JPN	12	10	11	12	11	10	24	25	28
DEU	29	27	34	18	14	14	12	13	18
SWE	33	38	47	2	2	2	14	16	22
NLD	55	58	67	5	5	5	15	24	34
GBR	26	27	28	8	7	7	25	25	31
USA	8	11	11	15	18	18	32	32	33

Note: Per cent Hinc OECD denotes countries exports of goods and services calculated as a percentage of total high income OECD trade in goods and services. All export figures calculated from constant 1995 US dollars.
Source: Export statistics: World Bank, *WDI Online*.

Turning to the third measure of export competitiveness and effort presented in Table 12.3 – high-tech exports as a per cent of manufacturing exports – a slightly more nuanced picture emerges. Japan, Germany and Sweden increased the high-tech component of their exports over the 1990s; and in the case of Japan high-tech shares are now within the range of the other model cases, while Sweden and Germany still lag behind. The trend rate of growth for Dutch high-tech exports was strong and by 2004 led all the other cases. The UK had a steady growth in the high-tech component of trade such that it managed to retain its relative position within the group, while the US for its part maintained its high-tech shares over the 1990s. On this measure, therefore, there is evidence of considerable improvement in the international competitiveness of the UK and especially the Netherlands. There is also evidence of improvement in the case of Japan and Sweden as well: to the point at which indeed, in the Japanese case at least, there is no appreciable gap between its performance and that of the other new model cases.

Table 12.4 provides two additional measures of overall international competitiveness. The first measure tracks the evolution of unit labour costs from 1980 to 2002. Clearly, over the 1980s, the old emulative models (Germany, Japan and Sweden) were faced with an increase in their unit labour costs while the new emulative models (the US, the UK and the Netherlands) were experiencing a downward trend in unit labour costs. This general pattern held until the mid-1990s, at which point the trend rates began to reverse; such that it is now the new emulative models that are faced with increasing unit labour costs relative to the other three cases.

Table 12.4 Comparative measures of export competitiveness

	1980	1985	1990	1995	2000	2002
Index of relative unit labour cost manufacturing sector						
JPN	44	49	61	100	101	87
DEU	78	70	83	100	93	92
SWE	151	130	149	100	89	83
NDL	110	92	99	100	93	97
GBR	125	112	117	100	145	146
USA	136	169	114	100	118	121
Current balance as a percentage of GDP						
	1980	1985	1990	1995	2000	2003
JPN	−1.0	3.7	1.5	2.1	2.5	2.9
DEU	−1.7	2.7	2.9	−1.1	−1.4	2.1
SWE	−3.2	−1.0	−2.5	3.4	3.9	3.7
NDL	−0.5	3.2	2.7	6.2	2.2	1.9
GBR	1.4	0.6	−4.0	−1.3	−2.1	−2.7
USA	0.1	−2.8	−1.4	−1.4	−4.2	−5.0

Source: SourceOECD, *Economic Outlook No. 74: Annual and Semi-annual data.*

The deterioration in the competitiveness of the new emulative models is reflected in their current account balance. The Japanese, despite weak domestic growth and an erosion of relative market share, managed to run current account surpluses from the early 1980s and increasingly so since the mid-1990s. The Germans appear to have turned the corner on their deficit, posting a strong surplus in 2003, with the Swedes posting strong surpluses since the end of the severe recession of the early 1990s. Despite strong performance in terms of high-tech exports, the trend implied by the current account data for the Netherlands suggests a continued erosion of their trade surplus. This is compatible with the mild erosion of their competitive advantage implied by the evolution of their unit labour costs. Turning to the UK, there appears to be little to no relief from the chronic current account deficits of the 1990s. Indeed the data for 2003 indicates that the position of the UK has further deteriorated, as its unit labour costs evolve in lockstep with the health of their current account. This suggests that over the 1990s the UK has suffered an overall decline in international competitiveness. The US performance mirrors that of the UK with less of a rise in unit labour costs but with a more severe deficit on the current account, such that by 2003 the trade deficit stood at 5 per cent of GDP. While it may be true that such a deficit does not portend a crisis, it does nonetheless indicate a weakness in terms of international competitiveness. In this sense, it is possible to speak of a structural weakness in the US macro-economy, even if it can be more than covered by the privilege of empire. For both these reasons, the US, in this regard, hardly stands out as an emulative model.

With the exception of Germany, the measures provided in this section resist easy generalizations across the model cases, or even easy generalizations for the individual model cases themselves. Clearly, the German model has stalled. Indeed, the severity of the German problem is evidenced by stagnation across both business cycles and by stagnant labour productivity growth. Given that manufacturing counts for the larger share of employment in Germany than in any of the other five models, the decline of manufacturing has no doubt contributed to the deteriorating conditions in the German labour market. The US, on the other hand, has not only seen an improvement in its international competitiveness in some areas, but by-and-large has managed to attain functional levels of open unemployment. What this section makes most clear is that it is not possible to draw any straightforward generalization about the overall success and failure, based on the relative empirical status and merits, of the macroeconomic performance of the emulative cases. And, in fact, success and failure ought not to be measured simply in these terms. For as was noted in Chapter 2, if success cannot be demonstrated by reference to improvements in the lives of working populations, both inside and outside of work, then to talk of 'success' at all here is misplaced.

'Model' labour markets: 'flexploitation' and 'functional' unemployment

The return of full employment or near full employment has been touted as one, if not the, central accomplishment of the model cases of the 1990s. As the data presented in Table 12.2 demonstrated, none of the model cases actually managed a return to full employment, at least as that term was once commonly understood in the post-war era. Given that so much of the battle over the superiority of the new model cases has been fought out on the terrain of unemployment, it is worth considering what the open unemployment rate actually measures, and why measuring unemployment in this way is increasingly a poor measure of the overall condition of labour markets.

The problem with the open unemployment rate is that it is a relative measure in both static and dynamic terms. Taking the static aspect first, the unemployment rate expresses the number of persons currently unemployed and actively seeking work (over a limited reference period) as a per cent of the total active labour force. The total active labour force, in turn, is comprised of those individuals that are currently employed (broadly defined as anyone receiving a minimal amount of paid employment during the reference period) plus all of those deemed to be unemployed. So given the expansive definition of what it means to be employed versus the narrow definition of what it means to be unemployed, there is a built-in downward bias in the static calculation of unemployment rates. In dynamic terms a problem arises because the size of the labour force tends to contract and expand. In practice, this means that a country may experience zero or negative employment growth while at the same time registering little or no increase in the open unemployment rate, simply because members of the unemployed have given up looking for work and hence are no longer considered in the labour force, so leaving a higher proportion of employed to unemployed in the labour force. Something like this has occurred in the US over the past three years – the labour market has been contracting, while at the same time a significant number of persons have left the labour force, effectively countering to some extent the upward pressure on the unemployment rate.

Outside the relative problems with standard or open definitions of unemployment, there is another way in which official unemployment data can be a poor indicator of conditions in the labour market. Given that only a minimal amount of paid labour within the reference period is required to count a person as employed, the open unemployment rate says virtually nothing about the quality (job security and stable hours) of employment. For example, some workers may be chronically underemployed and in search of full-time employment but are nonetheless regarded as employed. Once again, in the US, this is the case, to the extent that by the expanded definition of unemployment (one that includes underemployment and self-employment for economic reasons in its definition of unemployment) the rate of unemployment is almost double that of the rate recorded by the standard definition. For all the above reasons, and given the increased incidence of part-time and insecure labour contracts over the past two decades, the standard definition of unemployment has become less useful as a measure of conditions in the labour market. In the first part of this section, therefore, a critical assessment of the labour market performance of the emulative cases is made in an attempt to circumvent the serious limitations of unemployment as a measure of the overall performance of labour markets.

Employment and participation

While there has been a general decrease in the open unemployment rate in four out of the six cases over the latter half of the 1990s, such aggregate statistics obscure the degree to which pools of marginalized workers face labour markets in which there is a much higher incidence of unemployment. Among the top four model cases (the US, the UK, the Netherlands and Sweden) for example, youth unemployment rates were double or more national rates during the 1990s (see Table 12.5). Only in the case of the Netherlands did youth unemployment relative to total unemployment improve, and in the rest of the cases, including the US, it worsened. There is some irony here because both the UK and US instituted rather Victorian measures in an attempt to 'encourage' participation by the poor and young adult workers in the labour market via the introduction of extensive compulsory workfare

Table 12.5   Youth unemployment

	Youth unemployment rate		Total unemployment rate	
	1990s*	2002	1990s*	2002
JPN	7.0	10.0	3.6	5.4
DEU	8.1	9.7	8.1	7.7
SWE	15.6	12.8	6.9	4.0
NLD	9.0	5.9	5.3	4.1
GBR	13.4	11.0	7.4	5.1
USA	11.7	12.0	5.6	5.8

*1990s average cyclically adjusted.
Note: 1990s average cyclically adjusted.
Source: unemployment rate, OECD; Youth unemployment based on World Bank, *WDI Online*, and OECD *Employment Outlook 2003: Towards More and Better Jobs*: Statistical Annex (2003).

schemes. The effect of this was not so much to increase employment as to decrease the unemployment rate of young adults. In the US, the other major group excluded from the 'jobs boom' of the 1990s were African American and Hispanic workers. African American workers experienced double the rate of open unemployment (10.8 per cent) of their white counterparts over the 1990s, while the corresponding Hispanic unemployment rate was 8.6 per cent (Mishel *et al.* 2003: Table 3.1).

Leaving aside, for the moment, the fact that the 'successful' capitalist models are increasingly dumping unemployment on the politically marginalized (especially in the case of Sweden, the US and UK), there has nonetheless been significant improvement in the labour market for four of the six model cases. What we see here is not full employment certainly, but the achievement of what may be termed 'functional levels of unemployment' (FLU). A functional level of unemployment can be defined as a rate of unemployment which is sufficient to ensure overall price flexibility in wage rates, while at the same time being low enough so as not to be politically destabilizing or *ceteris paribus* excessively taxing on government spending.[2]

The question, however, is to what extent such levels of open unemployment are a function of the capitalist models' superior performance in terms of employment growth, or are merely attributable to other factors such as a decline in the hours of work or changes in labour force participation rates? Table 12.6 presents data that help answer this question. Three measures are presented which taken together go some way toward an explanation of the dynamics at play in each of the cases' employment performance. The first measure tracks the cyclically adjusted rate of employment growth which allows for a comparison of the job richness of each of the cycles for each case, and a comparison between the cases. Significantly, in all of the cases,

Table 12.6 Components of employment growth

	Employment		Working-age population		Labour-force participation	
	1980s	1990s	1980s	1990s	1980s	1990s
JPN	1.31	0.07	0.76	−0.01	0.54	0.38
DEU	1.23	0.40	0.57	0.22	2.46	2.22
SWE	0.57	−0.42	0.32	0.38	2.46	−0.57
NDL	1.05	1.96	0.92	0.49	0.28	1.14
GBR	0.55	0.42	0.42	0.22	0.33	0.02
USA	1.57	1.28	0.85	1.27	0.65	−0.07

Note: all figures cyclically adjusted; employment figures based on a common definition.
Source: SourceOECD, *Economic Outlook No. 73: Annual and Semi-annual data.*

except the Netherlands, employment growth was weaker over the 1990s than during the 1980s. The second measure presented in Table 12.6 is a straightforward measure of the rate of growth for the working age population. This measure allows for an assessment of the underlying demographic pressure: the potential supply of workers. On this measure, only in the case of the US was there a substantial increase in the potential supply of new workers during the 1990s, whereas in the rest of the cases the growth in the supply of labour was minimal and either stagnant or declining compared to their 1980s average. The third measure presented in Table 12.6 tracks the actual supply of new workers via changes in the growth of the participation rate.

In the UK, job growth was anaemic over both cycles – almost on par with the German performance during the 1990s. What then accounts for the success of the UK in reducing its unemployment rate? The answer the data suggest is that the growth of the working age population slowed relative to the 1980s along with an almost complete levelling out of the participation rate. There is therefore less of a New Labour economy at work here than there is a favourable change in the underlying demographic pressure (population growth) coupled with a decrease in the rate of labour force participation. Even this begs the question as to why and who left the labour market. The answer as to who is partly answered in Table 12.7. Male participation rates declined from 76 per cent during the 1980s to 72 per cent during the 1990s. In sum this means that the decline in male participation rates accounts for half of the decrease in male unemployment rather than being the result of an increase in employment. Further study has revealed that the bulk of men leaving the labour force are over fifty (Gregg and Wadsworth 1999: 59). Moreover, as is demonstrated later in this chapter, the other major exit route from British labour markets has been through entry into the disability

Table 12.7   Structure of employment and labour force participation

	Part-time*/ Full-time		Female part-time/Total part-time		Labour Force Participation Rates			
					M	M	F	F
	1980s	1990s	1980s	1990s	1980s	1990s	1980s	1990s
JPN	20%	28%	72%	68%	78	77	48	49
DEU	13%	17%	90%	87%	70	71	41	48
SWE	13%	11%	86%	82%	73	69	61	60
NDL	33%	41%	74%	75%	73	71	39	50
GBR	25%	29%	87%	82%	76	72	50	54
USA*	21%	22%	67%	67%	76	75	54	59

* US figures not strictly comparable based on national definition of dependent employment.
Note: all figures expressed as averages, non-cyclically adjusted.
Source: Part-time data calculated from OECD Corporate Data Environment, 'Labour Market Statistics: Employment by full-time/part-time distinction based on a common definition'; participation rates calculated from Bureau of Labor Statistics (BLS), 'Foreign Labor Statistics'.

system. Neither of these developments suggests improvement in the equality of opportunity that Labour's New Deal claims to deliver.

The German experience is instructive relative to that of the UK because employment and labour force growth rates were almost the same in the two economies, whereas the growth in labour force participation in Germany was 2 per cent higher than in the UK over the 1990s. Hence, it is worth speculating that, had the UK economy been faced with the same increase in labour force participation that Germany experienced over the past two cycles, whether the UK unemployment rate would have been any better. Indeed it might even have been worse.

The US performance on job creation, although worse than during the 1980s, nevertheless managed to track the increase in the underlying growth of the working age population. US unemployment rates decreased, as the data make clear, partly as a result of an overall decrease in the participation rate over the cycle of the 1990s: a result which is hardly suggestive of a strong economy eating away through its labour reserves towards full-employment. As the data on participation growth presented in Table 12.6 suggest, both the UK and the US were at least as successful in discouraging workers from entering the labour force as they were in providing jobs for all those who wanted one.

This brings us to the Dutch case, which has been heralded as nothing short of a jobs 'miracle' (Keman 2003). As the data in Table 12.6 make evident, not only did the Dutch manage to improve their job creation performance considerably during the 1990s, but they did so well in excess of the underlying pressures on labour force participation rates. Employment grew at almost twice the rate of labour force participation and over six times the rate of working age population growth.

However, more detailed labour market statistics provide an entirely different and more negative assessment of not only Dutch performance but also that of all the cases under review here. Two significant structural shifts have taken place in advanced capitalist labour markets. First there has been a general feminization of labour markets (see Table 12.7). Male participation rates have decreased while female participation rates have increased. This could be interpreted as a progressive structural change if female workers were gaining access to core 'golden age' jobs, but they were in fact not. What is more, this feminization has occurred in the context of the winding down of the core golden age sector for males: that is, a winding down of highly unionized, living-wage remunerated, secure full-time employment. Second, as is well known, there has been an overall growth in the relative share of service sector employment as a per cent of total employment. As the data in Table 12.8 also reveal, however, this too has been an equally gendered development. Excluding Germany and Japan, by the latter half of the 1990s well over 80 per cent of all female employment was in the service sector. These two structural shifts, more than any other factors, seem to be the key components of the new emulative models' capacity to generate functional levels of unemployment and the requisite degree of flexibility.

By 2003, fully one out of every two jobs in the Netherlands was either of the part-time or self-employed variety. Moreover, on a comparative basis, Dutch employers made extensive use of temporary labour contracts (Barrell and Genre 1999: 51). The 'Dutch miracle' it turns out then, was, and remains a chimera. Dutch employers have done a remarkable job in spreading work rather than creating full-time employment. In a detailed study of Dutch

Table 12.8   Distribution of employment by gender and sector

| | Service sector employment as % of total male and female employment | | | | | | Service sector employment as % of total employment | | |
| | 1981 | | 1991 | | 1998 | | 1981 | 1991 | 1998 |
	M	F	M	F	M	F	M & F	M & F	M & F
JPN	52	59	54	64	56	71	54	58	62
DEU	NA	NA	44	70	50	79	NA	55	62
SWE	47	82	53	85	58	86	63	68	72
NLD	54	83	60	85	63	84	63	70	73
GBR	50	78	53	81	59	86	62	66	71
USA	56	80	61	84	63	86	66	72	74

Source: Calculations based on World Bank, *WDI Online*.

labour market policies, including active labour market measures, Keman concluded that Dutch employment performance '...is not the direct result of an active labour market policy *per se*, but is rather the effect created by the relaxation of labour market regulation...insofar as one can speak of an above average performance by the Netherlands, this is due to the exceptional growth in part-time labour' (2003: 131). And as Keman further points out, part-time employment is negatively correlated with the capacity of individuals to receive full welfare benefits. As such 'the Polder model is not capable of bringing about a miracle in terms of both work *and* welfare' (2003: 132).

Part-time and self-employment growth have stabilized in the US, where they now account for one out of every five jobs created. However, when all forms of non-standard labour contracts are taken into account, the level of insecure part-time jobs in the US economy is substantially higher than even that: particularly for women, where fully 34 per cent of all jobs are of the non-standard variety (Mishel *et al.* 2003, Table 3.16). Some analysts have explained the levelling off in the use of part-time non-standard contracts as the result of the relatively lax regulations that govern US labour markets, such that American employers have less need of temporary and part-time contracts to achieve flexibility (see discussion in Peck and Theodore 2002).

As is clear from the data presented in Table 12.7, in every case except Sweden and the US the increase in female participation rates has occurred in tandem with a significant increase in part-time employment. What is equally interesting is that, within this sample, the gender distribution of part-time jobs is most skewed in the European countries, including the UK (see Table 12.7 for detail). Once the relatively low proportion of part-time employment in Germany and Sweden is taken into account, the UK and the Netherlands – the vanguards of the Third Way – stand out as the two most-gendered and 'flexploitative' of the model cases. Indeed, they are well 'ahead' of Japan, which is routinely singled out in the literature as having relied heavily on a part-time female labour force to provide overall labour market 'flexibility' (Burkett and Hart-Landsberg 2003). In this regard, Japan is closer to that of the US than it is to the other 'model' cases.

Hours, stress and quality of life

All of these measures only get at the broad structure of unemployment and employment in the model cases. What do assessments of life at the workplace reveal about job satisfaction and stress? Here the picture is even bleaker. The starting point for this phase of the investigation is cross-national data on work hours. There are several limitations to the data on average annual work-hours as used by the OECD. First, the national statistics on which they are based use different methodologies: the most problematic of which is that some use household surveys (such as the US), while other countries use establishment surveys (such as Japan). The difference between the two is that household surveys better reflect paid and unpaid overtime, while the latter only include paid overtime (Mizunoya 2001). One result is that the Japanese estimates are significantly lower than the actual hours worked. The second limitation to cross-national data on work hours is that they pool part-time and full-time employment when calculating averages. So in the case of the Netherlands, average annual hours have decreased partly because of the rapid increase in part-time employment. Similarly, given the UK's higher proportion of part-time workers relative to the US, meaningful comparisons are hard to draw at lower levels of detail.

Nonetheless, based on the published data, calculations for cyclically adjusted average annual hours of work are presented in Table 12.9. Despite the high incidence of part-time employment in Japan and despite the fact that unpaid 'service overtime' is not included, Japanese workers still worked the longest hours of any advanced capitalist workforce and of all the model cases studied here over the 1990s. The International Labor Organization (ILO) estimated that Japanese workers actually clock 350 hours more than the OECD statistics suggest (Kato 1995).

More recent estimates in a cross-national comparison of paid and unpaid overtime estimate that male workers in Japan provide an extra tenth, or 180–200 hours of service overtime annually (Mizunoya 2001). The problem of overwork was so pervasive in Japan over the 1990s that a new phrase entered the Japanese lexicon, 'Karoshi', which literally translated means 'death from overwork'. In a national poll, 48 per cent of the households surveyed said that they were concerned about themselves or a member of their family dying as a result of overwork (Kato 1995). Clearly there is not much more productivity that can be squeezed out of the Japanese labour force through intensified managerial techniques.

Among the economies studied here, American and British work hours were the second and third longest respectively (Table 12.9). The increase in female participation rates, coupled with the average hours worked per person, means that US and British households are now collectively engaged in more paid labour than at any other time. Hence, it is hardly surprising

Table 12.9 Average annual hours

	1980s	1990s
JPN	2065	1870
DEU	1653	1524
SWE	1529	1597
NLD	1571	1372
GBR	1751	1738
USA	1831	1838

Source: SourceOECD, *Economic Outlook No. 73: Annual and Semi-annual data.*

that in both countries work-time-related concerns of over-work and overtime are on the rise, and this has occurred across both sectoral and occupational lines.

Taking the American case first, 37 per cent of all full-time workers in the US feel overworked. The cost of overwork is not a trivial matter. With family members spending longer hours at work there is less time for family life, and higher degree of stress both at work and in the home. The recession and slow recovery since 2001 has only added to the general frustration over long hours of work, as US companies have shed employees and squeezed increased productivity out of their remaining workforce. Indeed, the level of overwork has become so pervasive in the US of late that employees have been fighting back through collective action lawsuits over unpaid overtime. As one Human Resource consultancy commented: 'companies hit by such lawsuits read like the Fortune 500. Settlements so far, include Starbucks paying its store managers $18 million, Pacific Bell paying engineers $35 million and $27 million to its sales managers, and Farmers Insurance paying $130 million to claims adjusters. Wal-Mart has 28 separate lawsuits pending against it'.[3] In the most recent of the Wal-Mart lawsuits to go to court, in which the retailer was found guilty, company officials defended their managerial practices by arguing that they were simply 'trying to encourage teamwork'.[4]

The data on average hours of work, presented in Table 12.9, obscure the full extent of increased hours because such data are averages, and therefore spread increased hours of work by some members of the labour force over the whole of the working population. Disaggregated studies of average working hours reveal that there has been a general increase in the proportion of males and females performing paid and unpaid overtime since the late 1980s. In 1989 for example, 43 per cent of full-time workers performed paid overtime, with 25 per cent reporting working unpaid overtime. By 1998, these figures had increased to 55 and 41 per cent respectively (Harkness 1999: Table 6.1a). The extent of unpaid overtime in the UK is now so pervasive that British workers performed £23 billion in unpaid over-time in 2003. Moreover, this increase in unpaid overtime has been registered across occupational categories, with the average unpaid overtime among professionals at 9.5 hours a week and among manual workers at between 5.5 and 6 hours a week. Given New Labour's continued insistence on exercising an opt-out from the European directive on work time, and, the labour cost advantage gained by capital, UK workers will likely continue to work longer hours for less pay than their European counterparts.

In a discussion paper put out by the Institute for the Study of Labor, a bi-national comparison of German and the UK rates of overtime found that overtime, unpaid and paid, 'was more prevalent in the UK than Germany' (Bell *et al.* 2000: 25). The contribution of unpaid overtime to the UK's professional service sector is not trivial. For example, once unpaid overtime is factored in, holding constant for education and experience, professional salaries are more than twice as high in Germany than in the UK. Moreover, female professionals in the UK with 10 years of experience earn one-third of what their counterparts in Germany earn (Bell *et al.* 2000: Tables 6 & 7). In a related report from the Joseph Rowntree Foundation based on a nation wide survey conducted by researchers at Cambridge, extensive job insecurity among professional workers was reported (1999). Such insecurity was intimately connected to work intensification, as a result of the increased volume of work being demanded of individual employees, and the corresponding long working hours to complete the tasks demanded of them by managers. Although not the focus of the report, it nonetheless mentions that the stress that professional employees were feeling was similar to that experienced by craft and operative workers during the 1980s.

For Germany, given the low incidence of part-time work, it seems safe to conclude there has been an overall reduction in hours worked although less than the data suggests, due to the increase in part-time work. Swedish hours actually increased over the cycle of the 1990s, which makes intuitive sense because Sweden actually saw a decrease in part-time employment during the 1990s. The actual path of work hours is hard to track in the case of the Netherlands, once again due to the high incidence of part-time work; but given the Dutch, like their German counterparts, have an active policy of work time reduction and job sharing, it would seem safe to conclude that average hours of full-time workers has decreased. However, in a study conducted by a Dutch research and consultancy firm, it was found that not only had contractual hours of work increased but that a further 9.5 hours of paid and unpaid overtime were being clocked by Dutch workers on a weekly basis in 2002, up from 6.5 hours in 2000 (TNO 2003). Dutch disability rates still remain twice the European average, despite a series of changes from the beginning of the 1990s that were designed to repeal the use of disability as a form of unemployment insurance (Barrell and Genre 1999). This suggests that despite the 'consensual' basis upon which flexibility has been pursued in the Netherlands, Dutch workplaces are not free from high stress and overwork.

Model welfare states and the modalities of 'flexploitation'

The central task of this section is to establish the link between private and public sector restructuring. The welfare state has no doubt been under severe *retrenchment* pressures but the real action has taken place in terms of welfare state *restructuring*. However, before proceeding directly to the behavioural changes embedded in welfare state restructuring across the individual model cases, it is useful to make a cursory analysis of changes in the size of the welfare state, as much of the debate on the relative fortunes of the model cases has hinged on the supposed 'crowding out' effect of the welfare state. The most interesting aspect of any such cursory analysis of the quantitative measures of the size of welfare states is that it inevitably reveals the absence of any necessary connection between the size of the welfare state and economic performance. That is, although the size of the welfare state may be fiscally unsustainable at certain levels of persistent unemployment, there is no 'iron law' that relates the nominal size of public social expenditure to economic growth, stagnation or decline.[5]

A simple confirmation of this is suggested in Table 12.10. Notice, for example, that Japan ran the leanest welfare state over the 1980s and, as illustrated above, had the best record on unemployment and GDP growth. In the 1990s, however, Japan continued to run the leanest welfare state but with one of the worst performances in terms of GDP and employment growth. Near the other extreme, the Netherlands during the 1980s combined a larger welfare state than all of the other cases, excluding Sweden, with one of the worst performances in terms of GDP and unemployment; and yet, during the 1990s, the Dutch had the best performance in terms of GDP growth and open unemployment, despite (or perhaps because of) an increase in the absolute and relative size of the welfare state. Even in the case of the US, there has been a moderate increase in the size of the welfare state. Clearly a range of growth and unemployment rates is compatible with a range of welfare state sizes, *sans* any cross-national or intra-national correlation between welfare state size and macroeconomic performance.

In fact, on both measures of public social expenditure provided in Table 12.10 there was an across-the-board increase in real welfare state program spending. On the third measure of welfare state size presented, however, which consists of a simple ratio of total population to number of government employees, there is some evidence of retrenchment. On this measure, Germany, the Netherlands and the UK showed strong signs of a decline in the size of the welfare state. In the case of the Netherlands, the decline in public sector

Table 12.10   Public social expenditure and government employees

	PSE (% of GDP)		PSE (per capita)		Ratio Pop: Gempl		Combined Rank	
	1980–89	1990–98	1980–89	1990–98	1980–89	1990–98	1980–89	1990–98
JPN	11.1	12.9	1999	3034	24:1	24:1	1.0	1.0
DEU	22.9	28.1	5207	6090	15:1	17:1	3.3	3.7
SWE	31.3	35.9	5634	7126	6:1	6:1	6.0	6.0
NDL	30.0	30.4	5233	6415	20:1	22:1	4.0	4.0
UK	23.0	25.8	3523	4815	8:1	11:1	4.0	3.7
US	13.6	15.3	3106	4212	14:1	14:1	2.7	2.7

Source: Public social expenditure figures calculated from ESDS; Government employment (Gempl) data from SourceOECD, *Economic Outlook No. 73: Annual and Semi-annual data*.

employment is somewhat surprising, given that it already had the second highest ratio of the six cases. In the case of the US, Sweden and Japan, there was little to no change in public sector employment relative to the population, with Japan continuing to lead with the highest population-to-government-employee ratio of the six cases.

If the link between welfare state size and economic growth is non-causal, then it also appears from the preceding data that there is also no necessary relationship between retrenchment, economic growth and unemployment. But from this observation, it should not be concluded that the present 'success' of the model cases has nothing to do with the configuration of their welfare states. The first factor that needs to be firmly kept in mind is that aggregate measures of welfare state spending may mask changes in the composition of that spending. Spending may be redeployed from direct universal cash benefits to selective targeted benefits, or it may be directed from one area of program spending to another, without affecting the overall level of public social expenditure. The movement away from universal to specific and targeted benefits has been the dominant characteristic of welfare reform in all the six economies under review here. The second factor that also needs to be kept in mind is that measures of welfare state spending, with population or GDP as the denominator, may be misleading because the key is to track benefit per beneficiary and not program spending per capita or as a per cent of GDP. Third, and closely related to the first, is that welfare state retrenchment needs to be understood as only one aspect of the broader phenomena of welfare state restructuring in general and labour market policy in particular.

In general, there are essentially two strategies that managers of the welfare state can employ to enforce the norms and size of capitalist labour markets. The first strategy involves the mobilization of *inactive* labour reserves: mobilizing those that have little to no attachment to the paid labour market – primarily individuals with some form of social assistance or disability allowance. The second strategy involves the mobilization of *active* labour reserves: mobilizing those who are attached to the paid labour market – the currently unemployed or underemployed. Modification of the behaviour of labour reserves in the aggregate (altering the set of 'choices' faced by members of the labour reserve) can be achieved through so-called 'passive' measures (that is, through a direct lowering of the duration and level of the benefit) and through 'active' measures, which alter the conditions attached to receipt of the benefit (mandatory skills training, job search, job placement and so on). Taken together, such measures can have a profound impact on labour force participation and unemployment rates, and the overall degree of flexibility within paid labour markets.

The data in Table 12.11 attempts to capture public social expenditure in those welfare programs (excluding unemployment insurance) that have a direct bearing on the level of inactive labour reserves. By these rather

Table 12.11   Spending on the maintenance of inactive labour reserves

	Sickness Benefit			Disability Benefit			Family Cash Benefit		
	1980s	1990s	1998	1980s	1990s	1998	1980s	1990s	1998
JPN	0.07	0.06	0.06	0.27	0.30	0.32	0.22	0.19	0.21
DEU	1.74	1.80	1.43	0.88	1.03	1.12	1.39	1.58	2.04
SWE	2.18	1.76	1.81	2.00	2.26	2.10	2.35	2.09	1.87
NDL	2.71	2.40	2.15	4.30	3.94	2.44	1.66	1.03	0.81
GBR	0.97	0.80	0.66	1.16	2.40	2.64	1.80	1.79	1.73
USA	0.27	0.25	0.23	0.69	0.82	0.86	0.33	0.28	0.22

Source: ESDS.

conservative measures, there has been, with some notable exceptions, a general retrenchment in welfare state spending, except possibly in disability spending. The Netherlands has seen an across-the-board reduction in all three program areas: markedly so in the case of disability and family cash benefits, which in 1998 was well below its 1980s level. The fall in Dutch disability spending was directly related to the retroactively applied tightening in criteria used to determine disability, and to an expansion in the definition of suitable employment for the disabled. The result of such changes was an immediate 8 per cent decrease in the number of disability recipients: which translated into nearly a quarter of million persons (OECD 1998). Such figures help explain the large growth of the Dutch labour force despite a relatively low growth rate for the working age population (refer back to Table 12.6). What the Dutch case illustrates is the degree to which public policy is linked to the relative size of passive and active labour reserves.

In all of the cases, there has been general clampdown in the access to sickness benefits, which has been offset to some degree, outside of the Netherlands, by an increase in spending on disability. This suggests that, despite the increased restrictions in access to sick benefits, some workers have been merely reclassified as disabled. Substantially, in the case of the UK, the over twofold increase in disability spending since the 1980s has been driven by a trebling in the number of working age persons on incapacity benefit (OECD 2004: 86–7). Such volume in turn suggests that the drop in the unemployment rate has been partially achieved through a reclassification of some of the unemployed as disabled. This also helps explain why the British labour force grew at one-tenth of the rate in growth of the working age population.

The other major component of passive labour reserve maintenance is family income support. In all cases, except Japan and Germany, where family cash benefits have been stable or increasing, recent years have seen reductions in the amount of spending on welfare (family cash benefits). In general, the reduction has come from two sources. The first has been through the direct reduction of benefit levels in order to force welfare recipients into the paid labour market. This has been especially so in the US, the UK and the Netherlands, and to some lesser extent in Germany. The second has been through the tightening in the criteria for benefit eligibility and restrictions on the duration of benefits. These changes prefigure the general move to recalibrate welfare state programs in such a way as, on the one hand, to clearly demarcate those deemed capable of being forced into the paid labour market from those considered incapable of labour force participation; and on the other hand, to attempt to 'activate' individuals within the passive labour reserves through implementation of mandatory workfare programs.

Just as 'Keynes plus the welfare state' came in many forms and sizes, the neoliberal workfare state has come in many forms and sizes. Indeed, what is crucial to an appreciation of welfare state restructuring in the model cases from the US to the Netherlands are not changes in the size of the welfare state per se, but, rather, the way in which welfare state program design and delivery has been altered so as to reinforce the coercive logic of capitalist labour markets. As Visser observes 'social policy must increasingly earn credits as economic policy and show how it helps to improve business performance and human capital development' (Visser 2000). Thus, the logic of welfare policy is no longer one of insulating workers from the vicissitudes of capitalist labour markets but rather one of, through a judicious use of behavioural carrots and a not so judicious use of material sticks, enforcing attachment to paid labour markets.

Meso-level theory and the persistence of limits[6]

Neo-institutionalists have recently stressed that the models of capitalism must be understood as historically determined institutional matrices which, owing to their individual particularities, have developed organizational capabilities which afford their respective social formations with 'comparative institutional advantages' (Hall and Soskice 2001). That is, embedded in each advanced capitalist country is a particular set of institutional arrangements, which, if properly exploited, confer comparative advantages that simultaneously provide the basis for the persistence of variation across the advanced capitalist zone and regulatory niche marketing opportunities for individual states. The logic here is quite straightforward: if the models themselves are only ideal-typical representations of spatially unique clusters of institutions (understood as corresponding to the geographic boundaries of the advanced capitalist state), which are themselves crystallizations of a unique set of historically contingent social relations, then it follows that the models are non-transferable from one national jurisdiction to another. Moreover, if individual models are understood as a totality of specific socio-historical relations, then even partial emulation (of a foreign financial complex, for example) will not embed the same socio-economic dynamic that it has in the model from which it is being transplanted. If true, therefore, the US is not likely to make the Social or Christian Democratic turn anytime soon; and likewise the European model cases are safe from cut-rate, wholesale, policy imports from abroad – in particular those emanating from the US.

There is indeed something to this logic. Take, for instance, the example of the US. The US has served as the competitive pole in the world market for more than a century. One of its dynamic sources has been the

> flexibility of its labour market, which has provided wide latitude for employer restructuring, larger degrees of wage dispersion, minimal degrees of union organization, and almost an infinite supply of labour from migration. The US has the capacity to employ the leading means of production in terms of scope and scale, and the flexibility of its labour markets allows extraction of longer hours of work than its economic rivals. (Fast and Albo 2003: 14)

Although these dynamic qualities may seem like hard, but ultimately not impossible, qualities to emulate, it is worthwhile to consider the structural conditions that support the US's flexible dynamism. As Jessop (in press) has cogently put the matter:

> the many conditions for US success, if such it be, cannot be repeated elsewhere. There can be only one world debtor running massive trade deficits among leading capitalist economies; only one economy able to print the most liquid international currency to finance its debts; only one major economy able to exploit a global brain drain to sustain its technological prowess despite decrepit public education; only one economy able to impose its definitions of intellectual property and other standards to benefit its own producers; and so forth.

All of this suggests that those countries which seek to emulate the macro-economic *performance* of the US will need to ensure that they are capable of transforming their comparative institutional advantages into competitive advantages *vis-à-vis* their rival economies. Hence, at this level of analysis at least, institutional convergence is blocked by not only the path-dependent nature of the developmental trajectory of individual advanced capitalist countries, but also by divergent responses to the competitive imperatives that arise from an integrated world market characterized as it is by a 'nested hierarchy' of space and scale. The comparison of interacting advanced capitalist countries – and hence welfare states and their labour markets – must take place within the context of an integrating world market, which in turn produces dynamic transformations of each case through time. These transformations, in their turn, provoke a variety of responses by individual states *ad infinitum*. This argument is quite consistent on the descriptive level (meso-level) at which it is cast, but itself is suggestive of a convergent logic operating at a broader level of analysis.

The convergent logic can be identified once the question is posed as to 'what is the underlying basis that makes possible a comparison of advanced capitalist countries?' National capitalisms are comparable precisely because they share common constraints and imperatives that arise from a similar set of social property relations which give rise to a comparable social logic of reproduction. The logic of capitalist reproduction can be understood in 'both its abstract determinations apart from particular cases and in its concretization in specific social formations, as part of an encompassing and interacting world market' (Fast and Albo 2003: 12). The regional, national and local specificities of capitalism derive from the fact that the

> spatial expansion of capitalist property relations occurs not against or apart from states, but rather is dependent upon states to guarantee the socio-economic property relations that make possible the organization of investment, production, distribution and exchange of goods and services between private actors. The uneven development and class conflicts forming a 'nested hierarchy' of specific institutional arrangements – from the local to the global – are both an internalization and a response to the common imperatives of capital accumulation in a world market. (Ibid)

This is the point of Brenner's observation that, to a greater or lesser extent, 'essentially every part of the capitalist world took part... in the unprecedented economic expansion of the epoch before World War I, was struck by the devastating interwar depression, partook of the great post-World War II boom, and has been weighed down by the structural crisis that began in the late 1960s' (Brenner and Glick 1991: 112).

To compare advanced capitalist countries, which are always the object of the VoC literature, is to compare a group of countries that have 'achieved' similar levels of capitalist 'maturity'. Such maturity is evidenced across a range of demographic and structural variables, which, taken together, allow for comparison based on a dynamic common to advanced capitalist development. To disregard the logic driving advanced capitalist development – the specificity in the way the domination of value over use value, private as opposed to substantive democratic control over the means of production and the social surplus, and so forth – and remain within the descriptive bounds of meso-level theorizations, however accurate and revealing they may be, disregards changing imperatives arising from the location of these countries within the global capitalist hierarchy and their own level of capitalist development. We need not go far to see the degree of convergence at this broader level: by the 1990s, all advanced capitalist countries had adopted conservative monetary policy regimes and all had instituted floating exchange rates, and deregulated capital and financial markets.

Institutional differences remain, but the more interesting question is to what end those institutions are being put. The Netherlands, for example, has been credited with using its distinctive brand of coordinated bargaining arrangements to achieve price stability. And while this represents, on the one hand, the continuing viability and variety of advanced capitalist institutional arrangements to raise the margins for capital, it nonetheless, on the other hand, is an example of a convergence in the logic driving institutional evolution, namely, price stability.[7] As Coates remarks, certain varieties of welfare capitalism in the current period 'may be a more civilised way of proceeding, but [they are] still ratcheting down ... we have to recognize that although the institutional structures of "trust based" capitalisms may remain in place, their substance will not' (2000: 260).

Notes

1. Reporting GDP per capita performance in relative terms to the US has the advantage of filtering out the long slowdown that set in during the mid 1970s.
2. From the worker's point of view such rates are rather like having a case of influenza: nothing that will kill you, just enough to wear you down. This concept can be usefully compared to the NAIRU.
3. Michael A Holzschu Overtime Liability: Can it Blowup in Your Face? Electronically accessed @ http://www.businessknowhow.com/manage/overtime.htm.
4. With 1.2 million employees, Wal-Mart is the largest service sector employer in the US (*Associated Press*, Wednesday, Feb. 18).
5. For econometric confirmation of this lack of relationship between welfare state size and economic growth, see A. Benabou, 'Inequality and Growth', NBER Macroeconomic Annual (Cambridge, MA: MIT Press, 1996).
6. This section relies heavily on a co-authored discussion paper presented at the Wake Forest conference on the *Convergence of Capitalist Economies: Competing Perspectives on the Organization of Advanced Capitalism in the New Century*. Wake Forest University, 2002. Fast, Travis, and Greg Albo. 'Varieties of Neoliberalism: Trajectories of Workfare in Advanced Capitalist Countries.'
7. It may be argued that coordinated bargaining arrangements were developed to maintain price stability so that the logic in the Dutch case has not shifted. Such a retort would, however, be remiss because coordinated bargaining arrangements were designed to pursue the *dual* spire of full-employment and price stability. For the Dutch, full employment was sacrificed on the spire of price stability. In this sense, there has clearly been a shift in the logic driving institutional evolution and it may be said of the same shift across high-income OECD countries: price stability over full-employment.

Conclusion: Choosing Between Paradigms – A Personal View

David Coates

If the arguments that underpin the design of this volume have any merit, it follows that the best of the scholarship that has emerged in comparative political economy in the last three decades has been *paradigmatically* anchored – using the term 'paradigm' in the way that Thomas Kuhn did in his pathbreaking arguments on the history of scientific thought (Kuhn 1970). Chapter 1 used the image of a stage illuminated by spotlights to establish this notion of paradigms. It visualized them as great ice-cream cones of light shining down onto the stage of contemporary reality: bringing the light of understanding to the stage of social action in exactly the way that Thomas Kuhn argued that first Copernicus and Newton, and later Einstein, did to a stage of natural phenomena that had hitherto been understood in the west largely through the paradigm of Catholic theology and Aristotelian thought. As Thomas Kuhn taught us, a well-developed paradigm – in both the social and the natural sciences – is anchored in a distinctive ontology and epistemology. It rests on a clear view of the human condition and of the kinds of knowledge of that condition that are open to the humans participating within it. A well-developed paradigm builds onto that ontological base, sets of core categories for use in analysis. It provides a dynamic conceptual universe, generative of more localized explanations that it creates by the deployment of those concepts to locate, isolate, measure and ultimately theorize empirical data. A well-developed paradigm also consolidates around itself agreed methodologies, a set of main texts, even a number of received truths.

Unfortunately it is often a feature of successful paradigmatic thought that in its moment of dominance it becomes invisible. Once established, those adhering to it often lose their understanding of the necessarily paradigmatic and relativistic nature of their own thought processes. They come to see the way that they think about the world as simply 'common sense': as a self-evident set of truths, and as the only possible set of methods for the under-standing of social reality. They even come to think of people working outside their paradigm as not simply wrong but as either ill-trained or, yet worse, ill-conceived. Paradigmatic thought, that is, is not only a route to enlightenment and new understanding, it can also be a route to intolerance and closure. We have seen that intolerance on many occasions in the history of the natural sciences – Galileo was, after all, obliged to recant – and arguably we are seeing it now in many branches of the social sciences as well.

Paradigms in the natural sciences tend to relate to each other in a temporal sequence. One replaces the other in time, as the new one satisfactorily answers that key set of issues by which practitioners of the old paradigm had been visibly and perennially defeated. But in the analysis of social phenomena, the relationship between paradigms is not synchronic in this fashion. It is diachronic. In the social sciences, paradigms perpetually struggle with each other for dominance; and that struggle is a permanent feature of the intellectual landscape. It is true that, even in the social sciences, paradigms rise and fall in dominance over time. But they do so while having to live, even when dominant, in competition with the others; such that, if a major paradigm is ignored, it is *not* normally because of its inadequacy as an explanatory vehicle. It is usually because the social forces whose interests would be best served by its dominance/consideration have been pushed out of the central loops of academic and political power.

That is what has happened recently across many of the social sciences, and even in the field of comparative political economy. In the space of my academic lifetime, the center of intellectual gravity has shifted dramatically to the *right*. It certainly has in the policy process. In the dominant finance ministries and the increasingly marginalized industry ministries of the advanced capitalist world, economic advice is invariably restricted these days to advocates of the old and new growth theories spawned from a neo-liberal analytical paradigm. It is all Adam Smith. Not Keynes anymore. Maybe a little Schumpeter now and then; but most of the time just various versions of only rational expectations economics. Academically, fortunately the field is wider; but even if we escape the desert of most modern economics departments, the major show in town is the clash between neoliberal growth theory and the right face of the new institutionalist scholarship. That clash is a vital one, as Chapter 1 made clear; but it is also one which is intellectually and politically impoverished. Which is why, in addition to holding that front, we need to begin to shift the center of intellectual debate back *left* again – to reposition it between the left face of the new institutionalism, and the radical scholarship of the Marxist tradition – the better to create an intellectual climate that might begin to widen the agenda of the policy debate once more, and strengthen the possibilities of radical and progressive change.

In the social sciences, the choice of paradigmatic framework for the organization of research and the advocacy of public policy is inherently a political as well as an academic endeavor. True, paradigms in the social sciences need to be judged initially, as in the natural sciences, for their explanatory openness, depth and range, but – as Table C.1 makes clear – they

Table C.1 Theoretical options: criteria for choice

Explanatory coherence
The number and quality of linkages in the explanatory chain
The number of unlinked elements in the explanation
The degree to which linkages stretch back to an organizing concept
The elegance and clarity of the explanation

Explanatory power
Capacity to handle evidence
Degree of vulnerability to facts
Clarity on counter-factual tests
Number of special exceptions being canvassed

Explanatory reach
Range of issues covered
Scale and importance of matters ignored/unexplained
Degree of depth – status of unexplained independent variable
Degree to which as range expands, coherence diminishes

Explanatory openness
Capacity to absorb new circumstances/new lines of research
Openness to articulation with additional lines of explanation
Degree to which that openness is compatible with original coherence
Openness to criticism and to self-reflection

Explanatory impact
The social consequences of applying its prescriptions
The pattern of winners and losers associated with its prescriptions
The interests privileged
The values structuring the approach

---

need also to be judged ultimately, as the paradigms of natural science are not, by their relationship to values.

The paradigms we choose reflect the values that we hold, and the proposals that we make on the basis of research developed within the paradigms chosen shape, the worlds in the manner of those values. Which is why it is time for us to ask of ourselves not only, in a narrow professional sense, do we do good research; but also, in a wider social sense, is the research that we do likely itself to do good. For the subject matter of our research is not anodyne, obscure, intellectualism for its own sake. Our research is about the conditions under which we can guarantee that, if people are sick, they can afford adequate medical care. It's about their certainty, or lack of certainty, of an adequate pension in old age. It's about their job security, about social justice, and about the ways in which we can act now to protect and develop those rights for our children and for theirs. There is too much unfinished business out there in the world for any of us to be satisfied with academic scholarship that itself remains unfinished.

We have arrived at that point in the development of comparative political economy where we need to do more than simply document and explain some pattern of important dependent variables by relating them back in a sophisticated manner to some unexplained or unexplored independent variable. With so much detailed scholarship behind us, and available to us, as comparative political economy explodes, now is the time to go after those independent variables – to tackle Maddison's ultimate level of causality – and to do so in ways that are consistent with the more focused explanations that we develop of proximate phenomena as we go. The various approaches laid out in this volume offer a range of routes to that more ambitious end; and in considering them, research students and policy advocates will need to make a judgment, not simply on the intrinsic qualities of each approach but also on the nature of the relationship between them. For ultimately, the issue to be settled here is whether a deeper understanding of the nature of our modern condition is best achieved by synthesis or by rupture. If the exercise is ultimately one of synthesis, then eclecticism is the order of the day; and scholarship will be advanced by the layering up of analysis, slice by slice: here starting with factor analysis, exploring rational choice modeling, adding institutional analysis, and finishing with a dash of class and structure. But if it is a matter of rupture, then the key research and policy question becomes that of in which paradigm intellectual and political activity should be anchored, and with which paradigm we should have no truck at all.

Speaking personally

To my mind, creative synthesis should be our first instinct, but some form of rupture will ultimately be unavoidable; not all the paradigms are of equal value in the pursuit of understanding here. Neoclassical economics is certainly not a serious runner here, as far as I can tell, for all its dominance in the corridors of power. Indeed, the central paradox of the modern age – in the area of growth theory and state policy at least – would appear to be that the ideational system most dominant in policy-making circles is the one least able to explain what is actually going on, and yet is at the same time the one least aware of its own limitations. It is not too much to say that many neoliberal economists now operate – to use Gramscian terminology – as the organic intellectuals of global capitalist classes, and as the main ideologues of the existing order. Certainly, the bulk of them have reconstituted themselves as a hermetically sealed and entirely self-referential priesthood, equipped with their own holy books, mantras, catechisms and modes of induction. They do seem to have reset themselves into what Galbraith recently called 'a kind of politburo for correct economic thought' (Galbraith 2000); and as such are broadly valueless for our purposes.

'So what is modern economics about?' Galbraith asked. His answer was that 'it seems to be mainly about itself' (Galbraith 2000: 2). The thought patterns into which neoliberal economists characteristically induct their students (and into which they themselves are inextricably locked) seem to act as an effective mental sealant against any recognition of the huge and deleterious social consequences of unregulated markets, and to invite a persistent preoccupation with the exchange of commodities once produced, rather than with their production per se. Indeed when viewed from outside, many of the university departments now spawning the new generation of neoliberal economists appear increasingly authoritarian (even potentially totalitarian) in their forms of thought and action: maintaining their credibility only by retreating into abstractionism and mathematical sophistry, shutting themselves off in the process from the scholarship and insights of the other social sciences, and proving increasingly intolerant of dissent from within their own ranks. There are some wonderful economists left, of course, networked together in schools of radical political economy; but as far as I can tell such networks no longer set the intellectual agenda of mainstream economics. And to the degree that that is true, so too is this: that whatever else the setting of the performance of capitalist models against contemporary explanations of that performance tell us, it certainly indicates that neoliberal growth theory is inadequate to the explanatory task and potentially dangerous in the policy process. As far as I can see, neoliberal economics is not part of any progressive solution to the problems of capitalist models, nor in truth any guide to understanding why such solutions are needed. It is actually part of the problem that the rest of us need to solve.

Which is why it is essential – if capitalist models are to be understood and their problems transcended – that neoliberalism be left behind: that we move on. How far we move on, and in which direction – and not whether we move on at all – seems to me to be the key issue that we actually face, as we seek stronger explanatory frameworks to guide political action. *We need to go left.*

We certainly need to explore the strengths and weaknesses of explanations that mix economic theories of a Schumpeterian or post-Keynesian kind with the institutional economic history of Douglass North and others. Such a mixture, limited as it is, is immeasurably superior, as a guide to the determinants of capitalist economic performance, to the simplistic gropings of even new growth theory (let alone old growth theory) for some way of measuring the 'X' factor that always lies beyond their abstracted theories of growth: that factor which time and again produces the last-paragraph throwaway line about 'other variables being beyond the model's reach and needing more research money to find.' Indeed, the superiority of any new paradigmatic mixture seems to depend on the degree of distance it establishes between itself and dominant neoliberal orthodoxies. It is clearly desirable to question the way markets work by confronting neoliberal arguments with arguments drawn from the writings of Schumpeter and Keynes. It is clearly advantageous to understand the cumulative interaction of economic variables and to add an institutional dynamic to our understanding of market processes. It is arguably even better to locate the entire neoliberal framework in its own finite (and now long gone) time and place (in the manner of Lazonick) – to treat its second coming as history once as tragedy, twice as farce – and then to switch the focus of analysis onto institutional dynamics of various kinds. Indeed, the big question is not whether to do all that. Such a move seems self-evidently essential. The big question is whether such an intellectual journey is itself enough; or whether the whole exercise can be given an enhanced level of understanding and insight by going the extra inch – by locating those institutional variables and dynamics in a deeper, more Marxist-inspired, level of analysis, one deploying a conceptual apparatus of classes and structures of accumulation, modes of production and social formations.

For myself, I find that last move both productive and essential. I find that the movement from 'proximate causes' to 'ultimate ones' (in the manner of growth accounting) is the proper move to make, if full understanding is our purpose; and I find too that such a move involves not simply a deepening of the argument but also its radicalization. Time and again of late in my own work, the insights of growth accounting have proved to be an important and valuable initial point of reference, but have themselves required to be 'thickened', supplemented and ultimately transformed by two further intellectual moves. The first is the move from factor analysis to the analysis of institutions, histories and growth trajectories, in the manner of the 'new institutionalism'. The second is the positioning of those institutional relationships in a 'deeper' set of class patterns and underlying structural processes, understood from a broadly Marxist perspective. For me, the full *explanatory* journey of why capitalist models perform differently is one that moves from 'growth accounting' through the 'new institutionalism' to Marxist explanations of combined and uneven economic development; and the underlying *theoretical* journey is one that rejects neoclassical economics entirely, and notes the insights of Schumpeterian and post-Keynesian explanations of growth, while ultimately remaining in a Marxist understanding of capitalism as a global system. As far as I can see, the post-war performance and contemporary difficulties of the various capitalist models manifest themselves at the level of factors of production, and are given expression in particular sets of institutional practices; but those practices are themselves driven by the balance and character of class forces by which they are infused, while the trajectory of the economies they sustain are centrally informed by the position occupied by those classes in the wider system of global accumulation characteristic of world capitalism as a whole.

So there is the question! Is our understanding of the varieties of capitalism in the modern age deepened enough if we merely add an institutional dimension to a neoliberal frame of reference? Or does that deepening require in addition that we replace a focus on markets with one on institutions; and/or then re-specify that market-institutional nexus as a social structure of accumulation with its own internal contradictions and global positioning? There are matters of judgment here, and scope for profound and prolonged disagreement. But that is as it should be. For the health and progress of the sub-discipline of comparative political economy, it is more important that the questions be asked than that the answers be agreed. Sub-disciplines come to maturity not with consensus but with self-reflection; it is time now for this sub-discipline to seek, not only knowledge of the world, but also knowledge of itself.

References

Abramovitz, M. (1956), 'Resource and output trends in the United States since 1870', *American Economic Review*, 46, 5–23.

Abramovitz, M. (1986), 'Catching Up, forging ahead and falling behind', *Journal of Economic History*, 46, 385–406.

Abramovitz, M. (1989), *Thinking About Growth*, Cambridge, Cambridge University Press.

Abramovitz, M. (1994), 'Catch up and convergence in the post-war boom and after', in W. Baumol, R.R. Nelson and E. Wolff (eds), *Convergence of Productivity*, Oxford, Oxford University Press, pp. 86–125.

Abramovitz, M. and David, P. (1996), 'Convergence and delayed catch-up: productivity leadership and the waning of American exceptionalism', in R. Landau, T. Taylor and G. Wright (eds), *The Mosaic of Modern Growth*, Stanford, Stanford University Press, pp. 21–62.

Aghion, P. and Howitt, P. (1992), 'A model of growth through creative destruction', *Econometrica*, 60, 323–51.

Aghion, P. and Howitt, P. (1998), *Endogenous Growth Theory*, Cambridge, Mass, MIT.

Aglietta, M. (1979), *A Theory of Capitalist Regulation: The US Experience*, London, New Left Books.

Aglietta, M. (1998), 'Capitalism at the turn of the century: regulation theory and the challenge of social change', *New Left Review*, 232, 41–90.

Albo, G. (1994), 'Competitive austerity and the impasses of capitalist employment policy', in R. Miliband and L. Panitch (eds), *The Socialist Register 1994*, London, Merlin Press, pp.144–70.

Albo, G. (1997), 'A world market of opportunities: capitalist obstacles and Left economic policy', in L. Panitch (ed.), *The Socialist Register 1997*, London, Merlin Press, pp. 5–48.

Albo, G. and Roberts, C. (1999), 'European industrial relations: impasse or model?', in E. Wood, P. Meiksins and M. Yates (eds), *Rising from the Ashes: Labor in an Age of Global Capitalism*, New York, Monthly Review Press, pp. 158–74.

Alesina, A. and Rosenthal, H. (1995), *Partisan Politics, Divided Government and the Economy*, Cambridge, Cambridge University Press.

Alesina, A. and Roubini, N. with Cohen, G.D. (1997), *Political Cycles and the Macro-economy*, Cambridge, MA, MIT Press.

Allan, J. and Scrugge, L. (2002), 'Political Partisanship and Welfare State Reform in Advanced Industrial Societies', unpublished, Department of Political Science, University of Connecticut.

Altvater, E. (2002), 'The growth obsession', in L. Panitch and C. Leys (eds), *Socialist Register 2002: A World of Contradictions*, London, Merlin, pp. 73–92.

Alvarez, R.M., Garrett, G. and Lange, P. (1991), 'Government partisanship, labor organization and macro-economic performance', *American Political Science Review*, 85 (2), 539–56.

Amable, B. (2000), 'Institutional complementarity and diversity of social systems of innovation and production', *Review of International Political Economy*, 7 (4), 645–87.

Ames, E. and Rosenberg, N. (1968), 'The Enfield arsenal in theory and history', *Economic Journal*, 78, 827–942.

Amsden, A. (1989), *Asia's Next Giant: South Korea and Late Industrialization*, Oxford, Oxford University Press.

Aoki, M. (2001), *Towards a Comparative Institutional Analysis*, Cambridge, MA, MIT Press.

Armstrong, P., Glyn, A. and Harrison, J. (1991), *Capitalism Since 1945*, London, Blackwell.

Arrighi, G. (1994), *The Long Twentieth Century*, London, Verso.

Arrighi, G. (2003), 'The social and political economy of global turbulence', *New Left Review*, II/20.

Arrow, K. (1962), 'The economic implications of learning by doing', *Review of Economic Studies*, 29 (3), 155–73.

Atkinson, A. (1970), 'On the measurement of inequality', *Journal of Economic Theory*, 2, 244–63.

Bakker, G. (2001), 'Entertainment Industrialized: Emergence of the International film industry, 1890–1940', unpublished PhD Thesis, European University Institute, Florence.

Ball, L. (1997), 'Disinflation and the NAIRU', in C.D. Romer and D.H. Romer (eds), *Reducing Inflation: Motivation and Strategy*, Chicago, Chicago University Press, pp. 167–85.

Baran, P. and Sweezy, P. (1966), *Monopoly Capital: An Essay on the American Economic and Social Order*, New York, Monthly Review Press.

Barrell, R. and Genre, V. (1999), *Labour Market Reform in the UK, Denmark, New Zealand and the Netherlands*, London, National Institute of Economic and Social Research.

Barro, R. (1998), 'Notes on growth accounting', *NBER Working Paper*, No. 6654.

Barro, R.J. (1997), *Determinants of Economic Growth*, Cambridge, MA, MIT Press.

Barro, R.J. and Sala-i-Martin, X. (1991), 'Convergence across states and regions', *Brookings Papers on Economic Activity*, 107–82.

Barro, R.J. and Sala-i-Martin, X. (1995), *Economic Growth*, New York, McGraw-Hill.

Baumgartner, F. and Jones, B. (1993), *Agendas and Instability in American Politics*, Chicago, University of Chicago Press.

Baumol, W.J. (1986), 'Productivity growth, convergence and welfare: what the long-run data show', *American Economic Review*, 76, 1072–85.

Baumol, W.J. (1994), 'Multivariate growth patterns: contagion and common forces as possible sources of convergence', in W.J. Baumol, R.R. Nelson and E.N. Wolff (eds), *Convergence of Productivity*, Oxford, Oxford University Press, pp. 62–85.

Baumol, W.J. (2002), *The Free-Market Innovation Machine*, Princeton, Princeton University Press.

Bell, D.N.F., Hart, R.A., Hübler and Schwerdt, W. (2000), 'Paid and Unpaid Overtime Working in Germany and the UK', IZA Discussion Paper Series (133).

Benabou, A. (1996), *Inequality and Growth*, Cambridge, MA, MIT Press.

Benhabib, J. and Spiegel, M. (1994), 'The role of human capital in economic development: evidence from cross country data', *Journal of Monetary Economics*, 34 (2), 143–73.

Berger, S. and Dore, R. (eds) (1996), *National Adversity and Global Capitalism*, Ithaca, NY, Cornell University Press.

Best, M. (1990), *The New Competition*, Cambridge, Polity Press.

Bethell, L. (ed.) (1998), *Latin America: Economy and Society since 1930*, Cambridge, Cambridge University Press.

Bhagwati, J. (2004), *In Defence of Globalization*, New York, Oxford University Press.

Blanchard, O.J. and Summers, L.H. (1988), Beyond the natural rate hypothesis, *American Economic Review*, 78 (May), 182–7.

Blanchflower, D. and Oswald, A. (1999), 'Well-being, insecurity and the decline of American job satisfaction', *NBER Working Paper*, No. 7487.

Blinder, A. and Yellen, J. (2001), *The Fabulous Decade: Macroeconomic Lessons from the 1990s*, New York, Century Foundation Press.

Block, F. (1977), *The Origins of International Economic Disorder*, Berkeley, University of California Press.

Blyth, M. (2003), 'Same as it never was: temporality and typology in the varieties of capitalism', *Comparative European Politics*, 1 (2), 215–25.

Bonefeld, W. (1999), 'Note on competition, capitalist crises and class', *Historical Materialism*, 5, 5–28.

Bonefeld, W. and Holloway, J. (eds) (1995), *Global Capital, National State, and the Politics of Money*, New York, St. Martin's Press.

Bowles, S. and Eatwell, J. (1983), 'Between two worlds: interest groups, class structures and capitalist growth', in D.C. Mueller (ed.), *The Political Economy of Growth*, New Haven, Yale University Press, pp. 217–30.

Bowles, S., Gordon, D. and Weisskopf, T. (1990), *After the Waste Land*, Armonk, M.E. Sharpe.

Boyer, R. (1990), *The Regulation School: A Critical Introduction*, New York, Columbia University Press.

Boyer, R. (1996), 'The convergence hypothesis revisited: globalization but still the century of nations?', in S. Berger and R. Dore (eds), *National Diversity and Global Capitalism*, Ithaca, Cornell University Press, pp. 29–59.

Boyer, R. (2001), 'The diversity and future of capitalisms: a regulationist analysis', in G. Hodgson, M. Itoh and N. Yokokawa (eds), *Capitalism in Evolution: Global Contentions – East and West*, Cheltenham, Edward Elgar, pp. 100–21.

Boyer, R. and Yamada, T. (eds) (2000), *Japanese Capitalism in Crisis: A Regulationist Interpretation*, London, Routledge.

Brenner, R. and Glick, M. (1991), 'The Regulation Approach', *New Left Review* 188, July–August, pp. 45–119.

Brenner, R. (1998), 'Uneven development and the long downturn: the advanced capitalist economies from boom to stagnation', *New Left Review*, 229, 1–265.

Brenner, R. (1999), 'Reply to critics', in Symposium on 'The economics of global turbulence', *Comparative Studies of South Asia, Africa and the Middle East*, XIX (2), 61–85.

Brenner, R. (2000), 'The boom and the bubble', *New Left Review*, II/6, 5–44.

Brenner, R. (2002a), *The Boom and the Bubble: The US in the World Economy*, New York/London, Verso.

Brenner, R. (2002b), 'The Neoliberal Economy after the Boom', paper presented at the Wake Forest Conference on the Convergence of Capitalist Economies, Winston-Salem, 27–29 September.

Brenner, R. (2003), 'Towards the precipice', *London Review of Books*, 6 February.

Broadberry, S.N. (1993), 'Manufacturing and the convergence hypothesis: what the long run data show', *Journal of Economic History*, 53, 772–95.

Broadberry, S.N. (1996), 'Convergence: what the historical record shows', in B. van Ark and N.F.R. Crafts (eds), *Quantitative Aspects of Post-War European Economic Growth*, Cambridge, Cambridge University Press, pp. 327–46.

Broadberry, S.N. (1997a), *The Productivity Race: British Manufacturing in International Perspective, 1850–1990*, Cambridge, Cambridge University Press.

Broadberry, S.N. (1997b), 'Forging ahead, falling behind and catching-up: a sectoral analysis of Anglo-American productivity differences, 1870–1990', *Research in Economic History*, 17, 1–37.

Broadberry, S.N. (1997c), 'Anglo-German productivity differences 1870–1990: a sectoral analysis', *European Review of Economic History*, 1, 247–67.

Broadberry, S.N. (1998), 'How did the United States and Germany overtake Britain? A sectoral analysis of comparative productivity levels, 1870–1990', *Journal of Economic History*, 58, 375–407.

Broadberry, S.N. (2003), 'Explaining Anglo-German Productivity Differences in Services Since 1870', unpublished paper, University of Warwick.

Broadberry, S.N. and Ghosal, S. (2002), 'From the counting house to the modern office: explaining Anglo-American productivity differences in services, 1870–1990', *Journal of Economic History*, 62, 967–98.

Brock, W.A. and Durlauf, S.N. (2001), 'What have we learned from a decade of empirical research on growth? Growth empirics and reality', *The World Bank Economic Review*, 15 (2), 229–72.

Brown, G. (2004), 'Speech by the Chancellor of the Exchequer, Gordon Brown, at the Advancing Enterprise Conference', QE2 Conference Centre, London, 26 January.

Bryan, D. (1995), *The Chase Across the Globe*, Boulder, Westview Press.

Bryan, R. (2001), 'Global accumulation and accounting for national economic identity', *Review of Radical Political Economics*, 33 (1), 57–78.

Bukharin, N. (1972), *Imperialism and World Economy*, London, Merlin, original publication 1917.

Burchell, B.J.D., D. Hudson, M. *et al.* (1999), *Job Insecurity and Work Intensification: Flexibility and the Changing Boundaries of Work*, York, Joseph Rowntree Foundation.

Burke, M. (2001), 'The changing nature of imperialism: the US as author of the Asian crisis of 1997', *Historical Materialism*, 8, 49–88.

Burkett, P. and Hart-Landsberg, M. (1996), 'The use and abuse of Japan as a progressive model', in L. Panitch (ed.), *The Socialist Register 1996*, London, Merlin Press, pp. 62–92.

Burkett, P. and Hart-Landsberg, M. (2000), *Development, Crisis and Class Struggle: Learning from Japan and East Asia*, New York, St. Martin's Press.

Burkett, P. and Hart-Landsberg, M. (2003), 'The economic crisis in Japan: mainstream perspectives and an alternative view', *Critical Asian Studies*, 35.3, 339–72.

Burnham, P. (1990), *The Political Economy of Postwar Reconstruction*, New York, St. Martin's Press.

Callinicos, A. (1999), 'Capitalism, competition and profits: a critique of Robert Brenner's Theory of Crisis', *Historical Materialism*, 4, 9–32.

Calmfors, L. (1990), 'Wage formation and macroeconomic policy in the Nordic countries: a summary', in L. Calmfors (ed.), *Wage Formation and Macroeconomic Policy in the Nordic Countries*, New York, Oxford University Press, pp. 11–60.

Calmfors, L. and Driffill, S. (1988), 'Bargaining structures, corporatism and macroeconomic performance', *Economic Policy*, 3, 13–61.

Campbell, J. and Pedersen, O. (2001), *The Rise of Neoliberalism and Institutional Analysis*, Princeton, Princeton University Press.

Campbell, J., Hollingsworth, R. and Lindbergh, L. (eds) (1991), *Governance of the American Economy*, Cambridge, Cambridge University Press.

Campbell-Kelly, M. (1992), 'Large-scale data processing in the Prudential, 1850–1930', *Accounting, Business and Financial History*, 2, 117–39.

Campbell-Kelly, M. (1998), 'Data processing and technological change: the Post Office Savings Bank, 1861–1930', *Technology and Culture*, 39, 1–32.

Carchedi, G. (1991), *Frontiers of Political Economy*, London, Verso.

Carlin, W. (1996), 'West German growth and institutions, 1945–90', in N.F.R. Crafts and G. Toniolo (eds), *Economic Growth in Europe since 1945*, Cambridge, Cambridge University Press, pp. 455–97.

Carnoy, M. (1984), *The State and Political Theory*, Princeton, Princeton University Press.

Carpenter, M. and Jefferys, S. (2000), *Management, Work and Welfare in Western Europe*, Northampton, MA, Edward Elgar.

Carroll, W. (2004), *Corporate Power in a Globalizing World*, Toronto, Oxford University Press.

Casper, S. (2001), 'The legal framework for corporate governance', in P. Hall and D. Soskice (eds), *Varieties of Capitalism*, New York, Oxford University Press, pp. 387–416.

Castells, M. (2002), *The Rise of the Network Society*, Oxford, Blackwell.

Castles, F. (1978), *The Social Democratic Image of Society*, London, Routledge & Kegan Paul.

Castley, R. (1997), *Korea's Economic Miracle: The Crucial Role of Japan*, London, Macmillan.

Chandler, A.D. Jr (1977), *The Visible Hand: The Managerial Revolution in American Business*, Cambridge, MA, Harvard University Press.

Chandler, A.D. Jr (1990), *Scale and Scope: The Dynamics of Industrial Capitalism*, Cambridge, MA, Harvard University Press.

Chang, H-J. (1993), 'The political economy of industrial policy in Korea', *Cambridge Journal of Economics*, 17, 131–57.

Chang, H-J. (1994), *The Political Economy of Industrial Policy*, London, Macmillan.

Chang, H-J., Park, H-J. and Yoo, C. (1998), 'Interpreting the Korean crisis: financial liberalization, industrial policy and corporate governance', *Cambridge Journal of Economics*, 22, 735–46.

Chatterji, M. (1992), 'Convergence clubs and endogenous growth', *Oxford Review of Economic Policy*, 8 (4), 57–69.

Chen, E. (1979), *Hyper-Growth in Asian Economies*, London, Macmillan.

Chibber, V. (1999), 'Building a developmental state: the Korean case reconsidered', *Politics and Society*, 27 (3), 309–46.

Chibber, V. (2003), *Locked in Place: State-Building and Late Industrialization in India*, Princeton, Princeton University Press.

Christiansen, P. and Rommetvedt, H. (1999), 'From corporatism to lobbyism?', *Scandinavian Political Studies*, 22 (3), 195–220.

Clarke, S. (1988), *Keynesianism, Monetarism, and the Crisis of the State*, Aldershot, Edward Elgar.

Clarke, S. (1999), 'Capitalist competition and the tendency to overproduction: comments on Brenner's "Uneven development and the long downturn" ', *Historical Materialism*, 4, 57–72.

Clarke, S. (2001), 'Class struggle and the global over-accumulation of capital' in R. Albritton, M. Itoh, R. Westra and A. Zuege (eds), *Phases of Capitalist Development*, New York, Palgrave, pp. 76–92.

Coates, D. (1994), *The Question of UK Decline*, Hemel Hempstead, Harvester-Wheatsheaf.

Coates, D. (1999), 'Labour power and international competitiveness: a critique of ruling orthodoxies', in L. Panitch and C. Leys (eds), *Socialist Register 1999: Global Capitalism versus Democracy*, London, Merlin, pp. 108–41.

Coates, D. (2000), *Models of Capitalism: Growth and Stagnation in the Modern Era*, Cambridge, Polity Press.

Coates, D. (2001), 'Capitalist models and social democracy', *British Journal of Politics and International Relations*, 3 (3), 284–307.

Coleman, W. (1988), *Business and Politics*, Toronto, University of Toronto Press.

Coleman, W. and Jacek, H. (1989), *Regionalism, Business Interests and Public Policy*, Beverly Hills, Sage.

Cortada, J.W. (1993), *Before the Computer: IBM, NCR, Burroughs and Remington Rand and the Industry They Created, 1865–1956*, Princeton, NJ, Princeton University Press.

Cox, R. (1987), *Production, Power and World Order*, New York, Columbia University Press.

Crafts, N. (2002), *Britain's Relative Economic Performance*, London, Institute of Economic Affairs.

Crepaz, M. (1992), 'Corporatism in decline?', *Comparative Political Studies*, 25 (2), 139–68.

Cronin, J. (2000), 'Convergence by conviction: politics and economics in the emergence of the "Anglo-American Model" ', *Journal of Social History*, XXXIII (4), 781–804.

Crouch, C. (1990), 'Trade unionism in the exposed sector,' in R. Brunetta and C. Dell'Aringa (eds), *Labor Relations and Economic Performance*, New York, New York University Press, pp. 68–91.

Crouch, C. (1993), *Industrial Relations and European State Traditions*, New York, Oxford University Press.

Crouch, C. (2001), 'Welfare regimes and industrial relations systems: the questionable role of path dependency theory', in B. Ebbinghaus and P. Manow (eds), *Comparing Welfare Capitalism*, London, Routledge, pp. 105–24.

Crouch, C. and Farrell, H. (2002), 'Breaking the Path of Institutional Development? Alternatives to the New Determinism', European University Institute Working Paper, SPS No. 2002/4.

Crouch, C. and Streeck, W. (eds) (1997), *The Political Economy of Modern Capitalism*, London, Sage.

Culpepper, P. (1999), 'Individual choice, collective action, and the problem of training reform', in P. Culpepper and D. Finegold (eds), *The German Skills Machine*, New York, Berghahn Books, pp. 1–34.

Daly, K. (2004), 'Euroland's Secret Success Story', Goldman Sachs Economics Paper, number 102, 16 January, Goldman Sachs Global Economics Website.

Daly, H. and Cobb, J. (1989), *For the Common Good: Redirecting the Economy Towards the Community, the Environment and Sustainable Development*, Boston, Beacon Press.

David, P.A. (1975), *Technical Choice, Innovation and Economic Growth*, Cambridge, Cambridge University Press.

David, P.A. (1985), 'Clio and the economics of QWERTY', *American Economic Review Proceedings*, 75, 332–7.

Davis, L. and North, D.C. (1971), *Institutional Change and American Economic Growth*, Cambridge, Cambridge University Press.

DeLong, B. and Summers, L. (2001), 'The "new economy": background, historical perspective, questions, and speculations', *Economic Review*, 4th Quarter, Federal Reserve Bank of Kansas City, 29–59.

Denison, E.F. (1962), *The Sources of Economic Growth in the United States and the Alternatives Before Us*, Washington DC, Brookings Institution.

Denison, E.F. (1967), *Why Growth Rates Differ*, Washington DC, Brookings Institution.

Denison, E.F. (1989), *Estimates of Productivity Change by Industry: An Evaluation and an Alternative*, Washington DC, Brookings Institution.

DiMaggio, P. and Powell, W. (1991), 'Introduction', in W. Powell and P. DiMaggio (eds), *The New Institutionalism in Organizational Analysis*, Chicago, University of Chicago Press, pp. 1–38.

Di Tella, R., MacCulloch, R. and Layard, R. (2002), 'Income, Happiness and Inequality as Measures of Welfare', mimeo, London School of Economics.

Due, J., Madsen, J., Jensen, C. and Petersen, L. (1994), *The Survival of the Danish Model*, Copenhagen, DJOEF Publishing.

Dumenil, G. and Levy, D. (2003), *Capital Resurgent: The Roots, Nature and Contradictions of the Neo-liberal Revolution in the Late Twentieth Century*, Cambridge, MA, Harvard University Press.

Durlauf, S.N. and Johnson, P.A. (1995), 'Multiple regimes and cross-country growth behaviour', *Journal of Applied Econometrics*, 10, 365–84.

Durlauf, S.N. and Quah, T. (1999), 'The new empirics of economic growth', *Handbook of Macroeconomics*, Volume 1A, Amsterdam, New York and Oxford, Elsevier Science, North-Holland, pp. 235–308.

Economic Policy Institute, *Datazone Database*, www.eipnet/org/datazone.

Eichengreen, B. (1996a), 'Institutions and economic growth: Europe after World War II', in N.F.R. Crafts and G. Toniolo (eds), *Economic Growth in Europe since 1945*, Cambridge, Cambridge University Press, pp. 38–72.

Eichengreen, B. (1996b), *Globalizing Capital*, Princeton, Princeton University Press.

Elbaum, B. and Lazonick, W. (1984), 'The decline of the British economy: an institutional perspective', *Journal of Economic History*, xliv (2), 567–83.

Esping-Andersen, G. (1990), *The Three Worlds of Welfare Capitalism*, Princeton, Princeton University Press.

Esping-Andersen, G. (1996), *Welfare States in Transition*, Thousand Oaks, CA, Sage Publications.

Esping-Andersen, G. and Regini, M. (eds) (2000), *Why Deregulate Labour Markets?* Oxford, Oxford University Press.

Estevez-Abe, M., Iversen, T. and Soskice, D. (2001), 'Social protection and the formation of skills: a reinterpretation of the welfare state', in P. Hall and D. Soskice (eds), *Varieties of Capitalism*, Oxford, Oxford University Press, pp. 145–83.

Evans, P. (1997), 'The eclipse of the state', *World Politics*, 50 (1), 62–87.

Fast, T. and Albo, G. (2003), 'Varieties of Neoliberalism: Trajectories of Workfare in Advanced Capitalist Countries', paper presented at the Annual Meetings of the Canadian Political Science Association, Congress of the Humanities and Social Sciences, Dalhousie University, Halifax, Nova Scotia, May.

Fei, J.C.H. and Ranis, G. (1964), *Development of the Labor Surplus Economy*, Homewood, IL, Irwin.

Feinstein, C.F., Temin, P. and Toniolo, G. (1997), *The European Economy Between the Wars*, Oxford, Oxford University Press.

Felipe, J. (1999), 'Total factor productivity in East Asia: a critical survey', *The Journal of Development Studies*, 35 (4), 1–41.

Felipe, J. and McCombie, J. (2003), 'How Sound are the Foundations of the Aggregate Production Function?', mimeo, Cambridge.

Field, A.J. (1996), 'The relative productivity of American distribution, 1869–1992', *Research in Economic History*, 16, 1–37.

Fields, K. (1995), *Enterprise and the State in Korea and Taiwan*, Ithaca, Cornell University Press.

Fine, B. (2002), 'Economics Imperialism and the new development economics as a paradigm shift?', *World Development*, 30 (12), 2057–70.

Fioretos, O. (2001), 'The domestic sources of multilateral preferences', in P. Hall and D. Soskice (eds), *Varieties of Capitalism*, Oxford, Oxford University Press, pp. 213–44.

Fligstein, N. (1990), *The Transformation of Corporate Control*, Cambridge, MA, Harvard University Press.

Fligstein, N. (2001), *The Architecture of Markets*, Princeton, Princeton University Press.

Florida, R. (2002), *The Rise of the Creative Class*, New York, Basic Books.

Flux, A.W. (1924), 'The census of production', *Journal of the Royal Statistical Society*, 87, 351–75.

Foster, J.B. (2002), 'Monopoly capital and the new globalization', *Monthly Review*, January, 1–16.

Frankel, M. (1957), *British and American Manufacturing Productivity*, Urbana, University of Illinois.

Freeman, C. (1997), 'The national system of innovation in historical perspective', in D. Archibugi and J. Michie (eds), *Technology, Globalisation and Economic Performance*, Cambridge, Cambridge University Press, pp. 24–49.

Freeman, A. (2001), 'Has the empire struck back?', in R. Albritton, M. Itoh, R. Westra and A. Zuege (eds), *Phases of Capitalist Development*, New York, Palgrave, pp. 195–214.

Friedman, M. (1962), *Capitalism and Freedom*, Chicago, University of Chicago Press.

Friedman, D. (1988), *The Misunderstood Miracle: Industrial Development and Political Change in Japan*, Ithaca, Cornell University Press.

Fukuyama, F. (1992), *The End of History and the Last Man*, New York, Free Press.

Fukuyama, F. (1995), *Trust: The Social Virtues And The Creation of Prosperity*, New York, Free Press.

Galbraith, J. (2000), 'How the economists got it wrong?', *The American Prospect*, 11 (7), 1–8.

Garrett, G. (1998), *Partisan Politics in the Global Economy*, Cambridge, Cambridge University Press.

Gereffi, G. (1996), 'Global commodity chains: new forms of coordination and control among nations and firms in international industries', *Competition and Change*, 4, pp. 1–22.

Gereffi, G. and Korzeniewicz, M. (eds) (1994), *Commodity Chains and Global Capitalism*, Westport, Praeger.

Gerth, H. and Mills, C.W. (1958), *From Max Weber: Essays in Sociology*, New York, Oxford University Press.

Giddens, A. (1979), *Central Problems in Social Theory: Action, Structure and Contradiction in Social Analysis*, Berkeley, University of California Press.

Gill, S. (1992), 'The emerging world order and European change', in R. Miliband and L. Panitch (eds), *The Socialist Register 1992*, London, Merlin Press, pp. 157–96.

Gilpin, R. (1987), *The Political Economy of International Relations*, Princeton, NJ, Princeton University Press.

Gindin, S. (2001), 'Turning points and starting points: left turbulence and class politics', in L. Panitch and C. Leys (eds), *The Socialist Register 2001*, London, Merlin, pp. 343–66.

Gindin, S. and Panitch, L. (2002), 'Rethinking crisis: a response to "slow growth, excess capital and a mountain of debt"', *Monthly Review*, 54/6, November, 34–46.

Gingerich, D. and Hall, P. (2001), 'Varieties of capitalism and institutional complementarities in the political economy', unpublished paper, presented at the American Political Science Association meeting, San Francisco.

Gingerich, D. and Hall, P. (2002), 'Varieties of capitalism and institutional complementarities in the macro-economy', unpublished paper, Department of Government, Harvard University.

Glyn, A. and Sutcliffe, B. (1972), *British Capitalism, Workers and the Profits Squeeze*, Harmondsworth, Penguin Books.

Golden, M. (1993), 'The dynamics of trade unionism and national economic performance', *American Political Science Review*, 87 (2), 439–54.

Goldsmith, R. (1977), *The Financial Development of India 1869–1977*, New Haven, Yale University Press.

Goldstein, J. (1988), 'Ideas, institutions, and American trade-policy', *International Organization*, 42 (1), 179–217.

Goldthorpe, J. (ed.) (1984), *Order and Conflict in Contemporary Capitalism*, Oxford, Clarendon Press.

Goodin, R.E. (2003), 'Choose your capitalism?', *Comparative European Politics*, 1 (2), 203–13.

Goodwin, R.M. (1967), 'A growth cycle', in C. Feinstein (ed.), *Socialism, Capitalism and Economic Growth*, pp. 54–8.

Gowan, P. (1999), *The Global Gamble: Washington's Faustian Bid for World Dominance*, London, Verso.

Gowan, P. (2001), 'Explaining the American boom: the roles of "globalisation" and United States global power', *New Political Economy*, 6 (3), 359–74.

Gowan, P. (2003), 'The American campaign for global sovereignty', in L. Panitch and C. Leys (eds), *The Socialist Register 2003*, London, Merlin Press, pp. 1–27.

Grahl, J. (2001), 'Globalized finance: the challenge to the Euro', *New Left Review*, II/8, 23–48.

Granovetter, M. (1985), 'Economic action and social structure: the problem of embeddedness', *American Journal of Sociology*, 91 (3), 481–510.

Granovetter, M. and Swedberg, R. (eds) (1992), *The Sociology of Economic Life*, Oxford, Westview Press.

Grant, W. (1989), *Government and Industry*, Brookfield, VT, Gower Publishing.

Greenfield, G. (2005), 'Bandung redux: the imperial alignment of anti-globalization nationalisms', in L. Panitch and C. Leys (eds), *Socialist Register 2005: Empire Reloaded*, London, Merlin (forthcoming).

Greenwood, J. (2002), *Inside the EU Business Associations*, New York, Palgrave.

Greenwood, J., Grote, J. and Ronit, K. (eds) (1992), *Organized Interests and the European Community*, Thousand Oaks, CA, Sage.

Gregg, P. and Wadsworth, J. (eds) (1999), *The State of Working Britain*, Manchester, Manchester University Press.

Greif, A. (1989), 'Reputation and coalitions in medieval trade: Maghribi Traders', *Journal of Economic History*, 49, 857–82.

Greif, A. (2000), 'The fundamental problem of exchange: a research agenda in historical institutional analysis', *European Review of Economic History*, 4, 251–84.

Griliches, Z. (1994), 'Productivity, R&D, and the data constraint', *American Economic Review*, 84 (1), 1–23.

Grimm, C. and Holcomb, J. (1987), 'Choices among encompassing organizations', in A. Marcus, A. Kaufman and D. Beam (eds), *Business Strategy and Public Policy*, New York, Quorum Books, pp. 105–18.

Grossman, G.M. and Helpman, E. (1994), 'Endogenous innovation in the theory of growth', *Journal of Economic Perspectives*, 8 (1), 23–44.

Gylfason, T. (1999), *Principles of Economic Growth*, Oxford, Oxford University Press.

Habakkuk, H.J. (1962), *American and British Technology in the Nineteenth Century*, Cambridge, Cambridge University Press.

Hacker, J. and Pierson, P. (2002), 'Business power and social policy', *Politics & Society*, 30 (2), 277–325.

Hall, M., Knapp, J. and Winsten, C. (1961), *Distribution in Great Britain and North America: A Study in Structure and Productivity*, Oxford, Oxford University Press.

Hall, P. (1993), 'Policy paradigms, social learning, and the state: the case of economic policymaking in Britain', *Comparative Politics*, 25 (3), 275–96.

Hall, P. (2001), 'Organized market economies and unemployment in Europe', in N. Bermeo (ed.), *Unemployment in the New Europe*, Cambridge, Cambridge University Press, pp. 52–86.

Hall, P.A. (1986), *Governing the Economy: The Politics of State Intervention in Britain and France*, Oxford, Oxford University Press.

Hall, P. and Taylor, R. (1996), 'Political science and the three new institutionalisms', *Political Studies*, 44 (4), 936–57.

Hall, P.A. and Soskice, D. (eds) (2001), *Varieties of Capitalism: The Institutional Foundations of Comparative Advantage*, Oxford, Oxford University Press.

Hall, P.A. and Soskice, D. (2003), 'Varieties of capitalism and institutional change: a response to three critics', *Comparative European Politics*, 1 (2), 241–50.

Hall, P.A. and Taylor, R.C.R. (1998), 'The potential of historical institutionalism: a response to Hay and Wincott', *Political Studies*, 46 (5), 985–62.

Hammermesh, D. (1990), 'Data difficulties in labor economics', in E.R. Berndtt and J.E. Triplett (eds), *Fifty Years of Economic Measurement*, The Jubilee of the Conference on Research in Income and Wealth, Studies in Income and Wealth, Vol. 54, Chicago, University of Chicago Press, pp. 273–97.

Harcourt, G. and Kitson, M. (1993), 'Fifty years of economic measurement: a Cambridge view', *Review of Income and Wealth*, 39 (4), 435–47.

Hardt, M. and Negri, A. (2000), *Empire*, Cambridge, MA, Harvard University Press.

Harkness, S. (1999), 'Working 9 to 5?', in P. Gregg and J. Wadsworth (eds), *The State of Working Britain*, Manchester, Manchester University Press, pp. 90–108.

Harrison, B. (1994), *Lean and Mean: The Changing Landscape of Corporate Power in the Age of Flexibility*, New York, Basic Books.

Hart, J. (1992), 'The effects of state-societal arrangements on international competitiveness', *British Journal of Political Science*, 22, 255–300.

Harvey, D. (1999), *The Limits to Capital*, London, Verso.

Harvey, D. (2003), *The New Imperialism*, Oxford, Oxford University Press.

Hassel, A. and Ebbinghaus, B. (2000), 'Concerted Reforms', unpublished paper, Europeanists Conference, Chicago.

Hay, C. (1997), 'Anticipating accommodations, accommodating anticipations: the appeasement of capital in the "modernization" of the British Labour Party, 1987–1992', *Politics and Society*, 25 (2), 234–56.

Hay, C. (2000), 'Contemporary capitalism, globalization, regionalization and the persistence of national variation', *Review of International Studies*, 26 (4), 509–31.

Hay, C. (2002), *Political Analysis*, Basingstoke, Palgrave.

Hay, C. (2004a), 'Theory, stylised heuristic or self-fulfilling prophecy: the status of rational choice in public administration', *Public Administration*, 81 (1), March 2004, 39–62.

Hay, C. (2004b), 'Common trajectories, variable paces, divergent outcomes? Models of European capitalism under conditions of complex economic interdependence', *Review of International Political Economy*, 11 (2), 231–62.

Hay, C. and Wincott, D. (1998), 'Structure, agency and historical institutionalism', *Political Studies*, 46 (5), 951–7.

Hayek, F. (1944), *The Road to Serfdom*, Chicago, University of Chicago Press.

Held, D. (1995), *Democracy and the Global Order: From the Modern State to Cosmopolitan Governance*, Stanford, Stanford University Press.

Henderson, J. (1993), 'Against the economic orthodoxy: on the making of the East Asia miracle', *Economy and Society*, 22 (2), 200–17.

Henley, A. and Tsakalotos, E. (1992), 'Corporatism and the European labour market after 1992', *British Journal of Industrial Relations* 30 (4), 567–86.

Henwood, D. (2003), *After the New Economy*, London, Verso.

Hicks, A. and Kenworthy, L. (1998), 'Cooperation and political economic performance in affluent democratic capitalism', *American Journal of Sociology*, 6 (May), 1631–72.

Hirsch, J. (1999), 'Class and the question of democracy', in L. Panitch and C. Leys (eds), *Socialist Register 1999: Global Capitalism vs. Democracy*, London, Merlin, pp. 278–93.

Hirst, P. and Thompson, G. (1999), *Globalization in Question*, Cambridge, Polity Press.

HM Treasury (2000), *Productivity in the UK: The Evidence and the Government's Approach*, London, HM Stationary Office.

Hodgson, G. (1996), 'Varieties of capitalism and varieties of economic theory', *Review of International Political Economy*, 3 (3), 380–433.

Hodgson, G. (2001), 'Frontiers of institutional economics', *New Political Economy*, 6 (1), 245–53.

Hollingsworth, J. (1997), 'Continuities and change in social systems of production: the cases of Japan, Germany and the United States', in J. Rogers Hollingsworth and R. Boyer (eds), *Contemporary Capitalism: The Embeddedness of Institutions*, Cambridge, Cambridge University Press, pp. 267–317.

Hollingsworth, J. (2000), 'Doing institutional analysis: implications for the study of innovations', *Review of International Political Economy*, 7 (4), 595–644.

Howell, C. (1992), *Regulating Labour: The State and Industrial Relations Reform in Postwar France*, Princeton, Princeton University Press.

Howell, C. (2001a), 'Approaches to Contemporary Political Economy: Varieties of Capitalism and Beyond', CSE Panel Proposal, Planning Document, 17 September.

Howell, C. (2001b), 'The Construction of Industrial Relations Institutions: Theoretical and Comparative Perspectives', unpublished paper, American Political Science Association, San Francisco.

Howell, C. (2003a), 'Varieties of capitalism: and then there was one?', *Comparative Politics*, 36 (1), 103–24.

Howell, C. (2003b), 'The state and institutional construction', paper presented at the conference on 'Politics and the Varieties of Capitalism', Wissenschaftszentrum Berlin, 31 October–1 November.

Huber, E. and Stephens, J. (1998), 'Internationalization and the social democratic welfare model: crises and future prospects', *Comparative Political Studies*, 33 (3), 353–97.

Huber, E. and Stephens, J. (2001), *Development and Crisis of the Welfare State*, Chicago, University of Chicago Press.

Huber, E., Ragin, C. and Stephens, J. (1993), 'Social democracy, Christian Democracy, constitutional structure and the welfare state', *American Journal of Sociology*, 99, 711–49.

Hutton, W. (1994), *The State We're In*, London, Cape.

Hutton, W. (2002), *The World We're In*, London, Time Warner Books UK.

Huws, U. (2003), *The Making of a Cybertariat*, New York, Monthly Review Press.

Imlah, A.H. (1958), *Economic Elements in the Pax Britannica: Studies in British Foreign Trade in the Nineteenth Century*, New York, Russell & Russell.

Immergut, E. (1990), 'Institutions, veto points, and policy results', *Journal of Public Policy*, 10 (4), 391–416.

Immergut, E.M. (1998), 'The theoretical core of the new institutionalism', *Politics and Society*, 26 (1), 5–34.

Ingham, G. (1996a), 'Some recent changes in the relationship between economics and sociology', *Cambridge Journal of Economics*, 20, 243–75.

Ingham, G. (1996b), 'The "new economic sociology"', *Work, Employment and Society*, 19 (3), 549–64.

Iversen, T. (1999), *Contested Economic Institutions: The Politics of Macroeconomics and Wage Bargaining in Advanced Democracies*, Cambridge, Cambridge University Press.

Iversen, T. (2000), 'Decentralization, monetarism and the social democratic welfare state', in T. Iversen, J. Pontusson and D. Soskice (eds), *Unions, Employers and Central Banks*, Cambridge, Cambridge University Press, pp. 205–31.

Iversen, T. (2001), 'The dynamics of welfare state expansion', in P. Pierson (ed.), *The New Politics of the Welfare State*, New York, Oxford University Press, pp. 45–79.

Iversen, T. and Pontusson, J. (2000), 'Comparative political economy', in I. Iversen, J. Pontusson and D. Soskice (eds), *Employers, Unions and Central Banks*, Cambridge, Cambridge University Press, pp. 1–37.

Iversen, T. and Soskice, D. (2001), 'An asset theory of social market preferences', *American Political Science Review*, 95 (4), 875–94.

Jackson, T., Marks, N., Ralls, J. and Stymne, S. (1998), 'Sustainable Economic Welfare in the UK, 1950–96', unpublished paper, Centre for Environmental Strategy, University of Surrey.

Jang, S.C. (2000), 'Driving Engine or Rent-Seeking Super-Cartel? The Business-State Nexus and Economic Transformation in South Korea, 1960–1999', unpublished PhD Dissertation, Michigan State University.

Jensen, M. (2000), *A Theory of the Firm*, Cambridge, MA, Harvard University Press.

Jessop, B. (1982), *The Capitalist State*, Oxford, Martin Robertson.

Jessop, B. (1990), *State Theory: Putting the Capitalist State in its Place*, Cambridge, Polity Press.

Jessop, B. (ed.) (2001), *Regulation Theory and the Crisis of Capitalism* (5 vols), Cheltenham, Edward Elgar.

Jessop, B. (in press), 'From Thatcherism to new labour: neo-liberalism, workfarism, and labour market regulation', in H. Overbeek (ed.), *The Political Economy of European Unemployment: European Integration and the Transnationalization of the Employment Question*, London, Routledge.

Jones, B. (2001), *Politics and the Architecture of Choice*, Chicago, University of Chicago Press.

Jones, L. and Sakong, I. (1980), *Government, Business and Entrepreneurship in Economic Development: The Korean Case*, Cambridge, MA, Council on East Asian Studies, Harvard University.

Jorgenson, D.W. and Griliches, Z. (1967), 'The explanation of productivity change', *Review of Economic Studies*, 34, 249–80.

Judis, J.B. (2000), *The Paradox of American Democracy: Elites, Special Interests and the Betrayal of Public Trust*, New York, Pantheon Press.

Kaldor, N. (1966), *Causes of the Slow Rate of Growth of the United Kingdom*, Cambridge, Cambridge University Press.

Kaldor, N. (1970), 'The case for regional policies', *Scottish Journal of Political Economy*, 17 (November), 337–48.

Kaldor, N. (1972), 'The irrelevance of equilibrium economics', *Economic Journal*, 382 (December), 1237–55.

Kang, M. (1996), *The Korean Business Conglomerate: Chaebol Then and Now*, Berkeley, Institute of East Asian Studies.

Kapstein, E.B. (1994), *Governing the Global Economy: International Finance and the State*, Cambridge, MA, Harvard University Press.

Kato, T. (1995, February), *Workaholism: Its not in the Blood*, retrieved, 2004, from the World Wide Web: http://members.jcom.home.ne.jp/katori/WORKAHOLISM.html.

Kato, T. (2001), 'Japanese Regulation and Governance in Restructuring: Ten Years after the "Post-fordist" Japan debate', paper presented at the East Asian Modes of Development and Their Crises: Regulationist Approaches, Tunghai University, Taiwan.

Katz, H. (1993), 'The decentralization of collective bargaining: a literature review and comparative analysis', *Industrial and Labor Relations Review*, 47 (1), 3–22.

Katzenstein, P. (1978), *Between Power and Plenty*, Madison, University of Wisconsin Press.

Katzenstein, P. (1985), *Small States in World Markets*, Ithaca, NY, Cornell University Press.

Keman, H. (2003), 'Explaining miracles: third ways and work and welfare', *Western European Politics*, 26 (2), 115–35.

Kendix, M. and Olson, M. (1990), 'Changing unemployment rates in Europe and the USA', in R. Brunetta and C. Dell'Aringa (eds), *Labour Relations and Economic Performance*, New York, New York University Press, pp. 68–91.

Kennedy, P. (1988), *The Rise and Fall of the Great Powers*, London, Unwin Hyman.

Kenny, C. and Williams, D. (2001), 'What do we know about economic growth? Or, why don't we know very much', *World Development*, 29 (2), 1–22.

Kenworthy, L. and Pontusson, J. (2004), 'Inegalitarian Market Trends and the Politics of Compensatory Redistribution in OECD Countries', unpublished paper, Department of Political Science, Cornell University.

Keynes, J.M. (1930), 'Economic Possibilities for Our Grandchildren,' subsequently published in *Essays in Persuasion*, New York, Norton (reprinted in 1963).

Keynes, J.M. (1940a), 'The concept of national income: supplementary note', *Economic Journal*, 197 (March), 60–5.

Keynes, J.M. (1940b), *How to Pay for the War: A Radical Plan for the Chancellor of the Exchequer*, London, Macmillan.

Kim, E.M. (1997), *Big Business, Strong State*, Albany, SUNY Press.

Kim, L. (1997), *Imitation to Innovation: The Dynamics of Korea's Technological Learning*, Cambridge, MA, Harvard Business School Press.

Kinderman, D. (2003), 'Pressure from Without, Subversion from Within: the Two-Pronged German Employer Offensive', unpublished paper, Department of Political Science, Cornell University.

Kindleberger, C.P. (1967), *Europe's Postwar Growth: The Role of Labor Supply*, Cambridge, MA, Harvard University Press.

Kindleberger, C.P. (1996), *World Economic Primacy, 1500 to 1990*, Oxford, Oxford University Press.

King, D. and Rothstein, B. (1993), 'Institutional choices and labor market policy', *Comparative Political Studies*, 26 (2), 147–77.

Kitschelt, H., Lange, P., Marks, G. and Stephens, J. (eds) (1999), 'Convergence and divergence in advanced capitalist democracies', *Continuity and Change in Contemporary Capitalism*, Cambridge, Cambridge University Press, pp. 427–60.

Kitson, M. and Michie, J. (1995), 'Conflict, cooperation and change: the political economy of trade and trade policy', *Review of International Political Economy*, 2 (4), 632–57.

Kitson, M. and Michie, J. (2000), *The Political Economy of Competitiveness*, London and New York, Routledge.

Kleinknecht, A. and ter Wengel, J. (1998), 'The myth of economic globalisation', *Cambridge Journal of Economics*, 22, 637–47.

Konings, M. (forthcoming 2005), 'Political Institutions and Economic Imperatives: Bringing Agency Back In', *Research in Political Economy*, Vol. 22, New York: JAI Press/ Elsevier Science, 2005.

Korpi, W. and Palme, J. (2003), 'New politics and class politics in the context of austerity and globalization: welfare state regress in 18 countries 1975–95', *American Political Science Review*, 97 (3), 425–46.

Kotz, D., McDonough, T. and Reich, M. (eds) (1994), *Social Structures of Accumulation: The Political Economy of Growth and Crisis*, Cambridge, Cambridge University Press.

Kuhn, T. (1970), *The Structure of Scientific Revolutions*, Chicago, University of Chicago Press.

Kwon, H. and Pontusson, J. (2003), 'Welfare Spending, Government Partisanship and Varieties of Capitalism', unpublished paper, Department of Government, Cornell University.

Lacher, H. (1999), 'Embedded liberalism, disembedded markets: reconceptualising the *Pax Americana*', *New Political Economy*, 4 (3), 343–60.

Lal, D. (1983), *The Poverty of Development Economics*, London, IEA, Hobert Paperback.

Lall, S. (1991), 'Marketing barriers facing developing country manufactured exporters: a conceptual note', *The Journal of Development Studies*, 27 (4), 137–50.

Lange, P., Wallerstein, M. and Golden, M. (1995), 'The end of corporatism?', in S. Jacoby (ed.), *Workers of Nations*, Oxford, Oxford University Press, pp. 1–26.

Lash, S. and Urry, J. (1987), *The End of Organized Capitalism*, Oxford, Polity Press.

Layard, R. (2003), 'Happiness: Has Social Science a Clue?', Lionel Robbins Memorial Lectures 2002/3, London School of Economics.

Layard, R., Nickell, S. and Jackman, R. (1991), *Unemployment: Macroeconomic Performance and the Labor Market*, New York, Oxford University Press.

Lazonick, W. (1991), *Business Organization and the Myth of the Market Economy*, Cambridge, Cambridge University Press.

Lazonick, W. (1992), 'Business organization and competitive advantage: Capitalist transformations in the twentieth century', in G. Dosi, R. Giannetti and P.A. Toninelli (eds), *Technology and Enterprise in a Historical Perspective*, Cheltenham, Edward Elgar, pp. 119–63.

Lazonick, W. (1994a), 'Social organization and technological leadership', in W.J. Baumol, R.R. Nelson and E.N. Wolff (eds), *Convergence of Productivity*, Oxford, Oxford University Press, pp. 164–96.

Lazonick, W. (1994b), 'Creating and extracting value: corporate investment behaviour and American economic performance', in M.A. Bernstein and D.E. Adler (eds), *Understanding American Economic Decline*, Cambridge, Cambridge University Press, pp. 79–113.

Lebowitz, M.A. (1999), 'In Brenner, everything is reversed', *Historical Materialism*, 4, 109–30.

Lebowitz, M. (2003), *Beyond Capital: Marx's Political Economy of the Working Class*, New York, Palgrave.

Lembruch, G. (1984), 'Concertation and the structure of corporatist networks', in J. Goldthorpe (ed.), *Order and Conflict in Contemporary Capitalism*, New York, Oxford University Press, pp. 60–80.

Levine, R. and Renelt, D. (1992), 'A sensitivity analysis of cross-country growth regressions', *American Economic Review*, 82 (4), 942–63.

Lewis, W.A. (1954), 'Economic development with unlimited supplies of labour', *Manchester School*, 22, 139–91.

Lijphart, A. and Crepaz, M. (1991), 'Corporatism and consensus democracy in eighteen countries', *British Journal of Political Science*, 21, 235–56.

Linder, S. (1986), *The Pacific Century: Economic and Political Consequenes of Asia-Pacific Dynamism*, Stanford, Stanford University Press.

Lipietz, A. (1987), *Mirages and Miracles*, London, Verso.

Long, W.F. and Ravenscraft, D.J. (1993), 'Decade of debt: lessons from LBOs in the 1980s', in M.M. Blair (ed.), *The Deal Decade: What Takeovers and Leveraged Buyouts Mean for Corporate Governance*, Washington, DC, Brookings.

Longstreth, F. (1988), 'From corporatism to dualism?', *Political Studies*, 36, 413–32.

Lucas, R.E. (1988), 'On the mechanics of economic development', *Journal of Monetary Economics*, 22, 3–42.

Lutz, S. (2000), 'From Managed to Market Capitalism: German Finance in Transition', Max Plank Institute Discussion Paper.

McCombie, J.S.L. and Thirlwall, A.P. (1994), *Economic Growth and the Balance of Payments Constraint*, London, Macmillan.

McCraw, T.K. (1996), 'Competition and "fair trade": history and theory', *Research in Economic History*, 16, 185–239.

McNally, D. (1999), 'Turbulence in the world economy', *Monthly Review*, 51 (2), 38–52.

Maddison, A. (1991), *Dynamic Forces in Economic Development*, Oxford, Oxford University Press.

Maddison, A. (1995a), *Explaining the Economic Performance of Nations*, Cheltenham, Edward Elgar.

Maddison, A. (1995b), *Monitoring the World Economy, 1820–1992*, Paris, OECD.

Maddison, A. (2001), *The World Economy: A Millennial Perspective*, Paris, OECD.

Maddison, A. (2003), *The World Economy: Historical Statistics*, Paris, OECD.

Magnusson, L. and Ottoson, J. (1997), *Evolutionary Economics and Path Dependency*, Cheltenham, Edward Elgar.

Mandel, E. (1975), *Late Capitalism*, London, Verso.

Mankiw, N.G. (1995), 'The growth of nations', *Brookings Papers on Economic Activity*, 1, 275–326.

Mankiw, N.G. (2003), *Macroeconomics*, New York, Worth.

Mankiw, N.G., Romer, D. and Weil, D.N. (1992), 'A contribution to the empirics of economic growth', *Quarterly Journal of Economics*, 107, 407–37.

Manow, P. (2001), 'Comparative institutional advantages of welfare state regimes and new coalitions in welfare state reforms', in P. Pierson (ed.), *The New Politics of the Welfare State*, New York, Oxford University Press, pp. 146–64.

Mares, I. (2001), 'Firms and the welfare state', in P. Hall and D. Soskice (eds), *Varieties of Capitalism*, Oxford, Oxford University Press, pp. 184–212.

Marshall, A. (1890), *Principles of Economics*, London, Macmillan.

Martin, C. (1991), *Shifting the Burden*, Chicago, University of Chicago Press.

Martin, C. (1995), 'Nature or nurture?', *American Political Science Review*, 89 (4), 898–913.

Martin, C. (2000), *Stuck in Neutral*, Princeton, Princeton University Press.

Martin, C. (forthcoming), *Corporatism from the Firm Perspective*.

Marx, K. (1848), *The Communist Manifesto*, London, Verso.

Marx, K. (1867/1961), *Capital, Volume 1*, Moscow, Foreign Language Publishing House.

Marx, K. (1973), *Grundrisse*, Harmondsworth, Penguin.

Mason, E., Perkins, D., Kim, K. and Cole, D. (1980), *The Economic and Social Modernization of the Republic of Korea*, Cambridge, MA, Harvard University Press.

Mayer, M. (2001), *The Fed*, New York, Free Press.

Meiksins, P. and Whalley, P. (2002), *Putting Work in its Place*, Ithaca, ILR Press.

Milgrom, P. and Roberts, J. (1992), *Economics, Organization and Management*, Englewood Cliffs, NJ, Prentice-Hall.

Miliband, R. (1969), *The State in Capitalist Society*, New York, Basic Books.

Mill, J.S. (1965), *Principles of Political Economy*, New York, Augustus M. Kelley: original publication 1848.

Mishel, L.R., Bernstein, J. and Boushey, H. (2003), *The State of Working America, 2002/2003*, Ithaca, ILR Press.

Mitchell, B.R. (1998), *International Historical Statistics: Europe, 1750–1993* (fourth edition), London, Macmillan.

Mizunoya, T. (2001), 'An international comparison of unpaid overtime work among industrialized countries' [trans], *Society of Economic Statistics*, 81.

Mokyr, J. (1990), *The Lever of Riches: Technological Creativity and Economic Progress*, Oxford, Oxford University Press.

Molina, O. and Rhodes, M. (2002), 'Corporatism: the past, present, and future of a concept', *Annual Review of Political Science*, 5, 305–31.

Moore, G.E. (1965), 'Cramming more components onto integrated circuits,' *Electronics*, 38 (8), 19 April.

Mosley, H., Keller, T. and Speckesser, S. (1998), *The Role of the Social Partners in the Design and Implementation of Active Measures* 27, Geneva, International Labour Office.

Myrdal, G. (1930), *The Political Element in the Development of Economic Theory*, London, Routledge & Kegan Paul.

Myrdal, G. (1957), *Economic Theory and Underdeveloped Regions*, London, Duckworth.

Nordhaus, W. and Tobin, J. (1972), 'Is growth obsolete', in *Economic Growth*, Fiftieth Anniversary Colloquium, National Bureau of Economic Research, New York, Columbia University Press, pp. 1–80.

Nordlinger, E. (1981), *On the Autonomy of the Democratic State*, Cambridge, MA, Harvard University Press.

North, D.C. (1990), *Institutions, Institutional Change and Economic Performance*, Cambridge, Cambridge University Press.

North, D.C. and Thomas R.P. (1973), *The Rise of the Western World: A New Economic History*, Cambridge, Cambridge University Press.

O'Brien, P.K. and Keyder, C. (1978), *Economic Growth in Britain and France, 1780–1914: Two Paths to the Twentieth Century*, London, Allen & Unwin.

O'Brien, P.K. and Prados de la Escosura, L. (1992), 'Agricultural productivity and European industrialization, 1890–1980', *Economic History Review*, 45, 514–36.

Odell, J.S. (1982), *U.S. International Monetary Policy: Markets, Power and Ideas as Sources of Change*, Princeton, NJ, Princeton University Press.

OECD (1998), *OECD Economic Surveys: Netherlands 1997–98*, Paris, OECD.

OECD (1999), *Employment Outlook*, Paris, OECD.

OECD (2003), *Employment Outlook 2003: Towards More and Better Jobs Statistical Annex*, Paris, OECD.

OECD (2004), *OECD Economic Surveys: United Kingdom 2004*, Paris, OECD.

Ohmae, K. (1990), *The Borderless World*, New York, Harper.

Olson, M. (1963), *The Economics of the Wartime Shortage: A History of British Food Supplies in the Napoleonic War and in World Wars I and II*, Durham, NC, Duke University Press.

Olson, M. (1982), *The Rise and Decline of Nations: Economic Growth, Stagflation and Social Rigidities*, New Haven, Yale University Press.

O'Mahony, M. and Wagner, K. (1996), 'Anglo-German productivity performance: 1960–89', in B. van Ark and K. Wagner (eds), *International Productivity Differences: Measurement and Explanations*, Amsterdam, North Holland.

O'Rourke, K. (1997), 'The European grain invasion, 1870–1913', *Journal of Economic History*, 57, 775–801.

Orren, K. and Skowronek, S. (2004), *The Search for American Political Development*, New York, Cambridge University Press.

Panitch, L. (1994), 'Globalization and the state', in R. Miliband and L. Panitch (eds), *The Socialist Register 1994*, London, Merlin Press, pp. 60–93.

Panitch, L. (2000), 'The new imperialist state', *New Left Review*, II: (2), 177–98.

Panitch, L. (2002), 'The impoverishment of state theory', in S. Aronowitz and P. Gratsis (eds), *Paradigm Lost: State Theory Reconsidered*, Minnesota, University of Minnesota Press, pp. 89–104.

Panitch, L. and Gindin, S. (2004), 'Global capitalism and American empire', in L. Panitch and C. Leys (eds), *Socialist Register 2004*, London, Merlin, pp. 34–46.

Panitch, L. and Leys, C. (eds) (2004), *The New Imperial Challenge; The Socialist Register 2004*, London, Merlin Press.

Panitch, L., Leys, C., Albo, G. and Coates, D. (eds) (2001), *Socialist Register 2001: Working Classes, Global Realities*, London, Merlin Press.

Peck, J.A. (2001), *Workfare States*, New York, Guilford.

Peck, J.A. and Theodore, N. (2002), 'Temped out? Industry rhetoric, labor regulation and economic restructuring in the temporary staffing business', *Economic and Industrial Democracy*, 23 (2), 143–75.

Penrose, E. (1959), *The Theory of the Growth of the Firm*, Oxford, Basil Blackwell.

Perez, S. (2000), 'From de-centralization to re-organization: explaining the return to national-level bargaining in Italy and Spain', *Comparative Politics*, 32 (4), 437–58.

Peters, G. (1999), *Institutional Theory in Political Science: The New Institutionalism*, London, Pinter.

Petras, J. and Morley, M. (1992), *Latin America in the Time of Cholera*, New York, Routledge.

Pierson, P. (1993), 'When effect becomes cause', *World Politics*, 45 (4), 595–628.

Pierson, P. (1994), *Dismantling the Welfare State?*, New York, Cambridge University Press.

Pierson, P. (ed.) (2000), *The New Politics of the Welfare State*, New York, Oxford University Press.

Piore, M. and Sabel, C. (1984), *The Second Industrial Divide*, New York, Basic Books.

Polanyi, K. (1944), *The Great Divide*, New York, Rinehart and Company Inc.

Pollin, R. (2003), *Contours of Descent: US Economic Fractures and the Landscape of Global Austerity*, London, Verso.

Pontusson, J. (1992), 'At the end of the third road: Swedish social democracy in crisis', *Politics and Society*, 20 (3), 305–22.

Pontusson, J. (1995a), 'Explaining the decline of European social democracy', *World Politics*, 47 (July), 495–533.

Pontusson, J. (1995b), 'From comparative public policy to political economy: putting political institutions in their place and taking interests seriously', *Comparative Political Studies*, 28 (1), 117–47.

Pontusson, J. (1997), 'Between neoliberalism and the German model: Swedish capitalism in transition', in C. Crouch and W. Streeck (eds), *Political Economy of Modern Capitalism*, London, Sage, pp. 55–70.

Pontusson, J. (2000), 'Labour market institutions and wage distribution', in T. Iversen, J. Pontusson and D. Soskice (eds), *Unions, Employers and Central Banks*, Cambridge, Cambridge University Press, pp. 292–330.

Pontusson, J. (2003), *Social Europe versus Liberal America*, Unpublished.

Pontusson, J. and Swenson, P. (1996), 'Labor markets, production strategies, and wage bargaining institutions', *Comparative Political Studies*, 29 (2), 223–50.

Porter, M. (1990), *The Competitive Advantage of Nations*, London, Macmillan.

Poulantzas, N. (1975), *Classes in Contemporary Capitalism*, London, Verso.

Prados de la Escosura, L., Dabán Sánchez, T. and Sanz Oliva, J.C. (1993), 'De te Fabula Narratur? Growth, structural change and convergence in Europe, 19th–20th centuries', Documentos de Trabajo D-93009, Dirección General de Planificación, Ministerio de Economia y Hacienda, Madrid.

Pritchett, L. (1996), 'Where has all the education gone?', *World Bank Research Working Paper*, No. 1522.

Putnam, R. (1993), *Making Democracy Work*, Princeton, Princeton University Press.

Puttnam, R. (2000), *Bowling Alone: The Collapse and Revival of American Community*, New York, Simon & Schuster.

Putnam, R. (ed.) (2002), *Democracies in Flux: The Evolution of Social Capital in Contemporary Society*, New York, Oxford University Press.

Radice, H. (2000), 'Globalization and national capitalisms: theorizing convergence and differentiation', *Review of International Political Economy*, 7 (4), 719–42.

Rees, A. (1969), *Real Wages in Manufacturing 1890–1914*, Princeton, Princeton University Press.

Regini, M. (1995), 'Firms and institutions: the demand for skills and their social production in Europe', *European Journal of Industrial Relations*, 1 (2), 191–202.

Reich, S. (1990), *The Fruits of Fascism: Postwar Prosperity in Historical Perspective*, Ithaca, NY, Cornell University Press.

Reuten, G. (1991), 'Accumulation of capital and the foundation of the tendency of the rate of profit to fall', *Cambridge Journal of Economics*, 15, 79–94.

Rhodes, M. and Mény, Y. (eds) (1998), *The Future of European Welfare: A New Social Contract?*, New York, St. Martin's Press.

Richards, A. and Waterbury, J. (1990), *The Political Economy of the Middle East*, Boulder, Westview Press.

Rodrik, D. (1995), 'Getting interventions right: how South Korea and Taiwan grew rich', *Economic Policy*, 55–107.

Romer, P. (1986), 'Increasing returns and long-run growth', *Journal of Political Economy*, 94 (5), 1002–37.

Romer, P. (1990), 'Are non-convexities important for understanding growth?', *NBER Working Paper*, No. 3271.

Romer, P. (1994), 'The origins of endogenous growth', *Journal of Economic Perspectives*, 8 (1), 3–22.

Romer, P.M. (1990), 'Endogenous technological change', *Journal of Political Economy*, 98, S71–102.

Rostas, L. (1948), *Comparative Productivity in British and American Industry*, Cambridge, National Institute of Economic and Social Research.

Rothstein, B. (1988), 'State and capital in Sweden', *Scandinavian Political Studies*, 11 (3), 235–60.

Rowthorn, B. (1992), 'Corporatism and labor market performance', in J. Pekkarinen, M. Pohjola and B. Rowthorn (eds), *Social Corporatism*, Oxford, Oxford University Press, pp. 82–131.

Roy, W. (1997), *Socializing Capital: The Rise of the Large Industrial Corporation in America*, Princeton, NJ, Princeton University Press.

Rude, C. (1999), 'The Volcker Monetary Policy Shocks: A Political-Economic Analysis', New School of Social Research, Unpublished.

Rueda, D. and Pontusson, J. (2000), 'Wage inequality and varieties of capitalism', *World Politics*, 52 (April), 350–83.

Sala-i-Martin, X. (2002), '15 years of growth economics: what have we learnt?', in N. Loaiza (ed.), *The Challenges of Economic Growth*, Central Bank of Chile.

Sandholtz, W. and Zysman, J. (1989), '1992: recasting the European Bargaining', *World Politics*, 42 (1), 95–128.

Sassoon, D. (1997), *One Hundred Years of Socialism*, London, Fontana Press.

Saul, J. (2001), *Millennial Africa: Capitalism, Socialism, Democracy*, Trenton, NJ, Africa World Press.

Sayer, A. and Walker, R. (1992), *The New Social Economy: Reworking the Division of Labor*, Cambridge, Blackwell.

Scharpf, F. and Schmidt, V. (eds) (2000), *Welfare to Work in the Open Economy*, New York, Oxford University Press.

Schmidt, V. (2000), 'Values and discourse in the politics of adjustment', in F. Scharpf and V. Schmidt (eds), *Welfare to Work in the Open Economy*, New York, Oxford University Press, 1, pp. 229–309.

Schmidt, V.A. (2002), *The Futures of European Capitalism*, Oxford, Oxford University Press.

Schmitter, P. (1981), 'Interest intermediation and regime governability in contemporary Western Europe and North America', in S. Berger (ed.), *Organizing Interests in Western Europe*, Cambridge, Cambridge University Press, pp. 285–327.

Schumpeter, J.A. (1942), *Capitalism, Socialism and Democracy*, New York, Harper.

Scott, A. (1998), *Regions and the World Economy: The Coming Shape of Global Production, Competition, and Political Order*, Oxford, Oxford University Press.

Scott, J. (1985), *Weapons of the Weak*, New Haven, Yale University Press.

Seabrooke, L. (2001), *US Power in International Finance: The Victory of Dividends*, New York, Palgrave.

Shaw, M. (2000), *Theory of the Global State*, Cambridge, Cambridge University Press.

Shonfield, A. (1965), *Modern Capitalism*, New York, Oxford University Press.

Skidelsky, R. (2000), *John Maynard Keynes, Vol. III: Fighting For Britain, 1937–46*, Basingstoke, Macmillan.

Skocpol, T. (1985), 'Introduction', in P. Evans, D. Rueschemeyer and T. Skocpol (eds), *Bringing the State Back In*, New York, Cambridge University Press, pp. 3–37.

Smelser, N. and Swedberg, R. (1995), *The Handbook of Economic Sociology*, Princeton, Princeton University Press.

Smith, A. (1776), *An Inquiry into the Nature and Causes of the Wealth of Nations*, London, Methuen and Co. (1904, fifth edition).

Smith, N. (1990), *Uneven Development: Nature, Capital and the Production of Space*, Oxford, Basil Blackwell.

Snow, D., Rochford, E. Jr., Worden, B., S. and Benford, R. (1986), 'Frame alignment processes, micro-mobilization, and movement participation', *American Sociological Review*, 51, 464–81.

Solow, R.M. (1956), 'A contribution to the theory of economic growth', *Quarterly Journal of Economics*, 70, 65–94.

Solow, R.M. (1957), 'Technical change and the aggregate production function', *Review of Economics and Statistics*, 39, 312–20.

Solow, R. (1966), 'Review of capital and growth', *American Economic Review*, 56 (4), 1257–60.

Solow, R. (1987), 'We'd better watch out', *New York Times*, 12 July.

Solow, R. (1988), 'Growth theory and after', *American Economic Review*, 78 (3), 307–17.

Soskice, D. (1990a), 'Reinterpreting corporatism and explaining unemployment: coordinated and non-coordinated market economies', in R. Brunetta and C. Dell'Arringa (eds), *Labour Relations and Economic Performance*, Basingstoke, Macmillan, pp. 170–211.

Soskice, D. (1990b), 'Wage determination: the changing role of institutions in advanced industrialized countries', *Oxford Review of Economic Policy*, 6 (4), 36–61.

Soskice, D. (1991), 'The institutional infrastructure for international competitiveness: A comparative analysis of the UK and Germany', in A.B. Atkinson and R. Brunetta (eds), *Economics for the New Europe*, Basingstoke, Macmillan, pp. 45–66.

Soskice, D. (1994), 'Reconciling markets and institutions: The German apprenticeship system', in L. Lynch (ed.), *Training and the Private Sector*, Chicago, University of Chicago Press, pp. 25–60.

Soskice, D. (1999), 'Divergent production regimes: coordinated and uncoordinated market economies in the 1980s and 1990s', in H. Kitschelt, P. Lange, G. Marks and J. Stephens (eds), *Continuity and Change in Contemporary Capitalism*, Cambridge, Cambridge University Press, pp. 101–34.

Soskice, D. (2000), 'Macroeconomic analysis and the political economy of unemployment', in T. Iversen, J. Pontusson and D. Soskice (eds), *Unions, Employers and Central Banks*, Cambridge, Cambridge University Press, pp. 38–74.

Steinmo, S. (1993), *Taxation and Democracy*, New Haven, Yale University Press.

Stiglitz, J. (1999), 'Whither Reform? Ten Years of the Transition', World Bank Conference, Washington DC.

Stiglitz, J. (2002), *Globalization and Its Discontents*, New York, W.W. Norton.

Storper, M. (1997), *The Regional World: Territorial Development in a Global Economy*, New York, Guilford.

Strange, S. (1989), 'Towards a theory of transnational empire', in E-O. Czempiel and J. Rosenau (eds), *Global Changes and Theoretical Challenges*, Lexington, Lexington Books, pp. 161–76.

Streeck, W. (1991), 'On the institutional conditions of diversified quality production', in E. Matzner and W. Streeck (eds), *Beyond Keynesianism*, Aldershot, Elgar, pp. 21–61.

Streeck, W. (1992), *Social Institutions and Economic Performance*, Beverly Hills, CA, Sage.

Streeck, W. (1996), 'Lean production in the German auto industry', in S. Berger and R. Dore (eds), *National Diversity and Global Capitalism*, Ithaca, NY, Cornell University Press, pp. 138–70.

Streeck, W. (1997), 'German capitalism: does it exist? Can it survive?', in C. Crouch and W. Streeck (eds), *Political Economy of Modern Capitalism*, London, Sage, pp. 33–54.

Streeck, W. (2001), 'Introduction', in W. Streeck and K. Yamamura (eds), *The origins of non-liberal capitalism*, Ithaca, NY, Cornell University Press, pp. 1–38.

Streeck, W. and Schmitter, P. (1985), *Private Interest Government*, Beverly Hills, CA, Sage.

Swan, T.W. (1956), 'Economic growth and capital accumulation', *Economic Record*, 32 (November), 334–61.

Swank, D. (2001), 'Political institutions and welfare state restructuring', in P. Pierson (ed.), *The New Politics of the Welfare State*, New York, Oxford University Press, pp. 197–237.

Swank, D. and Martin, C. (2001), 'Employers and the welfare state', *Comparative Political Studies*, 34 (8), 899–923.

Swenson, P. (2002), *Capitalists against markets*, Cambridge, Cambridge University Press.

Sylla, R. (2002), 'Financial systems and economic modernization', *Journal of Economic History*, 62, 277–92.

Temin, P. (1966), 'Labor scarcity and the problem of American industrial efficiency in the 1850s', *Journal of Economic History*, 26, 361–79.

Temin, P. (1971), 'Labour scarcity in America', *Journal of Interdisciplinary History*, 1, 251–64.

Temin, P. (2002), 'The golden age of European growth reconsidered', *European Review of Economic History*, 6, 3–22.

Temple, J. (1999), 'The new growth evidence', *Journal of Economic Literature*, 37, 112–56.

Thelen, K. (1998), 'Historical institutionalism in comparative politics', in N. Polsby (ed.), *Annual Review of Political Science*, 2, 369–404.

Thelen, K. (2001), 'Varieties of labour politics in the developed democracies', in P.A. Hall and D. Soskice (eds), *Varieties of Capitalism*, Oxford, Oxford University Press, pp. 71–103.

Thelen, K. (2003), 'The political economy of business and labour in developed democracies: agency and structure in historical-institutional perspective', in I. Katznelson and H. Milner (eds), *Political Science: The State of the Discipline*, New York, W.W. Norton, pp. 371–97.

Thelen, K. and Steinmo, S. (1992), 'Historical institutionalism in comparative politics', in S. Steinmo, K. Thelen and F. Longstreth (eds), *Structuring Politics: Historical Institutionalism in Comparative Analysis*, Cambridge, Cambridge University Press, pp. 1–32.

TNO (2003, mei), *Overwerk in 2001 en 2002 Sterk Toegenomen*, TNO, retrieved, 2004, from the World Wide Web: http://www.arbeid.tno.nl/perskamer/20030508.html.

Tourraine, A. (1985), 'An introduction to the study of social movements', *Social Research*, 52 (4), 749–88.

Triplett, J. (1999), 'The Solow paradox: what do computers do to productivity', *Canadian Journal of Economics*, 32 (2), 309–34.

True, T. (1992), *Participation in Public Policy-Making: The Role of Trade Unions and Employer Associations*, New York, Walter de Gruyter.

Turner, J. (1982), 'Towards a cognitive redefinition of the social group', in H. Tajfel (ed.), *Social Identity and Inter-group Relations*, New York, Cambridge University Press, pp. 15–40.

Unger, B. and van Waarden, F. (1999), 'Interest associations and economic growth: a critique of Mancur Olson's *Rise and Decline of Nations*', *International Review of Political Economy*, 6 (4), 425–67.

US Bureau of Labor Statistics (2003), 'International Comparisons of Manufacturing Productivity and Unit Labor Cost Trends, 2002,' 9 September.

US Bureau of Labor Statistics (2004), 'Industry Analytical Ratios and Basic Industry Data for the Total Economy', 6 May (folder available from Robert Brenner on-request).

US Government (various issues), *Economic Report of the President*, Washington, DC, Unites States Government Printing Office.

Visser, J. (2000), 'From Keynesianism to the Third Way: labour relations and social policy in postwar western Europe', *Economic and Industrial Democracy*, 21, 421–56.

Visser, J. and Hemerijck, A. (1997), *A Dutch Miracle: Job Growth, Welfare Reform, and Corporatism in the Netherlands*, Amsterdam, Amsterdam University Press.

Vitols, S. (2001), 'Varieties of corporate governance', in P. Hall and D. Soskice (eds), *Varieties of Capitalism*, Oxford, Oxford University Press, pp. 361–86.

Waddington, J. and Hoffmann, R. (eds) (2000), *Trade Unions in Europe*, Brussels, European Trade Union Institute.

Wade, R. (2003), *Governing the Market*, Princeton, Princeton University Press.

Walker, J. (1991), *Mobilizing Interest Groups in America*, Ann Arbor, University of Michigan Press.

Wallerstein, M., Golden, M. and Lange, P. (1997), 'Unions, employers' associations, and wage-setting institutions in northern and central Europe, 1950–1992', *Industrial and Labor Relations Review*, 50 (3), 379–401.

Walras, L. (1954), *Elements of Pure Economics*, Homewood, Richard Irwin, original publication 1874.

Watson, M. (2003), 'Ricardian political economy and the varieties of capitalism approach: specialisation, trade and comparative institutional advantage', *Comparative European Politics*, 1 (2), 227–40.

Webber, M.J. and Rigby, D.L. (1996), *The Golden Age Illusion: Rethinking Postwar Capitalism*, New York, Guilford.

Weber, M. (1947), *Social and Economic Organization*, New York, Free Press.

Weir, M. (1992), *Politics and Jobs*, Princeton, Princeton University Press.

Weir, M. and Skocpol, T. (1985), 'State structures and the possibilities for "Keynesian" responses to the great depression in Sweden, Britain and the United States', in P. Evans, D. Rueschemeyer and T. Skocpol (eds), *Bringing the State Back In*, New York, Cambridge University Press, pp. 107–63.

Weiss, L. (1998), *The Myth of the Powerless State*, Ithaca, NY, Cornell University Press.

White, E.N. (2000), 'Banking and finance in the twentieth century', in S.L. Engerman and R.E. Gallman (eds), *The Cambridge Economic History of the United States, Volume III: The Twentieth Century*, Cambridge, Cambridge University Press, pp. 743–802.

White, L. (1992), *Why Now? Change and Turmoil in US Banking*, Washington, DC, Group of Thirty.

Whitley, R. (2000), *Divergent Capitalisms: The Social Structuring and Change of Business Systems*, Oxford, Oxford University Press.

Wilensky, H. (1976), *The 'New Corporatism', Centralization, and the Welfare State*, Beverly Hills, CA, Sage.

Wilks, S. and Wright, M. (1987), *Comparative Government-Industry Relations*, Oxford, Clarendon Press.

Wilson, G. (1990), *Business and Politics*, Chatham, NJ, Chatham House.

Woo, J. (1991), *Race to the Swift: State and Finance in Korean Industrialization*, New York, Columbia University Press.

Wood, E.M. (1995), *Democracy against Capitalism*, Cambridge, Cambridge University Press.

Wood, E.M. (2002), 'Contradictions: only in capitalism?', in L. Panitch and C. Leys (eds), *Socialist Register 2002*, London, Merlin Press, pp. 275–93.

Wood, S. (2001), 'Labour market regimes under threat?', in P. Pierson (ed.), *The New Politics of the Welfare State*, New York, Oxford University Press, pp. 368–409.

Yates, J. (1989), *Control through Communication: The Rise of System in American Management*, Baltimore, MD, Johns Hopkins University Press.

Yeager, T.J. (1999), *Institutions, Transition Economies and Economic Development*, New York, Westview Press.

Young, A. (1928), 'Increasing returns and economic progress', *Economic Journal*, 38 (December), 527–42.

Zuege, A. (2000), 'The Chimera of the third way', in L. Panitch and C. Leys (eds), *Socialist Register 2000: Necessary and Unnecessary Utopias*, London, Merlin, pp. 87–114.

Zysman, J. (1994), 'How institutions create historically rooted trajectories of growth', *Industrial and Corporate Change*, 1, 243–83.

Index